DISCIPLINING
THE HOLOCAUST

SUNY series, Insinuations: Philosophy, Psychoanalysis, Literature

Charles Shepherdson, editor

DISCIPLINING
THE HOLOCAUST

KARYN BALL

Cover art: *The Agnew Clinic* by Thomas Eakins, 1889. Courtesy of the University of Pennsylvania Art Collection, Philadelphia, Pennsylvania.

Published by
State University of New York Press, Albany

For information, contact State University of New York Press, Albany, NY
www.sunypress.edu

Production by Diane Ganeles
Marketing by Michael Campochiaro

Library of Congress Cataloging-in-Publication Data

Ball, Karyn.
    Disciplining the Holocaust / Karyn Ball.
        p. cm. — (Insinuations: philosophy, psychoanalysis, literature)
    Includes bibliographical references and index.
    ISBN 978-0-7914-7541-6 (hardcover : alk. paper)
    ISBN 978-0-7914-7542-3 (pbk. : alk. paper)
    1. Holocaust, Jewish (1939–1945)—Historiography. 2. Holocaust, Jewish (1939–1945)—Germany—Influence. 3. Denkmal für die ermordeten Juden Europas (Berlin, Germany) 4. Holocaust memorials. 5. Psychoanalysis and culture. I. Title.

D804.348.B35 2008
940.53'18072—dc22   2007044486

10 9 8 7 6 5 4 3 2 1

*This book is dedicated to my parents, Philip and Tirzah Ball,
who have made everything possible. For their gift of loving discipline.*

Contents

Illustrations

Acknowledgments

Shorter versions of the first and fifth chapters, as well as parts of the third, previously appeared, respectively, in *Cultural Critique* 46 (2000): 124–52, in *Women in German Yearbook* 19 (2003): 20–49, and in *Witness and Memory: The Discourse of Trauma*, edited by Ana Douglass and Thomas Vogler (New York: Routledge, 2003), 249–73. I am thankful to the University of Minnesota Press, the University of Nebraska Press, and Routledge, respectively, for publishing the original versions of these essays. Leslie Morris, Lisa Disch, Ruth-Ellen Joeres, and Thomas Vogler deserve particular thanks for their astute feedback on various drafts of these articles.

It is perhaps all too fitting in a work devoted to discipline to acknowledge my many debts, which I have accrued in various cities over the span of years while this project came to fruition. In Minneapolis, I am grateful above all to Jack Zipes. I would have given up if it had not been for his encouragement and advice. As a cofounder with Anson Rabinbach and David Bathrick of *New German Critique*, he has contributed to the development of critical German studies in North America and helped to make much interesting and important work possible. To my former advisor, Jochen Schulte-Sasse, and to my unofficial mentor, John Mowitt, I owe an inestimable debt. Not only have they inspired me to see lines of inquiry that I would have otherwise left fallow, but they are also stellar models as intellectuals who do not disavow the historical and social density of theoretical questions. I also want to thank María Brewer, Maria Damon, Keya Ganguly, Timothy Brennan, Leslie Morris, Silvia Lopez, Andres Moreno, and Ole Gram for encouraging careful and honest scholarship even if my stubborn egotism does not always allow me achieve it. Over the years, Ole has been remarkably gracious about commenting on long-winded drafts and helping me with translations at the drop of a hat.

I am deeply grateful to the Social Sciences and Humanities Research Council of Canada for supporting new research as well as the revision and preparation of this manuscript for publication. I would also like to thank the Woodrow Wilson Foundation and the German Academic Exchange Commission (DAAD) for funding preliminary research in Berlin from 1995 to 1997. In Berlin, Manuel Köppen, Klaus Scherpe, Astrid Deuber-Mankowsky, Gertrud Koch, Nikolai Franke, Karin Lafferentz-Krueger, Christian Gänshirt, and Simone Ungerer facilitated an emotionally and intellectually complex engagement with the challenges of Holocaust memory in Germany. In more recent years, the DAAD has also supported my participation in six-week seminars organized by the Institute for German Cultural Studies at Cornell University. It was a privilege to take part in conversations and workshops in Ithaca on the Frankfurt School and visual representations of the Holocaust directed by Peter Uwe Hohendahl in 2001 and David Bathrick in 2003, respectively. I am also thankful to David for introducing the 2003 seminar participants to Anson Rabinbach, whose scholarship I have long admired and who remains an invaluable interlocutor.

Here in Edmonton, I would like to acknowledge my friends and colleagues John-Paul Himka, Christopher Bracken, Michael O'Driscoll, Per Anders Rudling, Clemens Ruthner, Andrew Gow, and the members of the Holocaust studies workshop for commenting on portions of this manuscript and for their enlightened conversation over the years. John-Paul deserves particular mention for organizing the Holocaust studies workshop where I have presented three chapters of this manuscript and for his courage as a scholar who regularly faces down contemporary deniers and apologists in our midst. Chris Bracken and Alifeyah Gulamhusein have been steady sources of solace and sensibility throughout these dessicating years in a province rife with egregiously high axles and fulsome barnyard grunts that stand in for human expression during hockey play-offs. Amy Swiffen, Jeff Kerr, Dianne Chisholm, Chrystia Chomiak, Leon Hunter, Janine Brodie, and Malinda Smith have raised my spirits over long periods of outrage fatigue in an Alberta run by an alcoholic and illiterate former premier and a United States co-opted by George W. Bush and Dick Cheney. For the record, I owe less than nothing to the latter even if they spurred my work by inciting my rage. In contrast, I wholeheartedly thank the surly Mark Woytiuk, who has provided pivotal research support throughout the preparation of this manuscript (and others) above and beyond the call of duty.

Finally, apart from my parents who have supported me in innumerable ways, and to whom this book is dedicated, I would also like to mention my aunt and uncle, Judith and Seymore Levin, who have alternated with my father in the role of devil's advocate. At the State University of New York Press, I am deeply grateful to Wyatt Benner and Diane Ganeles for their painstaking editorial work on the manuscript; and also to James Peltz and Charles Shepherdson for making its publication possible. There are, then, those whom I would like to acknowledge for implicit and explicit forms of solidarity and inspiration in recent years that have meant a great deal to me—Andrew Von Hendy, who commented on a prior draft of this project; Tom Cohen; Bettina Bergo; Krzysztof and Ewa Ziarek; Katherine Rudoph; Elizabeth Walden; Judith Feher Gurewich; Frances Restuccia; Yael Katz; Geoffrey Winthrop-Young; Scott Scribner; David Kaufmann; Ariana

Martin; Ivan Lerner; Maurice Stevens; Brad Prager; Eric Kligerman; Robert Shandley; Darcy Buerkle; Wendy Brown; and Judith Butler; and, last but not least, Hayden White, the most antipuritanical being I have ever met. I remain, as always, his adoring disciple.

If something is to stay in the memory it must be burned in: only that which never ceases to *hurt* stays in the memory. . . .

—Friedrich Nietzsche

One wants to get free of the past: rightly so, since one cannot live in its shadow, and since there is no end to terror if guilt and violence are only repaid, again and again, with guilt and violence. But wrongly so, since the past one wishes to evade is still so intensely alive. National Socialism lives on, and to this day we don't know whether it is only the ghost of what was so monstrous that it didn't even die off with its own death, or whether it never died in the first place—whether the readiness for unspeakable actions survives in people, as in the social conditions that hem them in.

—Theodor W. Adorno

"Speaking properly" appears to be an instance of the ideological work of acquiring skills, a process central to the formation of the subject. The "diverse skills" of labor power must be reproduced, and increasingly this reproduction happens "outside the firm" and *in school*, that is, outside production and in educational institutions. . . . The first mention of "conscience" . . . is linked to the acquisition of mastery, to learning how to "speak properly." . . . In this sense the rules of proper speech are also the rules by which *respect* is proffered or withheld. Workers are taught to *speak* properly and managers learn to speak to workers "in the right way." . . .

—Judith Butler citing Louis Althusser

What happens when acts or performances (discourse or writing, analysis or description, etc.) form part of the objects they designate? When they can give themselves as examples of that of which they speak or write? There is certainly no gain in self-reflexive transparency, on the contrary. An accounting is no longer rendered, nor a simple report or compte rendu given. And the borders of the whole are neither closed nor open. Their trait is divided.

—Jacques Derrida translated by Samuel Weber

Introduction

The self-effacing caveat to this project was already half written by someone else after I returned to the United States in spring 1997 from Berlin, where I had been conducting research on the Holocaust. That June, Norman G. Finkelstein published a scathing critique of the subject of my first chapter, Daniel Jonah Goldhagen's *Hitler's Willing Executioners*, in the *New Left Review*.[1] Finkelstein pinpoints the errors of logic, tacit admissions, minimizations, and misrepresentations that recur in Goldhagen's treatment of his sources. In Finkelstein's assessment, Goldhagen bamboozled us with what amounts to a grotesque work of "pseudo-scholarship" on "The Holocaust," a capitalization Finkelstein reserves for "literature" that promulgates a mythical and ideologically exploitative treatment of National Socialist crimes and has, consequently, no scholarly merit. These crimes are, in contrast, designated the "Nazi holocaust" with a lowercase *h* to signal their historical status. Here and elsewhere Finkelstein rages against those who exploit "The Holocaust" as a morally and emotionally saturated symbol of Jewish victimization for the purposes of officializing Zionist ideology and extorting financial gains disguised as restitution.[2]

Though I disagree with DePaul University's decision to deny Finkelstein tenure in 2007, the corrosive tone of many of his arguments casts serious doubt on the open-minded spirit of his research. There are, to be sure, various problems with Finkelstein's conspiratorial notion of a "Holocaust industry." In the first place, his excoriation of Goldhagen naturalizes his own chip-on-the-shoulder fixation as a son of survivors who has anointed himself the righteous defender of Holocaust memory. Finkelstein repeatedly authorizes himself as a redeemer of "true" memory in the face of trivializers and exploiters such as Goldhagen and Elie Wiesel (whom Finkelstein disparages as the nominal CEO of the Holocaust industry). These self-aggrandizing gestures suggest that Finkelstein falls prey to Goldhagen's tendency to take the blindsiding effects of his own proprietary resentment for granted.

In the second place, Finkelstein's criticism of the Holocaust industry reduces ideology among Holocaust scholars to Zionism narrowly identified with a Jewish-nationalist presupposition that anti-Semitism is eternal and with a concomitant presumption that Jews require Israel as a fail-safe sanctuary, an

1

end that justifies any means, including the expropriation and persecution of Palestinians. Though I agree that the mass murder of European Jews should not be deployed to rationalize the expansion of illegal settlements and the dire injustice of the Palestinian situation, his grinding of the anti-Zionist ax discounts the prospect that scholars use the Holocaust to further other critical or ideological interests.

This underlies a third source of my discomfort with Finkelstein. He gives militant expression to a climate of scorn among some platform leftist identity capitalists who have, over the years, personally asked me to face the demoralizing prospect that Holocaust studies is, in itself, "politically incorrect."[3] This backlash against the Holocaust's perceived privilege in academic and cultural contexts evokes an economic logic of scarcity. The assumption is that scholarship about the Shoah appropriates time, energy and public attention that would be more urgently invested in the analysis of immediate and ongoing problems. For this reason, regardless of my commitment to studying this genocide as a telling example of how society fails to stand up against state violence, my self-indulgent preoccupation with the (mass murder of) Jews aids and abets contemporary violence against the disenfranchised. I therefore proffer this book as evidence of my poor political discipline.

Whatever self-doubts his tendentious conclusions managed to stir up on my part, Finkelstein's otherwise acute critique of Goldhagen appeared to gain more credibility when it was republished the following year as a companion piece to "Revising the Holocaust" by Ruth Bettina Birn, whose impeccable credentials include her service as the chief historian in the War Crimes and Crimes Against Humanity Section of the Department of Justice in Canada.[4] Birn's expertise as a historian and her knowledge of the German language qualify her to weigh Goldhagen's statements against the documents he cites as well as the ones he leaves out and to discern errors of translation that exacerbate his distorting and reductive generalizations. What Birn shares with Finkelstein is a concern about how such obsessive pseudoscholarship abuses history, but her criticism is less fractious. She contends that the community of Holocaust scholars "is under a special obligation to counter the ongoing process of trivialization. Only by scrupulously differentiating between one's ego and the object of one's studies can the meaning of the Holocaust be preserved and protected."[5] The issue, as Birn implies, is how much we indulge in (unconscious) narcissism when we constitute our objects of inquiry as reflections of our beliefs. This is a structure of identification to which no one is completely immune. Yet Birn is seemingly uncritical in her endorsement of the ideal of nonegoistic scholarship that guides our professional training as experts. For example, she comments on Goldhagen's "use of nearly malicious language for the description of particularly terrible facts, presumably to convey sarcastic detachment." It is a style she finds "wholly undignified," suited only for "[a]n argument of immaculate circularity."[6]

Such a criticism raises thorny questions about what it could mean to want to fulfill the criterion of dignity as a professional ideal. What is at stake when scholars write about atrocities in a "dignified" manner?

This question vexes Finkelstein's attempt to use Goldhagen to recast the politics of a pugnacious alignment between truth and a presumably nonideological content in opposition to a suspiciously rhetorical form, which disavows the interdependency between them. Robert Eaglestone has recently endeavored to move us beyond this opposition in his defense of the critical value of "postmodernism" for opening up questions of legitimation.[7] Eaglestone's postmodernist role model is Hayden White, who is famous for his critique of the naively positivist ideals of historical objectivity and empirical transparency. White's work since the 1960s has encouraged critical skepticism vis-à-vis earnest proclamations in the name of science that posit a clear separation between substantive-epistemological criteria, on the one hand, and moral-rhetorical criteria, on the other. His attention to the rhetorical and ideological content of the *forms* of history (and theory) illuminates how all such protocols mediate both the representation of the past and each other. Every form (narrative, metaphor, order) will subtly persuade or fail to persuade others of the authority of the worldview, values, and judgments that the representation as a whole conveys.[8]

White's attention to the "inexpungeable relativity" of every referent informs his use of the term *emplotment* to underscore, with Roland Barthes, the rhetoricity of history as a poetic configuration of events that imitates generic models.[9] Insofar as such models construct texts by setting up the parameters according to which they are written, history, as Eaglestone asserts, "is not the past objectively reconstructed, but texts constituted by generic rules that claim to represent the past."[10] To Eaglestone's argument, I would add that we safeguard our authority as scholars only insofar as we consistently obey these rules that we learned as students and then as researchers imitating the paradigms that a particular disciplinary tradition and the shifting trends of intellectual history have placed before us. One of my principal claims is that such obedience is a function of a narcissistic investment in how we are perceived by others who might decide on the basis of our inadequate rigor to banish us from the circle of respectability. It is, in short, a risky matter of *speaking properly*, of suitable conduct, that might foster social acceptance, or deny it.

This is to emphasize that the protocols of professional scholarship are not only epistemological and logical, but are also social to the extent that they imply a standard of appropriate behavior. The performance of expertise is implicated in the sociogenesis of subjectivity, or what is more commonly referred to as subject formation. When Birn castigates Goldhagen for his "wholly undignified" style, she is calling attention to his failure to simulate a convincing *appearance of restraint*, which stipulates affect management. We must hide our feelings—or, at the very least, not let on to their intensity—

when we perform and thereby constitute our roles as authoritative experts. Of course, restraint as a sign of professionalism goes far beyond the ivory tower, where professors pass it along to their student disciples, since it is also a bourgeois norm that popular culture transmits to consumers, parents to their children, and employers to their workers.

An issue I bring to the fore in my analysis of Goldhagen's reception is that the dissemination of disciplinary codes transpires, not just in the production, but also in the reception of scholarship written with a particular audience in mind whose members' identities are thereby implied. The subtle enlistment of implied readers for particular lessons renders them susceptible to slippages between epistemological criteria and moral values about what should be represented and how. Whether readers identify with these protocols and values determines the persuasive force of the account. Yet persuasiveness is not merely effected by the logic, thoroughness, and precision of a presentation, since it is imbricated in culturally specific codes of good behavior. To respond with belief to a statement is also to react to its intelligibility as a by-product of conventions that have become familiar and thus acceptable through inherited and current paradigms. The commonplace I am reiterating here is that belief is, in part, a function of this feeling of familiarity that affirms the continuing power of role models to delimit notions of propriety and validity even when the information or ideas being conveyed are relatively new. Part of what is at stake in my use of the terms *discipline* and *disciplinary* is, thus, not only the field of inquiry that determines and is determined by the communities that heed particular rules for producing and presenting knowledge. I am also emphasizing the *imaginary* and *mimetic* dimensions of scholarship—what I am calling the *disciplinary imaginary*—that conscripts its producers and readers into reinvesting in particular models and protocols as the parameters of knowledge, authority, and social conduct.

My theorization of the disciplinary imaginary reopens the problematic hermeneutical legacy of what Wilhelm Dilthey called *Verstehen* (empathetic understanding) identified as a praxis specific to the human sciences. It might be recalled that Dilthey conjoins *Verstehen* with a reflection on the question of how "the mental construction of the mind-affected world make[s] knowledge of mind-affected reality possible." Understanding is, for Dilthey, "the rediscovery of the I in the Thou" whereby "the mind rediscovers itself at ever higher levels of connectedness." He adds that "this sameness of the mind in the I and the Thou and in every subject of a community, in every system of culture and, finally, in the totality of mind and universal history, makes the working together of the different processes in the human studies possible. In these," Dilthey declares, "the knowing subject is one with its object, which is the same at all stages of its objectification."[11] This definition already signals a tendency in the empathetic imagination to fall prey to an "identitarian" neutralization of differences, to a thematization of the other as a projection of the same. What becomes palpable from an analysis of debates about the Holocaust is that its emotional charge often incites a kind of projectile narcissism that not only blurs asymmetries between the I and the Thou, but also eclipses the other's perspective at the expense of both reality and justice. From the standpoint of ideology critique, such narcissism redoubles the difficulty of distinguishing epistemological criteria from moral criteria. In other words, when are moral judgments about the way the past *should be seen* (and how an implied "we" *should feel* about it) coded as descriptive statements about how things *actually were?*

My conception of the disciplinary imaginary is intended to foreground the social implications of the modes of idealization that are involved in formalizing traumatic history as an object of discourse. One of the impetuses of my approach derives from Michel Foucault's definition of the "principle of discipline" in "The Order of Discourse" (1970).[12] Foucault defines a discipline as "a domain of objects, a set of methods, a corpus of propositions considered to be true, a play of rules and definitions, of techniques and instruments. . . ."[13] In this conception, a discipline exerts "a principle of control over the production of discourse" that fixes its limits through "a permanent re-actuation of the rules."[14] This "re-actuation" perpetuates a discipline beyond its emergence in keeping with a contextual horizon that provisionally delineates its relation to what it excludes.

Foucault's delimitation of the "principle of discipline" emphasizes the importance of rules that regulate the formulation of valid statements and the determination of new knowledge. Foucault is committed to a formal appraisal of the political and material effects of discourse as a medium of knowledge, power, and subject formation. He is therefore careful to demarcate his understanding of disciplinary discourse from metaphysical views of intention and reference as originary essences. In a discipline, "what is supposed at the outset is not a meaning which has to be rediscovered, nor an identity which has to be repeated, but the requisites for the construction of new statements."[15]

In keeping with Foucault's standpoint on discursive formations, I understand a discipline as a methodologically distinct domain of inquiry by virtue of its practitioners' adherence to the rules that delimit the contents, form, and parameters of an object of inquiry. This object is created and institutionalized through a cross-referencing among public statements about it over time. In contrast to Foucault, however, I argue that scholars preconsciously rely on an idealized concept when they defend a "rigorous" mode of representing their object as if it were a static presence. The idealization I call the *object proper* is a selective admixture of interpretations, which serves as a *regulative fiction* for the expert enunciations that reactuate and reauthorize it.

In tracing the emergence of the text in structuralist and poststructuralist theories of the 1960s and 1970s, John Mowitt employs the term *disciplinary reason* to describe the ways in which "rules shade into norms" in producing the identity and institutional coherence of a community of scholars.[16] Extrapolating on the Foucauldian nuances of the term, Mowitt notes that the rules of scholarship become *disciplinary*, in the sense of punishing, when scholars criticize or ostracize those who do not adopt them. *Disciplinary reason* plays on the double sense of *discipline* for Foucault as a field of inquiry as well as a system of protocols that monitors (through punishments and rewards) discourse, knowledge, and subject formation in the human sciences.

In a 1976 interview, Foucault explains that his aim in *Discipline and Punish* is to show how, in the seventeenth and eighteenth centuries, "a new 'economy' of power was established" comprising procedures that allowed its effects "to circulate in a manner at once continuous, uninterrupted, adapted, and 'individualized' throughout the entire social body."[17] This "new" form of power is "efficient" from the standpoint of capitalist interests, because the technologies it deploys enhance the visibility of subjects, which impels them to internalize their own surveillance. Foucault derives his conception of disciplinary power partly from Jeremy Bentham's eighteenth-century design for a prison featuring a central watchtower with wide windows facing an inner "showcase" ring of prison cells. In Foucault's cinematic characterization,

> [a]ll that is needed, then, is to place a supervisor in a central tower and to shut up in each cell a madman, a patient, a condemned man, a worker or a schoolboy. By the effect of backlighting, one can observe from the tower, standing out precisely against the light, the small captive shadows in the cells of the periphery. They are like so many cages, so many small theatres, in which each actor is alone, perfectly individualized and constantly visible.[18]

Foucault's "microphysics" of discipline diffuses a notion of centralized power as the property of a repressive state to characterize how dispersed relations of control are rooted in a social network: they proliferate subject positions with their respective norms, and thereby produce discourse as well as "docile bodies" and even "populations" that behave in "the proper way" rather than merely hemming in identity, speech, action, and desire.

Mowitt's critique of disciplinary reason suggests that scholars imaginatively constitute an object of inquiry as a touchstone for judgments of validity and the principles of substantive or methodological inclusion and exclusion they perform; in this manner, they also establish an imaginary basis for membership in a discourse community. My emphasis, drawing on Mowitt, is that the imagined object is an idealized memory composite that determines the focus and scope of expert discourse about it. At stake in the defense of the object proper is thus a desire to standardize its contents and police its parameters as a foundation of inquiry and as an anchor of professional power.

Eaglestone has defended a "postmodernist" critical stance in studies of Holocaust discourse against those who use that term to reject peremptorily a loose blend of very different antifoundationalist theories about history, language, and identity. This amalgam is excoriated as ahistorical, amoral, and apolitical—in short, as relativistic—because it ostensibly seduces us into doubting the reality of historical referents.[19] Cathy Caruth paraphrases Paul de Man's 1982 essay "The Resistance to Theory" to remind us that "linguistically orientated theories do not necessarily deny reference but rather deny the possibility of modeling the principles of reference on those of natural law, or, we might say, of making reference like perception."[20] Caruth's remark eloquently pinpoints what is at stake in my post-positivist formulation of the proper. This formulation is based on Roland Barthes' 1957 essay "Myth Today," which offers a theory for the fixation of meaning through the ideological deformation of the sign.[21] Myth, or what other critics call *ideology*, is conveyed by discourse; it is not itself an object, a concept, or an idea; it is, rather, a mode of signification whereby a type of social usage "is added to pure matter."[22] Myth petrifies the concept and presents its social usage, its motive, as a neutral reason. In this way, the history that falls from the meaning to the concept assumes the appearance of a natural fact. Hence the modus operandi of myth as Barthes understands it: to transform a meaning into a form and thus convert history into nature.[23] Ultimately, however, it is the motivated character of mythic signification that distinguishes it from the arbitrary sign. Indeed, the "health" of language depends on this arbitrariness. What is nauseating about myth, according to Barthes, is precisely this *excess* of motivation that has been frozen and naturalized as fact.

As an imaginary touchstone for disciplinary inquiry, the object proper cannot altogether be separated from myth as Barthes defines it. In semiotic terms, the object proper is the ideological product of an attempt to fix the signified of an object. This signified is, then, an *idealized concept* that has been given the status of an already constituted neutral referent. The well-trained scholar seeks to reproduce this "anterior" ideal through a rigorous interpretation that is deemed successful to the extent that it manages to realize the "substance" or "essence" of the object proper. Before interpretation, the concept of an object of inquiry is a nebulous blur of aspects, details, and themes that assumes its provisional determinacy through a contextually mediated act of delimitation. When scholars make recourse to the proper, they are attempting to freeze and thereby eternalize a particular delimitation of the concept beyond the horizon of its emergence. In this manner, the idealized object proper memorializes the concept as a stable locus of disciplinary knowledge.[24]

The extremely traumatic violence of the Nazi atrocities against the Jews and other "racial inferiors" provokes disciplinary reason as scholars seek to control the moral significance of the past for different groups. In the five chapters that follow, I will be employing the concept of the disciplinary imaginary to describe the nexus of scientific, aesthetic, moral, and rhetorical ideals that scholars in different fields invoke as they defend an "appropriate" (rigorous and ethical) approach to the Holocaust. Part of my focus is on scholars' and critics' endeavors to regulate interpretation by excluding "insufficiently rigorous," "immoral," "profane," or "pornographic" representations of the Jewish genocide. When I speak of disciplining the Holocaust, I am referring to efforts to secure its moral and historical significance for "us" against potential trivializations over time.

The 1996 controversy that followed the publication of Daniel Jonah Goldhagen's *Hitler's Willing Executioners* provides a case in point for the disciplinary logic involved in the contestation over how to represent traumatic history.[25] As a bitter aftereffect of the Jewish genocide, Goldhagen's ressentiment challenges historians' reliance on logical criteria to define appropriate Holocaust historiography. I argue that part of what is at stake in the attack on Goldhagen is a refusal to allow his ressentiment to trouble "our" discipline. It is Goldhagen who therefore behaves "improperly" in his accusatory statements about "the Germans" who are his target. I am suggesting that we reconsider the theoretical implications of Goldhagen's "undignified" ressentiment as an understandable response to a genocide that destroyed families, communities, and future generations. The voluble academic reaction to Goldhagen's weak logic exposes the depth of academics' investment in the protocol of restraint, which is inextricably bound up with the epistemological ideal of rigor that governs professional scholarship as a mode of rational behavior.

The polarized reception of *Hitler's Willing Executioners* reveals that Goldhagen's angry argument about Germany's transhistorical anti-Semitism had very different impacts on nonacademic readers and academic readers, as well as on conservatives, liberals, and the New Left. In Germany, too, "the gap between academics and public was also a gap between the generations."[26] If Goldhagen "struck a chord" in Germany, as Geoff Eley contends, then it was not on substantive grounds, but rather because his book "regalvanized public attention for a self-critical perspective precisely as the countervailing pressures mounted for bringing Germany's struggle with its Nazi past to some final and reassuring closure." For this reason, Eley concludes, "*Hitler's Willing Executioners* will remain an event in the history of Germany's late-twentieth-century public culture long after the noise surrounding its scholarly credentials has faded away."[27]

It cannot go without saying that the histories of European and American imperialism and colonialism are punctuated by atrocities that have all too often approached a genocidal scale; however, because the Nazi crimes were perpetrated in a presumably "rational" and largely fair-skinned Europe, the West's traumatized complacency has variably manifested itself in philosophy and literary criticism as a sacralizing attitude about the "unrepresentability" of state-engineered mass death. Adorno played a seminal role in inaugurating this attitude when he disclaimed the possibility of writing lyric poetry "after Auschwitz." After his return to Germany, he published a statement in 1949 that has since been cited in nearly every subsequent discussion concerning the propriety and limits of representing the "Final Solution": "To write poetry after Auschwitz is barbaric. And this corrodes even the knowledge of why it has become impossible to write poetry today."[28] In *Negative Dialectics* (1966), Adorno softens the so-called *Lyrikverbot* (lyric prohibition), but puts forward still another critical absolute: "All post-Auschwitz culture, including its urgent critique, is garbage."[29] These two statements have sometimes been read as a postmetaphysical transliteration of the biblical prohibition against graven images of the sacred or divine.[30] Adorno's secularization of the Second Commandment disclaims identitarian and affirmative culture "after Auschwitz."

As his readings of Stefan George and Eduard Mörike in "On Lyric Poetry and Society" indicate, Adorno's critique was, as White paraphrases it, directed "against a certain kind of romantic, sentimental and schmaltzy kind of lyricism that used horrified comment on horrifying events as proof of the sensitivity of the commentator."[31] Yet Adorno does grant a critical dialectical potential to modernist literature that does not reproduce "the harmonious narrative of traditional realist forms," but rather, as Michael Rothberg characterizes it, enunciates "the rifts that realist mimesis represses."[32] The writings of Samuel Beckett, Franz Kafka, and Paul Celan repeat the forces of domination at the level of form, and thereby bring about a negative aesthetic experience of what exceeds or resists them. Art's unintelligible or visceral element refracts the social domination of inner and outer nature effected by an increasingly rationalized capitalist society. If "the work of art's detachment from empirical reality is at the same time mediated by that reality,"[33] then the very possibility of art is negatively determined by an encounter with the materiality of domination itself, which the form of the work simultaneously recapitulates and repudiates. By definition, then, this element cannot be assimilated to an axiomatic "meaning" or to an intuition of any kind that reduces the work to the consolation of individual freedom, which would betray the continuity and irremediability of suffering. In sum, Adorno's so-called lyric prohibition was not targeting lyrics or poetry *tout court*, but the possibility of "private" expressions of resistance that proclaim the individual's uniqueness in spite of and in complicity with a reified society that spawned anonymous mass murder in the death factories. As he writes in *Aesthetic Theory*, "It is the conciliatory element of culture in art that characterizes even its most violent protestation."[34] The "lyrical" representation of experience, which affirms the dignity of the "I" that frames it, is the precipitate of a metaphysical heritage, a commodity economy (including the sentimental tendencies of mass entertainment), and a universal history narrated as progress. The lyric therefore functions rhetorically for Adorno as the merely apparent exception that proves the rule for all potentially resistant creative culture.

Adorno's stance is ultimately more complicated than his isolated statements indicate. For example, he eschewed the morality forbidding art to forget even for a second that "pleasure can be squeezed" from "the so-called artistic rendering of the naked physical pain of those who were beaten down with rifle butts."[35] Such didacticism, as Adorno cautions, "slides off into the abyss of its opposite," since even "the sound of desperation pays tribute to a heinous affirmation."[36] In spite of these qualifications, the lyric prohibition's circulation in popular as well as many academic discussions about the Holocaust since the 1960s has consecrated a dogmatic premise that reflections about and representations of the Shoah must be governed by a negative aesthetic that scrupulously avoids the danger of identity-affirming representations. This rhetoric shapes the work of French theorists such as Jean-François Lyotard and Maurice Blanchot, whose references to Auschwitz are conspicuously influenced by Adorno. While Lyotard's reading of *Negative Dialectics* draws on Adorno's critique of Hegelian logic to connect Auschwitz to the aporetic "wound of nihilism" that skepticism opened in philosophy, Blanchot transposes Adorno through the dictum that there can be no fiction narrative about Auschwitz.[37] George Steiner also contributed to the institutionalization of Adorno in the United States as a mouthpiece for the impasse faced by art after Auschwitz, a catastrophe that hastened the downfall of tragedy proper in Steiner's terms.[38] For some staunch critics of the *Holocaust* miniseries (1978) and Steven Spielberg's *Schindler's List* (1993), Adorno's challenge to the possibility of an authentically resistant art after Auschwitz translated into an interdiction against film dramatizations of the Holocaust that arrogantly assume adequate "re-creations" of the genocide are possible and desirable as a means of moral enlightenment. James E. Young succinctly encapsulates the ethos of artistic expression about the genocide "after Adorno" as the question of "how to represent it without thereby recuperating it."[39]

During the last four decades, various forms of public discourse about the Holocaust in West Germany, France, and the United States have popularized the trope of the genocide's alleged "unrepresentability." Based on the logic that mass murder and the death-camp universe simultaneously fall outside of and break down commonplace and philosophical notions of experience, Auschwitz is sometimes constructed as incommensurable with everyday life and as "unrepresentable" (or "unspeakable") in its terms. Naomi Mandel facetiously spotlights the disciplinary valence of the rhetoric of unspeakability in Holocaust discourse played as an "identity game": "Who gets to call whom a 'Nazi'? Who can play the far more popular role of 'Jew'? Who gets to participate in a collective psyche that represses the Holocaust or is traumatized by it? Whose history is so horrific that it is, like the Holocaust, unspeakable?"[40] With this project, I join Mandel in declaring a moratorium on the melancholic fetishism of unrepresentability and unspeakability that deflects our complicity with the modes of conduct that facilitated the Holocaust and other genocides since 1945. My supplement to Mandel's argument is to demystify this clichéd rhetoric by stressing its intellectual lineages and cultural sedimentations, which have formed the horizon of the kinds of statements that might be made about the mass murder of European Jews.

This horizon coalesces in debates about Holocaust memorialization that concretize the social, cultural, political, and economic stakes of attempts to make public determinations of moral propriety—the question of how various groups should feel about the Nazi crimes. Young describes the conservative force of memorials as forms of public discourse that provide spatially fixed figurations of the collective memory of an event, group, and/or individual and regulate identifications with the past. This mode of fixation is key to my understanding of the object proper as an imaginary anchor for scholarly interpretations.

"In the eyes of modern critics and artists," Young observes, "the traditional monument's essential stiffness and grandiose pretensions to permanence doom it to an archaic, premodern status." "What seems worse" to Young "is the monument's insistence that its meaning is as fixed as its place in the landscape—its obliviousness to the essential mutability of all cultural artifacts and the way in which all art's significance evolves over time." In this respect, "monuments have rather sought to provide a naturalizing locus for memory, casting a state's triumphs and martyrs, its ideals and founding myths, in forms as naturally true as the landscape in which they stand." Yet as Young recognizes, these are merely the monument's "sustaining illusions, the principles of its seeming longevity and power." Ultimately, however, "neither the monument nor its meaning is really everlasting. Both are constructed in particular times and places, contingent on the political, historical, and aesthetic realities of the moment."[41]

Karen E. Till situates memorials in the category of "official urban landscapes of memory," including museums and monuments, or even the urban landscape itself.[42] Such rhetorical topoi, as M. C. Boyer calls them, are emblematic of the relationship between power and memory to the extent that they concentrate myriad complex meanings into a territorial and dramaturgical act.[43] Till observes that memorial rituals "'naturalize' a collective identity as citizens physically enact what is normal, appropriate or possible for a group at a particular setting."[44] Neither relics nor traces, they advance interested and typically sacralizing constructions of historical moments in a permanent public form. These meanings stand in for contradictory, differential, and diffuse collective memories that cannot be viewed simply as an accumulation of individual recollections, as Till remarks. Such memories reflect "the activities that go into making a version of the past resonate with group members" whose own identities are defined in part by social narratives that are always changing to accommodate "perceived group needs in the present and projected future."[45] Memorials thus seem to unify an existing collective memory while actually constituting its "proper" content as what must be passed along to future generations; they thereby convert the proliferative and dispersive differentiation of the past among various constituencies with conflicting relationships to its official interpretation into an immobile external form.

Enshrined on squares of concrete and grass, the conventional memorial freezes a lesson about the past so that it is empowered to survive beyond the context of its enunciation and thereby defer the eventual obsolescence of the interests that built it. The memorial thus sets itself against the fading of an affective investment in a particular version of a collective memory. Whether memorials are representational or abstract, their form congeals this investment in space in order to protect it over time. By defying the flux of remembering, memorials literalize Barthes' definition of myth: they transform a meaning into a form and thus convert history into nature.

In the second chapter, I will trace the instauration of a moral imaginary that emerges in the period immediately before and after Germany's reunification in discussions beginning in the late 1980s about the Berlin Memorial to the Murdered Jews of Europe designed by Peter Eisenman, which opened to the public in 2005. This discussion commenced in the wake of the 1986 Historians' Debate (*der Historikerstreit*) about the centrality of the Holocaust in German history and the ethical limits of the historian's role in determining the contents of national consciousness. The issues linking Jürgen Habermas's intervention in this debate before reunification with the reception of Goldhagen ten years later helped to forge the hegemonic power of a West German standpoint in defining an appropriate mode of working through the Nazi past. In effect, the discussions about the memorial initiated by the television journalist Lea Rosh in collaboration with the historian Eberhard Jäckel translated Habermas's insistence on a victim-centered (post)national imaginary in the writing of Third Reich history into aesthetic protocols governing the external form and content of an ethical historical consciousness. Academic experts, artists, and public officials succeeded in asserting their sense of taste over and against the "lowbrow" sentimentality of the nonacademic participants in finalizing the Berlin memorial's form. The interests of this taste favored a "deconstructivist" style exemplified by the Jewish architect Daniel Libeskind, who designed the Berlin Jewish Museum. It is not coincidental, then, that Eisenman, the winner of the memorial competition, has interpreted Jacques Derrida's critique of the metaphysics of presence as a "Hebraic" provocation to rethink architecture. Eisenman's "deconstructed minimalism" marks the power of the rhetoric of sublime unrepresentability associated with Adorno's negative aesthetics. The emergence of this arguably "Jewish" style as a negative memorial genre indicates that moral protocols have bled into aesthetic conventions that regulate the kind of sentiments viewers should experience while reflecting on the contemporary significance of German responsibility for the Third Reich's crimes.

Giorgio Agamben briefly critiques the rhetoric of unrepresentability in *Remnants of Auschwitz*, which has attracted a great deal of attention in recent years for its reconsideration of the stakes of Holocaust testimony in light of Foucault's theses on biopower.[46] For Agamben, the death camps illustrate the absolute reach of biopower as the capacity to administer the life and death of populations. In Foucault's words, biopower designates "what brought life and its mechanisms into the realm of explicit calculations and made knowledge-power an agent of transformation of human life." What might be called "society's 'threshold of modernity' has been reached when the life of the species is wagered on its own political strategies" and "modern man" has fatefully fulfilled a potential to become "an animal whose politics places his existence as a living being in question."[47]

In "The Birth of Biopolitics," Foucault conjoins biopower with his historicization of liberalism as a "principle and a method of rationalizing the exercise of government, a rationalization that obeys . . . the internal rule of maximum economy." Liberal rationalization begins from the premise that the activity of governing humans "in the framework of, and by means of, state institutions" cannot be its own end.[48] Rather, this end is aligned with society, "which is in a complex relation of exteriority and interiority with respect to the state."[49]

According to Agamben, biopower supplements sovereign power by enabling "bare life," the practices that reproduce the conditions of survival, to come under the purview of politics as its excluded condition. Nazi biopolitics collapsed the border between survival and political existence in pursuit of unlimited sovereignty. In the case of the Jews in Germany, as Carolyn Dean remarks, "many Germans supported the concentration camps in their midst because the regime presented them as an effective antidote to lawlessness."[50] The visceral realities of mass murder—acrid smoke and a drizzle of bony ash, the gradual reduction of a human body to the skeletal brink of death, the production of "life that does not deserve to live"—took place in the very midst of society. Nazi policies thereby suspended the difference between sociopolitical and bioeconomic survival in defining the right to *live with* (in a community) as the right to live at all.[51]

Agamben's elaboration on the biopolitical stakes of Holocaust testimony enjoins a reexamination of the ways in which the conditions for the "Final Solution" "arose within a world that remains ours," to borrow Mowitt's phrasing.[52] The administration of mass death continues as the supplement to the sovereign power of industrialized nations that permit famine and disease to ravage certain "other populations." Hence the apparent continuity and "ordinariness" of everyday life is the "grace" a dominant group confers on itself by derealizing the precarious situation of those "other populations" it harms.[53] My failure to act on empathetic feelings for their exceptionalized desperation and suffering hereby attains the status of a civilizing norm.

Yet despite his warnings against ontologizing Auschwitz as "a reality absolutely separated from language," it is hard to see how Agamben avoids that trap when he declares that Holocaust "survivors bore witness to something it is impossible to bear witness to," a "lacuna," or more precisely, a "caesura." This irremediable gap marks testimony about the concentration camps as paradigmatic enactments of biopower that absolutely separated the living from the speaking being when they transformed the human into a "a bare, unassignable and unwitnessable" subsistence, and the "inhuman" as such.[54] Agamben's vocabulary recalls the idiom of Lyotard, who preceded him by fifteen years with his analysis in The Differend (1983) of the silences that freight testimony about mass murders in the death camps. It is here, too, that Lyotard takes up the philosophical challenge posed by Robert Faurisson's negation of the historical reality of the gas chambers to the moral authority of death camp survivor testimony. "'Auschwitz' after Lyotard" (chapter 3) traces this figuration through Lyotard's critiques of the metaphysical and humanist assumptions that pervade phenomenological, empirical, and ontological formulations of experience.

In "Discussions, or Phrasing 'after Auschwitz'" (1980), Lyotard orchestrates a dialectic between Adorno and Derrida, which is philosophically overdetermined by a post-Hegelian and posthumanist critique of consciousness and experience that informed French philosophy after World War II. This is a lineage that, as Derrida has remarked in "The Ends of Man,"[55] amalgamated Hegel's, Husserl's, and Heidegger's phenomenologies into a reductive anthropologism. The influence of this critique compels Lyotard to read "Auschwitz" after Adorno as an event that derails metaphysical understandings of experience and the human proper. In The Differend, Lyotard's debt to Adorno is manifest again in the negative critical aesthetic that he derives from bringing Ludwig Wittgenstein's observations on language games to bear on Immanuel Kant's various considerations of judgment. This critical aesthetic is "negative" in a philosophical sense, since it emphasizes how the "truth content" of survivor testimony is vexed by the contingencies of its reception, which is why it only becomes intelligible as the affect evoked through its negation by dominant discourse—the feeling, as Lyotard understands it, that justice has been left in abeyance. This move is problematic because it potentially sacralizes the failure to comprehend mass murder by endowing it with the status of a sublime "sign of history" that opens the postmodern.[56]

Dorota Glowacka acknowledges that debates about Holocaust literature and art "have become the site where the relationships between ethics and aesthetics enter a hiatus." This hiatus takes the form of "a radical discrepancy between the piety of memory and the iconoclastic impetus of art called upon

to convey that memory."[57] In defending Lyotard against critics of his "panaes-
theticism of the sublime," Glowacka calls attention to the suppression of the
aesthetic dimension of representation in commentaries on Holocaust literature
and art that promote a "hegemony" of the ethical.[58] *The Differend* undermines
this "hegemony" by foregrounding the importance of affect for a philosophy of
testimony that contests the monopoly of cognition in the writing and reception of history. As Claire Nouvet has recently attested, the value of Lyotard's
focus in *The Differend* on the aesthetic dimension of hearing testimony lies
in his delineation of an "inarticulate" affectivity. This affectivity not only
ignores a referentiality that "presupposes interlocution," but also suspends the
determination of cause and effect by signaling only itself.[59] Because affect is
"tautogorical" in this sense, its singular testimony, according to Nouvet, is
"doomed to be judged both irrefutable . . . and equivocal" in logos: it either
produces belief or fails to in the absence of visible evidence.[60]

Nouvet's preliminary characterization of Lyotard's philosophy of testimony in *The Differend* identifies affect but "not libido" as the "monster
which scandalizes the very rules of philosophical cognition."[61] Yet Nouvet
herself recognizes that a distinction between affect and libido falls apart in
the context of Lyotard's own prior theorization of the libidinal economy
(1974).[62] My return to Freudian psychoanalysis after Lyotard is intended to
extend an inquiry about affect and its domestication in and beyond aesthetic
experiences as a by-product of the libidinal, imaginary, and social registers
of identification. In the fourth chapter, I examine the conditions and limits
of the psychoanalytic framework for evaluating traumatic affect in discourse
about the Holocaust.

In the early 1990s, Dominick LaCapra and Eric Santner proposed
compelling models of "working through" and mourning that incorporate
psychoanalytic concepts; however, because they are committed to holding
perpetrators responsible for their crimes while respecting the specificity
of the victims' suffering, both critics tend to foreground the ethical and
conscious valences of working through while expropriating Freud's theses
on the drives and fantasy. In this respect, they sidestep crucial questions
about traumatic affect that a psychoanalytic emphasis on the unconscious
commits us to ask. Chapter 4 therefore returns to Freud's theory of trauma
and compulsive repetition in *Beyond the Pleasure Principle* (1920) in order to
recover the role of the unconscious in the process of working through the
past. Trauma is primarily an "economic" problem for Freud that aggravates
a systemic need to regulate the quantity and force of tensions such as posttraumatic anxiety that pressure the psychophysical apparatus from within.
Because working through is inseparable from the economic aim of defusing
excess affect, it cannot be restricted to a process of achieving conscious critical awareness (premised on free will) as LaCapra and Santner understand
it. To take psychoanalysis seriously is to consider how critical reflection is
unconsciously organized.

In his observations of World War I veterans, Freud finds it remarkable that their traumatic nightmares force them to relive painful events. This thesis troubles his emphasis on unconscious wish fulfillment in *The Interpretation of Dreams* and leads him to posit an unconscious masochism in traumatic repetition. Freud subsequently speculates on this mechanism in "The Economic Problem of Masochism" (1924), where a primal destructive tendency figured by the death drive manifests itself in externally or internally directed aggressions. According to Freud, these aggressions are sexually "bound" through sadistic and/or masochistic pleasure. Sadomasochistic fantasies thus provide an imaginary forum for exorcising and enjoying aggressions against a social order that demands their repression and for the play of self-images that simultaneously enact, resist, and regulate and that are, in their turn, regulated by a subject's desire for social acceptance.

My argument, following Judith Butler, is that this desire fosters a susceptibility to internal surveillance that Foucault identified as an effect of disciplinary power. In *The Psychic Life of Power* (1997), Butler has observed that Foucault's *Discipline and Punish* restricts subjectification to the symbolic register.[63] He thereby distances himself from Louis Althusser's conception of ideological interpellation as an imaginary and a material process. Yet Foucault's stress on the material impact of the practices that render the subject visible in relation to a network of discursively constructed categories does not offer a satisfying explanation for how the process of becoming a subject of discipline is consolidated by the imaginary and its pleasures.

Freud provides a prospective answer to this question in identifying a "moral" form of masochism as an internalization of the judgmental and punishing force of social norms and constraints. This disciplinary masochism indicates a primary destructive (i.e., "death-driven") impetus for the self-critical scrutiny of past behavior and decisions. In my reading, Freud's speculations about the death drive as a primal urge to revert to a state of inorganic stasis might be viewed as a *refraction* of the force of norms that require the management and suppression of affect, the very protocol of self-restraint that Goldhagen in his "undignified" anger oversteps. Freud's understanding of moral masochism thus provides the basis for my argument that internalized self-surveillance is involved in critical reflection as a process of evaluating the propriety of personal conduct from symbolizations of the past. So conceived, such symbolizations of traumatic events may deepen the insinuation of an internalized punitive gaze into memories, which makes it difficult to determine where moral masochism ends and critical reflection begins.

Ultimately, then, my return to Freud allows me to rethink memory as an imaginary and socially mediated venue of disciplinary formation. This is to view memories as signs that are inflected by contexts of interpretation along with the expectations and conventions that attend them. Memories are *sociographic* (borrowing from Mowitt) in this sense even as they are selectively constituted in the imaginary, which is the site of fantasies and narcissistic identifications. This standpoint on memory's potentially disciplinary force brings me full circle and back to the question of my own desire to study the Holocaust in particular and traumatic memory more generally. This desire is fueled in part by my "Jewish" outrage about disavowed violence against vulnerable groups in the past and present, but also, perhaps, by a narcissistic "wounded liberal attachment," to echo Wendy Brown,[64] to seeing myself as a person who cares about injustice and sympathizes with "the victims." In this connection, the last chapter, "Unspeakable Differences, Obscene Pleasures: The Holocaust as an Object of Desire," extends my inquiry governing the disciplinary role of fantasy in enabling sympathy with victims of persecution. This chapter foregrounds the agency of feminist protocols governing the representation of sex and gender in the professionalization of sympathy among critics who are committed to examining the historiographical implications of women's testimony about genocide. My critical method involves treating my own associations as symptomatic of a disciplinary imaginary shaped by the legacies of Foucault, deconstruction, psychoanalysis, and identity politics. This confessional performance extracts the rules of critical conduct that I have inherited from training in the histories and rhetorics of theory, but also from a confessional culture that constructs self-awareness, particularly where sexual desire is at stake, etiologically and progressively. The issue, then, is whether my discipline, my enlightened ability to "speak properly," is genuinely altered by the impact of new knowledge about the Nazi crimes.

Tim Cole invokes the term "Shoah business" to criticize the ways Americans are being sold a sugarcoated and redemptive myth rather than a historical reality. He observes that "[d]ue to the nature of this past, the craving for meaning . . . verges on the obsessive." Half a century later, "there is far more guilt about the 'Holocaust' than there is understanding."[65] A performative contradiction that I do not avoid is that this project arises from the pressure to "work through" my own truculent obsession with the betrayal of the European Jews and other groups targeted by the Nazis for genocide. Mine is a paranoid and guilt-ridden rage that is reignited by similar betrayals in more recent times, similar failures of empathy as Dean might describe them, that have taken place with alarming frequency since "we" said "never again." Dean's analysis of the "fragility" of empathy after the Holocaust invites us to contemplate the anxiety that surrounds our seemingly constrained ability to respond meaningfully to injustice and violence against others in a society bent on managing affect, and, I would add, in the expert discourses devoted to masking it as a dirty professional secret. Jacques Lacan warns against the rationalization of affect in discourse that rebounds against any attempt to theorize it: "Should analysis ever expose its weakness," Lacan writes, "it would be advisable not to rest content with recourse to 'affectivity.' This taboo-word of dialectical incapacity will, along with the verb 'intellectualize' . . . , remain, in the history of the language, the stigmata of our obtuseness regarding the subject."[66] The challenge I have set for myself in this book is to uncover instances of what Nietzsche decried as a dearly bought, blood-limned "mastery over the affects" and "the whole somber thing called reflection," without perpetuating the illusion of an Archimedean scientific stance that raises me above the disciplinary logics I examine.[67] *Disciplining the Holocaust* is, in the end, an attempt to fathom how our earnest and high-minded scholarship about traumatic history already stoops into cruel obtuseness, an inner coldness that Adorno derided as "the basic principle of bourgeois subjectivity, without which there could have been no Auschwitz."[68]

1

Disciplining Traumatic History

Goldhagen's "Impropriety"

The revered German historian Hans Mommsen concludes his critique of Daniel Goldhagen's *Hitler's Willing Executioners*[1] with a carefully considered judgment: "The corrosive sharpness with which Goldhagen charges the Germans with a will to 'demonic anti-Semitism'—and to make them out not as accomplices but as generally eager perpetrators—is certainly not suited (*sicherlich nicht geeignet*) to laying *ressentiment* to rest (*stillzulegen*) and is anything but helpful in facilitating a sober confrontation with the past directly in light of the present."[2] Mommsen condemns his young American colleague for inappropriately making blanket statements about "the Germans" and contends that Goldhagen's method of representing them as enthusiastic perpetrators is unsuitable for the task of quieting *ressentiment*. This judgment follows a discussion that begins with the thesis that Goldhagen's book does not really justify the inflamed debate surrounding it. Indeed, it "plainly lags behind the current state of research, rests on broadly insufficient foundations, and brings no new insights to bear on answering the question of why it became possible for an advanced and highly civilized country to relapse into barbarism, into the systematic liquidation of millions of innocent human beings—here, primarily, of Jews."[3]

Given these considerable problems, one is struck with the book's success in provoking the likes of Mommsen without being worth the ink that he and others spill in its name. Surely, the inflamed territorial tendencies of professional historians cannot account for all of the sound and fury in the discussion preceding and immediately following the publication of its German translation in August 1996. Moreover, the historians' responses contrast curiously with the book's popularity among the German public—after it was translated, it immediately sold out. Geoff Eley and Atina Grossmann have coined the term "*Goldhagen effect*" to characterize the almost ecstatic public enthusiasm that greeted the German version and its author's triumphal speaking tour, restricted to (formerly) West German cities. Eley surmises that by bringing "the sober and meticulous institutional histories of policy-making down to the ground, showing what they meant in the actions of deliberate and willful individuals," Goldhagen "made it harder to escape the upsetting reality of Holocaust violence,"[4] or, in Jane Caplan's sharp phrasing, the "unmediated moment of individual choice" as the perpetrators "faced and destroyed their victims: as Germans slaughtered Jews."[5]

Writing in *Ha'aretz* in 1997, Ilana Hammermann highlights Goldhagen's tendency to magnify the details of how the perpetrators singled out the Jews in face-to-face interactions of violence and murder. In this manner, he seemingly "calls upon the reader 'to reach for his sword . . . and take revenge against the monster' but at the same time enables him 'to calm himself, since there is no one to slay anymore.' "[6] Hammermann's caustic observation postulates an angry longing for revenge as the underlying ground for the popular response to Goldhagen's "pamphlet" (as she dismissively refers to it), particularly among American Jews, who, as Omer Bartov reminds us, were "probably Goldhagen's most avid consumers in the United States."[7] Caplan supports this interpretation when she points to Goldhagen's frequent use of the pronoun "we" along with his "repeated 'thick' descriptions of the subjective experience of killing," which "are calculated to induce both negative and positive identifications on the part of the reader: a repudiation of the motives and choices that underlay the horrifying acts of the killers, and an empathetic identification with the suffering of their victims." Goldhagen invites his American readers in particular to take comfort in knowing that they "stand on the morally sound side of the partitioned world of guilt and innocence that it presents"—to see themselves as the "heirs of Enlightenment values" while distinguishing themselves from the "alien values and 'radically different' culture" of the Germans. Such ploys are what constitute for Caplan the core strategy of *Hitler's Willing Executioners*: "the logic of how it positions its readers."[8]

Hammermann's and Caplan's comments emphasize Goldhagen's ability to mobilize readers' identifications with a righteous anger and desire for revenge, albeit futile, against "the Germans." It is this effect that has apparently touched a tender nerve of Holocaust historiography: the persistence of Jewish ressentiment that sixty-five years of liberal-democratic rehabilitation in Germany have failed "to put to rest" (*stillzulegen*).[9] Though critics have typically derided the "viscerality" of Goldhagen's style,[10] his rage tends to fall outside of the theoretical purview of the illustrious historians focusing on the book's methodological flaws, of which, to be sure, there is no dearth. In this chapter, I want to reflect on the antidisciplinary status of Goldhagen's ressentiment, which seemingly eludes historicization.

Goldhagen's Impropriety

It is not surprising that historians would blanch at the baldness of Goldhagen's tone. The expression of ressentiment in a scholarly work troubles the unspoken etiquette that historians typically respect in attempting to produce objective-seeming accounts. This is the case insofar as historical writing should at the very least appear not to take sides in order to be considered objective. "Appropriate" history might not be able to escape the task of making judgments, but it avoids grandstanding. "Proper" history implicitly condemns without offending.

Mommsen claims that Goldhagen's approach is unsuitable for a historical reflection that should seek to defuse rather than to fan the fires of ressentiment. This assessment connotes that Goldhagen transgresses the tacit codes of acceptable scientific communication and conduct, that it is, somehow, *improper*. On the flip side, reproaching a survivor's son for expressing anger about German cruelty during the Third Reich also seems "inappropriate" in failing to respect the traumatic impact of mass murder. For while one might expect a Harvard scholar to examine opposing evidence and arguments, is it not unjust to demand polite composure in the case of genocide? Indeed, why should historians be courteous and neutral when describing mass murder and other atrocities? Should not the magnitude of such crimes be allowed to derail the rules of civility respecting scholarly discourse?

Admittedly, this way of posing the problem is misleading. In the case of recent history such as the Holocaust, there is no question of "allowing" this trauma to affect historical writing. Assessing its impact on the writing of history belongs to the work of understanding the specificity of the Shoah as an historical event. For this reason, Goldhagen's ressentiment should not be punished and summarily dismissed as a failure of rationality, but might instead be taken seriously as an object of inquiry in its own right.

I stage this defense of the scientific and moral propriety of Goldhagen's ressentiment in order to highlight the behavioral and stylistic codes that determine acceptable approaches to the Holocaust. When scholars have recourse to notions of propriety, they draw on a nexus of models, expectations, and protocols that define a *disciplined* (i.e., *consistently rigorous*) approach to an object of inquiry. The ideal of rigor thus exerts a normative power to determine the parameters of the object of inquiry, to establish the ethics of its representation, and to regulate membership in the discourse community that focuses on it. As Robert Eaglestone understands it, historical rigor is not scientific; rather, it "stems from the genre or discourse rules of the discipline of history itself."[11] Though I agree with this distinction, I find that historians tend to use the terms *rigor* and *science* interchangeably in debates about historiography. When such rules are broken down in terms of their function, it nevertheless becomes clear how "science" operates as an implicitly moralizing regulative ideal and as a rhetorical effect that professional scholars can reproduce if they obey the rules (as Eaglestone contends).

These functions might be differentiated in accordance with the following rubrics. In the first place, there are *substantive* criteria that demarcate the spatial, temporal, and otherwise factual and thematic contents of the historical object. In the second place, there are *epistemological* criteria that dictate how and to what extent the object of inquiry can be validly known.[12] Third, the fairness and persuasive force of any history will be assessed on the basis of *moral* criteria, which determine the *propriety* of these representations as bearers of social and cultural meanings and as vehicles for furthering certain ethical and political aims. Here and in the four subsequent chapters, I use the term *moral* to refer to the force of deeply held, emotionally charged, and not always fully conscious ideas about the way things should be. The term *morality* is sometimes distinguished from *ethics*, which translates values into codes of conduct for specific situations. In effect, disciplinary protocols are always ethical in this sense, since values mediate decisions about what aspects of an event should be included or merit more attention than others. Fourth, insofar as no one account can depict every aspect of the past, *stylistic* and *rhetorical* conventions guide the work of historians seeking to produce an *intelligible*, *persuasive*, and *sufficiently complete* representation of the available scholarship.

It should be noted that the four functions involved in the judgment of disciplinary propriety can be distinguished formally but are, in practice, inextricably bound: all four sets of standards inform decisions about which facts will be excluded and how those included will be ordered and weighed in the interests of emphasis and readability. As Hayden White contends, the "governing metaphor of an historical account could be treated as a heuristic rule which self-consciously eliminates certain kinds of data from consideration as evidence."[13] My emphasis, as an extension of White's standpoint, is that the metaphors and narratives that organize content are also social to the extent that they regulate scholarly writing as a mode of professional conduct. Hence the judgment of appropriate behavior is also at stake in evaluations of historical accounts as "just" (valid, reliable, thorough, fair, or respectful) representations of an object.

It will be difficult to say anything about the relationship between scientific and moral propriety that has not already been anticipated by White's keen observation that "historical narrative has as its latent or manifest purpose the desire to moralize the events of which it treats."[14] My interest in the Goldhagen controversy centers on the problems that arise when scientific protocols are alternately opposed to or confused with an ethics of representation in Nazi-period historiography. The locus of this problematic is a perceived split or convergence between scientific and moral notions of propriety where the former derives from the rules for evaluating and configuring evidence and the latter from a feeling that we must respect the traumatic magnitude of mass murder and not discount its perpetrators' responsibility. This problematic conspicuously informs reactions to Goldhagen's refusal to honor the protocols of a scientifically neutral approach when he allows his ressentiment to distort his presentation of German atrocities.

There are, to be sure, numerous substantive and methodological justifications for the "chorus of dismissal" among professional historians commenting on Goldhagen's overhyped scholarly "intervention."[15] In contrast to his nemesis, Christopher Browning, whom Goldhagen treats arrogantly, he refuses to weigh the prospect of ambivalent readings of the documents he examines. He consequently produces a monocausal picture of *certain* Germans' behavior and then compounds this "baldest of essentializing generalizations"[16] by extending it to the wartime German populace as a whole. Goldhagen's assertion of the primacy of German anti-Semitism as a spur to genocide is not a new insight, and Mommsen has a point when he calls the younger scholar's self-proclaimed originality into question. Anson Rabinbach notes that Goldhagen "offers a version of German history as a long preamble to murder, an approach that dismisses the Holocaust as a 'modern' event" in presenting it "as a passionate crime of ethnic hatred deeply rooted in Germany's long history of anti-Semitism."[17] Yet even though Goldhagen forsakes a comparatist approach in portraying the long-term evolution of a virulent "eliminationist" anti-Semitic *Weltanschauung*, "religious in origin, which, since the time of Martin Luther, had festered beneath the surface of German society,"[18] he fails to engage the so-called *Sonderweg* ("special path") thesis that attributes Germany's early twentieth-century authoritarian and illiberal "deviation" to its belated development as a unified state in comparison with other liberal Western nations.[19] Michael Brennan remarks that Goldhagen offsets "a universal[izing] agency for domination" among the Germans by a reified notion of Jewish victimhood. He thus " 'exoticizes' the Holocaust as an exclusively Jewish and German affair" while foreclosing "wider considerations of communities implicated in events"—among them, those who resisted, non-Jewish victims, and those who also collaborated.[20] Moreover, in the few instances where he cites contradictory evidence, Goldhagen does not allow it to qualify his argument about "ordinary" Germans.[21] Indeed, the prevailing rhetorical gesture of the book is a flat and flippant dismissal of opposing research, the discussion of which Goldhagen typically leaves to the footnotes while "aggressively blazing his lone path" as a "fighter against an established and self-satisfied academic elite."[22] The painful lack of intellectual integrity is not helped by his recourse to ironies that are at once too easy and too pointed. Ultimately, poor editing makes these problems all the more annoying because they are repetitive.

Mommsen raises the question as to how it became possible for "an advanced and highly civilized land" to liquidate millions of innocent people, and the Jews "above all," yet in Goldhagen's view, the answer to Mommsen's question "goes without saying": the Germans murdered the Jews because they were thoroughly, relentlessly, and transhistorically anti-Semitic.[23] When commanded to massacre entire villages, to drive humans into cattle cars, and to shoot small children at point-blank range, they could only justify their obedience as the reversal of all other deeply entrenched value systems through a remorseless belief that the Jews were not, in fact, human. They were reviled as *Fremdkörper* (alien bodies) suited for slavery, experimentation, and extermination.[24]

While Mommsen's criticism of *Hitler's Willing Executioners* obviously does not deny these facts, he cannot validate Goldhagen's rage. Instead, he worries that Goldhagen's book will reinforce ressentiment rather than quieting it: his "portrayal of sadistic and gruesome violence releases a certain voyeuristic moment that serious research about the Holocaust has deliberately avoided in its restrained portrayal of the crimes, particularly since it translates at best into mere *Betroffenheit* (affectation of dismay) and contributes little toward real explanation."[25] Mommsen's anxiety may be justified, as the following passage suggests, since Goldhagen minces no words in establishing the personal and sadistic disposition of German cruelty:

> The men of Police Battalion 309 used the marketplace near the Jewish districts to assemble the Jews. . . . *The Germans* took hundreds of Jews from the marketplace to nearby sites, where they shot them. Yet the killing was proceeding too slowly for *the Germans'* taste. . . . *The Germans*, without precise orders about the methods by which to achieve their ends, took their own initiative (as they so often were to do during the Holocaust) in devising a new course of action. . . . The men of Police Battalion 309's First and Third Companies drove their victims into the synagogue, the less compliant Jews receiving from *the Germans* liberal blows of encouragement. *The Germans* packed the large synagogue full. The fearful Jews began to chant and pray loudly. After spreading gasoline around the building, *the Germans* set it ablaze; one of the men tossed an explosive through a window, to ignite the holocaust. The Jews' prayers turned into screams. A battalion member later described the scene that he witnessed: "I saw . . . smoke, that came out of the synagogue and heard there how the incarcerated people cried loudly for help. I was about 70 meters' distance from the synagogue. I could see the building and observed that people tried to escape through the windows. One shot at them. Circling the synagogue stood the police members who were apparently supposed to cordon it off, in order to ensure that no one emerged." Between 100 and 150 men of the battalion surrounded the burning synagogue. They collectively ensured that none of the appointed Jews escaped the inferno. They watched as over seven hundred people died this hid-

eous and painful death, listening to screams of agony. Most of the victims were men, though some women and children were among them. Not surprisingly, some of the Jews within spared themselves the fiery death by hanging themselves or severing their arteries. At least six Jews came running out of the synagogue, their clothes and bodies aflame. *The Germans* shot each one down, only to watch these human torches burn themselves out.

With what emotions did the men of Police Battalion 309 gaze upon this sacrificial pyre to the exterminationist creed? One exclaimed: "Let it burn, it's a nice little fire (*schönes Feuerlein*), it's great fun." Another exulted: "Splendid, the entire city should burn down."[26] (My emphasis)

A quick glance at Goldhagen's language in this passage reveals a tone that embraces its own exclamation points and almost seems to rejoice in its failed sobriety. Yet while his illustrations are not subtly presented, neither are they patently exaggerated even as he moves into narrative high gear. His language is openly condemning, and it allows for no exceptions or ambivalence. He crafts his images with dramatic precision, careful to emphasize (and reemphasize) *the Germans'* initiative in carrying out this genocidal "innovation." Goldhagen defends this emphasis in his introduction as a method of stressing the perpetrators' identity and agency. In practice, it has the force of an accusation with each repetition.

The young Harvard scholar is certainly not shy about employing emphatic modifiers to increase our horror in response to the actions of Police Battalion 309 as they burned Jews alive in the Bialystok synagogue. Phrases such as "fiery death," "sacrificial pyre," and "human torch" resonate with the lurid figures of pulp fiction, what Norman G. Finkelstein calls "Holoporn" and Ruth Bettina Birn describes as "the style used in bad historical novels."[27] In fairness to his critics, one wonders why an episode that is so tragic and grotesque nevertheless requires dramatic intensification. Does Goldhagen think that his readers will be bored? Or does he assume that they are too simple to imagine that a death by burning is "hideous and painful," and that they will remember the perpetrators' nationality only if he insistently reminds them of it?[28]

Eley observes, "There are also genuine issues of taste, strategy, and ethical choice involved in choosing to present this in all its vivid awfulness, particularly given the pornographic discourse sometimes associated with the circulation of such images." While he acknowledges the legitimacy of such graphic descriptions, Eley also sympathizes with Goldhagen's predecessors, who were irritated by an approach that effaced "the ethical seriousness" of their work.[29] Eley's reference to "taste" clearly targets Goldhagen's "low-brow" conduct, an assessment that reverberates throughout the reviews. The historians are condemning Goldhagen's lack of *class*—his failure, in other words, to

respect what Grossmann refers to as the *Schamgrenze* (shame borders) that
well-behaved historians have traditionally honored while recounting the Nazi
crimes. Writing for the *New York Review of Books*, the publisher-editor of *Die
Zeit*, Josef Joffe, reiterates Jürgen Kocka's observation that "[m]ost historians
have used more cautious language" or have, at the very least "scrupulously
stopped pointing at 'the Germans' " in the modern literature on the Holocaust.
Yet here was Daniel Goldhagen, "slicing through such comforting shibboleths
as 'Hitler and his henchmen,' fingering 'the Germans' again."[30] "A half century
later," Franklin Littell insists, "when the Holocaust . . . is remembered and
discussed, sensitivity and *a low tone of voice* are preferable to arrogance and
self-righteousness" (my emphasis). The American historian goes still further,
implying that Goldhagen's approach exploits "the historical record to undergird
a distorted view of 'the Germans,' " which Littell decries as "wrong, morally,
academically and politically."[31]

The language of a few of these criticisms beckons us to sexualize
Goldhagen's impropriety by insinuating that he enjoys his rage about German cruelty toward the Jews.[32] Joffe quotes the "German-Jewish scholar"
Dan Diner, who remarks that Goldhagen "describes the cruelties of the
perpetrators in all of their opulence." Joffe also cites the sociologist
Y. Michal Bodemann, who called the book "pornography" because it "drives
home the 'pleasure derived from murder and torture' in a 'voyeuristic narration.' "[33] Grossmann likewise suggests that Goldhagen obtained "moral
authority" among his nonacademic readers through "what seemed to his
critics a grotesque, lurid, virtually pornographic language of witness, which
could proclaim a certain docudrama authenticity." He "got down to the
nitty-gritty graphics of gushing blood and flying body parts with a gusto
from which most historians would recoil."[34]

Carolyn J. Dean observes that his critics' designation of "pornography"
renders Goldhagen's language of witness "inextricable from far more suspect
pleasures."[35] "Calling something 'pornography,' " Dean argues, "is a way of
putting aside arguments about the nature of representation in favor of a
vague but palpable sense that this image or that text elicits an improper
response." It is a label that "passes for an argument about the relation
between moral and political perversion where there is really no argument
and attributes responsibility for Nazism and fascism implicitly to particular
sorts of illicit, sexual emotions."[36] Unlike "historians whose allegiance to
a neutral narrative voice restrains moral judgment, encouraging a cognitive rather than emotive mode of apprehension," Dean writes, "Goldhagen
inserts himself into the action, asking the reader to imagine in the most
vivid terms how a German soldier must have felt as he shot a young Jewish child, and he describes the murder in gruesome detail." She infers that
the historians' attribution of *pornography* became a way of speaking about
his "unrestrained moralism" in a book "that simply did not subscribe to any
serious historiographical conventions about distinguishing clearly between

the event and one's subjective judgment of it, between history writing and the evocation of (in this case traumatic) memory."[37]

What is striking about some of the criticisms of Goldhagen's "pornographic" style is that they also problematize the role of fantasy in historical visualization. Hammermann, for example, "accuses Goldhagen of inventing details of horror that do not exist in his sources, 'a consequence of that (certainly unconscious) seductive pull of the dark need in people's souls to peep as closely as possible, with a mixture of horror and pleasure, at the atrocity being perpetrated on others.' "[38] Bartov affirms there is no doubt that certain elements of Goldhagen's description "seem to reflect his own fantasies—themselves most probably the product of (over)exposure to media representations of the Holocaust and other massacres—rather than the information culled from the documentation he cites." He writes: "Goldhagen wants us to imagine with him the thoughts that went through the minds of a German policeman and the little girl he shot, he wants us to imagine what the shooting actually looked like; in short, he demands that we fantasize atrocity and be morally outraged by the horrors conjured up in our minds."[39]

Such comments are extremely revealing, because they not only enunciate the phantasmatic aspects of Goldhagen's descriptions, but also the ways in which his graphic visualizations *imply a reader who will share them.* In Dean's view, these condemnations of Goldhagen's style suggest that "explicit portrayals of violence must produce a disingenuous emotional response (*Betroffenheit*)," or what she refers to as "corrupted empathy." By implication, the restrained portrayal of violence would instead evoke "proper feelings, though it is not clear why exactly this is the case or what those feelings should be."[40] Ultimately, however, "whether Goldhagen is a hypocrite or a saint is really beside the point," as Dean observes, "since the text's real difficulty is that its very logic refuses any simple choice between the moral numbness equated with voyeurism and the moral integrity equated with empathy." In effect, those historians who "accuse Goldhagen of being a charlatan or an overly vigilant prosecutor demand that we finally take the side of either good or bad history, of moral numbness or integrity when what the book really exposes is the difficulty involved in writing the history of the genocide of European Jewry." Indeed, as Dean surmises, "[i]t is as if the venom historians' directed at Goldhagen's celebrity was thus a means of disavowing the very difficult question of how best to represent historical knowledge about the Holocaust, a question whose answer was taken to be self-evident. . . ."[41]

Dean's analysis of comparisons with pornography in Goldhagen's reception demonstrates how discourse about the Holocaust operates as an index of anxiety about the limits or "fragility" of empathy. Thus, in her assessment, the term *pornography* ultimately attests to critics' "frustration about the inadequacy of conventional moral language to address the Holocaust." This frustration is then "projected onto a bad object: onto Goldhagen's work in particular, but also onto its commercial success and thus onto all those nameless and faceless readers who apparently can't distinguish between titillation and moral gravity, emotional appeals and serious historical work."[42] This contention betrays the root of Goldhagen's "pornographic" tendency. The problem lies with "us" as his "morbidly fascinated" implied readers—with the suspected inadequacy or impropriety of our feelings and perceptions—rather than with any *intrinsic* impropriety on his end.[43] It is "we" readers who worry about feeling hailed into identifying too closely "either with the suffering of victims or with the hatred of perpetrators,"[44] and it is "we" who feel ashamed of being implicated in his tasteless (low-class) behavior, his poor discipline, and also, most acutely perhaps, in the *jouissance* that saturates his lushly detailed spectacles of German cruelty and Jewish agony.

This image of Goldhagen's implied reader locates part of the seductive force of *Hitler's Willing Executioners* in the opportunity it provides for its consumers to satisfy a scopophilic fascination with transgressive violence and to relish alternately sadistic identifications with perpetrators and masochistic identifications with victims. The warm reception of the book indicates that his German and American audiences likely took advantage of the occasion for voyeuristic pleasure that the professional historians rejected with disgust; nevertheless, as Bartov notes, Goldhagen's "insistence on the most explicit aspects of the horror must have, at the same time, been quite familiar to [American] readers exposed to a tremendous number of real and staged representations of violence in the media." For Americans, Goldhagen's "fortress mentality" reproduces "representations of 'Germans' and 'Jews' as two absolutely distinct abstract principles that have been locked in an eternal struggle whose outcome can only be total victory or total defeat—*Sieg oder Untergang*."[45] Paradoxically, then, it is precisely because of entertainment's desensitizing impact that "Goldhagen's images of horror remained sufficiently distant to prevent alienation through anxiety and disgust." Among German readers, however, the prospect for sadomasochistic identification with these abstractions may coincide with an "almost perverse pride" in their shameful history, what Heinrich August Winkler alluded to as "negative nationalism."[46]

To obtain a clearer sense of how traumatic history might be written in the absence of ressentiment, it is illuminating to compare Goldhagen's depiction of the Bialystok synagogue burning with Browning's narration of the same incident:

> What started as a pogrom quickly escalated into more systematic mass murder. Jews collected at the marketplace were taken to a park, lined up against a wall, and shot. The killing lasted until dark. At the synagogue, where at least 700 Jews had been collected, gasoline was poured at the entryways. A grenade was tossed into

the building, igniting a fire. Police shot anyone trying to escape. The fire spread to nearby houses in which Jews were hiding, and they too were burned alive. The next day, thirty wagonloads of corpses were taken to a mass grave. An estimated 2,000 to 2,200 Jews had been killed. When General Pflugbeil sent a messenger to Major Weis to inquire about the fire, the major was found drunk. He claimed to know nothing about what was happening. Weis and his officers subsequently submitted a false report of the events to Pflugbeil.[47]

In contrast to Goldhagen's description, Browning's prose is self-effacing and its use of adjectives and other intensifiers sparing. This is not to suggest that Browning's description lacks a coherent narrative structure or dramatic tension: the staccato sequence of matter-of-fact sentences builds a unifying parallelism into a description of the actions, causes, and effects with a clearly linked beginning, middle, and end; however, the deadpan irony elicited by the concluding fragment of indirect conversation seems geared to provoke tempered disgust and reflective judgment rather than incite moral outrage. In short, Browning has maintained a civil, detached tone that neither calls attention to itself nor offers much in the way of affective content. The problem with this style is that it incongruously applies to the barbaric actions of the reservists themselves. Do these "ordinary men" really deserve the courtesy that Browning extends to them by mitigating their agency through his recourse to the passive voice?

While I object to this aspect of his narrative style, I generally appreciate Browning's account for its nuanced and evenhanded consideration of the disavowals, ambivalences, overcompensations, coldness, and unabashed savagery that inflected the police reservists' metamorphosis into mass murderers. Goldhagen, for his part, is justified in eschewing the passive voice in order to emphasize their agency. He is also right to insist upon the moral and practical meaning of German cruelty toward the Jews during killing operations and on the death marches as an index of the unique virility of German anti-Semitism at that time. For Goldhagen, if the state-authorized orders are of secondary significance in understanding the motivations of the perpetrators, it is because these orders are not sufficient to explain the thoroughness and enjoyment with which soldiers and reservists rounded up their victims young and old, forced them to strip in the woods, and shot them in mass graves dug at gunpoint by the Jews themselves. In the same vein, the deeply ingrained will to obey authority cannot fully clarify the behavior of male and female guards who continued to starve and beat their Jewish prisoners to death on pointless marches at the end of the war even after Himmler ordered an end to the killings.

Goldhagen's exposure of the Germans' enjoyment of a brutal process whose explicit aim was extermination may provide something of a corrective to the work of scholars in recent years who have gone too far in separating themselves from "intentionalist" understandings of the Holocaust. In Eley's definition, intentionalists "personalized the explanation of the 'Final Solution' around Hitler's ideological outlook and dictatorial will."[48] In contrast, so-called functionalist or structuralist readings shift attention from a demonic Hitler and his high command to focus instead on the institutional and economic structures and contingencies that propelled participation in the genocide, particularly at the bureaucratic level. In this manner, historians have sought to qualify what they correctly see as an overemphasis on the central role of Hitler and his inner circle in orchestrating the atrocities and in manipulating and enforcing mass obedience. Conversely, the functionalist approach has sometimes been marred by a socially deterministic view of the perpetrators' actions. In Moishe Postone's view, functionalist approaches "take for granted what needs to be explained—that a program of complete extermination could even become thinkable."[49]

Dominick LaCapra acknowledges that "the stress on industrialized mass murder, the machinery of destruction, technology, (pseudo-)science and bureaucracy (as well as peer pressure and careerism) do not fully account for the forces Goldhagen obsessively and graphically depicts and imaginatively projects or enhances."[50] Against this backdrop, Goldhagen's Manichaean outlook had the peculiar merit of reminding historians and other scholars that the killers were either anti-Semitic or acquiesced in anti-Semitic convictions when they followed orders to murder. Brennan observes that "Goldhagen's thesis involves an explicit rejection of accounts" exemplified by Raul Hilberg's that "explain the Holocaust as involving emotionless and bureaucratic 'production-line killing' or as the inner potentiality of modernity to reverse gains made during the Enlightenment," à la Zygmunt Bauman. Goldhagen, Brennan says, also repudiates accounts that focus on Hitler's charisma and the cult of personality, sociologistic standpoints that emphasize the Germans' deeply ingrained will to obey authority or resist collectively applied and state-ordained peer pressure as explanations for a "temporary suspension of 'civilized' behavior under totalitarian conditions, in which all opposition was effectively (and decisively) crushed."[51] By maniacally reciting the nationality of the perpetrators, Goldhagen, as Bartov characterizes it, "led a frontal attack against all of those scholars who had apparently become wholly incapable of seeing what the general public had intuitively known all along, that it was 'the Germans' who had done it, that they had always wanted to do it, that they did it because they hated Jews, and that once called upon to do it, they did it with great enthusiasm and much pleasure."[52] In short, Goldhagen's "unrestrained moralism enabled the reader to cut through complexity and hold the perpetrators accountable in an emotionally satisfying fashion."[53]

It was the fog engulfing questions about individual and collective motivation that Goldhagen strove to pierce.[54] According to Jäckel, Goldhagen "wants to avoid the 'clinical' perspective which restricts itself to numbers and place-names" and chooses instead "to convey the horrors of these atrocities which others have neglected."[55] Jäckel grants that Goldhagen is justified in doing so and also acknowledges that Goldhagen's graphic treatment of the atrocities committed by police battalions and by the guards during the death marches (the principal part of the book, in other words) succeeds in providing "some penetrating passages." However, his responsibilities as a historian do not end there: "The main task of research is, after all, to explain the connections. Goldhagen has neglected to make these connections; the Police Battalions' place and participation [in these events consequently] remain unclear."[56] The book is, moreover, "riddled with errors"[57] and Jäckel unhesitatingly condemns it as "little more than a step backward to positions long since passed by; even worse," Jäckel continues, "it is a relapse to the most primitive of all stereotypes."[58] In short, as Jäckel bluntly asserts at the outset of his review, *Hitler's Willing Executioners* "is not on the cutting edge of research and does not satisfy even mediocre standards; it is simply bad."[59]

The stridency of Jäckel's condemnation gives me reason to pause. Goldhagen's ride on a megalomaniac "wave of hyperbole" is not a sufficient reason to dismiss the book as a whole.[60] Nor is the fact that he contributed to a sensational marketing campaign on the book's behalf that commercializes the seemingly inexhaustible potential for the Jewish genocide to instigate controversy—to capitalize, in Littell's words, on the "brute fact that today 'there's no business like Shoah business.' "[61] It is important to recall that Goldhagen's book found an extraordinarily receptive audience among the mainstream media and nonacademic readers. By the end of the first year of its publication in English, it had been translated into twelve languages. Not only was Goldhagen's the first scholarly examination of the Shoah to become an international best seller, it was also the first "asserting a long genealogy of German evil" since the veteran U.S. foreign correspondent William L. Shirer's *The Rise and Fall of the Third Reich* (1961) to have achieved this degree of commercial success.[62] Grossmann reports: "Eighty thousand copies of the German edition were sold in the first month, and by the time of the book tour, 3000 books a day were flying off the shelf."[63] As Goldhagen packed expansive "venerable" high-culture venues in Hamburg, Berlin, Frankfurt, and Munich, Grossmann writes, "people of mixed generations fought for tickets to the panel discussions as if they were headed to a rock concert."[64]

Such success is particularly remarkable when one considers with Caplan that academic books in the United States "never break through into this kind of mass market."[65] Goldhagen was even awarded the Democracy Prize by the journal *Blätter für deutsche und internationale Politik* at a ceremony in Bonn on March 10, 1997, where the head of the Hamburg Institute for Social Research, Jan Philipp Reemstma, a leading philanthropist of the Left, conferred the prize, and no less illustrious a figure than Jürgen Habermas gave the *Laudatio* before an audience of two thousand.[66]

Grossmann observes that Habermas's *Laudatio* is "full of qualifiers and defense mechanisms."[67] It commences with the grounds for bestowing this prize on Goldhagen, who, "through the 'urgency, the forcefulness, and the moral strength of his presentation,'" has "'provided a powerful stimulus to the public conscience of the Federal Republic'" and "sharpened 'our sensibility for what constitutes the background and the limit of a German normalization.'"[68] Hence the prize reflects "the contributions that an American, a Jewish historian, has made toward Germans' search for the *proper way to come to terms with a criminal period of their history*" (my emphasis).[69] Habermas deflects the widespread criticisms of *Hitler's Willing Executioners* by celebrating the book's pedagogical effects and disclaiming his right to assume the authority of a professional historian in adjudicating its merit as a historical work. In this way, Eley asserts, "the impact of Goldhagen's book was co-opted into the political pedagogy Habermas, Reemtsma, and other left intellectuals had been practicing in their various ways since earlier in the 1980s."[70] Despite his qualifications, Habermas's ceremonial role did not shore up his credentials with leftist scholars, who share the historians' negative judgment of Goldhagen's book and therefore viewed the former's praise as yet another example of his "anachronistic anti-fascism."[71]

Habermas goes on to contest the criticism that "Goldhagen's intentionalist argument overextends the credit of his empirical work,"[72] an allegation that for Eaglestone enjoins us to grant that "there is something to overextend." "It is only because the work claims to be historical," Eaglestone writes, "that its moral elements—the 'urgency, the forcefulness, and the moral strength of his presentation'—are deemed important."[73] Eaglestone advocates for Goldhagen's admission into the bastion of "reasonable" historians on the grounds that his method—at once "cultural cognitive" and explicitly moral—is based on his view of human nature, an ethics and worldview that shapes his choices without undermining the historical status of his statements. In keeping with a postmodernist stance modeled by White and Jean-François Lyotard, Eaglestone stipulates that "being a 'reasonable historian' and producing history means following the rules of the genre" of historical writing as a sophisticated narrative about the past. The conventions of this narrative prioritize certain modes for weighing evidence and, as Eaglestone notes, these rules "can be followed more or less well."[74] If Goldhagen's book was important, Eaglestone argues, it was because it followed the rules and was therefore regarded as a history, albeit flawed.

The predominant tendency in the historians' reception of *Hitler's Willing Executioners* contradicts Eaglestone's assessment. The impact of the book is significant precisely because it was deemed *unreasonable*: in the minds of his peers, he did not follow the professional historian's rules consistently or sufficiently and, as Eley puts it, "he dismissed the normal requirements of evidence."[75] Birn, the chief historian in the War Crimes Against Humanity Section of the Canadian Justice Department and former adviser to the

U.S. Office of Special Investigations, insisted "that by using Goldhagen's method of handling the evidence, one could easily find sufficient citations from the material he used to demonstrate the exact opposite of what Goldhagen maintains."[76] Jacob Neusner even goes to the length of lambasting *Hitler's Willing Executioners* as a "hysterical" and "shoddy" work, full of "such pretension and violent emotion," "pseudo-scholarship and bad arguments" that it "calls into question the scholarly integrity of Harvard's doctorate."[77] Clearly, in Neusner's eyes, Goldhagen failed to produce the generic effect of reasonableness that results from adhering to disciplinary protocols—quite the opposite, actually. Such an unequivocal pronouncement underscores how the purview of scientific rigor extends beyond the treatment of evidence to behavior, and not just among professional scholars, but also to such readers who will be influenced by the beatitude of experts modeling judiciousness.

By implying that Goldhagen's expression of traumatic affect leads him to poor professional conduct, these assessments speak to the antidisciplinary status of his ressentiment, which, I want to argue, might provoke us to reexamine our commonsense understanding of the codes of acceptable conduct that historians introject and simulate as *signs of reason*. His impropriety invites us to consider professional subjectification as a *generic* operation that codifies expectations about how best to imitate the "reasonable scholar" model. Our imaginary identification with this model induces us to internalize and at least partially obey generic conventions of style as behavior.

In what follows, I will consider the imaginary valence of this identification as the crux of disciplinary mimesis. I borrow the psychoanalytic term *imaginary* from Jacques Lacan to refer to the register wherein memories, fantasies, idealizations, and identifications are created and screened. Foremost among them is the *imago* or *ideal ego* (self-image) as the nucleus of an infantile narcissistic desire. This register shapes and is shaped by the *symbolic* as the realm of language, discourse, norms, and surveillance that are absorbed and introjected in the form of an *ego-ideal*. It is the reciprocal relation between the symbolic and the imaginary that is at work in the disciplining of scholarly identifications and interpretations. The *real* is Lacan's term for the inassimilable and refractory force of the repressed, which "extimately" resists yet also striates the commerce between the two other registers that foreclose it. One of its signs in discourse and other practices is repetition, since the real is that which always returns to the same place. Of interest here for psychoanalytic theorists and cultural critics is the pattern that emerges in behavior that signals the insistent logic of a fantasy that simultaneously structures and exceeds reality.[78]

LaCapra figures the Goldhagen controversy as the real when he insists that it has received "too much attention" and likens it to a "recurrent dream" with "the tendency not to be laid to rest but to reappear. To the extent that this is the case," LaCapra adds, "it may indicate that there are aspects of the book and the debate it provoked with which we have still not come sufficiently to terms."[79] From a psychoanalytic standpoint, the particular hurdle that historiography is challenged to confront in the specter of Goldhagen's traumatic affect is how the return of the "impossible real" troubles the civility of disciplinary identifications "wie ein Stachel im Fleisch" ["Like a Thorn in the Flesh"] as Han-Ulrich Wehler entitled his review of the book.[80] What is the destiny of Goldhagen's ressentiment in the disciplinary imaginary?

Trauma and the Disciplinary Imaginary

I have been leading up to the question of how historiography reinscribes its limits as a mode of professional subject formation by discouraging historians from querying their methods for assessing the imaginative and affective dimensions of representation. This line of inquiry is indebted to Wilhelm Dilthey, when he delimited *Verstehen*, or imaginative understanding, as a mode of investigation specific to history as a human science. One of the aims of this chapter is to extend the "critique of historical reason" that Dilthey inaugurated when he invited historians to consider the question of how "the mental construction of the mind-affected world make[s] knowledge of mind-affected reality possible."[81] It is the regulative power of this "mental construction of the mind-affected world" that is at stake in my conception of the disciplinary imaginary. Another goal is to conceptualize the affective undercurrents of this praxis as an object of inquiry in their own right.

Historians adopt a crude form of *Verstehen* in the course of imagining events and describing motivations. "Vulgar" (i.e., distorted and reductive) historicist *Verstehen*, as Caplan explains, claims empathetic knowledge of historical actors.[82] While ressentiment is widely recognized by historians as a bristling motive of ongoing social and political tensions,[83] the theoretical issues that it raises are shuffled off onto other disciplines, or to reiterate Dean's point above, onto "bad objects" such as Goldhagen. The affective residues of the past, it seems, comprise an "improper" object of historical explanation, because they fall between the demands for a logical and verifiable examination of archival evidence. The methods for investigating such detritus are the slippery territory of other more theoretical disciplines (such as cultural studies and psychology), which many historians view with suspicion (there are certain disciplines that are more "proper" than others, after all).

LaCapra is one significant exception to this generalization. The historical status of traumatic affect is an explicit departure point for his adaptation of psychoanalytic terms to create a critical framework for studies of traumatic history.[84] In a recent book, *History in Transit*, LaCapra asks, To what extent one can determine "what precisely in the work of a historian can be related to his or her own experience?"[85] It is apparent to LaCapra that Goldhagen's mode of *Verstehen* in *Hitler's Willing Executioners* is not critically nuanced by such a question. Goldhagen recognizes the "alterity" of the perpetrators' perspective but projects their actions through the eyes of certain (Jewish) victims "with whom Goldhagen identifies" and whose experience of the events he "phantasmatically recounts."[86] Hence, while the book is "ostensibly a contribution to perpetrator history, the basis of its argument is an excessive, unchecked identification" with Jewish victims and an imaginative introjection of their reactions.[87]

LaCapra's observations resonate with Hammermann's and Bartov's suspicions, cited earlier, that elements of fantasy are imbricated in Goldhagen's graphic visualizations of events. From LaCapra's perspective, Goldhagen's resentful tone and phantasmatic style might be read as a form of *acting out* whereby his subject position as a survivor's son becomes something of a "total identity." Possessed by his father's past, he cannot control his compulsion to repeat it as though it were fully present.[88] This is clear from the bitterness that appears to overwhelm his ability to make balanced judgments about his own evidence. Conversely, while Jäckel scrutinizes the validity of Goldhagen's individual claims, he avoids the painful truth behind this "simply bad" best-selling book—that Germany's democratic recuperation cannot heal wounds left by ostracism, dispossession, deportation, enslavement, torture, and genocide.

LaCapra suggests that scholarship focusing on recent extremely traumatic events is more likely to evince heightened "transferential" identifications with the object of inquiry as researchers alternately deny, act out, and work through its effects. He notes that this "transferential problem revealed itself as particularly intense" in the case of Goldhagen's book and its reception.[89] My own analysis of the Goldhagen controversy is indebted to LaCapra's adaptation of the psychoanalytic concept of transference to describe the ways in which the varying subject positions of historians and other scholars differentially reflect the traumatic impact of their object of inquiry. Notably, for LaCapra, transference is no longer limited to the clinical context with the analyst playing the omniscient surface for the projection of various oedipal scenes. Transference is also a disciplinary phenomenon whereby "the historian or analyst tends to repeat with more or less significant variations the problems active in the object of study."[90] Above and beyond many other events, "the Holocaust presents the historian with transference in the most traumatic form conceivable—but in a form that will vary with the difference in subject-position of the analyst."[91] For this reason, while certain statements "or even entire orientations may seem appropriate for someone in a given subject-position," they will not seem appropriate for everyone:

> Whether the historian or analyst is a survivor, a relative of survivors, a former Nazi, a former collaborator, a relative of former Nazis or collaborators, a younger Jew or German distanced from more immediate contact with survival, participation, or collaboration, or a

relative "outsider" to these problems will make a difference even in
the meaning of statements that may be formally identical. . . . Thus,
while any historian must be "invested" in a distinctive way in the
events of the Holocaust, not all investments (or cathexes) are the
same, and not all statements, rhetorics, or orientations are equally
available to different historians.[92]

It is in light of such incommensurable investments that LaCapra views the
Holocaust as a *limit case* with respect to the work of critical historicization.
For if the injustice of genocide cannot be repaired, then historians will
inevitably confront, defer, or deny this limit in the course of their analyses.
In any case, "the point is not to deny transference or simply to act it out,
but to attempt to work through it in a critical manner."[93]

LaCapra's understanding of working through evolves from Freud's
durcharbeiten as the self-conscious processing of disavowed, repressed, or denied
aspects of the past.[94] However, LaCapra insists on giving working through
a critical dimension that distinguishes it from the ideological project of
"mastering the past" (*Vergangenheitsbewältigung*). In this formulation, working
through counteracts compulsive acting out through an explicit and critically
controlled process of repetition. This process has the power to alter life in
significant ways by enabling "the selective retrieval and modified enactment
of unactualized past possibilities" and "a more viable articulation of affect
and cognition or representation, as well as ethical and sociopolitical agency,
in the present and future."[95]

LaCapra's remarks bear on the ways in which standards of moral
propriety decide not only *what* may be said about recent traumatic history,
but also *how* and *by whom*, which is why, in the case of the Holocaust,
historians' national, religious, and ideological backgrounds become an issue.
Obviously, the well-established German historian Mommsen will relate to
this limit differently than the Jewish-American Goldhagen, who is also
a relative newcomer to the historical field. In the same vein, American
historians do not share the same motivations for debunking Goldhagen's
argument that German historians do. It is impossible to view Browning's
critical issues with Goldhagen in the same way as Mommsen's. In contrast
to his older German colleague, Browning, an American, does not feel a
need to vindicate Germany by invoking its successful reintegration into the
West. Reciprocally, the perspective of descendants of murdered or surviving
Jews will typically differ from the views of Jews without a direct connection
to the genocide, as will the sensibilities of German historians of different
generations and political leanings, not to mention of different Germanys
before 1990.[96]

However, this is not to suggest that such investments and perspectives
are fixed within any generation or even any particular group. In extending
the theoretical implications of LaCapra's polemical points, I would like to

emphasize that scholars' subject positions are intimately bound up with collective memories that change not only between generations, but also within the scope of an individual's lifetime. Maurice Halbwachs has observed that personal memory has a collective dimension insofar as an individual's sense of the past at any given moment is determined and inflected by his or her differential membership in multiple groups that are themselves in flux.[97] One might therefore speak of memory's "fragility" as a quality of the variable influences of different contexts that are as provisional and finite as the communities who define them.

The various interpretations of the past precipitated by a scholar's transference with his or her object of inquiry will reflect the repressions, exclusions, and fixations peculiar to the collective memories of the communities to which he or she belongs. Another way of saying this is that meaning, like memory, is a function of the alterity or dehiscence of socially mediated investments in the object at stake.[98] As collectivities change and/or disperse, so too does the quality and degree of a historian's commitments to the concerns of those communities with which he or she is affiliated. To observe that collective memory is a practice as much as it is a product of interpretation, reconfiguration, and displacement is, thus, to emphasize its historicity as a socially contingent force.

The reciprocity between interpretation and collective memory has an important bearing on the problem of theorizing the disciplinary imaginary. This is the case insofar as the ideal of disciplinary propriety draws its normative power from the institutionalization of moral, aesthetic, and/or scientific standards. Disciplinary traditions are institutionalized collective memories that establish a horizon of interpretation by positing models that are worth imitating and questions that are valid to pose. If teachers or mentors do not render this phenomenon explicit, students and aspiring scholars will passively inherit tradition as an unacknowledged limit that naturalizes the power of particular interpretations and standards of judgment and thus circumscribes the individual's freedom to adopt or contest various ideas without being beholden to it. The task of becoming conscious about a discipline's horizon is thus a social as well as a hermeneutical problem.

In *Representing the Holocaust: History, Theory, Trauma*, LaCapra problematizes institutionalized structures of interpretation, but he is more interested in deducing the symptomatic configuration of texts from their "ideologically reinforcing" elements.[99] He therefore rejects a teleological historicist temporality, because its rigid reliance on contextualization disables it from accounting for anachronisms or ideological symptoms in texts and other artifacts. In its place, LaCapra adopts a psychoanalytically attenuated Nietzschean temporality to read ideological symptoms as the "return of the repressed."[100] The result is a concept of *repetitive temporality*, or what he calls "history as displacement," that draws on the *Nachträglichkeit* (belatedness) of historical understanding. For LaCapra, the belatedness of historical understanding enables us to see things or to ask questions that "were not available to oneself or others in the past." In this respect, belatedness is "bound up both with traumatic effects and with the very ability to learn from an exchange with the past."[101]

LaCapra's attention to the retroactive temporalities at stake in instances of traumatic history is valuable for emphasizing the way in which trauma operates as a kind of *affective horizon* for Holocaust historiography. In his words, the conceptualization of time as repetition with change "allows for a recognition of the need to act out problems 'symptomatically' in a post-traumatic context and for the significance of trauma in history which may be particularly marked in the recent past." By the same token, it "allows for the way in which trauma limits history and historical understanding, notably in its disruption of contextualization and dialogic exchange."[102] In this manner, LaCapra calls attention to the connection between trauma, ethics, and ideology in scholarly interpretations of the Holocaust. Incommensurable subject positions will effect incommensurable meanings whose moral propriety and substantive value will need to be judged on a case-by-case basis. Historians and critics must therefore consider their relative implication in the object and its context without losing sight of the way in which the object "answers back": texts should not become mere pretexts for "one's own undoings and unfashionings," as LaCapra warns.[103] For LaCapra, the ability to work-through traumatic history ultimately depends on this hermeneutical self-discipline.

LaCapra distinguishes individual motivation and intention from ideology as a general framework of meaning, which, as Postone points out, "is important when psychoanalytic categories are used to illuminate social and historical phenomena";[104] however, this distinction does not account for the ways in which not all meanings are altogether intended or how they become unconsciously ideological, hence symptomatic. Intention and ideology are difficult to distinguish from each other because even critical scholars presuppose a certain level of "common sense" as an intuitively self-evident set of truths. Yet it is precisely the subterranean disposition of this intuition that perpetuates the positivistic assumption that a nonideological standpoint is possible. It may be that the psychoanalytic theory of the unconscious renders the distinction between intention and ideology moot. This standpoint presumes that the unconscious places subjects under the spell of individual and inherited fantasies that generate a nexus of imaginary and symbolic identifications; meaning is therefore unconsciously bound up with ideological horizons of interpretation. The concept of the unconscious therefore suggests that the field of actions and desires is only intentional to the extent that individuals "choose" to activate a largely inherited cultural repertoire of images as well as the laws, familial structures, idioms, and social conventions that precede and frame consciousness and inclination. In what follows, I will make a preliminary attempt to theorize how scientific and moral intuitions are mediated by imaginary and sociohistorical identifications, which foster the regulatory force of the object of inquiry as a centrifuge of discipline and desire.

Historical writing subjects the information available from artifacts, documents, and testimony to hermeneutical and logical criteria. To the extent that these criteria reflect a historian's training in institutions of higher learning and in the line of accruing scholarly experience, his or her transferential and narcissistic exchange with the object of study will be informed by institutional affliliations and values along with generational, ethnic, religious, and political ones. Freud writes that narcissism is not a perversion, but rather "the libidinal complement to the egoism of the instinct of self-preservation, a measure of which can be attributed to every living creature."[105] While primary narcissism refers to the individual's unconscious enthrallment with an idealized image of self, what Lacan calls the *imago*, secondary narcissism entails a more conscious identification with the desires and expectations of others who have the capacity to confirm or detract from self-love. The concept of secondary narcissism offers a way of thinking about identifications with objects of inquiry, intellectual lineages, scholarly protocols, and institutional collectivities. Such disciplinary identifications stem from a desire for social acceptance as a necessary condition for sustaining self-love and ego survival. The compiled influence of these groups and their respective expectations is an *introjected critical gaze* that renders a historian or any scholar sensitive to the demands of the symbolic: in Lacan's terms, the order of signs, conventions, and laws, as well as familial and institutional relations.

By identifying with disciplinary expectations as the criteria of scientific validity, a historian empowers them to delimit the horizons of both interpretation and meaning in his or her work. This is the sense in which an object of scholarship might be said to "look back": the gaze *specularizes* the historical object as the mirror of rigor. This "mirror" is often distant and blurry—the contours of the object shift as new angles and data emerge. The key aspect of this identification that I want to foreground here is that the desire propelling it is *mimetic*: the scholar seeks to create the ideal interpretation in a manner that will reinforce his or her membership in a disciplinary community. So conceived, the disciplinary gaze is not merely the conveyor and producer of meaning; it is also a medium of the fluctuating power of social structures as forces of proliferation, convention, and constraint. Because it is idealized, scientific rigor has a phantasmatic dimension that reinforces its function as a normative hinge of disciplinary praxis.

My characterization of the disciplinary gaze is indebted to John Mowitt's explanation of *disciplinary reason* and the narcissistic structure of academic discipleship. In general, Mowitt is interested in extending the implications of Michel Foucault's thinking on the generation of disciplinary objects as "instances of the social production of subjectivity" and the subjection of agency. Disciplinary reason is the reflex of a power-knowledge matrix that regulates the interplay between academics and their objects.[106]

Thomas Kuhn's notion of the *paradigm* from *The Structure of Scientific Revolutions* and "Second Thoughts on Paradigms" provides a crucial step in Mowitt's theorization of the need among members of a discipline to "have a framework within which even their intellectual differences take on significance." The paradigm designates "that characteristically elusive level of 'scientific' experience embodied in the symbolic inscription of community," while at the same time "uncoercively managing internal dissension" about what lies outside it.[107] Yet insofar as Kuhn does not consider the power relations that make the paradigm effective as a mode of subjectification, Mowitt finds this definition insufficient for understanding the dynamic of disciplinary reason. He therefore draws on René Girard's "From Mimetic Desire to the Monstrous Double"[108] in order to conceptualize the sacrificial violence through which scholarly identity is secured. In Mowitt's extrapolation from this essay, the disciplinary object is the sacralized product of a rivalry between persons or groups over possession of the object of inquiry. This rivalry threatens to implode the object as well as the power structure that subjects "disciples" to those who train them. It also displaces the object with the gnarled intersection of narcissistic projections. A scapegoat must consequently be constructed who doubles the monstrous aspects of the object by embodying and externalizing the forces that threaten it from "within," including competing demands on a scholar's "identificatory economy."[109] The elimination of this scapegoat functions to cement individual and group identity against a common (profane) enemy; it thus fosters a misrecognition of the object as a sacred fetish that binds "the group together through the role of the norm."[110]

Mowitt's reading of Girard emphasizes the structures through which academics desire, identify with, and thereby invest in their objects of study. He also accounts for how the scholarly devotion to the disciplinary object obscures "subjectivity's own grounding in the sociogenesis of objects"—that is to say, in the emergence, delineation, and institutionalization of fields of inquiry.[111] His analysis thus goes a long way in explaining the attack on Goldhagen as a disciplinary deployment of the scapegoat mechanism. Goldhagen's anger, "overbearing attitude,"[112] or "pornographic" style are pathologized as lapses of discipline that threaten the unity of the scientific community.

While keeping Goldhagen's methodological and logical fallacies in mind, I want to propose that his ressentiment eludes critical historicization insofar as it pressures the protocols of civil society to which scientific culture and professional criticism belong. The ideal of social propriety defined as an unemotional, thus "rational," civility, requires individuals to repress feelings that make demands on unaffected individuals for sympathetic understanding. Such embarassing demands threaten to disrupt the smooth and efficient progress of social interactions, which suits the normalizing inclinations of those groups for whom the persisting anger of minorities may raise disturbing questions about responsibility for and complicity with a history of privilege steeped in prejudice and persecution. By castigating Goldhagen's emotionalism, the historians "retain something of the collectivity which preserves individuals from pathological symptoms." "The sickness is socialized," to borrow Max Horkheimer's and Theodor W. Adorno's phrasing, as an allergic reaction to the alien yet all too familiar signs of anxiety, vulnerability, and precariousness among the victims we create.[113] Horkheimer's and Adorno's critique of subjects who harden themselves internally in mimetic conformity with the repressive effects of external domination illuminates a larger issue about how scientific values and protocols might be deployed as a means of controlling the "isolated, shameful residues" of history.[114] This is a critique that was deflected by Goldhagen's critics.

The Frankfurt School's theses about the internalization of "outer" domination bears the traces of Max Weber's influence. It was in *The Protestant Work Ethic* that Weber famously (and problematically) characterized Calvinism as a form of ascetic Protestantism that defines "grace" as "a status that separates man from the depravity of the creaturely and from the 'world.'" It must be proven in "a specific form of conduct unambiguously distinct from the style of life of the 'natural' man," which is to say, through systematic self-denial and a methodical monitoring of natural urges. The consequence for the individual was "the drive to *keep a methodical check* on his state of grace as shown in how he conducted his life and thus to ensure that this life was imbued with *asceticism*."[115]

Weber's argument suggests that when professional scholars expropriate emotion as instinctual excess, they seem to conflate reason with a concept of grace that belongs to the Christian lineage of discipline. From the standpoint of the disciplinary imaginary, "grace" is a sign of election that signals the worthiness of one's dedication to a "calling"—a commitment to professional specialization as an end in itself. Rage against those who singled Jews out for mass murder and those who let it happen is a thorn in the side of Christian-stoic ideologies that set the implicit codes of bourgeois behavior. It is almost as if scholars have inherited a kind of covert Calvinism in the secular form of a work ethic that blurs the difference between rigor and moral rectitude and puritanically punishes feelings as a sinful indulgence that corrupts disciplined praxis. Such covertly Calvinist ideologies define a "proper" analysis as an emotionally ascetic inquiry that sticks humbly to the facts and sacrifices socially "burdensome" personal issues to the demands of modesty and reason. In this manner, disciplinary etiquette ensures that historical anger is unlikely to disturb us when we least expect it.

Goldhagen's gracelessly "Jewish" ressentiment would rather predictably become the target of a legacy of monitoring and neutralizing the voices of those whom religious chauvinism has systematically marginalized. In defending the moral validity of Goldhagen's rage, then, my intention is not to dismiss the evidence of his book's logical and methodological flaws; but neither do I want to proclaim the comparative objectivity of alternate accounts that are officially governed by the ideal of scientific neutrality, which, is, in part, a rhetorical and aesthetic effect of style or, to put it still more brashly, the covertly Calvinist ideal of grace. It is the ascetic valence of professional reason as a secular permutation of grace that I am opening up to scrutiny in this chapter. My aim is to provoke more sensitivity about the social and aesthetic dimensions of the ideal of scientific rigor that enhance its power to decide the membership and conduct of the professional Elect (those who have been Called). This power is typically disavowed when scholars have intuitive recourse to an ideal of scientific propriety as if it were a nonideological core of "common sense." Institutional training at the graduate and post-graduate level indoctrinates us with the initiative to police our own work as a proof of proper behavior that authorizes our access to particular communities and domains of inquiry. Such policing is disciplinary because it indicates the effect of internalized surveillance.

My conception of the disciplinary imaginary emphasizes how this internalized surveillance reinforces the phantasmatic agency of the object of inquiry as a regulative fiction. The "object proper" is a malleable figure, a composite memory image that reflects a nexus of moral, aesthetic, scientific, and ideological standards; it is at once the result and anchor of these standards that delimit disciplinary discourse. Yet because the object proper takes shape through repeated references over time, it is fraught with the alternately real and virtual contingency of its eventual appropriation. While members of a disciplinary discourse community might treat the object as though it were unified, their struggle over it reveals the provisionality of its interested construction. Hence the sign of a shared commitment to an object in the history of ideas is actually dissensus as often as consensus.[116]

The ethical issue that debates about the Holocaust enunciate is whether scholars have a responsibility to ensure that genocidal histories retain their capacity to shock as a means of inspiring the vigilance of "never again" in the face of complacency and indifference. Unfortunately, the attempt to institutionalize this traumatic aura creates other issues for a scholar such as Goldhagen, who repudiates alternative historical accounts because they do not conform to the image of his own ressentiment proffered as a "new fact." Conversely, when Mommsen and Jäckel expropriate Goldhagen's demonizing portrait of a transhistorical German anti-Semitism in the name of scientific rigor, they sidestep the task of theorizing the historiographical status of the anger that saturates his approach and that attests to the visceral aftereffects of the Jews' betrayal to a mass death.[117] Yet as Mommsen himself grants, the attention that Goldhagen's award-winning book received "teaches us that the emotional aftereffect of the German murder of the Jews still lingers after decades" in Western nations.[118]

Finally, I presume that I merely restate the obvious when I insist that the intersubjective character of meaning precludes the possibility that any single image of history or any affective relation to it can be universal for all the groups concerned. For this reason, despite scholars' desires to institute certain interpretations as normative, their definitions of propriety will inevitably vary as a function of the social, political, cultural, and economic interests inflecting their collective identifications. In this respect, at least, Holocaust historians are not unique. The self-interested dimension of meaning is always an implicit issue for researchers who engage in the very practices at stake in their description and analysis of actions and relations. The aim of this book is to demonstrate how the traumatic impact of the Holocaust makes this issue explicit as historians, philosophers, and critics weigh moral, institutional, and other normative impulses against one another. If some historians argue that Goldhagen "crossed the line" when he blurred the distinction between scientific and moral judgment, their interdiction of his affective "excess" inadvertently exposes the punishing power invested in institutionalized norms for the restrained presentation of expertise, which produces it both as a form and a mirror of proper behavior.[119] It is incumbent upon us to reassess the value of this professional protocol if it reproves rage against mass murder as bad behavior. Does such discipline not imitate the domestication of emotion in the workplace that facilitated the administration of genocidal policies on every level of German society?

As I intimated before, Goldhagen's ressentiment is antidisciplinary in revealing the limits of professional boundaries and political allegiances as well as liberal ideals of tolerance and conduct. I therefore agree with Dean's assessment that Goldhagen's impropriety merely diverts historians from "theoretical and methodological questions that might incapacitate moral judgment" and plunge "historians into murky waters by taking them into areas of philosophy and psychology beyond their realm of expertise."[120] The question of whether or not angry responses to traumatic events should be labeled "irrational" is itself a sociocultural symptom of the reification of knowledge and its division into "subjective" and "objective" disciplines. The social-scientific style that valorizes a repudiation of emotion and an attendant appearance of self-mastery is part of the ideological baggage of the Enlightenment's prioritization of secular reason. It is in this respect among others that discipline in the narrow sense of scientific rigor is implicated in the historical development of technologies of subject formation. Restraint ranks high in a disciplinary code that mediates between the social and economic domains, so that the former increasingly imitates the latter as the condition and aegis of success from a social Darwinist standpoint: the "fittest" are those "knights of industry" whose shouts for bloody sacrifice are as "cold-blooded as business."[121] Goldhagen exposes a professional ethos that hardens us against the traumatic "excrescences" of persecution and mass death. Yet it is worth questioning the assumption that mourning for genocide can be subject to a statute of limitations and that the statements of those affected are authoritative only when feelings do not color their perceptions. Goldhagen's impropriety is a symptom of posttraumatic anxiety among members of a vulnerable group, the rage of the betrayed minority clamoring at the gates of a self-entitled majority that aided or turned its back on murder. Traumatic events challenge historians to open these gates by divesting themselves of a scientistic equanimity that is barbaric in the face of genocide.[122]

2

The Aesthetics of Restraint

Peter Eisenman's "Jewish" Solution to Germany's Memorial Question

Portraying a breach in civilization by means of art is difficult, perhaps even impossible. But for the act that seeks its symbolic expression here, there is no better medium than that of visual art—the abstract formal language of modern art, whose brittle self-containment is more likely than any other to guard against solecisms and trivializations. Anything more tangible would risk the pitfall of false abstraction.

—Jürgen Habermas

In commenting on the "tortured fate of the 'German-Jewish symbiosis,'" Atina Grossmann observes that we have, in the last two decades, witnessed a "'surfeit of memory,' in which official West German identity, arguably, has become as dependent on the Holocaust as Jewish identity." The debate about German guilt since the war's end in 1945 is "hardly a history of silence and amnesia," according to Grossmann, since "in every decade, albeit in different ways, remembering Jews has been linked to (and necessary for) the rehabilitation of Germans."[1] The German/Israeli historian Dan Diner has noted the "cyclically recurring debates and periodic outbursts" in the Federal Republic, "which are often prompted by questions concerning the interpretation and representation of the Holocaust."[2] This evidence of compulsive repetition confirms Dominick LaCapra's insights about the transferential dimension of traumatic discourse, particularly in Germany, where debates about the Nazi past exemplify entrenched patterns of "acting out" and "working through." From an American academic perspective, what is perhaps most remarkable about the German public sphere is that, in contrast to the "talking head" media format that prevails in the United

States, scholarly views and debates are published in major newspapers such as *Die Zeit* and the *Frankfurter Allgemeine Zeitung*. Social theorists, historians, and cultural critics capture the attention of educated non-academic readers and influence government decisions.

Geoff Eley identifies the 1986 Historian's Depate (*der Historikerstreit*) as the most influential of the controversies that resulted when "left liberals, social democrats, and others further to the Left" spoke out against the "tendentious apologetics" of a certain conservative sector of German opinion that called for an end to the "voracious demand for literary and visual memorials to the drama and suffering of the Nazi period." The debate about the uniqueness of the Holocaust and its centrality in German history "powerfully influenced public life in 1986–87, including the election campaigning of early 1987."[3] It continues to be significant for many scholars of German memory politics because it revealed that collective remembrance about the Third Reich's crimes is vulnerable, not only to public forgetting and repression, but also to ideological manipulations by the very scholars whose self-professed task it is to examine the past disinterestedly. Yet as Mary Nolan suggests, while the debate seemed to have "ended in victory for those who argued that the past should not pass away, that the Holocaust was unique, and that the Federal Republic must maintain its commitment to a postnational identity," the sense of security this victory may have imparted was false: "Controlling the past did not give liberal historians control of the future," she writes, "for although the past did not pass away, the present did."[4] In short, if the *Historikerstreit* proved anything, it was the potential divisiveness of Germans' commitments to acknowledging a criminal history.

In reflecting on the Historians' Debate a decade later, Anson Rabinbach observes that "[t]he political battle to ensure the 'singularity' and 'uniqueness' of the Holocaust against its public 'relativization' might have been won in the public media, but at the cost of binding future scholarly interpretations to the somewhat restrictive terms of what Habermas had referred to as the 'consensus' of the Federal Republic of Germany."[5] The philosopher and social theorist established himself in this debate as "the conscience of the republic"[6] through his insistence that an explicit acknowledgment of German responsibility for Auschwitz remain a fulcrum for a critical consciousness and continuing vigilance. He also helped to institutionalize a decidedly West German model of memory politics during the first two decades after reunification.

Grossmann historicizes Habermas's impact on the West German context by highlighting key "Holocaust moments" that affected his standpoint. She reminds us that the "silent" 1950s culminated in "outbreaks of antisemitic vandalism and desecration of Jewish cemeteries and synagogues" that seemed to demonstrate the failure or severe limits of denazification during the Adenauer era. This failure deeply influenced Habermas's view of this period as "morally and politically bankrupt," a stance that "explains a good deal about his soft spot for Daniel Goldhagen" as well as his recourse to Adorno in the context of the Historian's Debate. As Grossmann observes, "It was in that apparently precarious context [of the late 1950s] that the re-emigré T. W. Adorno asked, in a public lecture to the Society for Christian-Jewish Cooperation (later a radio broadcast), 'Was bedeutet: Aufarbeitung der Vergangenheit? (What does coming to terms with the past mean?).'" He thus "echoed Arendt's earlier injunctions against 'willful forgetting,' 'loss of history,' and 'eradication of memory'" that became, as Grossmann recalls, "an integral part of the commemoration process."[7] If, for Grossmann, Goldhagen seems to have played the role of the admonishing and accusing Jew that Cilly Kugelmann once identified as a key figure in the "theatrical self-understanding of the Germans' public portrayal of themselves,"[8] then Adorno preceded him, albeit with more authority among leftist circles.

Habermas's 1986–87 intervention in the Historians' Debate translated Adorno's standpoint on the pedagogical aims of working through as a mode of critical remembrance into a protocol of ideal citizenship. In keeping with this concept, Habermas's redefinition of a properly "postnational" historical consciousness functioned as an ethical counterpoint against arguments for normalization and reconciliation during Helmut Kohl's chancellorship in the 1980s and 1990s, which bridged the pre- and postunification periods. This period was punctuated by the Bitburg controversy, the Historians' Debate, the fall of the Berlin Wall, the rededication of the *Neue Wache* after reunification, Steven Spielberg's *Schindler's List*, the reception of Goldhagen, the traveling exhibit on the Wehrmacht's supplemental and active role in National Socialist atrocities, and the publication of Victor Klemperer's Nazi-period journals in the same year, 1999, as the completion of Daniel Libeskind's Jewish Museum. These events shaped discussions about the Memorial to the Murdered Jews of Europe that were instigated in the late 1980s in the wake of the Historians' Debate by the television journalist Lea Rosh in collaboration with the historian Eberhard Jäckel. The memorial initiative thus bookends the close of the Bonn republic in a West Germany that, as Nolan notes, had been "built and ruled by the Wehrmacht and Hitler Youth generations," but was, "however reluctantly, a nonnational or perhaps a postnational state."[9]

The processes that culminate in memorials exemplify how the contradictory composition of collective memories is ultimately overridden by an official figure for the past that is intended to structure appropriate public identifications. Here, when I say *figure*, I include inscriptions on plaques that contain names and dates and little else and thus bestow writing with iconic properties or, as is the case with Peter Eisenman's minimalist Memorial to the Murdered Jews of Europe, the concerted absence of writing that stresses the "unrepresentable" magnitude and depth of Jewish loss.

Eisenman's designs have frequently been associated with the utopian radicality of Derridean deconstruction, an association he shares with his contemporaries Daniel Libeskind, Bernard Tschumi, Coop Himmelb(l)au, Zaha Hadid, Frank Gehry, and Rem Koolhaas, who were featured with him in the "Deconstructivist Architecture" exhibit at the Museum of Modern Art in 1988.[10] In 1983, Tschumi invited both Derrida and Eisenman, who had never previously met, to participate in planning one of the thirty-five freestanding pavilions comprising his "Urban Park for the Twenty-First Century" project at La Villette on the 125-acre former site of slaughterhouses in the northeast corner of Paris. In a transcript of their conversations, Eisenman affiliated the "Hebraic" ban on graven images with Derrida's deconstruction of the metaphysics of presence, which the architect adopted as a personal challenge to rethink the agency of absence and negation architectonically.[11] This affiliation accrued leverage in a milieu informed by Adorno's and Claude Lanzmann's influential reinterpretations of the Second Commandment to proclaim the unrepresentability of mass murder.[12] As I have argued elsewhere, the authority of their negative aesthetic was reinforced in the 1993–94 debate about the authenticity of Schindler's List, which some critics lauded for its documentary style as a partial fulfillment of a "watered-down" image prohibition.[13]

For the generation of postwar artists and cultural critics who were subjected to the melodramatic Holocaust miniseries and the more sophisticated, but slickly entertaining, Schindler's List, Lanzmann's almost obsessive tendency to dwell on the absences left behind by the apparatus of mass murder continues to offer a model that seems consonant with Adorno's translation of the image prohibition into a negatively sublime repudiation of redemptive and identitarian affirmations. In different ways, then, Adorno and Lanzmann supplemented the attraction of minimalist and abstract forms to ensure suitably restrained Holocaust representation, though certainly the legacy of modernist architecture and its functionalist repudiation of ornament also played a significant role.[14]

Despite his ironically self-acknowledged "political incorrectness,"[15] the minimalist form and intentionally sublime effect of Eisenman's Memorial for the Murdered Jews of Europe might be viewed as in keeping with his investment in the discipline of an *image-prohibition aesthetics* that obtained influence in West Germany before the fall of the Berlin Wall and during the decade thereafter. Thus far, I have described the disciplinary imaginary as a confluence of personal and cultural image repertoires that shape identifications and thereby enter into processes of subject formation. The disciplinary force of what I am defining as image-prohibition aesthetics in the newly unified Germany becomes evident from the discussions about the memorial, which was completed in 2005. These discussions propelled the selection of Eisenman's deconstructive design as a tastefully "Jewish" venue for achieving the Habermasian ideal of a victim-centered critical remembrance.

While writing about the Jewish Museum in Berlin, James E. Young notes that Libeskind studied with the "founders" of deconstructivist architecture—John Hejduk and Eisenman at the Cooper Union in New York[16]—a lineage to which Libeskind's own characterizations of his praxis repeatedly attest. Perhaps because of Libeskind's and Eisenman's shared preoccupation with deconstruction, the memorial's form obtains part of its intelligibility and persuasiveness from its comparison with Libeskind's Jewish Museum in Berlin. The conceptual conjuncture between their Berlin projects instaurates a genre of "deconstructed minimalism" that conjoins a critique of the metaphysics of presence with image-prohibition aesthetics to render visible the repressed absence of murdered Jews through an allegedly Jewish form. In this chapter, I consider how the memorial's form officiates Habermas's adaptation of Adorno's model of *Verarbeitung*, or critical remembrance, as a prerequisite of responsible German citizenship. I will begin by spotlighting key moments in memorial culture before and after the fall of the Berlin Wall that augmented the power of this regulative ideal for remembering and identifying with "the Jews" above all.

Memorial Culture before and after Reunification: Between Revisionism and Jürgen Habermas's "Western Consensus"

To follow the debates, controversies, and scandals surrounding the Nazi past that have punctuated the German public sphere since the late 1960s is to recognize the tenacity of German efforts to work through a shameful past. Writing about the Goldhagen controversy, Grossmann quips, "[T]he more one reads backward, the less surprising the 'Goldhagen effect' appears. It becomes difficult to distinguish what was indeed new and different, and what was another version of the same old, same old—some sort of initiation rite that every generation of postwar Germans has to undergo."[17] Yet as she also acknowledges, "Public excitability—always characterized by an ambivalent mixing of denial, defensiveness, obsession, contrition, and the proverbial *Betroffenheit* (being deeply affected)—about the Nazis and their crime is a recurrent, if not constant, feature of German politics and culture, and it shows no sign of abating as the next millennium approaches."[18] As soon as " 'Goldhagen' fades," Grossmann predicts, "another debate, another controversy, another scandal moves in to occupy the political economy of Holocaust memory."[19]

Grossmann's remarks resonate among those of us who "make a habit of observing Germany's tussles with its past" and who "remain intrigued by a moving target, swinging between anxious resentment and resentful denial, that just won't go away and keeps mutating, seemingly with increasing speed and intensity."[20] A decade before the Goldhagen controversy, the problem of historicizing the Nazi period was already the theme of a debate about the suspected abuse of history in the writings of German conservative historians.

The Historians' Debate began in 1986 after the *Frankfurter Allgemeine Zeitung* published the philosopher-historian Ernst Nolte's canceled Römerberg talk, "The Past That Will Not Pass: A Speech That Could Be Written But Not Delivered." The critical theorist Habermas responded in *Die Zeit* with "A Kind of Settlement of Damages (Apologetic Tendencies)."[21] Nolte's canceled talk challenged the Holocaust's "persistent" centrality in the writing of German history. Habermas attacked Nolte along with Michael Stürmer and Andreas Hillgruber for attempting to minimize the genocide as the pivotal event in twentieth-century German historiography. In the ensuing months, their exchange touched off a generational conflict among right- and left-leaning German historians in West Germany about the ethical limits of the historian's power as an expert to determine the significance of Nazi-period history and thereby decide the content of national consciousness.

Writing in 1988, Charles Maier characterized the historians' controversy as "a reminder that there are spurious as well as genuine ways to work through the past."[22] The "revisionist" and "antirevisionist" positions on the proper historical representation of the Nazi period enact attempts to determine "not merely which version of the past is valid, but what historical themes are legitimate or worthy of study."[23] Though a considerable amount of substantive scholarship has already been published on it, I hope I will be forgiven for briefly returning to a debate that defined key issues for the ensuing discussions about the memorial. Both cases enact a struggle over whose image of the past will prevail in a world of competing narcissisms and as an answer to the question of whose identity "counts" in the writing of history.[24]

Eley alludes to a leftist political pedagogy that emerged in the 1980s and that "aimed at heading off the initiatives for building a conventional German patriotism, by insisting on the indissoluble ethical unity between Germany's democratic vitality and continuing to take responsibility for the crimes of the Third Reich."[25] Habermas's 1986 interventions in the Historians' Debate successfully entrenched these parameters for West German consciousness after Auschwitz. In "A Kind of Settlement of Damages: (Apologetic Tendencies)" and "Concerning the Public Abuse of History," Habermas reprimands Alfred Dregger, along with the historians Stürmer, Hillgruber, Nolte, and Klaus Hildebrand, for appropriating history in the service of a "positive" West German national identity.[26] The brunt of Habermas's critique falls on Stürmer, Hillgruber, and Nolte, who are taken to task for instrumentally exploiting their status as experts in a pluralist public sphere to propagate morally questionable interpretations of the Nazi period as expert "historicizations" that aim to defuse reflection on the Holocaust's singularity and professionally cleanse history as a foundation of national unity.

The opening paragraph of Habermas's "A Kind of Settlement of Damages" criticizes the inscription on the memorial stone of Bonn's North Cemetery and Dregger's April 25, 1986 speech to the Bundestag. It was in the course of this speech that the former chairman of the Christian Democratic

Union (CDU) dismissed the need to distinguish between victims and culprits in the dedication of the Bonn memorial "To the Victims of Wars and the Rule of Violence." Habermas denounced the apologist interests informing Dregger's remarks and the inscription, which condoned an abstraction that crudely blurs the difference between dead veterans, including Nazi perpetrators, and the people whom they persecuted and murdered.[27] The memorial would, in Habermas's view, institute this abstraction as a collective memory over and against a victim memory that contests such a "cohabitation." Ultimately, then, by effacing distinctions that recall German crimes, the plans for the Bonn memorial put an interested and partial memory in the service of a positive national image in order to provide the citizens of the "perpetrator nation" with a symbolic means of downplaying a criminal period in their past.[28]

It is worth noting that Habermas's criticism of Dregger's speech is consonant with Adorno's moratorium in the third section of *Negative Dialectics* on the logic of *Sinnstiftung* as a compensatory and identitarian provision of "higher meaning." For Adorno, the mass-murdered must never become fodder for the logic of identity. The widespread and inappropriate "settling of accounts" about guilt (*Schadensabwicklung*) is a form of this logic that seeks to reconcile the particular with the totality. Such a logic repeats a redemptive emplotment of consciousness that bestows a higher meaning on the promise of reconciliation and unity. Adorno emphasizes that the particular has a concreteness that eludes identification with the universalizing concept. To remain vigilant, thought must bear witness to the impossibility of subsuming the particular under the universal. Adorno's figure for this impossibility is Auschwitz: "after Auschwitz, our feelings resist any claim of the positivity of existence as sanctimonious, as wronging the victims; they balk at squeezing any kind of sense, however bleached, out of the victims' fate. And these feelings do have an objective side after events that make a mockery of the construction of immanence as endowed with a meaning radiated by an affirmatively posited transcendence."[29] For Adorno, our "feelings" should bristle at the collapse of immanence into a redemptive transcendence that sweeps an unassimilable suffering under the carpet of collective fates in order to reaffirm progress in the face of barbarism. The memory of the murdered must instead be preserved as a thorn in the side of modern conscience.

One point remains consistent in Adorno's varying statements about Auschwitz: he calls for a recognition that the materiality of suffering can only be experienced negatively, since cultural forms of expression, including not only an ostensibly individualized lyric poetry but also cultural criticism itself, are complicit with forces of domination that perpetuate reification, or the hardening of feeling, as an adaptive mechanism. Such a recognition would thus involve a determinate negation of its own condition of possibility: critique is negative and dialectical in order to remain vigilant against its tendency to capitulate to generalization or, in aesthetic experience, the identitarian inclination to affirm reason, as in the Kantian sublime, which transcends a failure of imagination by asserting reason's power to discern this limit.

Adorno's "Education after Auschwitz" was initially delivered as a radio lecture in 1966. Its concerns are consonant with those of "The Meaning of Working Through the Past" (1959), where Adorno criticizes the desire among Germans to put the shame of national crimes against the Jews behind them. Both essays target a sensibility that he noticed with no small degree of disgust was already emerging in the early 1950s, when non-Jewish Germans disavowed or otherwise sought to minimize their responsibility for the horrors of their all too recent past. Adorno was thus addressing those Germans who acted as though a superficial and typically forced confrontation with the mass murders were a finite procedure that could be checked off like a distasteful chore. He was also reproaching a postwar tendency among Germans to broker their own suffering during the air bombings and expulsions as equalizing collateral against shame for the irreparable harm that they caused or with which they were complicit. Such attitudes trivialize the German crimes against the Jews and others while failing to consider their significance for modern Western society. The death camps revealed the nightmare horizon of an Enlightenment dream of progress in the instrumental reason of the National Socialist agenda to "exterminate" the Jews efficiently.

Because the 1959 and 1966 pieces are chiefly polemical in intent, Adorno is less committed than elsewhere to fleshing out the philosophical density of his terms. However, in the 1959 essay, he does take care to distinguish between "improper" and "proper" modes of confronting the past as a process related to the Freudian concept of *durcharbeiten* (to work through). Adorno distinguishes *durcharbeiten* from *Aufarbeitung*, when the latter denotes a bureaucratic *Erledigung* (dispatching) of an unpleasant obligation. In the mouths of politicians, it also suggests an arrogant desire to "master" and transcend the mass murders of the Jews. *Aufarbeitung* as *Vergangenheitsbewältigung* (mastering of the past) is therefore to be distinguished from *verarbeiten*, defined as to work upon and come to terms with the past through critical reflection. Adorno's *verarbeiten* is, thus, a regulative ideal that should govern German responses to Auschwitz.[30]

Adorno identifies the aim of "Education after Auschwitz" as a critical process that would prevent a recurrence of the Holocaust by fostering an "intellectual, cultural, and social climate" wherein "the motives that led to the horror would become relatively conscious."[31] In addition, education must labor against a lack of reflection and thereby dissuade people from falling prey to those mechanisms that compel them to vent on others their anger about being dominated. In this respect, the only education "that has any sense at all is an education toward critical reflection."[32] Facilitating such reflection is the goal of education after Auschwitz.

Adorno's influence on Habermas is striking in the latter's denunciation of Stürmer among other members of the Right who deploy a conciliatory rhetoric of transcendence in pursuit of a national *Sinnstiftung*. Part of Stürmer's notoriety in leftist circles stems from his role as a speechwriter for Chancellor Kohl, a Christian Democrat. In Stürmer's view, a divided Germany requires historical continuity to foster nationalist values.[33] Historians should therefore offer a unifying image that can cement a fractured society.[34] In short, he preaches a regression to conventional nationalism as a precondition of collective identity whereby history becomes an ersatz religion that replaces lost values.[35] In keeping with Adorno, Habermas is quick to jump on the Christian concept of abstract justice at the heart of Dregger's remarks above, which assumes the infallible judgments of a pluralist God granting equal treatment to one and all on the Day of Judgment. The modern connection between individuality and equality derives from this abstraction, along with the "universalistic" basis for the West German constitution.[36] Dregger thus appealed "to deep-seated moral intuitions" when he leveled the differences between the culprits and victims of the Nazi regime.[37] The suffering of the particulars might be held in common only once their particularity has been collectively effaced.

In Habermas's analysis, Dregger's celebration of collective fates is a symptomatic repetition of the controversial Bitburg incident triggered by President Reagan's diplomatic trip to West Germany in May 1985. The morning hours were filled by a quick excursion to Bergen-Belsen that was essentially an afterthought in the diplomatic itinerary—an inept concession to outraged Jewish groups, veterans, and media critics. The main event was Reagan's May 5 commemorative visit in Chancellor Kohl's company to the Bitburg Cemetery, which is known to contain the graves of SS members, a criminal organization responsible for orchestrating and carrying out the mass murders. With Kohl and Reagan standing by, American and German veteran generals performed the ritual conciliatory gesture of shaking hands. In his speech, the American leader memorialized the victims on both sides who lost their life under Hitler's dictatorship. Reagan briefly mentions the forty-eight SS graves in passing, before entering into a reflection on the tragic fates of "simple soldiers."

As I will discuss below, the 1996 "War of Annihilation: Crimes of the Wehrmacht, 1941–1944" exhibit coordinated by the Hamburg Institute for Social Research has since promoted awareness of the fact that these "simple soldiers" not only provided a military shield for the SS, but also participated in deportations and killing operations. Reagan's speech clumsily elided the Third Reich's atrocities as a goodwill gesture to the conservative Kohl's West Germany and thus abused his privilege as a powerful public official to write over historical wrongs. He also affirmed the Federal Republic's "new" identity as a fully recuperated member of the civilized, democratic, and capitalist West.[38] In Reagan's Christian dramaturgy, Kohl's Federal Republic could serve to consolidate U.S. moral sovereignty by playing the prodigal son to the president, cast as a forgiving father. By presiding over a ritual reconciliation, Reagan thus handed apologists an opportunity to draw a longed-for *Schlußstrich* (concluding line) under the Nazi past.[39]

The Bitburg affair was a significant episode in West German memory politics because it officiated a language of reconciliation that gilded over the perpetrators' agency with sentimental rhetoric about the suffering caused by war. From Habermas's perspective, the incident provided a preview of subsequent conservative efforts to appropriate historical consciousness for the sake of German national esteem in the government planning of new memorials and museums in the 1980s, which engaged the expert services of historians.[40] Habermas objected to professional historians being "given their fixed role in the process of ideological planning" and the "bureaucratic production of meaning" that positioned them to withdraw from the bank of "suitably positive pasts" and to project an image of a Federal Republic "firmly anchored in the Atlantic community of values" with which Germans could legitimately identify.[41] Kohl's former political advisor, the conservative historian Stürmer, codified the politics of normalization when he called for the dissemination of "positive" images of the past in order to coin a confident national consciousness for the future. This orientation shaped a memorial culture in West Germany as well as Kohl's specific plans to donate a museum of German history to Berlin "as part of his effort to nurture a 'normalized' national identity for the Germans, to sanitize Germany's past."[42] Such plans were, as Maier sees it, emblematic of an inclination to "package and subdue [German] history by suitably arranging its relics."[43]

Though the voice of Adorno is audible in Habermas's criticisms of this climate, it is worth remarking the limits of the former's influence when the latter defends the "unfinished project" of modernity. Elsewhere he notoriously chides his Frankfurt School forebears for the pervasive "Nietzschean" tendencies they manifest in "their blackest book," the *Dialectic of Enlightenment*.[44] Horkheimer's and Adorno's *Dialectic* "holds out scarcely any prospect for an escape from the myth of purposive rationality that has turned into objective violence."[45] "The suspicion of ideology becomes *total*," Habermas declares, "but without any change of direction." It is instead "turned not only against the irrational function of bourgeois ideals, but against the rational potential of bourgeois culture itself, and thus it reaches into the foundations of any ideology critique that proceeds immanently." Hence the *Dialectic's* argument is paradoxical in Habermas's reading, "because in the moment of description it still has to make use of the critique that has been declared dead."[46] This performative contradiction confirms his "suspicion that Horkheimer and Adorno perceive cultural modernity from a similar experiential horizon, with the same heightened sensibility, and even with the same cramped optics that render one insensible to the traces and the existing forms of communicative rationality."[47]

In the course of Habermas's intervention into the Historian's Debate, Adorno's critique is itself rationalized and liberalized to the extent that his "experiential horizon," with its "heightened sensibility" and "cramped optics," is expropriated and his critical ethos is rendered "constructive." Not surprisingly, this intervention reiterates the value of communicative rationality while nevertheless borrowing the authoritative force of Adorno's arguments against citing Germans' war trauma during the aerial bombings as a means of "settling accounts" with respect to their own genocidal past; it also reiterates Adorno's repudiation of Germans' immediate postwar attempts to posit a redemptive, identity-affirming sense of closure with respect to the National Socialist crimes. A genuinely critical engagement with the mass murders must be distinguished from a superficial and self-congratulatory claim of mastery over the past, which is one of the negative connotations of *Vergangenheitsbewältigung*. In addition, Habermas translates Adorno's prioritization of a genuinely critical working through into the foundation of postnational (enlightened European) citizenship. To be sure, Adorno's formulation of this aim is consonant with the "heightened sensibility" of a self-identified German critic forced into exile as a "Jew," yet Habermas rewrites it as a basis for a (Western) democratic consensus and a postconventional identity for Germans who are called upon continuously to evaluate their investments in particular traditions rather than passively accept them.

Adorno's "after Auschwitz" pedagogy continues to inflect Habermas's writing of the moral and liberal imaginary that has surfaced in more recent debates about the Memorial to the Murdered Jews of Europe. In Adorno's spirit, Habermas repudiates versions of the Nazi past "which transform comparisons into balancing accounts" and thereby eradicate the German historical legacy oriented toward the victims and their suffering.[48] Suffering, in his view, "is always concrete suffering; it cannot be separated from its context."[49] Mourning and recollection secure those traditions that have been formed by experiences of mutual distress; however, this does not mean that mourning is always mutual or that suffering is experienced in the same way by all individuals and groups. The asymmetry between perpetrators' and victims' experiences produces incommensurable memories in a nation's reckoning with its past, and elicits differing forms of mourning and regret.

For this reason, Habermas argues, even though the task of mourning might include the work of reconciliation, the burden of this work is differentially shared. Such a task is more ambivalent for those groups who lived under repressive circumstances and who maintained themselves by "usurping and destroying the lives of others." At the same time, an "undifferentiated form of remembrance" continues this usurpation by disavowing the gap between victims and perpetrators.[50] The oppressed should not be further victimized through an enforced reconciliation; neither should they be blotted out through a compulsory integration. The past leaves behind an irreversible debt to the dead, and it is the *intersubjective legacy* of this debt that haunts the fortuitousness of survival:

> Our own life is linked inwardly, and not just by accidental circumstances, with that context of life in which Auschwitz was possible. Our form of existence is connected with the form of existence of our parents and grandparents by a mesh of family, local, political and intellectual traditions which is difficult to untangle—by an historical milieu, therefore, which in the first instance has made us what we are and who we are today. No one among us can escape unnoticed from this milieu, because our identity both as individuals and as Germans is inextricably interwoven with it . . . there is the obligation we in Germany have . . . to keep alive the memory of the suffering of those murdered at the hands of Germans, and we must keep this memory alive quite openly and not just in our own minds. These dead have above all a claim to the weak anamnestic power of solidarity which those born later can now only practice through the medium of the memory which is always being renewed, which may often be desperate, but which is at any rate active and circulating. If we disregard this Benjaminian legacy, Jewish fellow citizens and certainly the sons, the daughters and the grandchildren of the murdered victims would no longer be able to breathe in our country.[51]

There is no question of *Schuld* in the sense of collective guilt for Habermas but rather as a *liability* or *debt* "for the distorted life circumstances which grant happiness, or even mere existence" at the cost of other lives.[52] Hence the "indebtedness of memory" implies a contract between the living and the dead, which is, itself, a measure of a common milieu of life-forms. In this view, Germans should consider themselves responsible for the genocide as long as they share the same life-forms as those who perpetrated the Nazi crimes. Indeed, since the conditions that enable present life also enabled Auschwitz, the death camps remain an ineluctable force in the formation of postwar identity.

Habermas acknowledges that the shock of Auschwitz shredded the naive Western faith in human solidarity and thereby altered the conditions for historical continuity in both Germany and the West. By anchoring nationalism in an instrumentally purged history, the conservative revisionists refuse this legacy, renounce a moral consensus based on respect for the memory of the murdered, and thus betray a national obligation to honor the victims of Nazi persecution, which is the premise for Germany's democratic rehabilitation. Before the Historian's Debate, this premise not only grounded the Federal Republic's "official self-image" according to Habermas; it also delivered West Germany's "greatest" postwar intellectual achievement: "the unreserved opening to the political culture of West."[53] This opening established the conditions for a constitutional patriotism determined by universalistic principles that represents the "only patriotism which does not alienate [Germans] from the West."[54]

In Habermas's view, the Federal Republic's renewed relation with the West was made possible only after and because of Auschwitz—a rapprochement that transpired in the shadow of the death camps.[55] This rapprochement is, then, a politically and morally desirable "credit" earned through conscientious remembrance. It is in this sense that Habermas casts the morality of remembrance as a form of debt payment that reflects the bourgeois-ideological link between responsible citizenship and the "civility" of free-market commerce that underlies his references to rapprochement and "the West."

Habermas's adaptation of Adorno's ideal of critical remembrance reinforces the hegemonic privilege of a West German standpoint that carries over into the memorial debates. In the first place, such references in 1986 construct the legitimacy of the Bundesrepublik Deutschland (the former West Germany) at the implicit expense of its undemocratic Deutsche Demokratische Republik "other" (the former East Germany). In the second place, West Germans *must adopt* this ideal or forsake their duties as responsible (well-behaved, debt-paying) citizens of Europe and the world. Hence, despite his repudiation of *Sinnstiftung* logic when it is exercised by the Right, Habermas replays it in calling upon contemporary Germans to "pay off" the crime of Auschwitz through indebted memory, which additionally assumes a compensatory meaning as a herald of reconciliation. To the extent that Auschwitz is retroactively assessed as the "price" Germans paid (and will continue to pay) for a democratic future, it henceforth becomes the means to the end of rehabilitating West Germany as a European democracy. For Habermas, it would therefore seem that only the bourgeois values of rationality and responsibility could shield Holocaust memory from the slings and arrows of the revisionists' perspectivalism that alters the contours of events in accordance with the interests of the present moment.[56]

Habermas's 1986 intervention was partly fueled by the 1980s memorial culture under Chancellor Kohl, who also presided over the reunification of Germany. As Karen Till observes, normalization in this period "came to mean that Germany should be simultaneously defined as a cultural nation," which "implies Western ideas of individual freedom and national self-determination," and as a European state, which "demands surrendering certain sovereign rights to such supranational organizations as the EU and NATO."[57] This orientation was most concretely enacted in the 1984 Bitburg affair, which I discuss above, and it certainly did not disappear when the Berlin Wall fell. After reunification, Kohl redesignated the *Neue Wache* on Unter den Linden in the former East Berlin as the "Central Memorial of the Federal Republic of Germany for the Victims of War and Tyranny." The memorial thereby assumed the commemorative function previously proposed for the Bonn memorial in the former West Germany. It was also consistent, as Elke Grenzer suggests, with prior employments of the site as a venue for naturalizing and affirming the state's coherent self-representation and dominance.[58] Till reports that criticisms of the *Neue Wache* focused on the proper function and form of the memorial as a public institution and on the question of which dead should be commemorated, concerns that carried over into concurrent discussions about the Berlin Holocaust memorial. It is worth reviewing the circumstances surrounding the rededication in order to understand how they were transferred into more recent debates in the newly anointed capital city.

The *Neue Wache* dates back to the aftermath of Napoleon's defeat when, in 1817, King William III commissioned the architect Karl Friedrich Schinkel to build a guardhouse across from his palace, which was initially conceived as "part of a larger vision of *Unter den Linden* as a parade ground that demarcated the power of the king in the heart of a Prussian empire."[59] Following the German capitulation in 1918, a simple granite pillar crowned with a black and silver oak wreath was added, and Otto Braun reinaugurated the memorial to honor the fallen soldiers of the Great War. Under Hitler, an oak cross was installed above the central pillar, which converted the memorial into an altar valorizing Germany's dead and legitimizing his fiction about the Third Reich as a successor to the Holy Roman Empire.[60] In 1957, this "tainted relic of the Nazi past" was modified once again. The oak cross was replaced with a hammer and sickle to officialize its status as a symbol of a German-Soviet alliance, and the memorial was "reframed as a *Mahnmal für die Opfer des Faschismus und Militarismus*" to naturalize the grounding of the German Democratic Republic.[61] After reunification, the hammer and sickle were removed and an enlarged reproduction of Käthe Kollwitz's fifteen-inch sculpture of a seated and mourning mother holding the corpse of her dead son was installed in the interior chamber. Officially deemed secular, the *Pietà*-like mother figure enveloped in a kerchief clasping her lifeless son's body to her breast nevertheless touched off discussions about the use of Christian imagery to symbolize grief, which some read as expropriating the Jews (again).

The chancellor's cabinet approved the rededication of the *Neue Wache* in January 1993 without debate in the federal parliament and without formal hearings or a public assessment of competing proposals. As a concession to various outraged victims' groups, passages from former president Richard von Weizäcker's Bundestag speech on May 8, 1985, to commemorate the end of World War II were inscribed on bronze plaques in eight languages affixed to the right of the entrance. The importance of this compromise should not be underestimated. As Till remarks, Weizäcker's speech has been held up as a model for an appropriately nuanced public acknowledgment of the differences between social groups who had suffered under the Nazis. Because he delivered the speech in the Bundestag months after the Bitburg affair, it was also heralded by critics of the Kohl administration, including Habermas, as a deserved reprimand to the chancellor's politics of normalization.[62] Since the rededicated *Neue Wache* had originally been planned to coincide with Dregger's vision for the Bonn memorial "To the Victims of Wars and the Rule of Violence," the addition of the Weizäcker inscription reflects a fraught compromise between the former CDU chairman's call for an undifferentiated recognition of war suffering and the ideal of critical citizenship that Habermas defined in the context of the Historians' Debate.[63] This compromise appears to be strategic in responding to an emergent pressure to mitigate a threatening image of a reunified Germany in the eyes of its European neighbors through demonstrations that it had humbly learned the lessons of its arrogant and violent past.

In addition, the recourse to Weizäcker's speech from 1885 confirms Till's contention that, since the reunification of Germany, a West German standpoint continues to be hegemonic in debates about memorialization. Since the fall of the Wall in 1989, German *Erinnerungspolitik* (the manipulation of collective memory for political reasons) has not departed from West German conventions governing public discussions about the Nazi past. These conventions have, if anything, become more rather than less entrenched since reunification. In discussions about the *Neue Wache*, for example, "the possible opinions of East Germans were not reported by the press because they were not recognized by the media (or perhaps by the reading 'public') as legitimate and authoritative actors," Till writes. East German standpoints were represented only "when they fitted existing interest group categories."[64] For all intents and purposes, then, the rededicated *Neue Wache* excised the East Germans and abolished signs of the previous government's expressions of official ideology.

Nolan presents the Goldhagen controversy along with the "War of Annihilation: Crimes of the Wehrmacht, 1941–1944" exhibit as crucial incidents in the trajectory of German memory politics following reunification. For while "Goldhagen exposed the actions of the SS and reserve police battalions," Nolan writes, the exhibit that opened in 1996 "attacked the myth of the clean Wehrmacht" as noncriminal defenders of the German people.[65] The exhibit was coordinated by the Hamburg Institute for Social Research, "whose iconoclastic director and patron, Jan Philipp Reemstma, was an early and energetic supporter of Goldhagen's work."[66] It comprised nearly a thousand photographs depicting Wehrmacht personnel "ordering, passively watching, logistically enabling, often actively participating, and always legitimating" the murder of Jews and partisans "by shooting, hanging, and the burning of homes and villages." The photographs in the exhibit accompanied excerpts from army orders, reports, letters, and diaries. The photos also contained "endless columns of POWS and newly dug mass graves filled with newly shot victims of a campaign fought outside the rules of war."[67] Such evidence countered a widely held popular belief that the

Wehrmacht stood apart from "the Nazi system, the SS, and the genocidal war those institutions waged. Rather, the Wehrmacht was a thoroughly Nazified institution, from its officer corps through its enlisted men and draftees."[68] As a further testament to the marginalization of the former East Germany in postreunification memory politics, the exhibit toured major and smaller cities in the former West Germany and also in Austria, but "virtually bypassed the former GDR."[69]

One possible partial explanation for this marginalization, as Till surmises, is that "communist societies were not structured by the Western dualism of public/private spheres, but rather by state/family arenas. East Germans therefore may have found it difficult to enter media-driven 'public' debates, even if they wished to, because they did not have a history of participating in this West German memory tradition."[70] The Historians' Debate of the 1980s had been "an exclusively West German event," as Nolan observes: "There were no comparably explosive reconsiderations of the Nazi past in the closing decade of the German Democratic Republic. Nor did the subsequent controversies about Goldhagen, the Wehrmacht exhibit, and the Mahnmal"—and, I would add, the debate about Steven Spielberg's *Schindler's List*—"involve the former East extensively."[71]

In her analysis of the *Neue Wache* and the 2005 memorial, Grenzer has commented on the "boom in memorials" marking "the absence and loss produced by the Holocaust," a boom that steadily displaced the emblems of the former East Germany since the fall of the Berlin Wall.[72] From a West German standpoint, as Till characterizes it, a memorial is viewed, theoretically at least, "as the outcome of a *public process* of working through the past, not just an official staging or representation of history."[73] Kirsten Harjes notes that Berlin memorials are "expected to represent a new generation of politicians and citizens committed to historical responsibility for the Holocaust and the fight against contemporary racism." Their functions are threefold: "to mourn and commemorate the dead, to educate their audiences, and to politically and socially represent contemporary German citizens." In this respect, Harjes observes, "Holocaust memory has usually been regarded as an exercise in specifically German citizenship."[74]

The terms of a "specifically German citizenship" were a consistent focal point of discussions about the Berlin Memorial to the Murdered Jews of Europe. In part because they were initiated in the wake of the Historians' Debate, these discussions culminated in a memorial that attests to the influence of Habermas's intervention, which promoted continuing respect for the singularity of the "Final Solution" as a fulcrum of a critical citizenship that would be affectively "indebted" to (i.e., identified with) the suffering of the predominantly Jewish victims of the Third Reich. This pedagogy adheres to Adorno's model of *verarbeiten* as a form of critical Holocaust remembrance over and against a redemptive politics of normalization that would denigrate victim memory by sweeping all wartime bereavement under the same equalizing rubric. In addition, Habermas constructs a national commitment to vigilance in light of Auschwitz as a medium for German rapprochement with the democratic West. Though this agenda was, in part, a reaction against the "normalization" of victim memory under Kohl, this aspect of his administration's politics necessarily shifted in the aftermath of the fall of the Berlin Wall, the reunification of the former East and West, and the election of Chancellor Gerhard Schröder with his Red-Green coalition in 1998, which ended the sixteen-year Kohl government. In this period of transition, as Harjes observes, the idea of a Holocaust memorial "came to be associated with the unified government's wish to set a signal of integration: the integration of east and west German [sic] collective memory, and Germany's peaceful integration into the European Community and its leading role in it." The prospect of a national Holocaust memorial was increasingly being perceived as a means for Germany to officiate its commitment to a "distinctly democratic form of collective memory."[75]

Rosh began collaborating with Jäckel in 1987 when they formed the Perspektive Berlin initiative to promote the memorial for the murdered Jews of Europe as "a visible sign in the country of the perpetrators."[76] From their agenda, it would appear that Jäckel, a contributor to the Historians' Debate, had been persuaded by Habermas's advocacy for Adorno's post-Auschwitz pedagogy. In the intervening period before ground was finally broken for the memorial on April 1, 2003, the initiators succeeded in promoting their aim to dedicate the memorial exclusively to the Jewish victims of the Third Reich. The memorial that was opened on May 10, 2005, officially functions to acknowledge the necessity of open-ended, yet informed remembrance as a venue of critical citizenship in a unified Germany. Its form is intended by the *Förderkreis*, a foundation set up to promote a monument to the Jewish genocide, to mark a wound in the landscape of German consciousness; and it is intended by Eisenman to precipitate a sublimely vertiginous encounter with the "unrepresentability" of mass murder. It commemorates the murdered Jews above all, with the Information Center also acknowledging how Nazi genocidal policies extended to other groups. The debates that deferred the memorial's completion foregrounded the question of whose response to genocide "should" be commemorated and thus idealized so as to prevail over time: Jews versus other victims, Jewish versus non-Jewish Germans, war generations versus future generations, and former West German versus former East German investments or counterinvestments in critical remembrance. Next, I will turn to the contestation around the content, form, and aims of the memorial to highlight the discursive contingencies as well as the taste and class interests that determined the selection of Eisenman's design as the most appropriate venue for assuring critical remembrance of the "Final Solution."

"What have we done to ourselves by doing away with the Jews?": The Memorial and Its Interlocutors

The Kohl government's decision to back the Förderkreis's insistence on dedicating the Holocaust memorial exclusively to the murdered Jews was the pragmatic fruit of a concession to Ignatz Bubis, the late president of the Central Council of the Jews in Germany from 1992 to 1999, who threatened to boycott the opening ceremony for the rededicated *Neue Wache* in November 1993. As Young notes, the federal government and the Berlin senate backed the project of commemorating the genocide of European Jews, because they recognized that it "might serve as a strategic counterweight to the *Neue Wache*."[77] Rosh retrospectively writes that she and Jäckel "wanted to remember the crime, the million-fold murder, and to honour the memory of the dead, to give them back their names." They hoped the memorial would "prevent Germany from simply getting down to the business of reunification, rebuilding, affluence—as if nothing had happened. But," she admits, "that would not be easy. Because at no other time in history had a nation, a people, admitted to and visibly documented such a tremendous crime committed in its name."[78]

Rosh is not exaggerating the challenges she and Jäckel faced. Over the course of the seventeen years the initators required to see it to completion, the memorial project was plagued by moral, territorial, and economic issues. From early on, Gerd Knischewski and Ulla Spittler observe, "there was an argument over the appropriate form for remembering the Nazi past which manifested itself as a competition between two grassroots initiatives for scarce resources (including claims to the site), and at the same time between different concepts for remembering, i.e., documentation of the Nazi repression system versus artistic memorialization of its victims."[79] The memorial was initially proposed for the current site of the "Topography of Terror" in Berlin, which maps the National Socialist administrative headquarters and pivotal institutions, including the Gestapo and the Central Office of Security of the Reich. The fall of the Berlin Wall opened the prospect of placing the memorial in one of the reunified capital's "most sought-after pieces of real estate": at the site of the Ministers' Gardens, a plot of twenty-thousand square meters between the Brandenburg Gate and Potsdamer Platz.[80]

There were also those who worried that the memorial would siphon off government funding from already existing memorial projects, including the "Topography of Terror," the documentary installation at the Wannsee villa that opened in 1992, the book-burning memorial on Bebelplatz (1995), and sites of deportations and former concentration camps such as the Grünewald train station (1992), and the Columbiahaus concentration camp (1994). The decision to purchase antigraffiti protection from Degussa, the sister firm of the company Degesch that had produced Zyklon B for the gas chambers, sparked intense arguments. Sibylle Quack, who had expressed critical concerns about the "danger of 'erasing the past in the process of remembering,' " quit her position as the executive director of the Foundation "Remembrance, Responsibility and Future" (established in 2000) during the Degussa controversy.[81] The decision to permit Degussa to stay on the project was, in part, a result of economic considerations, but it also acknowledged the company's initiative in contributing to compensation funds for forced and slave laborers before the Foundation "Remembrance, Responsibility and Future" required it and in publishing a 2004 book, Peter Hayes's *Die Degussa im Dritten Reich*, that documented its role in realizing Third Reich genocidal policies.[82] The decision to retain Degussa is significant, as Knischewski and Spittler remark, since it can be read as connoting a reconciliation with the circumstances in which the German economy profited from the National Socialist system.[83] According to Günter Schlusche, "[T]he main motivation for this decision was the fact that, in the country responsible for the Holocaust, there could be no clinically pure memorial that would be completely free, down to the last detail, of associations and burdens related to the past."[84]

Even as these issues were being resolved, the content and address of the memorial's exclusive dedication to the Jews remained the subject of heated contention and political posturing. In the third of three colloquia held by the organizers, Rosh remained adamant about commemorating the Jews alone because, as she writes, "the central goal of National Socialist genocide policy was the destruction of Jewry. This was Hitler's most important aim, more important to him than winning the war. The consummation of 2,000 years of anti-Semitism on this continent and the figure of six million Jewish victims demanded a memorial dedicated to the Jews."[85] Jäckel stood by Rosh in insisting that the decades-long anti-Semitism that prepared for the "extermination" had been the kernel of Nazi ideology and practice.[86]

The Central Council of the Jews in Germany as well as the World Jewish Congress supported Rosh and Jäckel on this point, while others criticized them for imposing an ethnocentric victim hierarchy, which relegates the Sinti and Roma, among others, to the status of "second-class" victims even though their murders were motivated by the same racist ideology.[87] Claus Leggewie and Erik Meyer deride this hierarchy premised on the "tasteless" notion that "a 1000-year culture has been ripped out of the heart of Europe" and left an "enormous loss and emptiness" behind.[88] They cite Henryk Broder's caustic inversion of this solipsistic premise: "What have we [Germans] done to ourselves by doing away with the Jews?"[89]

Representatives of the Sinti and Roma, as well as Reinhart Koselleck, Christian Meier, Jürgen Kocka, and the prominent Jewish commentators Salomon Korn, Micha Brumlik, Michael Wolffsohn, Rafael Seligmann, and Broder, challenged Rosh's and Jäckel's insistence on dedicating the memorial exclusively to Jewish victims. As Habermas understood their position, Koselleck and Meier, along with Korn, Brumlik, and Broder, were still reacting against the initial premise behind the rededication of the *Neue*

Wache to the Victims of War and Dictatorship, which threw perpetrators and victims together under one "unbearable" abstraction. Yet it is worth noting that the architect Korn was also questioning a central commemoration of the victims as opposed to the crime and its perpetrators, a gesture of disavowal in his eyes. "It is certainly more pleasant for descendants of the perpetrators to have a memorial to the victims than to construct a warning against the crimes committed by their own people," he contends.[90] Korn also worried that the project's supporters were promoting a reified victim-centered morality while acting on the motive to bind their names for perpetuity with a conventional, "eternal" public form.[91]

Up until his death in 2006, the historian Koselleck was admired as one of the most important theorists in Germany. In contrast to Korn, he underscored the problematic address of a "death-cult of memorials" that should present "remembrance and remorse, warning and reminder, in a lasting manner." For Koselleck, this address is fraught with the differences between the dead—an all-encompassing category (the *Neue Wache*), "innocent civilians" or prisoners of the Nazis, or even specific groups among the victims themselves.[92] The memorial's exclusive reference to the murdered Jews, from its critics' standpoint, would inflict an injustice on the Sinti and Roma, political prisoners, euthanized mentally challenged, gays and lesbians, Jehovah's Witnesses, and deserters that could only be made good again through individual memorials to these ignored groups. In addition, as Wolfgang Benz remarks, there were the Soviet prisoners of war along with the Ukrainian and Belorussian victims to whom politicians seldom refer when they mention the National Socialist crimes.[93] The prospect of individually commemorating each of these groups spurred the Lord Mayor of Berlin, Eberhard Diepgen, to refer sarcastically to Berlin as a " 'capital of repentance' with a 'memorial mile.' "[94] Regardless of its cynicism, this statement made those involved attentive to the impossibility of responding with individual memorials to a demand for an equal treatment of all the Third Reich's victims.[95] During the months preceding the autumn 1998 elections, Diepgen deflected decisions about the memorial and its construction time line; however, the June 25, 1999, parliamentary resolution (with a majority of 314 votes to 209) compelled him to accept decisions along these lines.[96] In 1999, the German parliament nevertheless overrode Mayor Diepgen's objections and decided to endorse the interests of the Förderkreis members, who wanted to institutionalize a wounding recognition of the Jewish genocide.

The right-wing mayor was not the only politician to enter the fray. The liberal polemicist Michael Naumann was named to assume the newly created post of minister of culture for Gerhard Schröder prior to the latter's election in September 1998. Citing the monumentality of Eisenman's design, Naumann compared it to Albert Speer's architectural plans and proposed educationally oriented alternatives, such as a library or archive that could house the Leo Baeck Institute for Jewish History, an exhibition, and a "genocide watch institute." Significantly, Naumann also questioned the interests of a project that had been deferred for so long that its intended effects would only fall upon those who were not involved in the atrocities associated with World War II. His democratic posturing was seemingly intended to capture the hearts and minds of postwar "new center" voters who wanted to stop wallowing in guilt and to draw a *Schlußstrich* between themselves and the past. Such polemics were largely regarded with suspicion by liberal newspapers such as *Die Zeit* and *Der Tagespiegel*, which depicted them as callous examples of *Kulturpolitik*. Schlusche describes Naumann as "a man of letters" who "bore a certain mistrust towards the educational potential of fine arts and architecture" and is seemingly sympathetic to his concern for combining "the aesthetic value of Eisenman's field of stelae with the classical medium of information, literature, and other educational elements."[97] Whatever his motivations, Naumann's intervention was important in prompting the addition of a "Place of Information," to which Eisenman reluctantly agreed.[98]

In October 1998, Martin Walser entered into the memorial debate on the occasion of receiving the Peace Prize of the German Book Trade Association in Frankfurt. The esteemed novelist used the occasion of his acceptance speech to warn his fellow Germans against the "instrumentalization of our shame" and the use of Auschwitz as a "moral cudgel" by the media. As Knischewski and Spittler paraphrase it, Walser also "maintained that only the individual could sincerely remember and that the state should not prescribe a way of ritualized mourning." He therefore "rejected the memorial as an attempt to 'monumentalize the German shame.' "[99] Walser was accused of "moral arson" by an outraged Bubis, who, up until his death in 1999, was sometimes treated as a Jewish weather vane for German improprieties.[100] In proclaiming a German entitlement to move beyond sensitivity about the Nazi crimes, Walser joined Diepgen and Naumann in challenging notions of moral propriety that prioritize the victims' perspective to enjoin remembrance of their losses. While I agree with Walser that the state's interest in regulating collective memory should be questioned, his acidic language resonates with Diepgen's and Naumann's rhetoric to create a sense that a climate had emerged in the late 1990s in which politicians and writers had come to share Nolte's resentment against a compulsive focus on the Nazi crimes against the Jews. In this respect, Walser's complaint, as Grossmann recalls, was only one recent example of how "Germans presented themselves as victimized and marginalized in the face of disproportionate attention devoted to Jews and their fate."[101]

Walser's apparent resentment about "dwelling" on the mass murder is, of course, a luxury. While the traumatic charge of genocide might fade away for contemporary Germans who are seeking to construct a European identity for themselves, passing time cannot simply erase the irreparable legacies of mass murder for groups whose families and, in many cases, entire communities were wiped out. Third Reich Germans, Austrians, and their collaborators not only decimated the Jewish, Roma, and Sinti communities of Europe, but also their future generations.[102] The resulting destruction of culture and extended community does not disappear for the affected minorities after the passage of a few decades, and it continues to be painful for many members of these groups, who, despite their diminished numbers, are still subject to archaic stereotypes, particularly in former Eastern Bloc countries. According to a May 2005 poll, 43 percent of contemporary Poles believe that Jews wield too much global economic power, despite their minority status.[103] Roma and Sinti still endure segregation and marginalization that circumscribe their chances to survive economically.[104] Quite obviously, too, the Holocaust's continuing traumatic force has fed a vicious cycle of bloodshed in the Middle East, where the civilian populations of Israel and the Palestinian territories are at the mercy of ideologues and militants on the respective sides of a life-or-death struggle. One cannot help but wonder what a Holocaust memorial would look like that seriously engaged this dimension of the genocide's legacy. In any case, such an interest would have been perceived as "incorrect" for the acting members of the Förderkreis, whose subject positions as Germans called on them to perform an unmitigated recognition of national responsibility for the mass murder of European Jews. In this conclusion, their position mostly coincides with Habermas's standpoint on the memorial debate, which contends that Third Reich history calls on Germans *in particular* to attend to the specificity of the damage inflicted on the Jews *in particular*.

Though my own position on a victim-centered critical remembrance is in many aspects commensurate with his, I want to call attention to the disciplinary power of Habermas's contributions to German memory politics. The epigraph to this chapter is a quotation from Habermas's "Der Zeigefinger: Die Deutschen und Ihr Denkmal" ("The Finger of Blame: The Germans and Their Memorial"), which was published in *Die Zeit* in March 1999. It is the first prose appearing in Hélène Binet's "photo essay" that accompanies Lukas Wasserman's "photo impressions" in a large-format art book with the title *Holocaust Memorial Berlin* coauthored by Hanno Rauterberg and the Eisenman Architects.[105] The book's blithe celebration of the memorial's somber beauty is only enhanced in Rauterberg's commentary, "Building Site of Remembrance," and Eisenman's "The Silence of Excess," with the latter printed on parchment-quality paper that contrasts with the glossy pages of Binet's and Wasserman's photo essay. The book obviously belongs to the commercial genre of art and architecture texts featuring highly aestheticized images of important buildings by important architects—that is to say, a genre geared toward unhampered fetishistic consumption. Nevertheless, the decision to cite Habermas apart from all those who participated in the more than fifteen years of debate about the memorial underscores the influence his pronouncements have obtained in discussions about the ethics of Holocaust representation since the 1980s.

In "Der Zeigefinger," Habermas comments on the "passionate controversy over the planned memorial," and, in particular, on the issue of whether the memorial should be dedicated exclusively to the Jews. He also reaffirms the need to recognize the specificity of the Third Reich's exterminatory anti-Semitism as a necessary element in the development of a properly postnational identity:

> Do we, the citizens of the Federal Republic of Germany, who remain the politico-legal and cultural heirs of the state and society of the 'generation of perpetrators,' accept a historical accountability for the consequences of their acts? Do we bear in self-critical remembrance Auschwitz—and the vigilant reflection on the events associated with this name—making it an explicit part of our political consciousness? Do we accept the disturbing political responsibility that accrues from the break in civilization, which was committed, supported, and tolerated by Germans, to those born after it as an element of a broken national identity? "Broken" in as much as this reponsibility means the will to abandon mindsets [we inherited] from the continuity of our own traditions that led us astray. As descendants sharing liability we tell ourselves "never again." The break in the continuity of our sustaining traditions is the prerequisite of recovering our self-respect.
>
> Should the planned memorial be the answer to these questions, then it makes no sense that we in the land of the perpetrators commemorate the Jewish victims in the same fashion as the victims' descendants in Israel and the U.S., as conscientious people all over the world. It cannot be the point that "Jews get a Holocaust memorial from us Germans." In the context of our political culture, such a memorial needs to have a different meaning. Through this memorial, the generations of the perpetrators' descendants avow a political identity branded [into them] not only by their predecessors' actions—the crime against humanity committed and tolerated during National Socialism—but also by the shock of the unspeakable done to the victims that persistently disquiets and admonishes us.[106]

Habermas is, in part, positioning himself against a "crime and crime-centered" meaning of the memorial by reiterating the terms of his 1986 intervention into the Historians' Debate, where he called upon Germans of all ages to accept responsibility for the atrocities of previous generations by maintaining memory of the Nazi atrocities as a permanent fulcrum of sociopolitical self-understanding. It is therefore key, for Habermas, that the memorial will address the perpetrators' descendants and not seem to serve as a compensatory gift to their victims. He once again promotes Adorno's understanding of critical remembrance by prioritizing the victims' standpoint while renouncing the desire for consolation: "The unconditional moral impulse towards remembrance must not be qualified through the context of self-assurance. We can only think of the victims seriously, and properly, when we think of them for their own sake."[107] His imagery is visceral: the shock of the Third Reich Germans' crimes must be *branded* (*eingebrannt*) into German identity as a persistent reproach.[108] Habermas hereby exemplifies a protective investment in a West German leftist construction of Auschwitz as the symbol of Germany's unsurpassed record of evil that Heinrich August Winkler has derided as a mode of "negative nationalism."[109]

Habermas's didactic optimism contrasts with Young's skepticism about the pedagogical ends of the memorial. Young's essay, "Germany's Memorial Problem—and Mine," plots his reflections about the seemingly interminable contestations over the memorial and the transformation of his skepticism into something approaching appreciation for the final result of a long and vexed process. In an address at the third colloquium in April 1997, Young remarks that if "the aim of a national Holocaust memorial in Berlin is to draw a bottom line under this era so that a reunified Germany can move unencumbered into the future, then let us make this clear." However, if it is "to remember for perpetuity that this great nation once murdered nearly six million human beings solely for having been Jews, then this monument must also embody the intractable questions at the heart of German Holocaust memory rather than claiming to answer them."[110] Young initially worried that the memorial would serve as "a hermetically sealed vault for the ghosts of Germany's past" and that, instead of eliciting memory of murdered Jews, "it would be a place where Germans would come dutifully to *unshoulder* their memorial burden" in order, then, to "move freely" into the next century. He accedes, "A finished monument would, in effect, finish memory itself."[111]

Young's self-reflections spotlight a publicly exhibited design competition in April 1994 that was organized by the Federal Ministry of the Interior, the Science Research and Culture office of the Berlin senate, and the Förderkreis. The projects submitted for this first competition bear some comment. Till notes that despite "the large number of proposals and the significant public interest in the competition, there was a notable lack of creativity by the artists: most used Jewish symbols (Stars of David, the menorah, the twelve tribes of Israel), created large graves or gashes in the earth, or used concentration camp icons (barracks, train tracks, cattle cars, concentration camp gates, ovens)."[112] Rauterberg complains about the "abysmal kitsch" distinguishing many of the entries to this competition, which, in his view, wallowed in "self-chastisement" and a "contrived artiness" that "thwarted all hopes of achieving anything even approximating a fitting memorial."[113] Young writes that "submissions ran the gamut of taste and aesthetic sensibilities, from the beautiful to the grotesque, from high modern to low kitsch, from the architectural to the conceptual."[114] He dwells on a radically provocative proposal by the "negative memorial" artist, Horst Hoheisel, who previously commemorated the Jews deported from Kassel, Germany. Hoheisel proposed to blow up the Brandenburger Tor, to grind its stone remains into dust, and to sprinkle the dust on its former site, which would thereafter be covered with granite plates.[115] Dani Caravan, designer of the 1994 Walter Benjamin monument in Portbou, Spain, proposed a Jewish star-shaped field of yellow flowers. The Berlin artists Renata Stih and Frieder Schnock mapped a series of "bus stops" where visitors could wait for coaches to take them to "sites of actual destruction in Berlin, Germany, and Europe." One entry stipulated a 130-foot-tall empty vat as a vessel for the blood of the murdered.

Two first prizes were awarded to Simon Ungers and Christine Jacob-Marks in the March 1995 competition, though Jacob-Marks's design prevailed. Ungers proposed an 85 x 85 meter square structure of steel corner girders raised on concrete blocks. The names of the concentration camps would be cut out of the steel so that sunlight could cast them into the center area. Jacob-Marks's winning proposal featured a 23-foot-thick and 300-foot-square concrete gravestone tilted at an angle running from 6 to 20 feet high, respectively, at its farthest ends. The tilted gravestone would be engraved with the names of 4.5 million murdered Jews. In addition, eighteen stones from Masada in Israel, where Jews committed collective suicide at the end of their revolt against the Romans in 66–73 CE, would mark its surface, in keeping with the Jewish tradition of leaving small stones at grave sites. The design that Korn aptly referred to as the *Mega-Grabplatte*, (mega gravestone)[116] was derided as "too big, too heavy-handed, too divisive and finally just too German," according to Young. Bubis hated it and exercised his Jewish-moral veto right when he told Chancellor Kohl that "the winning design was simply unacceptable." Kohl was compelled to rescind government support for this "too big and undignified design."[117] Young himself felt relieved at the time: "Better a thousand years of Holocaust memorial competitions and exhibitions in Germany than any single 'final solution' to Germany's memorial problem. This way," he adds, "instead of a fixed icon for Holocaust memory in Germany, the debate itself—perpetually unresolved amid ever-changing conditions—might now be enshrined."[118]

Young reports how "jurors subsequently told of rancorous, biting debate, with little meeting of the minds." Class and educational differences came to the fore: "The citizens' group resented the intellectuals and experts on the jury, with what they regarded as their elitist taste for conceptual and minimalist design. . . . Meanwhile, the intellectuals sniffed at the layjurors' middle-brow eye for kitsch and monumental figuration, their philistinian emotionalism; and the Bundestag's appointees glanced at their watches as the right political moment seemed to be ticking away."[119] Young asserts, "What had begun as an intellectually rigorous and ethically pure interrogation of the Berlin memorial was taking on the shape of a circular, centripedally driven, self-enclosed argument. It began to look like so much hand wringing and fence sitting, even an entertaining kind of spectator sport."[120]

The development of the memorial project was also marked by three public colloquia in January, March, and April 1997 attended by "distinguished artists, historians, critics and curators to address the most difficult issues and to suggest how the present designs might best be modified,"[121] by parliamentary debates in 1996 and 1999 that attempted to settle financial and design issues, and by endeavors among both conservative and liberal politicians to undermine it. The completed memorial by Eisenman is the hard-won compromise that resulted from a second design competition in 1997. A five-member *Findungskommission* composed of Werner Hofmann, Josef Paul Kleihues, Dieter Ronte, and Christoph Stölzl and led by the token Jewish-American professor, Young, ultimately selected a design by the New York architect Eisenman in collaboration with the New York based sculptor Richard Serra, who left the project to Eisenman's sole direction after June 1998.[122]

Young comments acerbically on his identity capital as "the only foreigner and Jew" who was invited to participate in the expert commission on the memorial. He asks himself, "[W]as I invited as an academic authority on memorials, or as a token American and foreigner? Is it my expertise they want, or are they looking for a Jewish blessing on whatever design is finally chosen?"[123] One might likewise speculate on the conjuncture of motives and contingencies that led the experts to choose Eisenman's and Serra's initial design, or what is referred to as Eisenman I. My hypothesis is that despite its "deconstructivist" agenda, Eisenman's "excess of silence" appeals to a conventional mimetic longing to find a properly "Jewish" form to correspond to respectful identifications with the murdered Jews. Certainly, Eisenman's own professed commitments speak to this interest.

In a transcript of a 1985 conversation with Derrida, the architect acknowledges that he had "recently begun to consider Hebraic thought and its implications for architecture." He goes on to conjecture that "[t]here were no graven images in the temple," and, as he understands it, "the Hebrew language contains no present tense of the verb 'to be'—only 'was' and 'will be.'" "Thus Hebraic thought," he simplistically concludes, "deals more with absence than presence." This definition inspires him "to try to construct a relationship between Hebraic and architectural thought" that, in consonance with Derridean deconstruction, would take place as a "critique of the operation of presence in architecture." It is the *idea* of a "Jewish" deconstruction that seemingly spurs Eisenman's attempt to respond to the question of why "architecture is so resistant to decentering," since, as Derrida suggests, it "seems to have nothing to do with absence."[124] It is, in Eisenman's words, "a system of presences" that represses *différance* as what "requires the simultaneous operation of both presence and absence. If this is the case," Eisenman adds, "then architecture has been one of the arenas in which *difference* [*sic*] is most repressed."[125]

Such comments are more in keeping with the majority of Eisenman's self-characterizations than with subsequent remarks in which he dissociates himself from Derridean deconstruction (a de rigueur gesture among deconstructivists). J. Hillis Miller and Derrida himself comment on Eisenman's proclaimed resistance to his affiliation with deconstruction, which he so explicitly embraced in their collaboration entitled *Chora L Works* for Tschumi's Park de la Villette project mentioned above.[126] In a letter to Eisenman dated October 12, 1989, Derrida reappropriates deconstruction as his (philosophical) domain when he paternalistically chastises the architect for remarks about the "presence of absence" in the context of *Moving Arrows, Eros and Other Errors* (Eisenman's "Romeo and Juliet" project in Verona, Italy).[127] "This discourse on absence, or on the presence of an absence, perplexes me," Derrida writes, "not only because it bypasses so many tricks, complications, traps that the 'philosopher,' especially if he is a bit of a dialectician, knows only too well and fears to find you caught up in again, but also because it has authorized many religious interpretations, not to mention vaguely Judeo-transcendental ideologizations of your work."[128] Derrida goes on to cite the architect's seemingly disingenuous disclaimer in an interview that he never talks about deconstruction.[129]

Eisenman's miffed tone is audible in his patently deconstructive response to the absent father's reproach. He replies that Derrida's "deconstruction of the presence/absence distinction is inadequate to architecture," which must confront a third term, what Eisenman calls *presentness* to designate "neither absence nor presence, form nor function, but rather an excessive condition between sign and being." It is, for Eisenman, "the possibility of another aura in architecture, one not in the sign or in being, but a third condition of betweenness."[130] Whereas traditional architecture "collapses presentness into presence and has always viewed their separation as dangerous," his architecture seeks to release the excess of presentness from "the strong bond between form and function" that represses it, not to deny functionality, but to allow architecture to function without symbolizing it.[131]

Derrida's criticism seems tendentious in moments—anarchically or possessively intent on distancing himself from Eisenman's projections of a work "in common" based on *his* (not Derrida's) interpretation of *chora* while protesting that the philosopher's reproach "is a sign of love."[132] His jab at Eisenman's "vaguely Judeo-transcendental ideologizations" applies to the architect's remarks from *Chora L Works* about the putatively "Hebraic" disposition of deconstruction and his own architecture by extension. To press this point, Derrida quotes Libeskind at length to illustrate the implicit theological quality of the "the void, absence, negativity" around which the Jewish Museum is organized in order to render visible the invisible repression of the fatal German-Jewish cultural relationship.[133] For Derrida, "a void that represents is no longer a void proper."[134] The philosopher hereby hints at a problematic conjuncture between Libeskind's literalization of perished Jews in a "Jewish" architectural space and Eisenman's minimalist allegiance to the image prohibition. Derrida also questions Libeskind's avowedly metaphoric construction of Jewish culture as the avant-garde. The logic of exemplarity informing this construction makes the philosopher anxious, because it exacerbates a slippage between annihilated Jewish life and the Holocaust as a Jewish destiny. I imagine Libeskind's cryptically inane response did not put this anxiety to rest: "To me the void is much closer to the avant-garde, by which I really mean Moses," Libeskind confesses. "The avant-garde is a people under God without any mediating circumstances, no explanation as to why, and no possibility of relinquishing it. I think this is not a concept of the avant-garde but an experience of it—one either has it or one does not."[135]

Noah Isenberg is also troubled by the exemplarist logic fomented by the architect and his audience: "Much like the position that Daniel Jonah Goldhagen assumed in Germany, Libeskind's stance in relation to his predominantly non-Jewish audience is that of the 'authentic' Jew who communicates in the voice of a child of Holocaust survivors."[136] Libeskind hails as an "authentic Jew" by virtue of a quintessentially diasporic background: he is the son of survivors, was born east of Berlin, in Lodz, Poland, and lost most of his family to the Nazis. He emigrated to Tel Aviv and then, as a virtuoso pianist in the company of Itzhak Perlman, to the United States, Libeskind abandoned music for the study of architecture in New York, and then came to Berlin to build his first commissioned project, the Jewish Museum.[137]

With the museum in Berlin completed in 1999, Libeskind had already set the stage for Eisenman to concretize his flimsy link between "Jewish" architectural motifs and Derridean deconstruction. Because of the aleatory overlap between the development of the two projects, one *might* draw the conclusion that Libeskind's Jewish Museum and Eisenman's memorial propose suitably "Jewish" forms for the capital of a reunified Federal Republic of Germany to acknowledge the irreparable harm caused by the Third Reich's genocidal policies. The question that such a contingency raises is whether the construction of a "Jewish" genre of built forms does not mainly serve to locate the impetus of German critical reflection in the authenticating organ of a Jewish body. In what follows, I speculate on how Libeskind's museum contributed to the intelligibility of Eisenman's design for the memorial as a realization of a "Jewish" aesthetic that furthers a pedagogical desire to structure German moral-affective identification with the sublime magnitude and depth of Jewish suffering. How do Libeskind and Eisenman inadvertently naturalize the idea of "the Jew" (and, specifically, the absent murdered Jew) as a disciplinary vehicle for German national and historical consciousness?

Deconstructivist Architecture between Libeskind and Eisenman: Toward a "Jewish" Antimemorial Genre?

Writing in 1997, Young observes, "[T]he possibility that art might redeem mass murder with beauty (or with ugliness) or that memorials might somehow redeem this past with an instrumentalization of its memory continues to haunt a postwar generation of memory-artists." Hence Germany's " 'Jewish question' is now a two-pronged memorial question: How does Germany remember events it would rather forget, and how does it build a new and just state on the bedrock memory of its horrendous crimes?"[138] According to Young, the answer to this question should not be expressed through traditional monuments whose "grandiose pretensions to permanence" and "demagogical rigidity and certainty about history" continue "to recall traits too closely associated with fascism itself." Rather than insisting that "its meaning is as fixed as its place in the landscape," a monument against fascism would "have to be a monument against itself: against the traditionally didactic function of monuments, against their tendency to displace the past they have us contemplate, and finally, against the authoritarian propensity toward monumental spaces that reduce viewers to passive spectators."[139]

Young favors a generation of artists who engage in the design and installation of what he calls "counter-monuments": "brazen, painfully self-conscious memorial spaces conceived to challenge the very premises of their being."[140] This generation cannot tolerate the prospect of reducing historical trauma to "exhibitions of public craftsmanship or cheap pathos." In addition, they "contemptuously reject the traditional forms of and reasons for public memorial art, those spaces that either console viewers or redeem such tragic events, either indulging in a facile kind of *Wiedergutmachung* or purporting to mend the memory of a murdered people. Instead of searing memory into public consciousness," Young writes, "these artists fear, conventional memorials seal it off from awareness altogether; instead of embodying memory, memorials may only displace it." In sympathy with these artists, he declares: "To the extent that we encourage monuments to do our memory-work for us, we become that much more forgetful. What these artists believe, in effect, is that the initial impulse to memorialize such an event as the Holocaust may actually spring from an opposite and equal desire to forget it."[141]

Young's recent writings on antimemorial practices in Germany attests to the rise of deconstruction in the 1980s, which had manifestly shaped an intellectual milieu in the late 1990s among scholars and artists working on questions of public memory. Deconstructionist ideas and strategies contributed to an ideological horizon that determined what statements (and values) would resonate in debates that carried over from the two decades before German reunification.

Derridean deconstruction targets the "ontotheological" premises that confound truth with presence, essence, self-sameness, and origin. This postmetaphysical perspective also repudiates idealized notions of a "proper" or "authentic" humanity and a unified subject. Derrida's persuasive critiques of anthropocentrism and his overturning of the metaphysical subordination of absence, negation, and difference to presence and determinacy have inclined scholars and artists to think more carefully about the flux of memory as a multifaceted, socially inflected, and often contradictory basis of historical consciousness and collective identification. His impact is evident from a constellation of negative or dissonant aesthetic inclinations that recur in discourse about "deconstructivist" or antimonumental approaches to Holocaust memorialization.

One point that is less obviously pertinent where architectural and memorial forms are concerned is Derrida's emphasis on the supplemental agency of writing as a mode of spacing. Derrida's early analyses of Rousseau and Saussure, among others, demonstrate that writing is just as much at stake in the creation of meaning as speech. Intelligible differences in speech at once presuppose and eclipse its dependency upon the "silent" letters in phonetic writing (and the spaces between them).

In *Derrida's Haunt: The Architecture of Deconstruction*, Mark Wigley emphasizes Derrida's subversion of the metaphysical subordination of the space of writing to the time of speech by depicting deconstruction as a mode of *spacing* (a *becoming* space—which is to say, a *movement* of displacing, setting aside, demarcating and inverting borders, and of reversing interiors and exteriors rather than a thing).[142] "The traditional sense of space," Wigley writes, "is only produced in the very gesture of its subordination." Hence, to "interfere with that gesture is to produce a very different sense of space, a sense that at once disturbs and produces the tradition."[143] It is deconstruction's agency as spacing that endows it with a power to challenge the fundamental premises of architecture as a theorization of space, a mode of figuration, and an institutionalized praxis. For if, as Wigley argues, metaphysics "is no more than a determination of place, the production of the sense of a pure interior divided from an improper exterior, a privileged realm of presence uncorrupted by representation," then "[w]hatever disrupts metaphysics disrupts this sense of interior."[144]

In keeping with deconstructive protocols, Libeskind views his architecture as process rather than a product. Before the museum was commissioned, Libeskind had established a reputation for drawings and designs—the *Micromegas* of 1978 and the *Chamber Works* of 1983, for instance—that self-consciously explore the relationship between a "pre-objective" intuition of geometric structure and "the possibility of formalization which tries to overtake it in the objective realm."[145] As Dalibor Vesely remarks with reference to Libeskind's 1980 "deconstructive constructions," the architect enunciated "constructive possibilities on the boundary of actual and imaginary space" as a process of transition "from the space of real possibilities to the space of possible realities."[146] In self-consciously "emulating avant-garde practice," Stanley Allen observes, "Libeskind marked out for himself a territory at the margin, but in so doing, inscribed his practice deeply and insistently in fundamental questions of the discipline and its boundaries." He thereby implied "that a disciplinary framework that would marginalize his own production was itself corrupt and arbitrary."[147]

Libeskind sees designs and models as tools for theorizing that are as potentially antidisciplinary as they are utopian in exposing the limits of the buildable, if not of imagination itself.[148] Though it is his first commissioned project, the design for the Jewish Museum is no exception. The "museum ensemble" is "always on the verge of *becoming*—no longer suggestive of a final solution."[149] The impact of Derridean deconstruction and what in anglophone criticism came to be referred to as poststructuralism was entrenched in the North American milieu by the 1990s when Libeskind was building the Jewish Museum and Young was continuing to establish an international reputation as the foremost American expert on Holocaust memorials. This confluence is particularly marked in Young's enthusiastic contemplation of Libeskind's design for the Jewish Museum. Young characterizes the museum as a "twisting and jagged lightning bolt of a building" while reprising Libeskind's own deconstructive self-referencing: "In its series of complex trajectories, irregular linear structures, fragments, and displacements, this building is also on the verge of unbecoming—a breaking down of architectural assumptions, conventions, and expectations."[150]

Nevertheless, while it favors abstract and broken forms, Isenberg suggests that one might view initial incarnations of Libeskind's design "as a bold attempt to prove, on a concrete and institutional level, the existence of a German-Jewish symbiosis."[151] Certainly, the "Jewish" identity of Libeskind's concept is enhanced through his orchestration of critical allusions connecting Jewish with non-Jewish "bearers of immense hope and anguish" who affirm "the permanent human tension polarized between the impossibility of the system and the impossibility of giving up the search for a higher order." The "zigzag" of the Jewish Museum's broken six-point Star of David connects the site with the street addresses of prominent contributors to Berlin's German-Jewish cultural history. In this vein, Libeskind claims that the buildings' very lineaments are imbued with the "tragic premonition" of Heinrich von Kleist, the "sublimated assimilation" of Rachel Varnhagen, the "inadequate ideology" of Walter Benjamin, the "mad science" of E. T. A. Hoffmann, the "displaced understanding" of Friedrich Schleiermacher, the "inaudible music" of Arnold Schönberg, and the "last words" of Paul Celan. These emblematic names, Libeskind insists, "constitute the critical dimensions that this work [the museum] as discourse seeks to transgress."[152] In addition, the larger of the two courtyards is named after Celan and features natural stone paving in a pattern derived from an image by the poet's widow, Gisele Celan-Lestrange. The Garden of Exile and Emigration consists of forty-eight columns planted with willow oaks and filled with the earth of Berlin to signify the formation

of Israel in 1948, except for a forty-ninth central column, which contains
earth from Jerusalem and stands for Berlin.[153] Likewise, the designation of
the garden after Hoffmann, whose story, "The Sand-Man," was used by Freud
to elaborate the uncanny, reinforces its link with the experience of exile.

Hailed as the "last architectural masterwork in twentieth-century Berlin,
and its foremost building for the twenty-first,"[154] the museum that people
described "as a zigzag or a blitz, surely an image only seen by an angel," was
plotted as an "irrational matrix" of four "aspects": the first is the building
itself, which references a broken and distorted Jewish Star; the second alludes
to the cutoff of Act 2 of Schönberg's *Moses and Aaron*, a brooding work
"that culminates with the not-musical fulfillment of the word,"[155] according
to Libeskind; the third reflects the "ever-present dimension of the deported
and missing Berliners"; and, the fourth cites Walter Benjamin's elusive "urban
apocalypse along the *One-Way Street*" from 1928.[156] The underground interior
of the matrix is divided by the Axis of Continuity leading through Berlin's
history and the museum's exhibition spaces, the Axis of Exile running to
the E. T. A. Hoffmann Garden of Exile and Emigration, and the Axis of the
Holocaust, which moves inexorably toward "an abrupt deadend"[157]: the free-
standing, 27-meter-high, raw-concrete Holocaust Tower. This acutely angled,
dark, austere, and unheated void is dimly illuminated by a crack of daylight
from a high window that is obscure to the visitor, who can nevertheless
make out the muffled sounds of the (indifferent) city life outside.[158]

The shattered Star of David, the garden's forty-eight columns signifying
Israel's birth, and Libeskind's allusions promulgate the perceived "Jewishness"
of his design. Isenberg notes that both Libeskind and Schönberg "wrestle with
the biblical proscription against graven images"—"images of an inconceivable
God" and "the unimaginable horror," respectively—"to render the invisible
fleetingly palpable."[159] Isenberg cites public mentions of Libeskind's "power of
revelation" and "kabbalistic bent" that led the architecture critic Philip Noble
to laud him as the "Mystic of Lindenstrasse."[160] The project was officially
designated the Jewish Museum, but Libeskind referred to it as "Between the
Lines" to emphasize his configuration of "two lines of thinking, organization,
and relationship. One is a straight line, but broken into many fragments; the
other is a tortuous line, but continuing indefinitely."[161] "As the lines develop
themselves through this limited-infinite 'dialectic,' " Libeskind asserts, "they
also fall apart—become disengaged—and reveal themselves as separate." The
intended effect is of an impenetrable void running "centrally through what is
continuous [that] materializes outside as something that has been ruined, or
rather, as the solid residue of an independent structure, as a voided void."[162]
It is a void, as Andreas Huyssen confirms, that "will always be there in the
minds of the spectators crossing the bridges that traverse it as they move
through the exhibition space." Thus, "[T]he spectators themselves will move
constantly between the lines."[163]

Inside the Jewish Museum Berlin, the Holocaust tower, © Jewish Museum Berlin.
Photo by Jens Ziehe.

In 1997, during the height of rebuilding in the new capital, Huyssen
observed that "[t]here is perhaps no other major Western city that bears
the marks of twentieth-century history as intensely and self-consciously as
Berlin. This city text," part palimpsest and part *Wünderblock*, "has been
written, erased, and rewritten throughout this violent century, and its
legibility relies as much on visible markers of built space as on images and
memories repressed and ruptured by traumatic events."[164] Huyssen insists
that "the notion of Berlin as a void is more than a metaphor, and not just
a transitory condition," in part because the Wall required a no-man's land
with its land mines "that wound their way through the very center of the
city and held its Western part in a tight embrace," but also because West
Berlin itself "always appeared as a void on East European maps" while West
German television "for a long time represented the GDR as an absence."[165]
After the fall of the Wall, Potsdamer Platz metamorphosed from a cascade of
cranes into the fierce glitz of corporate capital, while conservative architects
standardized antimodernist protocols for renovation and new construction.

Against such a "lack of imagination and vision" seemingly aimed "at the erasure of memory rather than its imaginative preservation," Libeskind was the "one architect" according to Huyssen, "who understood the nature of this empty space in the center of Berlin."[166] As Libeskind himself recognizes, the "torn shards" of his ensemble "never existed as some prior whole (either in the ideal Berlin or in the real one) nor can they be reassembled in some hypothetical future." Rather the "fragmentation is the spacing, the separation brought about by the history of Berlin, which can only be experienced as the absence of time and as the fulfillment in time of what is no longer there." The Holocaust is, for Libeskind, the "*absolute* event of history." It marks the "incineration of meaningful development for Berlin and for humanity" that "shatters this place while bestowing a gift of that which cannot be given by architecture: the preservation of the sacrifice and the offering: guardian or night watch over absent and future meaning."[167]

Young shares Huyssen's admiration for the "structural rib" of Libeskind's concept: the "straight void-line running through the plan [that] violates every space through which it passes, turning otherwise uniform rooms and halls into misshapen anomalies, some too small to hold anything, others so oblique as to estrange anything housed within them. The original design also included inclining walls, at angles too sharp for hanging exhibitions."[168] In building a void into the heart of its design, Libeskind thus succeeds, for Young at least, in fulfilling his intention "to represent a space empty of Jews that echoes an inner space empty of the love and values that might have saved Berlin's Jews."[169] He not only "highlights the spaces between walls as the primary element of his [deconstructivist] architecture," thereby subtending its authoritative "presence"; he also employs deconstruction in the service of mimetic correspondence: to "capture," as Young puts it, "a void so real, so palpable, and so elemental to Jewish history in Berlin as to be its focal point after the Holocaust—a negative center of gravity around which Jewish memory now assembles."[170]

In contrast to Huyssen and Young, Isenberg is less ardent in his judgment: "A 'prism' colored so dramatically by the Shoah," he believes, "can hardly be an effective, let alone accurate, way for Berlin's history to be presented to the world."[171] Isenberg contends that Libeskind has mainly replaced the dominant narrative of German-Jewish symbiosis with another type of "master narrative" revolving around the Shoah that literalizes Dan Diner's concept of a negative symbiosis.[172] In sympathy with Isenberg, I would also ask whether a form so unmistakably forged in a "Holocaust vernacular,"[173] so concertedly intended to correspond with the dissonant and irremediable "truth" of Germans' repression of "their" murdered Jews, can be considered genuinely deconstructivist. Indeed, does not such a discourse mainly serve to naturalize deconstruction as *the* genre of Holocaust memorialization par excellence, thereby establishing its regulative power as the model of "antinormative" and "avant-garde" praxis?

The traces of psychoanalysis in deconstruction contributed to a parallel inclination among scholars of traumatic memory and, by extension, the Holocaust to examine German responses to signs and irruptions of their repressed or disavowed criminal past. Derrida was, by his own repeated admission, beholden to psychoanalysis. In his reading of the figuration of building and dwelling in deconstruction, Wigley highlights a footnote in "The Double Session" in which Derrida connects "its account of undecidability as a 'rereading' of Freud's essay 'The Uncanny' (*Das Unheimliche*), which, as is well known, describes the uneasy sense of the unfamiliar within the familiar, the unhomely within the home."[174] "We find ourselves constantly being brought back to that text," Derrida acknowledges, "by the paradoxes of the double and of repetition, the blurring of the boundary lines between 'imagination' and 'reality,' between the 'symbol' and the 'thing it symbolizes.' "[175] He quotes Freud's famous realization that "*[h]eimlich* is a word the meaning of which develops towards an ambivalence, until it finally coincides with its opposite, *unheimlich*. *Unheimlich* is in some way or other a sub-species of *heimlich*."[176]

The slippage between *heimlich* and the *unheimlich* that is pivotal to Freud's conception of the uncanny as a sign of the return of the repressed provides a model for Derrida's consideration of the contradictory philological lineages of binary oppositions that render the subordination of one term to the other undecidable (in the relation between memory and writing in "Plato's Pharmacy," for example). Derrida's self-consciously paradoxical performance of *différance* as a signifying movement disarticulates the opposition between identity and difference. This disarticulation extends Freud's lesson about the latent and potentially uncanny force exerted by traces of the repressed in a manner that speaks to Heidegger's critique of the essence of truth as a contingent revealing that also simultaneously conceals Being. Like the uncanny, deconstruction disturbs the relationship between the known and the unknown, the near and the far.[177] Indeed, as Wigley notes, "Derrida repeatedly, one might almost say compulsively, identifies the undecidables that uncannily intimate the violence within the familiar domain"—what Wigley connects via Heidegger with the institutionalization of metaphysics through (and as) the repression of an "originary" violence.[178] To the extent that Derrida's critical praxis would become the conscience after Heidegger that confronts and exposes such a repression, "[t]he question of deconstruction is," as Wigley stresses, "first and foremost a question of the uncanniness of violence."[179]

Given the paradigmatic significance of Freud's theorization of the uncanny for Derridean deconstruction, it is, perhaps, predictable that this lineage insinuates itself into Young's deployment of Libeskind to elaborate the protocols of an antimemorial genre. To this end, early on in his chapter on Libeskind, Young quotes Freud's characterization of the uncanny as an effect that signals "in reality nothing new or alien, but something which is familiar and old-established in the mind and which has become alienated from it only through the process of repression. . . . The uncanny [is] something which ought to have remained hidden but has come to light."[180] He also cites Anthony Vidler's "magnificent reading of the architectural uncanny" to illuminate Young's own understanding of " 'uncanny memorial architecture' as 'a metaphor for a fundamentally unlivable modern condition.' "[181] Drawing as well on Robin Lydenberg's theory of "uncanny narrative," Young subsequently distinguishes this genre by its effects: "[T]he stabilizing function of architecture, by which the familiar is made to appear part of a naturally ordered landscape, will be subverted by the antithetical effects of the unfamiliar. It is a memorial architecture that invites us into its seemingly hospitable environs only to estrange itself from us immediately on entering."[182] By extension, then, "the memorial uncanny might be regarded as that which is *necessarily anti-redemptive*. It is that memory of historical events which never domesticates such events, never makes us at home with them, never brings them into the reassuring house of redemptory meaning" (my emphasis). And, with more poignancy: "It is to leave such events unredeemable yet still memorable, unjustifiable yet still graspable in their causes and effects."[183]

Young's chapter on the Jewish Museum is devoted to reiterating how Libeskind's design fulfills the deconstructive conventions of the memorial uncanny. He alludes to Libeskind's protocol that the walls of the voids facing the exhibition walls will "remain untouched, unusable, outside healing and suturing narrative."[184] Instead, the exhibition narrative must be planned to allow the voids to interrupt it wherever intersections take place. In this manner, the voids make palpable "that much more is missing here than can ever be shown" through an "aggressively antiredemptory design, built literally around an absence of meaning in history, an absence of the people who would have given meaning to their history."[185] In addition, the dissonant meanings of exhibited objects are redoubled through juxtaposition: "[L]*ike uncanniness itself*, such artifacts and works when thus contextualized will always contain their opposites" (my emphasis).[186] Libeskind's voided spaces create uncertainty in visitors, who "are never where they think they are." The aim of such voids is "not to reassure or console but to haunt visitors with the unpleasant—uncanny—sensation of calling into consciousness that which has been previously—even happily—repressed." Yet if they are *not* didactic, as Young claims, the voids are, nonetheless, "reminders of the abyss into which this culture once sank and from which it never really emerges."[187]

What is striking in Young's moves to codify the memorial uncanny is that, without mentioning his name, he has converted Adorno's repudiation of consolatory impulses in culture after Auschwitz into a (morally? aesthetically?) *necessary* convention of this genre. Yet if one looks more closely, it becomes clear from a missing step in Young's logic that there is no logically "necessary" relationship between the uncanny and the antiredemptive. This insistent articulation of two otherwise unrelated ideas is only forceful by virtue of a

discursive formation and a milieu through which the uncanny might assume
an appearance of necessity among Young's antimemorial motifs as an aesthetic
effect of deconstruction.

According to Young, Germany's "attempts to formalize the self-inflicted
void at its center—the void of its lost and murdered Jews"—are *intrinsically*
and *necessarily* uncanny. He writes: "At least part of the uncanniness *in* such
a project stems from the sense that at any moment the 'familiar alien' will
burst forth, even when it never does, thus leaving one always ill at ease, even
a little frightened with anticipation—hence the constant, free-floating anxiety
that seems to accompany every act of Jewish memorialization in Germany
today."[188] Young's deployment of Libeskind as the model for the memorial
uncanny hereby conceals its status as an aesthetic effect—a phenomenon that
transpires on the side of the viewing subject rather than "in" the object.

Wigley reiterates Freud's insight that the supposed security of the home
and the homely harbors an impropriety "that is horrifying if exposed, precisely
because it does not befall an innocent subject," but one who confronts
"something which is familiar and old-established in the mind and which has
become alienated from it only through the process of repression."[189] Hence,
the uncanny does not merely indicate that "the subject is frightened. Rather
it is the constitution of the subject that is frightening."[190] By locating the
uncanny in the building itself as a figuration of voided memory, however,
Young misses the opportunity to theorize the constitution of this frightened
and frightening subject. Is it a German viewer haunted by the repressed
and thus "all too familiar" inner Nazi after embracing a less-authoritarian
democratic state or by the ghosts of murdered Jews and other "spooky
revenants," to borrow Huyssen's phrasing?[191] Could non-Germans, Jews among
them, also experience a clammy-fingered dawning of their own uncanny
potential to walk the halls as perpetrators rather than as innocent stalkers
of enlightened memory?

It is telling that Young concludes his chapter by reinscribing the
uncanniness of Libeskind's museum between Adorno's critical aesthetics
(reduced here to a fragment of an observation about estrangement) and
Freud's theses about the secret familiarity of the repressed. Young writes: "If
'estrangement from the world is a moment of art,' as Adorno would have
it, after Freud, then we might say that the uncanniness of a museum like
Libeskind's crystallizes this moment of art."[192] By conjoining Libeskind, Freud,
and Adorno, Young prepares for his final emphasis on the uncanny "condition
of a contemporary German culture coming to terms with the self-inflicted
void at its center—a terrible void that is at once all too secretly familiar and
unrecognizable, a void that at once defines a national identity, even as it
threatens to cause such identity to implode."[193] The Jewish Museum is hereby
constructed as a vehicle for German subject formation "after Auschwitz":
it is properly mimetic with respect to an uncanny and dissonant German
Holocaust memory while transliterating between modernist aesthetics and

deconstructivist architecture, between estrangement and a postmetaphysical subversion of presence.

Among the many awards and honors bestowed on Libeskind for this project in Germany alone over the last decade are the Berlin Cultural Prize (1996), the Deutsche Architekturpreis (1999), the Goethe Medallion for cultural contribution (2000), and an honorary doctorate from Humboldt University.[194] Vidler has recently declared the Jewish Museum on Lindenstrasse in Berlin a "humanist memory theater" that "resonates with all the aura of the terrifying sublime, and that, perhaps more than any modern work of architecture [Vidler has] ever seen, manages to hold the visitor in spatio-psychological suspense, the closest experience to what [he] imagine[s] a religious experience of architecture might be."[195] Young's and Vidler's apotheosis of Libeskind attests to the milieu partly created by contributors to Holocaust memorial debates who do not always distinguish between Derrida's performance of undecidability, Adorno's modernist preoccupation with defamiliarization and his insistence on the irredeemability of anonymous mass death, and Lanzmann's ban on dramatizing the Holocaust. This inadvertent amalgamation of postmetaphysical and modernist critiques of traditional representation enhanced the persuasive power of "deconstructed minimalism" as an antimemorial style best suited to indicate how the repressed memory of mass murder could only be rendered intelligible by a negation of presence, or, as Robert Storrs characterizes Rachel Whiteread's work, "in the solid shape of an intangible absence."[196] It also fostered a receptive audience for Eisenman's and Serra's initial submission for the second memorial competition in 1997, two years before the completion of the Libeskind museum.

Like the Jewish Museum, Eisenman's memorial is concertedly intended to confront the visitor with the impossibility of creating a monumental presence to depict Jewish life in Germany and Europe. The memorial consists of 2,711 high quality concrete slabs, or stelae, that are 95 centimeters (37 inches) wide and 2.98 meters (9 feet 9 inches) long. Because they are arranged on an uneven surface, the height of the stelae varies between .5 and 4.7 meters (15 feet 15 inches), which gives Wolfgang Thierse, former president of the Bundestag (1998 to 2005), the impression of an "endless sea of stone blocks."[197] This site, spanning 19,073 square meters, or the breadth of two football fields, displaces the no-man's land of the Berlin Wall, between the Brandenburg Gate and Potsdamer Platz, "a stone's throw from Hitler's bunker and the former nerve center of the Third Reich's administration."[198] The undulating paths between the 54 axes from north to south and 87 axes from east to west are paved, 180 lighting units are sunk into the ground, and 41 trees on the western side connect the memorial to the Tiergarten. The cost of the construction, including the Information Center with its exhibition area, lecture rooms, a bookshop, and offices, came to 27.6 million euros.[199]

Eisenman successfully resisted demands that he add names to the stelae, which, as Juli Carson notes, "would have literalized them as gravestones."[200]

He has also refuted interpretations of the memorial as a cemetery for the murdered Jews, even going so far as to claim that the memorial is a "place of no meaning."[201] According to Joachim Schlör, the memorial site offers "no instructions for the proper or 'correct' use."[202] Yet, of course, Eisenman's "rigor" of the undefined reproduces a generic convention associated with modernist attempts to allow the rational impulse of form-giving to become a vehicle for creating the effect of irrationality and perspectivalism. The architect's "restraint" is thus in keeping with the sensibility of antimonumental memory artists whose projects inscribe the importance of the sublime as a "proper" response to the Holocaust. Eisenman remarks:

> Each plane is determined by the intersections of the voids in the pillar grid and the gridlines of the larger site context of Berlin. In effect, a slippage occurs in the grid structure, causing indeterminate spaces to develop within the seemingly rigid order of the monument. These spaces condense, narrow, and deepen to provide a multilayered experience from any point in the gridded field. The agitation of the field shatters any notions of absolute axiality and instead reveals an omni-directional reality. The illusion of order and security in the internal grid and the frame of the street grid are thus destroyed. . . . The uncertain frame of reference that results further isolates individuals in what is intended to be an unsettling, personal experience.[203]

Eisenman's pronouncements indicate that this project continues his homage to Derrida's praxis of fostering undecidability over and against interpretative closure. Yet by emphasizing the disorientation he hopes to provoke among visitors to the memorial, Eisenman's description also serves to link the aesthetic of the uncanny with the protocols of the genre of "deconstructed minimalism." As defined by Libeskind's Jewish Museum and Eisenman's memorial, this is an antimemorial genre that emerges at the intersection of a modernist predilection for minimalist abstraction and Derrida's deconstruction of the metaphysics of presence. Whether he explicitly intends it or not, Eisenman's uncanny minimalism reasserts his submission to a deconstructive variant of the "Hebraic" discipline of the image ban. This variant is configured along the same lines as Adorno's negative sublime, which partly hinges on a revision of Immanuel Kant's definition.

In Kant's *Critique of Judgment*, his description of the sublime narrates a distinct order of mental events: a situation, scene, or historical phenomenon exceeds the power of the faculty of imagination to comprehend in a unified image what it mathematically (quantitatively) or dynamically (affectively) apprehends. This insufficiency paves the way for the hero of the story, reason, to claim a redemptive victory in exercising its power to create and hold fast that which "the senses and the imagination despair of grasping and representing," in John Paul Richter's phrasing.[204] As Kant emphasizes, "*Sublime is what even to be able to think proves that the mind has a power surpassing any standard of sense.*"[205] In adopting an overwhelming encounter with the infinite as its departure point, Kant's sublime tacitly revises a Christian topos in which faith through suffering and humility brings about a renewed sense of rapprochement between the uncertain mortal and a distant and eternal God.

In Adorno's emplotment of the sublime, in contrast, an unsettling failure of imagination is not redeemed by a *Sinnstiftung* of reason. Instead of confirming reason's supremacy, the experience of failure is sustained as a determinate recognition of the impossibility of achieving an unmediated (and thus unreified) relation to the singular reality of any object or event. Adorno derides the easy pleasure of overcoming the "tension between the potential presence of the infinite and the finitude of our sensible experience."[206] The reality of domination and suffering is cheapened rather than illuminated by plots that end in consolation.

Kant links the mathematical sublime with the cognitive agitation arising from the judgment of an object, while the dynamic sublime refers this agitation to the power of desire.[207] The memorial's rows of stelae of various heights seem explicitly structured to sustain the viewer's failure to comprehend the mathematically sublime magnitude and dynamically sublime depth of Jewish suffering without solace and thus adhere to Adorno's negative aesthetic. In Eisenman's words: "Today, an individual can no longer be certain to die an individual death, and architecture can no longer remember life as it once did. The markers that were formerly symbols of individual life and death must be changed, and this has a profound effect on the idea of memory and the monument. The enormity and horror of the Holocaust are such that any attempt to represent it by traditional means is inevitably inadequate. The memory of the Holocaust can never be one of nostalgia."[208]

Eisenman's contribution to the foundation's glossy, large-format *Materials on the Memorial*, published after its completion, almost overtly literalizes a standpoint Adorno articulated in *Negative Dialectics* about the death of the beautiful death and the impossibility of representing anonymous mass murder. Eisenman's statement is thus performative on three levels: first, it posits Adorno's pronouncements about anonymous death as intrinsic to the focus of the memorial; second, it confirms the anagogical propriety of the negative sublime for bearing witness to the Holocaust's unrepresentability; and third, it reinscribes this aesthetic as a convention of the antimemorial genre.

The names that Eisenman drops function rhetorically to authorize his antimemorial aesthetics for a negative commemoration of murdered Jews in keeping with the Second Commandment. In this vein, he identifies the intended experience of the memorial with Henri Bergson's conception of time as duration in contrast to a chronological narrative temporality.

Eisenman also alludes to Marcel Proust's *In Search of Lost Time* to demarcate the memorial's "living memory" from a "nostalgia located in the past touched with sentimentality that remembers things not as they were, but as we want to remember them." If successful, Eisenman's Bergsonian and Proustian reconfiguration of time and memory on a monumental scale would elicit an experience that adheres to Adorno's repudiation of compensatory thematizations of anonymous mass death: "[T]here is no goal, no end, no working one's way in or out," Eisenman declares. "[T]he duration of an individual's experience of it grants no further understanding, since understanding is impossible."[209]

Eisenman's statements promote his alignment with meaning-evacuated abstraction and thus (for him) connotatively Hebraic and deconstructive forms, as distinguished from conventional memorial modes of progressive narrative temporality and imagery. Notably, this alignment recurs not only in Eisenman's assertions about his intentions, but also in reviews of his design and the completed memorial itself. Carson observes that "Conventional memorials, especially those constructed to commemorate the victims of the Holocaust, typically combine metaphor (a slab for a gravestone, for instance) and didacticism (the obligatory timeline and list of names)." Such aesthetics, she writes, "are consistent with the 'never forget' imperative, whereby the documentation of atrocities is inevitably presented within an aesthetic interpretation of the sublime."[210] Grenzer remarks that "the failure to tame the source of the trauma is accentuated by the erasure of specificity and the impossibility of adequately bearing witness to the millions of victims of the Holocaust. . . . This absence of the mark upon the surface of the monument gives expression to 'the mute and the ambivalent' as a sublime landscape that seeks to redress the failure of communication itself."[211]

The absence of inscriptions on the minimalist stelae does not, of course, undermine their resemblance to tombstones for some viewers. Schlusche states the obvious: "The memorial is a place of remembrance dedicated to an unimaginably large number of dead human beings. In that respect, it represents the tradition of the gravestone or tomb."[212] *The New York Times* architecture critic, Nicolai Ouroussoff, suggests that the memorial's grid "can be read as both an extension of the streets that surround the site and an unnerving evocation of the rigid discipline and bureaucratic order that kept the killing machine grinding along. The pillars, meanwhile, are an obvious reference to tombstones."[213] Young observes that even if Eisenman "prefers that the pillars, though stone-like, remain under-determined and open to many readings," their abstract forms will "accommodate the references projected onto them by visitors, the most likely being the tombstone." Young nevertheless affirms Eisenman's decision to waive the inscriptions: "With written text, they might begin to look very much like tombstones, in fact, and so might generate a dynamic demanding some sort of formal treatment as tombstones, even symbolic ones."[214]

The motif of sublime or uncanny disorientation in the reception of Libeskind's Jewish Museum resurfaces in assessments of Eisenman's memorial. The title of Ouroussoff's review, "A Forest of Pillars, Recalling the Unimaginable," inadvertently connects Eisenman's memorial to descriptions of Libeskind's "Garden of Exile" at the Jewish Museum. The garden is also described as "a close-packed *forest of pillars* open to the sky where no surface is exactly horizontal or vertical," which creates "a sense of the exile's disorientated view of the world."[215] Because it was finished after Libeskind's museum, Eisenman's "forest of pillars" seems to mimic the garden's effect.

While arguing that Eisenman truncates minimalism's traditionally antisymbolist or "symbol full" tendencies, Carson foregrounds the memorial's "spatial *narrativization of affect*," which is intended "to let one know what it's like to fight a losing battle." The tops of the stelae are "cut at various oblique angles meant to provoke a disorienting affect [*sic*] on viewers negotiating their way through the labyrinth." The monument is "demarcated from the surrounding functional landscape" at the periphery, "but at the center any view of the city is virtually lost. When one emerges, the bodily memory of slowly getting lost—a crisis encroaching upon you—would be the souvenir that stays with you."[216] These effects evince Eisenman's desire to keep faith with the perspective of those "who walked alone at Auschwitz, who saw their parents taken away, who felt lost to the world, lost to reality, lost to any kind of explanation."[217] Notably, Carson's impressions also resonate with Harjes's, which herald Eisenman's success in mobilizing the visitor's sense of being emotionally overwhelmed by a "large and stunning" site that "alters the cityscape to a large degree." She writes: "It is intended to elicit a somatic, corporal form of memory, based not primarily on reflection but on emotional experience." Though they might expect an "emotional 'ride,' " Eisenman "expects visitors walking among the thousands of narrowly spaced stelae to experience feelings of claustrophobia and oppression reminiscent of the experience of Jews in the concentration camps."[218]

Rauterberg enthusiastically proclaims the sublime impact of the memorial, which "belies description as an undulating field of stelae . . . a place that presents nothing, where nothing is finished, and with which the Germans may not so easily find closure." Associations are fleeting here, since they "founder in the unfathomable mass of stelae and their painstaking alignment." The sublime is again evoked in Rauterberg's announcement that "the eye cannot take it in, nor can the camera capture it. . . . We are abducted into an in-between place beyond the imagery of the familiar, beyond categorization." There is "[n]o sense of occasion, no discernible aim, no entrance, no exit," he writes. "It does not lend itself to state ceremony or wreath-laying. . . . All that is seen here is that nothing is to be seen. And that in itself is a significant achievement."[219] For Rauterberg, the memorial's success stems from its adherence to the ethics of the image prohibition, which enjoins a restrained form so as to occasion an unsettling experience of the unrepresentable.

Garden of Exile, detail © Jewish Museum Berlin, photo by Jens Ziehe.

View of the Field of Stelae, November 2004. Photo by Dietmar Gust. Foundation Memorial to the Murdered Jews of Europe.

It would seem, then, that the negative counterpoint to conventional memorials has obtained a conventionality in its own right in the Memorial to the Murdered Jews of Europe. The memorial's satisfied admirers attest over and over again that it stirs up a sense of the "unrepresentable" magnitude of mass death in painfully unresolved dynamic tension with its absolute finality—in other words, that it adheres to the plot of Adorno's unreconciled sublime. This plot has come to function as a generic code for Holocaust memorialization that reproduces and is reproduced by a supposedly antimemorial ethos and prioritizes mimimalist abstraction over monumental representative designs as a signal of taste and sophistication. To the extent that he satisfies such conventional expectations, Eisenman undercuts his proclamation in a 2004 interview that he is "against the Holocaust industry" and the "kitchifying" nostalgia he associates with it.[220] By adopting the rhetoric of unrepresentability in his voluble declarations of his intentions, Eisenman has entered into the domain of "metakitschification," if you will: the "kitschification" of Adorno's repudiation of identitarian consolation in aesthetic experiences.

Yet while Eisenman's abstraction orchestrates a sublime homage to the difficulty of imagining mass murder, the site's timing raises questions about its intended audience beyond visitors to the new capital. As Habermas articulates the problem: "Who will actually express what with this memorial and to what aim? For what purpose should it serve and to whom is its message directed?" Young asks: "Will it be a place for Jews to mourn lost Jews, a place for Germans to mourn lost Jews, or a place for Jews to remember what Germans once did to them?"[221] In the words of Charlotte Knoblauch, the president since 2006 of the Central Council of the Jews in Germany: "No member of the postwar generations should feel guilty." "Because," she adds, "whoever cannot feel proud of his or her nation, will become susceptible to the words of the radical right."[222] Knoblauch's reprieve calls for a frank confrontation with the question of why the generations born after the war should become the addressees of the memorial's message of responsible remembering as if they could compensate for its stubborn repression among the generations who were complicit, not only with the crimes themselves, but also with a widespread failure to punish criminal individuals, groups, and businesses after the war. In addition, the progeny of the perpetrator generation who remain to learn the memorial's lessons have grown up in the relative absence of Jews and cannot concretely mourn their loss. As Harjes suggests, "Those with little knowledge about or interest in the Holocaust—which describes most young people in Germany today—are unlikely to have the intended emotional experience."[223] The memorial nevertheless places on their shoulders the burden of educating themselves about national complicity with the mass murder of European Jews.

Since Knoblauch is a spokeperson and leader of the Jewish community in Germany, her comment would likely relieve a scholar such as Grenzer, who contends that the past must be put to rest so that its "hyperbolic resonance" does not " 'suck the living down with the dead.' "[224] Because she is a member of a postwar generation, Grenzer's plea for a limit (in keeping with her family name, which could translate as a colloquial term for "border guard")[225] is more acceptable (or perhaps less unacceptable) than Nolte's instrumental injunction to allow the past to pass in the name of scientific objectivity and normalization or Stürmer's advocacy under Kohl for positive national images.

Finally, the issue raised in the debates that the memorial's completion leaves unanswered is whether Habermas's prioritization of a victim-identified critical remembrance serves the reconfiguration of Germany's self-presentation more than it furthers a "postnational" agenda to promote vigilance about prejudice and genocide. As Grenzer articulates it, "[m]astering unified Germany through the principles of a coherent, naturalized narrative is an attempt to affirm not just the past, but self-representation itself—its power and glory—as a reflection of the state's dominance."[226] A minimalist aesthetic signals that the recently unified Federal Republic remains cognizant of its past arrogance despite its growing power. The memorial's form therefore functions as a venue of *Erinnerungspolitik* to convey the state's humble accommodation of international pressures against forgetting.

Despite the architects' published self-identifications, it remains dubious to assert the existence of a "Jewish" memorial style that might be called "deconstructive minimalism" or the "memorial uncanny," as if a natural and inevitable link exists between Libeskind "the Jew," Eisenman "the Jew," Derrida "the Jew," Freud "the Jew," or even Young "the Jew." The ascription of cultural capital to ethnic origins begs the question of whether a non-Jewish architect (or even a convert to Judaism) could assume the authority to design a "Jewish" building if he or she fulfilled the genre's conventions. Would a Jewish critic like Young then need to be called in to authorize it? One might also ask whether it would be possible to recognize the "Jewish" features of this genre in the creations of non-Jews if it had not been for the overlap between Eisenman's and Libeskind's Berlin projects—which is to say, if the genre's themes and conventions were not first defined and exemplified by its Jewish-identified (and presumably circumcised) practitioners.

In his critique of the Libeskind phenomenon, Isenberg comments on a growing sense of resentment among German Jews toward the "shameless importation of American Jews—and American Jewish institutions—to assist the Germans (and, by extension, German Jews) in dealing with their past." This importation "allows American Jews to feel righteous about their cause, German gentiles to sense relief at having 'authentic' envoys to aid them in working through their past, and German Jews to remain by and large on the sidelines."[227] This premise, he predicts, would make it impossible for non-Jewish Germans to criticize "Jewish" designs by Jews without being branded anti-Semites.[228] I would add that it also construes ethnicity as a source of disciplinary authority. It was this philosemitic notion that facilitated the conjuncture between Libeskind's museum and Eisenman's memorial and thereby reinforced the latter's intelligibility and appeal at a particular historical moment. Of course, the resilience of this notion lies as much with the aura of the producing bodies that authenticate it as it does in the force of the connections the architects harness among Jewish traditions, the intersecting languages of philosophy and artistic practice, and German-Jewish, Jewish-American identity politics. "We Jews" can congratulate ourselves on our good fortune in sharing a history that has culminated in such a "tastefully" minimalist yet iconoclastic style. Wigley's warning might therefore be particularly apt here: Does not "good taste" merely conceal the forbidden pleasure of its nether "distasteful" side? Is the "Disneyland aesthetic" that Julius Schoeps attributes to the Libeskind museum a "classic example of blind Jewish fetishism among Germans," as Broder pronounced it? Was Libeskind born to create what Thomas Lackmann calls "Jewrassic Park"?[229] Does Eisenman's truncated minimalism not merely recode a superegoic enjoyment of the image prohibition, or perhaps even a melancholic pathos over a broken identity when "the Jews" became "the Murdered Jews of Europe"?

Grenzer contends that since "any commemorative site 'presents' itself as an event in the terrain it marks out in the present, *the field of the present can only bring the past forward through its own lens in a way that invariably condemns it to lose the past.*" For Grenzer, this "means that it is gratuitous to ask if the present loses the past, since loss of the past is an integral feature of the environment of any present."[230] In contemporary Germany, recent debates about memorials reflect competing desires to commemorate the magnitude of genocide and to mark a distance from the Third Reich's crimes as a sign of moral progress in the present. In this context, as Grenzer notes, commemoration risks two types of fetishism: it either treats the past *as if* it were not mediated by a present perspective, or foregrounds the present as if it inherits no traces of the past. "In both cases," Grenzer adds, "the relationship integral to the representation of the past *in* the present is effaced."[231]

Such fetishism is promoted in efforts to sustain (or disregard) the affective force of traumatic history by "spatializing" it in the mind in the form of a fixed ideal. The spatialization of the traumatic event as a consistent or unified image is, nevertheless, under siege by the nature of time, which constantly transforms interpretations of the past despite and because of particular interests. Beyond the academic domain of Holocaust studies, generic or highly aestheticized images increasingly replace the accounts of the survivors among other members of the generations who lived through the Second World War. The fading of first-person-witness memories exacerbates the problem of how scholars choose (to the extent that they are able) to shape a responsible historical consciousness in and beyond Germany—to remember the victims in order to avoid making new ones. At stake is history's power to teach the living after memories of the piles of the dead lose their traumatic aura. The memorial debates thus leave us with the question of whether the affective charge of a particular experience of suffering—in this case, that of the European Jews—can or should be sustained to promote the pedagogy of "never again." Should scholars and teachers seek to protect its traumatic significance from the vicissitudes of history and ideology? Or should the "Final Solution" be given less attention to "make room" for the consideration of present and future horrors?

"More than anything else," Koselleck observes, "memorials erected permanently testify to transitoriness."[232] Now that the memorial in Berlin is open to the public, there are few living survivors to testify to the events that Stürmer, Dregger, Nolte, Diepgen, and Walser insist that Germans are entitled to transcend. Arguably, Eisenman's antimemorial belatedly addresses the repression of the "Final Solution" that has been passed down through the decades from the perpetrator generations and that was already taking place even in Hitler's closest quarters.[233] In a cultural context replete with late confessions among the last aging members of the war generation (including Günther Grass's recent admission that he had been a member of the SS), Eisenman's memorial succeeds, but not so much as a lesson to contemporary Germans who were not involved. It is, as Young observes, "a deliberate act of remembrance, a strong statement that *memory must be created* for the next generations, not only preserved."[234] To Young's appreciative assessment, I would add that this creation functions as a *formal negation* of the disavowal among the wartime and postwar Germans of the magnitude of the loss endured by groups whom the Third Reich "exterminated."

In *The Holocaust and the Postmodern*, Robert Eaglestone asks how one could "prove or disprove the claim that the Holocaust was a watershed in human history."[235] Eaglestone contends that "our way of thinking, criticizing, doing history itself, the discourses that our debates inhabit and the horizons which orient these debates, are still striving to respond to the Holocaust."[236] He consequently favors a postmodernist approach that focuses "on both the act of comprehending, seizing, covering up, and on the resistance to that act—the emergence, if only momentarily, of otherness." This focus informs postmodernism's concern "with reason, its rules, and its limits" and a concomitant preoccupation "with the edges and outsides of discourses: where the philosophical, literary, historical meet, where what can be spoken of and what cannot meet."[237] Eaglestone acknowledges the influence of Jean-François Lyotard, who has translated Ludwig Wittgenstein's reflections on language games into a theory of the role of genres in determining the stakes, aims, and rules by which knowledge is produced and evaluated. As Eaglestone's adaptation of Lyotard suggests, one of the questions that postmodernism raises is how the figuration of Auschwitz as a limit event shapes and is shaped by a history of philosophers reading and rewriting their predecessors.

Naomi Mandel observes that while "the Holocaust's challenge to comprehension and cognition might sit uneasily with the proliferation of works on the topic, much Holocaust scholarship tends to affirm this challenge rather than dispel it."[238] She argues against a rhetoric that places the Holocaust "beyond the limits of language," a strategic designation that "facilitates a certain safe distance of the object of study from the study itself, paradoxically reinforcing atrocity's inaccessibility to knowledge."[239] This "fossilized" rhetoric, as Mandel characterizes it, continues to hold sway in the prevailing wisdom that "traumatic events make their impact largely in the form of *gaps* in understanding rather than a legacy with a clear and stable representational content," as Moishe Postone and Eric Santner have recently emphasized.[240] Dan Diner asserts, "The integration of the Holocaust into the course of history, the construction of an appropriate historical narration for an event unprecedented in its brevity and extremity, somehow disconnected from past and future, still remains an insurmountable task." It therefore seems to Diner that "the only serious attempt to deal with it historiographically is to accept its fundamental irreconcilability with the saeculum's core narratives."[241]

The question the adherents to this standpoint invite but never seem to take up is whether all representations of Nazi cruelty *should* or *must correspond* to a heightened awareness about the "insufficiency of cognition in the encounter with the reality of what happened" and the assumption that "knowledge itself produces gaps, opens onto the unimaginable."[242] The implication here is that an experience of knowledge about historical trauma is *inevitably* sublime—that our apprehension of the event transcends our ability to comprehend it, to reiterate Kant's formula. This construction is problematic because it makes trauma into the occasion for an aesthetic experience that is only possible from a contemplative distance that would not be available for the actual victims of violence and persecution. In addition, this aesthetic merely inverts and negates a correspondence theory of truth in replacing it with an experience that ineluctably exposes the limits of cognition. Through such a construction, Auschwitz has sometimes been taken as the "proof" for late twentieth-century skeptical or "postmodernist" philosophy. My concern is that such a figuration vitiates the pedagogical impetus to understand what specific lessons genocide holds for a disciplinary society that encompasses, among other things, the subject-forming discourse of skeptical philosophy.

The task of the next chapter is to demonstrate that the prevailing wisdom about the "insurmountability" and "irreconcilability" of the "caesura" of Auschwitz is not inevitable, but is rather the sedimentation of intellectual lineages that articulate and instill postmetaphysical values. Though I have thus far focused on the German context, I leave it now for late twentieth-century France[243] in order to consider Lyotard's postmodernist appropriation of Adorno's negative sublime. Lyotard's Adorno provides a bridge between the German and French contexts of post-Holocaust thought in converting the Frankfurt School theorist's critical aesthetic into a postmodernist politics.

In "Discussions, or Phrasing 'after Auschwitz,'" Lyotard places Adorno's reflections on metaphysics "after Auschwitz" in *Negative Dialectics* in dialogue with Derrida's post-Hegelian deconstruction of the humanist subject. In *The Differend*, Lyotard cements the critical value of a negative emplotment of the sublime in bearing witness to situations in which the validity of victims' testimony is expropriated and justice is thereby left in abeyance. *The Differend* is particularly pertinent to this project, because it is here that Lyotard foregrounds the pivotal role of affect in the reception of testimony about traumatic history. My reading of Lyotard will pressure a philosophical discourse that, despite its antifoundationalist discipline, sacralizes the death camp experience and all that it implies about modern reason in and beyond its history in philosophy. Lyotard's "Auschwitz" is the locus of a violence that transcends speech and the moral imagination because it exposes the subject's vulnerability in a biopolitical order that equates citizenship with humanity.

3

"Auschwitz" after Lyotard

I have analyzed thousands of documents. I have tirelessly pursued specialists and historians with my questions. I have tried in vain to find a single former deportee capable of proving to me that he had really seen, with his own eyes, a gas chamber.

—Robert Faurisson, 1978

When Robert Faurisson invoked a positivistic bias toward "hard evidence" to deny the existence of the gas chambers in 1978, he took advantage of the silence of the murdered, who could not repudiate his claims. His denial deployed a naive "seeing is believing" logic to dispute the authority of survivor testimony about the death camps.[1] One might assume that Faurisson's scandalous remarks did not win any converts in France. Yet as Omer Bartov observed in 2000, such statements were not "an ephemeral phenomenon that could be relegated to a fanatic, pro-fascist fringe"; members of both the Left and the Right, among them people with university degrees and "often-impressive intellectual credentials," commonly dismissed the historical and moral specificity of the crimes against the Jews.[2] The late French historian François Furet resurrected a 1950s argument that collapsed Nazism with Stalinism; the Sorbonne philosophy professor Alain Brossat denigrated the Jewish insistence on "their" Holocaust to assert a direct causal link between the "Final Solution" and the Palestinian refugee camps.[3]

Yet there is another aspect of the French intellectual milieu that struck a nerve among those, like Bartov, who argue for the centrality of the Holocaust in Europe's history of anti-semitism. Faurisson's relativistic denial of evidence resonated uncomfortably with a posthumanist skepticism that by the late 1970s had become influential amongst the generation of French philosophers who witnessed World War II, the news of Stalin's atrocities, the Algerian struggle, and the events of 1968 in Paris. The writings of Jacques

Derrida, Michel Foucault, and Jean-François Lyotard are overtly influenced by Friedrich Nietzsche's call for the destruction of metaphysics and his critique of the modern subject and by Martin Heidegger's turn toward language, which also inflected Jacques Lacan's critique of structural linguistics and his revision of Freudian psychoanalysis. This milieu fostered a repudiation of the metaphysics of truth conceptualized as a lost originary presence while encouraging vigilance about essentialist definitions of the human subject. To the extent that this vigilance also targeted the categories of experience, consciousness, and intention in Hegelian and Husserlian phenomenology, and Sartrean existentialism, what needed to be defended in the wake of Faurisson's denial was not the historical facticity of the gas chambers, but rather the value of posthumanist skepticism for grappling with testimony about a crime that extinguished most of its firsthand witnesses.

One means of authorizing such testimony might be to emphasize its "authenticity" as a measure of a witness's proximity to the events in question. Yet from Derrida's postmetaphysical perspective, this criterion is suspect, since it conflates "truth" with an "immediate" and "originary" presence. This conflation is "ontotheological" because it is beholden to the topos of a prelapsarian intimacy with the Word of God as the all-present origin of meaning. Anything short of this communion with full presence is less "true" and thus less "authentic."

The drive to safeguard a "proper" understanding of an object against the contingencies of interpretation is "ontotheological" insofar as it is fixed on the prospect of mimetically reactivating its presence-in-meaning. The object proper is, in effect, an idealized interpretation that orients disciplinary mimesis in keeping with a nexus of epistemological, moral, and aesthetic constraints. When scholars make recourse to this idealization on moral or scientific grounds, they are seeking to arrest *différance* as a movement of spatiotemporal differentiation that defers the prospect of closure for any referent. *Différance* subtends the sign as a substitution for the thing or event itself, a substitution that is, at once, secondary, provisional, and differential. The sign, as Derrida observes, is a problematic "detour" for metaphysical conceptions of reality that identify truth with the ideal of unmediated presence.[4]

Derrida's "Différance" was first published in 1968, a momentous year that further politicized the *Tel Quel* group's literary and philosophical engagement with issues of power and productivity in textual praxis. Lyotard's response to Faurisson is an attempt to weigh the consequences of an antifoundationalist approach to the problem of historical judgment in the context of a post-World War II, post-'68, posthumanist juncture that reinforced an ongoing philosophical turn toward the sign. This intervention by Lyotard is conspicuously marked by his dialogues with Adorno and Derrida, whose Nietzschean inclinations sharpened their critiques of frameworks that neutralize difference for the sake of an identitarian certainty.[5]

To counter the negationist threat, Lyotard does not suggest that scholars defend the authenticity of testimonial narratives. Nor does he encourage historians to abandon their efforts to evaluate the facticity of different narratives and modes of representation altogether. Instead, he stresses the asymmetries among epistemological, moral, and aesthetic judgments that pressure their legitimacy as consensus-based acts. Previously, in *The Postmodern Condition* (1979), he identifies a split between scientific and moral aims as an aspect of a "crisis of legitimation" that defines the current tendency of knowledge.[6] One implication of this crisis is that allegedly scientific or objective statements do not, in themselves, justify moral imperatives, which modify reality by guiding social and political actions.[7] For Lyotard, judging historical reality is, in the end, a political issue: it involves the task of deciding which protocols and whose aims will govern the judgment of a given claim. This is a question of *genre*, which Lyotard defines in *The Differend* as a rubric that supplies "rules for linking together heterogeneous phrases, rules that are proper for attaining certain goals. . . ."[8] Lyotard demonstrates how the constitution of any phenomenon as a referent depends on such linkages. This empowers genres of discourse to establish reality insofar as they not only determine the criteria for synthesizing and validating knowledge, but also control the "reins" of judgment in aesthetic, moral, and scientific discourses. However, while linkage between phrases is necessary in a logical sense, the genre that determines its rules and aims is not. Lyotard will therefore emphasize the power relations involved in the imposition of one genre over others, which ultimately decides a referent's validity. A danger of injustice arises when the referent is crimes against victims whose goals will not influence judgments of validity. This situation raises philosophical-pragmatic issues for Lyotard, who will cut to the heart of the matter: the adjudication among genres and their attendant aims.

Lyotard argues that the conflict between scientific, moral, and aesthetic modes of presentation cannot be resolved without first presupposing the primacy of one set of rules and aims over others—that is, without reverting to the genre of "positive reason" in assuming a synthesis of the multiple as a one. In this position, he is partially indebted to Theodor W. Adorno, whose *Negative Dialectics* (1966) conspicuously marks Lyotard's recourse to the sublime in his definition of postmodernism. In "Discussions, or Phrasing 'after Auschwitz' " (1980), Lyotard reads Adorno's *Negative Dialectics* as a post-Holocaust extension of the destruction of metaphysics that disarticulates philosophical prioritizations of unity and identity over difference.[9] Lyotard's Adorno enunciates the ambivalence that inflects Hegel's privileging of the genre of "positive" or synthetic reason as the condition of understanding as well as the method and end of a speculative logic. According to Adorno's "Meditations on Metaphysics," the synthetic logic that overrides difference and particularity is no longer desirable or possible "after Auschwitz." To the extent that he adopts Adorno's periodization of metaphysics after the death camps, "Auschwitz" functions as a historical model for Lyotard's crisis of legitimation: it reveals the limits of understanding as the goal of positive reason.

As Michael Rothberg suggests, one of "the later Adorno's most important insights is that the Holocaust forces a confrontation between thought and the event from which neither philosophy nor history can emerge unscathed." With *Negative Dialectics*, Adorno "represents modern history as a traumatic shock, a shock that leads to a critical reformulation of enlightenment." Lyotard adopts Adorno's reconfiguration of the critical faculty and political practice, which as Rothberg writes, "pushes his modernist philosophy and aesthetics to their outer limits."[10] Lyotard's postmodernism is over-determined by Adorno's Nietzschean inclination to subtend the false morality of a circular logic that equates truth with a reconfirmation of pregiven categories. Against the "truth drive" so defined, Lyotard will advocate for a critical "anti-identitarian" aesthetic that he derives from Adorno, for whom "Auschwitz confirmed the philosopheme of pure identity as death."[11]

In *The Differend* (1983), Lyotard considers the philosophical consequences of Faurisson's denial of the gas chambers for Holocaust testimony in particular and for judgments of truth and justice in general. Lyotard views Faurisson's disbelief as a sign that the event of anonymous mass death cannot be understood or validated on the basis of empirical and ontological concepts of experience. He consequently reflects on the *aesthetic* conditions for defending the validity of testimony about mass death in the gas chambers when the language of experience is inadequate to represent it. This defense implicitly adopts Adorno's philosophically negative revision of the aesthetic of the sublime that stresses the failure of imagination to encompass a whole through a single intuition and that does not permit a redemptive moment of mastery for the faculty of reason, as in Kant's definition. Adorno's "negativity" is also mediated by a Jewish-messianic rejection of the present order in favor of what Rothberg characterizes as the difference of a utopian promise to be fulfilled in "a post-totalitarian world that has not yet arrived."[12] Lyotard's fealty to Adorno's negative aesthetic propels him to stress the fragility of the gas chambers as a historical referent that cannot be understood empirically or ontologically. *The Differend* thus continues the critique of the metaphysics of experience launched in "Discussions, or Phrasing 'after Auschwitz' "[13] as a means of reflecting on the limits of validating testimony about the "Final Solution."

In both "Discussions" and *The Differend*, Lyotard critiques the assumptions underlying various philosophical and social frames of reference through which knowledge about mass death might be presented. My aim for this chapter is to open up Lyotard's densely intertextual configuration of "Auschwitz" as a negative philosophical and historical sign. In "Discussions," this figuration serves as the cornerstone for his construction of skepticism as the latent traumatic condition of critical philosophy. The focal question here will be how Adorno's periodization of metaphysics "after Auschwitz" in *Negative Dialectics* troubles Lyotard's parallel engagement with the posthumanist ethos of Derridean deconstruction. The dialectics he orchestrates between Adorno and Derrida allows Lyotard to disassemble the Hegelian synthetic conception of experience and the humanist *we* in the name of "Auschwitz," while appropriating the Holocaust as the cracked mirror of late twentieth-century critical philosophy. What will become clear is that Lyotard's Adorno endows the trauma of the death camps with the wounding power of skepticism to expose the limits of judgment. Henceforth "Auschwitz" becomes the sublime proof of an irreparably damaged moral consensus that negatively regulates and thus "disciplines" postmodernist philosophy.

The Wound of Nihilism

Before turning to Lyotard's writings on Auschwitz, it will be helpful to introduce the key terms in his consideration of language and judgment. This vocabulary signals Lyotard's reaction against the rationalist tradition of philosophies of language, which assume that communication requires an ideal ground or consensus. For Lyotard, in contrast, "[t]here is no 'language' in general [i.e., in the structuralists' sense], except as the object of an Idea [in the Kantian sense]."[14]

To separate himself from the rationalist tradition, Lyotard adopts a Wittgensteinian perspective to stress the agonistic and rhetorical aspects of communication as a series of *language games*. Wittgenstein employed this term in *Philosophical Investigations* to foreground the roles of context and convention in guiding contingent relations among various categories of utterance. Following Wittgenstein, Lyotard defines these categories "in terms of rules specifying their properties and the uses to which they can be put—in exactly the same way as the game of chess is defined by a set of rules determining the properties of each of the pieces, in other words, the proper way to move them."[15] Modifying the rules changes the game, while utterances that do not abide by the rules are said not to belong to the game that is based on them. By implication, then, "every utterance should be thought of as a 'move' in the game" wherein "to speak is to fight, in the sense of playing."[16]

Lyotard's metaphor of "play" stresses a social bond that "is composed," in Anne Barron's words, "not of the exchanges of free-standing, self-possessed individuals, but of the 'moves' within a multiplicity of language games, which, because innumerable, unstable and interlocking, produce a plurality of identities. . . ."[17] Within this framework, the term *linkage* or, specifically, *phrase linkage* is Lyotard's attempt to purge his discourse of all traces of an agent who might be understood as playing language games as well as being played by them. Instead, he favors the *phrase* as a purely contingent and absolutely spontaneous occurrence, a neutral "happening" or "arrival" in language that "expresses" no necessary content. Indeed, the contingency of phrasing constitutes the practical condition of a thought that at once defines and is defined by the situating of its addressee, addressor, referent, and sense "instances" in a phrase "universe."[18]

A rhetorical standpoint spurs Lyotard to focus on the provisional modes in which different phrases are connected and to foreground the role of rules that determine possible connections between various phrases. Accordingly, phrases are subject to the rules of their respective *phrase regimens* or *regimes* including reasoning, knowing, describing, showing, and prescribing. By distinguishing between phrases in terms of their regime, Lyotard emphasizes the productive power of the aims that govern phrases and determine their relations. Lyotard also stresses that phrase regimes are not translatable into one another. Heterogeneous phrases can, however, be linked "in accordance with an end fixed by a genre of discourse" that provides the rules for such articulations.[19]

Although linkage between heterogeneous phrases is sometimes difficult, linkage "happens," and is, in fact, unavoidable. For this reason, there is no "last phrase" in Lyotard's universe, since even the silence that would follow the last phrase is itself a phrase, and since a phrase would then be required to affirm that the penultimate was the last.[20] But if, for Lyotard, linkage between phrases is necessary (in the logical sense), the mode of their linkage is not. Hence the constant conflict between genres of discourse does not merely reflect the contestation over the value of a phrase and its orientation. As I have suggested, in Lyotard's view, it also exposes a crisis of legitimation whereby no proper mode of presentation can be determined without first presupposing the primacy of one genre and one intention over others—that is, without presupposing a synthesis of the multiple as a one.

In "Discussions, or Phrasing 'after Auschwitz,' " Lyotard reads Adorno's critique of this presupposition as a critical intervention into the history of metaphysics. In the remarks that Lyotard places under the title "after Auschwitz" in *Negative Dialectics* (a subheading that does not appear in the German original), Adorno reflects on the antimetaphysical import of the "Final Solution."[21] Auschwitz emerges here as Adorno's emblematic figure for a thought that derails an affirmative and redemptive logic that overrides difference: "After Auschwitz, our feelings resist any claim of the positivity of existence as sanctimonious, as wronging the victims; they balk at squeezing any kind of sense, however bleached, out of the victims' fate. And these feelings do have an objective side after events that make a mockery of the construction of immanence as endowed with a meaning radiated by an affirmatively posited transcendence."[22] Adorno repudiates the desire to appropriate the moral significance of the death camps through an identitarian logic that confirms an individual's relationship to society while striving toward "an affirmatively posited transcendence," a compensatory sense of closure after a traumatic event (*Sinnstiftung*). In Adorno's view, the self-aggrandizing bid for transcendence, which is ubiquitous in culture (including critique), trivializes the mass murders by reducing them to a conventional identity-confirming theme. Such a thematization is or should be impossible after Auschwitz, since it presumes a universe in which life has dignity and deaths are mourned. The anonymous gassing of the Jews should have destroyed this illusion of dignity, along with its emplotment of experience as a progressive accumulation of events that culminates in a beautifully mourned death. To the extent that the synthetic logic of metaphysical speculation adheres to this plot, it too must be cast away in the aftermath of industrialized genocide.

In "Discussions," Lyotard keeps faith with Adorno's rejection of *Sinnstiftung* by emphasizing the *exteriority* of the death camps. This topos functions to highlight the inaccessibility of the death camps to conventional modes of judgment and representation. In *The Differend*, Lyotard will articulate this inaccessibility aesthetically through the sublime negativity of "Auschwitz" as a historical sign. In "Discussions," he defines it as the condition that encloses "every situation of obligation posited in terms of subjectivity."[23] Thus, exteriority figured as the impossibility of thinking the "within" of the death camps from a position "outside" them—or, as the case may be, "after" them—spurs Lyotard's response to the question of what kind of text could "link onto" "Auschwitz."

For Lyotard, this question is inseparable from the problem of determining the conditions of possibility for a philosophy that bears witness to the name *Auschwitz* without being destroyed by the "wound of nihilism" that skepticism inflicts on thought. "This wound is not an accidental one," Lyotard declares, since "it is absolutely philosophical."[24] Skepticism is therefore not merely one philosophy among others; indeed, it has "traumatized" Western philosophy since the ancients. As Hegel observed in 1802, skepticism is " 'in an *implicit* form . . . the free aspect of every philosophy.' "[25] Part of Lyotard's agenda in "Discussions" is to reaffirm this traumatic freedom against Hegel himself. Ironically, he chooses the path of greatest resistance by pursuing this agenda dialectically, a move that self-consciously stages his own failure to avoid a synthetic logic.

To understand how Lyotard dialectically links skepticism as a negative science with the exteriority of "Auschwitz" as a historical sign, it will be helpful to rehearse Lyotard's examination of Hegel's shifting attitude toward skeptical thought. Citing an 1802 article, "Verhältnis des Skeptizismus zur Philosophie," Lyotard foregrounds Hegel's affirmation of skepticism as a mode of reflection that recognizes the philosophical necessity of contradictions in the connections among concepts.[26] He observes that Hegel still approves of this 1802 article on skepticism in paragraph 39 of his *Encyclopedia of the Philosophical Sciences* (published in 1816 and revised in 1827 and 1830), but he will subsequently repudiate skepticism as a "negative science" in paragraph 78, where he also identifies the dialectic as " '*an essential element of affirmative science.*' "[27] Lyotard notes that Hegel already "corrected" his 1802 position on skepticism in *The Phenomenology of Mind*, where he defines its negative aims. Accordingly, skepticism is that " 'which always sees in the result only *pure nothingness*, and abstracts from the fact that this nothing is determinate, is the nothing of *that out of which it comes as a result.*' "[28]

It is significant for Lyotard that Hegel does not always respect the distinction between affirmative and negative dialectics, for it allows him to interpret Hegel's eventual solidification of the distinction as a trace and a symptom of the "wound of nihilism" that skepticism inflicts on philosophy. Presumably, it was this wound that compelled Hegel to denigrate skepticism by categorizing it as a "negative science"; yet, as Lyotard observes, speculative discourse is also a mending of this breach that made philosophy vulnerable to despair. Indeed, speculative philosophy is *constitutively compelled* to cauterize this "wound" by sublating skeptical doubt. Paradoxically, skepticism hereby assumes the status of a repressed trauma to positive reason, which is also its driving force. The repression of skepticism is thus depicted as a *generic principle* or aim that negatively motivates and delimits science proper.

In considering skepticism's paradoxical status, it is worth recalling Hegel's distinction between positive and negative science that follows from his definition of *understanding* in the *Science of Logic.*[29] According to Hegel, understanding is that which "*determines*, and holds the determinations fixed." Reason is "negative and *dialectical*" to the extent that it "resolves the determinations of the understanding into nothing; it is positive because it generates the universal and comprehends the particular therein."[30] In short, concepts are rendered determinate once they are comprehended by the universal. Because determinacy is a condition of understanding, it depends on positive reason.

Hegel's distinction between the respective effects of positive and negative dialectics is clearly crucial to Lyotard's consideration of the genre of speculative discourse, or what he alternately refers to as "positive reason." According to Lyotard, positive reason is the genre within which Hegel "encloses" his dialectical logic and which Adorno critiques under the name of "affirmative dialectics." Adopting a Wittgensteinian standpoint on the contextually determined parameters of communicaton allows Lyotard to analyze this genre as a "language game" that is governed by three rules. First, the "rule for forming terms" in a dialectical phrase requires that each has at least two signifieds. Second, the "rule of immanent derivation" enjoins that negations or oppositions be immanently derivable from the given principles. Third, the "rule of expression" entails a movement of double immanent derivation that permits the synthesis of a *Resultat*: the unifying effect of closure to which the displacements and disintegrations enacted by the dialectic implicitly aim.[31] Because the *Resultat* is the goal of these operations from the beginning, each permutation in the dialectic expresses the identity of preceding ones and thereby confirms the unity of the logic that links and resolves them through its inherent teleology. In accordance with these rules, positive reason generically pursues a systemic confluence between method and aim, which expresses a two as a one—that is, which reduces differences and contradictions to a single unified phrase. In presupposing this "one" as its expression and result, speculative discourse overrides any existing dissensus and thereby neutralizes the grounds for "true discussion."[32]

Though Lyotard will develop this line of argument more fully in *The Differend*,[33] "Discussions" is significant because it demonstrates Lyotard's intellectual debt to Adorno, which has moral and logical implications for the French theorist's treatment of "Auschwitz." Lyotard's critique of positive reason is consonant with Adorno's emphasis on the negativity of the concrete particular in *Negative Dialectics* to reverse Hegel's privileging of affirmative dialectics. But here I want to avoid the error of inadvertently assuming Hegel's conflation between skepticism and negative science. The implication of this conflation is that Adorno self-consciously embraces skepticism when he privileges negative over positive dialectics; however, this observation misses the materialist aspect of Adorno's commitment to dialectics. Adorno locates a moment of truth in the particular, which is negative insofar as its specificity and materiality elude or resist subsumption by the abstract and totalizing universal. Adorno's insistence on the materiality of the particular is what distinguishes his "negative science" from one that converts "something into nothing." Indeed, Adorno strives after the opposite: to model a means of thinking the ways in which the negative intelligibly indicates the real.

Adorno's prohibition against any move to establish a conciliatory "higher" meaning (*Sinnstiftung*) for the Holocaust is imbricated in his critique of affirmative dialectics as a synthetic, result-driven logic. In "Discussions," Lyotard not only deploys Adorno's repudiation of *Sinnstiftung* for the purpose of critiquing the legitimacy of speculative discourse; he also bestows this repudiation with a regulative power. Faithful to Adorno, Lyotard will emphasize that "Auschwitz" is an event wherein the speculative requirement of a result is "disappointed and driven to despair."[34] The implication is that the "Final Solution" inflicted a wound on Western consciousness that cannot and should not be absolved. So constructed, "Auschwitz" assumes the power of skepticism to break up positive reason as a genre of logic that enjoins the identity of concepts through a unification of heterogeneous phrases. In this manner, Lyotard's "Auschwitz" "both 'refutes' the speculative dialectic . . . and remains in a sense continuous with Hegel and partially explicable via Hegel," as Geoffrey Bennington contends.[35]

Lyotard's "Auschwitz" is at once discontinuous and continuous with Hegel's concept of understanding, which, as I have mentioned, depends on the synthetic function of positive reason to establish conceptual stability. Lyotard assumes this definition when he observes that positive reason is constitutively driven to supersede the wound that nihilism opened in metaphysics. By extension, understanding would then be the result of a supersession that sutures nihilistic doubt. When Adorno insists that "Auschwitz" is an event that defies such a supersession, he is asserting that the death camps abolish or annul positive reason; however, insofar as understanding requires positive reason, Adorno's argument implies that the death camps cannot be "understood" in Hegel's sense. On the basis of this connection, Lyotard will identify "Auschwitz" not only as a symptom, but will also adopt it as the *model* of skepticism, which he represents as an irremediable wound to speculative philosophy. It remains to be seen how Lyotard will endow this traumatic model with a generic power to regulate the linkage of phrases in critical philosophy.

In his preface to *Negative Dialectics*, Adorno states that the "Meditations on Metaphysics" section is devoted to *Modelle* that are intended "to make plain what negative dialectics is and to bring it into the realm of reality, in line with its own concept." Since models do not elucidate general reflections, they must be distinguished from examples; however, they are also like examples in that they "serve the purpose of discussing key concepts of philosophical disciplines and centrally intervening in those disciplines."[36] "Auschwitz," by definition, is not an example—it does not *illustrate* negative dialectics; it is, instead, a model in *realizing* that which it illuminates.[37]

To suggest that models both intervene in and enact disciplines is to grant them a generic power not only to orient, but also to redirect and create knowledge. This institutional and institutionalizing power is paradoxical in the case of negative dialectics insofar as it "blurs the figures of the concept (which proceed from affirmation) and scrambles the names borne by the stages of the concept in its movement."[38] By extension, negative dialectics wields the power to destabilize the concepts that orient disciplinary fields. In constituting "Auschwitz" as the model of this undoing, Lyotard's reading of *Negative Dialectics* constructs it as an *antidisciplinary sign* that introduces a principle of dissolution into any discipline that adopts it as an object of inquiry.[39] Adorno thus indirectly provides Lyotard with a philosophical apparatus for constructing "Auschwitz" as a model and an anticipation of poststructuralist reading practices that traverse the boundaries among objects of inquiry along with the genres and disciplines that would contain them.[40]

Here it should be reiterated that the phrase "after Auschwitz" is intended as a citation of the first subsection of Adorno's "Meditations on Metaphysics," the third and final part of *Negative Dialectics*, though, as mentioned, there is no title for this subsection in the German version. Lyotard's employment of quotation marks to demarcate *Auschwitz* throughout the essay enunciates the critical lineage and rhetorical valence of this citation. Hence "Discussions" is not merely a reflection on the implications of Adorno's thought. It is also a self-conscious commentary on the *dissemination* of this thought through Lyotard's own text.

Of course, *dissemination* is Derrida's metaphorical correlative for the differentiation, deferral, and displacement of meanings and identities through their iterations over time. Derridean deconstruction self-consciously destroys metaphysical notions of an original, stable meaning by enunciating the provisionality and historicity of signification, which inverts binaries and relativizes idealizing logics. In "Discussions," Lyotard highlights the correspondence between dissemination and deconstruction as though to suggest that the very act of disseminating Derrida's critique performs deconstruction; however, as Lyotard himself acknowledges, he cannot elude speculative dialectics even while imploding the logic of identity. Adorno's anti-identitarian figuration of "Auschwitz" will hereby become the scene of a vexed cohabitation between negative dialectical and deconstructive thought.

The opening section of "Discussions" stages a dialectical exchange between Adorno and Derrida through three "chains" of phrases: one drawing from Derrida's writings and two from Adorno's. Each of these chains highlights the conventions that organize deconstruction and negative dialectics as genres of critical logic. The elaboration that follows the Derrida chain cites his definition of deconstruction as a strategic " '*overturning* of the classical opposition [between terms such as speech/writing, presence/absence, etc.] *and* a general *displacement* of the system.' "[41] Lyotard argues that this double operation performs "the work of speculative dialectics itself" if it is read literally.[42] This connection subsequently serves as a premise and conclusion for Lyotard's dialectical argument that links Derrida's deconstructive skepticism with Adorno's challenge to the viability and moral validity of metaphysics "after Auschwitz."

To follow this point, it will be helpful to consider that Adorno's and Derrida's respective engagements with Hegel's logic do not simply repudiate dialectics, but instead reappraise and rework Hegel's formulation of a dialectically determined negativity. In the *Science of Logic*, Hegel explicitly reinforces his thesis that what is posited is determined through what it subordinates or excludes—that is, negates. What Adorno will refer to as a *determinate negation* is the intelligibility that a conscious recognition of these negated aspects and their formative role obtains once it is incorporated into critical reflection. The process of negation entailed by thought thus assumes a positive status in and for it.

Lyotard locates the principal difference between Adorno and Derrida's thinking on negativity in Adorno's emphasis on the *legibility* and Derrida's on the *illegibility* of the determinate negation. Lyotard's figuration of "Auschwitz" bears witness to this difference as he follows through on Adorno's suggestion that it would be impossible to affirm a positive "result" in the aftermath of "Auschwitz." This declaration reiterates Lyotard's emphasis on the exteriority of the death camps (which is to say, their incomprehensibility for those who

did not experience them); he nonetheless concedes that this exteriority
cannot avoid assuming the form of a negative result in its translation
into philosophical discourse. Indeed, as Lyotard remarks at the outset of
this essay, the very word *discussions* in his title "announces" the genre
of dialectical discourse.[43] Lyotard does not disclaim the apparent necessity
of this discourse; instead, he interrogates it dialectically through Adorno
and Derrida's writings.

In simultaneously opposing and revising Hegel, Adorno and Derrida
both seek to radicalize the "free aspect" of skepticism through an interrogation
of the traditional metaphysical opposition between negativity and truth
construed as presence. Adorno excoriates positivist thought as a form of
result-driven logic privileged by a market-driven, functionalist economy.
In targeting the instrumentality of this logic, this critique foregrounds the
rationalizing impact of the physical sciences on the human sciences, which
contributes to the reification of the social relations that they investigate.
As *The Postmodern Condition* demonstrates, Lyotard shares a significant
stake in the ongoing critique of a positivist thought that is complicit with
the capitalist overvaluation of efficient and profitable productivity—what
he terms "performativity." In "Discussions," Adorno's negative figuration of
the Holocaust serves Lyotard's critique of performativity by articulating it
with the result-driven genre of speculative reason.

Both Adorno and Derrida reconceptualize the category of the negative
within and in opposition to Hegel to unsettle the urge toward unity that
defines the Hegelian subject in their eyes.[44] The dialectic that Lyotard stages
between Adorno and Derrida extends the implications of this critique to
Adorno's figuration of "Auschwitz" in *Negative Dialectics*; however, its staging
is vexed by Lyotard's attempt to finesse a rapprochement between Derrida's
deconstruction of the proper name and Adorno's rejection of *Sinnstiftung* in
the name of Auschwitz:

> This model [Auschwitz] . . is the name of something (of a para-
> experience, of a paraempiricity) wherein dialectics encounters a
> non-negatable negative (*un négatif non niable*), and abides in the
> impossibility of redoubling that negative into a "result." Wherein
> the mind's wound is not scarred over. Wherein, writes Derrida, "the
> investment in death cannot be integrally amortized."
>
> The "Auschwitz" model would designate an experience of
> language which brings speculative discourse to a halt. The latter can
> no longer be pursued 'after Auschwitz,' that is, 'within Auschwitz.'
> Here would be found a name "within" which we cannot think,
> or not completely. It would not be a name in Hegel's sense, as
> that figure of memory which assures the permanence of the *rest*
> when mind has destroyed its signs. It would be a name of the
> nameless. . . . It would be a name which designates what has no

name in speculation, a name for the anonymous. And what for speculation remains simply the anonymous.[45]

Lyotard's figuration of "Auschwitz" as a "para-experience" and "anonym" in this passage overtly echoes Derrida's deconstruction of the proper name as a designator of a unique entity or human subject. Derrida's deconstruction also targets its metaphysical heritage as a mimetic ideal and place-holder for signification. This heritage presents the proper name as a reliable designator and anchor of substantive, determinate identities and as a sign of past experience. Lyotard will subsequently undertake an intensive analysis of the relationship between names and historical experience in "The Referent, the Name" chapter in *The Differend*. In "Discussions," Lyotard briefly alludes to the problem of the proper name in his elaboration on negative dialectics following the first Adorno chain. In that context, Lyotard cites Adorno's views on the function of *micrology* as the study of the particular. According to Adorno, the micrological view defies a totalizing logic that reinforces itself by isolating and negating the particular. He therefore affirms its critical agency as an anti-identitarian strategy that cracks the "shells" of this isolation. The micrological standpoint explodes identities that have been negatively determined in relation to a subsuming concept and thereby frees the particular from its limited status as a "specimen" of the universal.[46]

Lyotard contends that the question of the specimen is "decisive" because it raises the question of the proper or factual name. Adorno is committed to protecting the proper name's specificity from the violence of a speculative thought that looks for an "intelligible, dialectical phrase" to "replace" it. In doing so, it "presupposes a reversal by which the particular becomes an example of the generic" and thereby sacrifices the difference represented by the name to a totalizing synthesis.[47] The name *Auschwitz* is already vulnerable to this logic because it refers to the scene of anonymous mass murder. Adorno's rejection of attempts to endow the Holocaust with a higher or transcendent meaning (what I have been calling *Sinnstiftung*) serves to guard the specificity of the victims' suffering against instrumental, synthetic, and redemptive appropriations that efface it. His privileging of the micrological over and against the universal rewrites this rejection as a critical strategy.

Employing Adorno's repudiation of *Sinnstiftung* as an anti-identitarian departure point, Lyotard argues that the discourse produced by the model "Auschwitz" disputes the speculative's generic requirement of a result. It nevertheless remains unclear how Lyotard's figuration of "Auschwitz" as a "para-experience," an "experience of language," bypasses this requirement,[48] for if language bears the trace of the speculative in aiming toward unified expression, then his dialectical approach would necessarily fail to register the annihilating logic that "Auschwitz" allegedly models.

In designating "Auschwitz" as a "para-experience," Lyotard obeys Adorno's prohibition by separating the death camps from Hegel's phenomenological and dialectical understanding of memory and experience. Despite its emphasis on language at the expense of an empirical and ontological subject, such a designation does not trivialize the extremity of existence in the death camps; instead, it emphasizes their power to refute the speculative logic of progression presupposed by Hegel's phenomenology of consciousness. This power derives from Lyotard's identification, following Adorno, of the ideal of a "beautiful death" with the "speculative element" in Hegel's concept of experience and thus as the by-product of a " 'dialectical process which consciousness executes on itself.' "[49] The "beautiful death" is an end of the finite that opens a revelation of the infinite. From Adorno's perspective, "Auschwitz" was the place wherein the law of the finite (anonymous) mass death declared the impossibility of a beautiful death and thereafter negates its anticipation. Speculative notions of experience governed by this anticipation are irrelevant "after Auschwitz": they cannot properly divulge the chasm that the death camps open in Western thought.

Ultimately, however, the requirements of expression supersede his ability to write on the borders of decidability, as the aim to identify the conditions and limits of judgment collapses philosophical skepticism into traumatic history. By means of this synthesis, Lyotard contructs "Auschwitz" as the mirror of a philosophy that is always already traumatized by skepticism. The latent trauma of skepticism would therefore constitute the negative aim of all critical philosophy, which the gas chambers "merely" realized historically.

In consonance with Derrida's critique of the humanist subject in "The Ends of Man," Lyotard's reflections on the trope of the beautiful death pursue a negative dialectical confrontation with the Hegelian, Greek, and Heideggerian emplotments of human mortality.[50] This confrontation is orchestrated as a double movement that affirms skeptical freedom in attesting to the negativity of anonymous mass murder, which darkly inverts the sublime sense of magnitude conventionally effected by a tragic end. There can be no redemptive closure for an event that shattered bedrock illusions of a civil consensus that would guarantee an individual's dignity in both life and death.

Improper Ends

> Man is that which is in relation to his end, in the fundamentally equivocal sense of the word. Since always. The transcendental end can appear to itself and be unfolded only on the condition of mortality, of a relation to finitude as the origin of ideality. The name of man has always been inscribed in metaphysics between these two ends. It has meaning only in this eschato-teleological situation.
>
> —Derrida

"Discussions, or Phrasing 'after Auschwitz' " is a transcript of a lecture that Lyotard delivered in Cerisy-la-Salle in the context of "Les fins de l'homme" colloquium in 1980 devoted to Derrida's work. The colloquium's title cites Derrida's "The Ends of Man," which explores the humanist subject implicit in the writings of Hegel, Husserl, and Heidegger. "Discussions" explicitly draws on this essay while enunciating the reverberations among Lyotard's titular references.

"The Ends of Man" was first delivered in October 1968 at the colloquium "Philosophy and Anthropology" in New York. As Derrida remarks, this presentation took place a few months after the student occupation of the Paris universities in May of that same year. In acknowledging this juncture within the text itself, Derrida stresses the historicity of its production and delivery. He thus inscribes the events of 1968 within the lineaments of his critique of humanism.[51]

Lyotard has also attested to the significance of 1968, a date he designates as a "sign of history."[52] This designation applies to those events that, according to Lyotard, liberate judgment and consequently evoke a feeling of the negative sublime. Auschwitz, Budapest 1956, and Paris 1968 open[ed] abysses in historical-moral judgment. Such events are negative insofar as judging them must take place in the absence of a criterion and *as if* they were indices of historical progress.

In the first section, I elaborated on the construction of "Auschwitz" in "Discussions" as a philosophical-historical sign. This construction allows Lyotard to act out the recursive tendency of traumatic memory as an affective precipitate of wounding pasts. If fixed, this traumatic sign obtains the power to regulate present and future interpretations, a power that is not unilateral, since current and subsequent events determine not only when but also how the past is selectively recalled. The events of 1968 were sedimented by the traumatic impact of World War II and the Algerian struggle for independence. Nevertheless, it is not just "Auschwitz" that teaches Lyotard how to read the events of 1968, but also the sign "1968" (which he also encloses in quotes), that teaches him how to read "Auschwitz."

The indexical function of "1968" within "Discussions" is evident in Lyotard's choice of citations. While Lyotard delivers "Discussions" in 1980, his citations of Derrida's writings draw mainly from the essays collected in *Marges de la philosophie* (1972), all of which were first presented or published between 1967 and 1972.[53] In addition, Lyotard cites Adorno's *Negative Dialectics*, which appeared in German in 1966. In speculating on "Auschwitz" through Derrida's work from the late 1960s and early 1970s, "Discussions" reinforces the centrifugal impact of "1968" as a sign that guides subsequent interpretations of history. In this respect, the 1980 colloquium on Derrida provides Lyotard with an occasion to reconvene the "spirit" of 1968 through Derrida's deconstruction of the humanist subject.

Lyotard's conspicuously post-Hegelian repudiation of phenomenological formulations of experience is consistent with a critical attitude that Derrida marks as the horizon of "1968." In "The Ends of Man," he characterizes this horizon as a "cross-section" of the trends that permit his reading of the period's "dominant motif," which emerged in reaction to Sartre's influence following the publication of *Being and Nothingness*. Among Derrida's principal objections to Sartre's project is that it fails to examine the concept of the "unity of man." As a result, Sartre inadvertently naturalizes man as a sign without historical, cultural, or linguistic limits.[54]

Derrida points out that the unified subject of humanist existentialism grounded various philosophical projects of the day: spiritualist and atheist existentialisms, philosophies of value, right-learning and left-leaning personalisms, and classical Marxism. A critical reaction against the humanistic-existentialist faith in the "unity of man" produced an anthropologistic reading that collapses Hegel, Husserl, and Heidegger. Derrida dissociates himself from this reductive amalgamation of different phenomenologies with humanistic existentialism, yet he remains interested in historicizing this conflation in relation to posthumanist critiques of phenomenology. According to Derrida's account, these critiques took their direction from Husserl's and Heidegger's delimitations of anthropologism; however, in forgetting this philosophical heritage, they produce what Derrida refers to as an "amalgam" of metaphysics, phenomenology, and humanism.

This amalgam was, for Derrida, mistaken in three respects. In the first place, it incorporated Hegel's *Phenomenology of Spirit* as a "science of man" rather than a "science of the experience of consciousness" (Hegel's original title for the *Phenomenology*). The amalgam thus ignored Hegel's own division of the *Encyclopedia* into the *Anthropology*, the *Phenomenology of Spirit*, and the *Science of Logic*. Second, despite Husserl's authority in postwar France, his critique of both empirical and transcendental anthropologisms was not only missed, but also, ironically, turned against him after passing through a reductive reading of Heidegger. This is the case even though it was actually Husserl who contributed to this misreading when he "precipitously interpreted" *Being and Time* as "an anthropologistic deviation from transcendental phenomenology."[55] Heidegger's *Being and Time* was deprived of its phenomenological aspects and thereby downgraded to a mere anthropologism. On the contrary, Derrida notes, Heidegger explicitly targets humanism as a component of the metaphysics and classical ontology that his "Letter on Humanism" purports to destruct.[56]

Clearly, Heidegger's proclaimed "destruction" of humanism and the postwar French reaction against the ideal of the "unity of man" factor crucially into Derrida's critical commitment to exposing modern residues of a metaphysical predilection for seeing the one in the many. Derrida views the organicist desire for the unity of essence and appearance as a reprise of ontotheological nostalgia for the communion between God and man. Despite this recognition, Derrida in "The Ends of Man" avoids systematically repudiating the various readings of Hegel, Husserl, and Heidegger that produced its reductive conflation, which he analyzes as a *symptom* of the "subterranean" anthropocentric and humanist assumptions in their phenomenologies. In short, he reads it as a sign that they "appear to belong to the very sphere of that which they criticize or de-limit."[57]

As in his other essays, Derrida adopts a Heideggerian strategy of continually shifting among the varying and sometimes divergent denotations and connotations of metaphysical language to deconstruct the specter of a human essence that Hegel, Husserl, and Heidegger defer. Derrida objects to the *we* implicit in this ideal subject that negates those whom it excludes. More generally, Derrida is concerned about its power to effect a violent "closure" or finalization of meaning that endangers the openness of thought. This is a danger against which Heidegger explicitly warned and which Derridean deconstruction actively seeks to thwart.

Derrida's "The Ends of Man" supplements Lyotard's reading of Adorno's "Auschwitz" as the scene of the "death of the beautiful death," which is a significant motif in "Discussions." Lyotard uses this trope to link Derrida's deconstruction of the humanist subject to Adorno's critique of the phenomenological concept of experience. The beautiful death figures here for a heroic emplotment of experience that delimits the dignity proper to being human. Its "death" in "Auschwitz" exposes the danger of defining the human for moral, political, or philosophical ends.

It is relevant to recall here that death has a peculiar status for the existentialism affiliated with Heidegger's name. In *Being and Time*, *Dasein* is most "true" to its ontological nature when it reflects on its "ownmost" end. Resoluteness (or impassivity) before an ever imminent death is the criterion of ontological authenticity. While he shares Adorno's suspicion of the cult of authenticity that goads *Being and Time*,[58] Derrida's work embraces Heidegger's concern with the pressure exerted by the ontic-ontological difference on the thought of Being as a whole. One of the strategies pursued by Derrida in "The Ends of Man" is to adopt Heidegger's "Letter on Humanism" as a call for the death of the humanist subject, a passing that Derrida's title heralds as an aim.

In "Discussions," the speculative-Hegelian emplotment of beautiful death is redoubled by Derrida's dialogue with Heidegger's "fundamental ontology," wherein authentic existence is realized in the anxiety of Being-toward-death. This dialogue folds Heidegger's existentialist reflection on mortality into Hegelian dialectics and the Greek ideal of the beautiful death that surfaces in Hegel's reading of *Antigone*. The result is a philosophical emplotment of the meaning of human ends and the human as such redeemed by death and its attendant rituals.

As Derrida observes, there is, in the end, that other "plot": the grave that is both an aperture in and a closure of human aims. In *Being and Time*, *Dasein* is "authentic" when it confronts its anxiety before death as the end of existence and a limit of thought.[59] It is, at once, the destiny and boundary of mortal life and the unsurpassable limit of Heidegger's fundamental ontology: that which would complete this project if it could be "fundamentally" thought within it. In this respect, death is not just an ending, but also an aim of thought about the meaning of Being, a reflection that is essential to humans as mortals destined/sent (*geschickt*) to death.

The implication of Heidegger's reflections on the ontology of death in *Being and Time* is that anxiety before death is essential to *Dasein* as the personification of a fundamental ontology marked by an "ecstatic" dispersion in time. In Hegel's writings, in contrast, a proper death is one that establishes the sense of an ending for a tragic or heroic life. Death not only ends or "cancels" life, but also completes and "sublates" it in the various contradictory senses of the German verb *aufheben*: to raise, hold, lift up; to annul, abolish, destroy, cancel, suspend; and, to keep, save, and preserve. An *Aufhebung* of life implies a recognition of death through mourning rituals that give the individual loss an identity in relation to a community. Mourning affirms the individual's membership in society, yet it also, ultimately, absolves his or her particularity within the unity and spirit of the social order as a whole. Mourning, for Hegel, reflects on the meaning of finitude that opens onto infinity; it functions dramaturgically as a cathartic ritual that attributes a higher meaning to death in affirming the continuity of the community that mourns.

The *Sinnstiftung* proper to death is suggestive of Aristotle's definition of catharsis as a purgative release from an accumulation of tragic pathos connected with a protagonist's death. Indeed, just as the *Aufhebung* is a "result" that defines the genre of speculative logic, catharsis is an affective goal that demarcates the genre of tragic drama. It is significant that the Hegelian emplotment of the beautiful death as defined by Lyotard-Derrida simultaneously conforms to the speculative genre in enacting the tragic rationale of striving toward catharsis as a cumulative "result" for the audience. In classical Greek tragedy, the protagonist's death permits the community to survive and thus transcend the turmoil that his or her actions precipitated.[60] Its lesson-bearing spectacle at once stages and resolves the repercussions of hubris.

Aristotle stipulates that a tragic plot must fulfill the standards of "proper magnitude" in its imitation of noble and complete action.[61] Furthermore, character is secondary in tragedy insofar as it supplements the imitation of action. It would therefore seem that character development, for Aristotle, merely serves to reinforce the lesson introduced by the action. Indeed, tragic dramas achieve their unity through their transcendence of obstacles typically instigated by the protagonist's hubris. Such an "excess" of individuality threatens to unsettle the public's faith in community along with the rules that cement its identity. This might explain why Aristotle argues that the finitude of character might be "sacrificed" to the infinity of divine destiny. Catharsis permits an *Aufhebung* of the opposition between human finitude and the divine and thus restores the conditions for a moral-social synthesis.

To view death as the *Aufhebung* of an individual's existence is to construct it as a unifying result—as if life were also governed by the rules of speculative discourse. Derrida translates the Hegelian *Aufheben* with *relever*, which plays on *relève* as relief, *relèvement* as uprighting or rebuilding, and the past participle *relevé* as (up)lifted, elevated, or raised up.[62] This interplay opens various connotative possibilities for reading the trope of the beautiful death as an *Aufhebung* that completes and relieves life. In addition, through its proximity to *se relever de*, Derrida's translation accrues the nuances of recovering from, getting over, and/or rising from the ashes. Connecting Hegel's understanding of death as *Aufhebung* with Derrida's translation of *Aufhebung* as *relève/relevé* suggests that the sickness and cares of existence, as well as mourning, anger, or shame can be affirmed, relieved, and transcended through a beautiful death.

It is worth noting that *relèvement* might also denote a plotting of one's position (as in *faire une relèvement de sa position*), perhaps in keeping with an economic end. The anticipation of a beautiful death would, in this instance, fall into the pejorative category of a calculated redemption (as connoted by the notion of *Wiedergutmachung*, making good again, in the German postwar context). In Adorno's view, it is precisely this kind of calculation that should be prohibited after Auschwitz. There is / should be no relief from the shame of genocide; neither is there a "relief guard" that might take over for (*prendre la relève de quelqu'un*) the vigilant memory that pays homage to the murdered. A final settling of accounts would be impossible when the bill (*relevé*) of repair can never be made good. Catharsis as an *Aufhebung* of the Holocaust would, for Adorno, be improperly plotted.

Derrida's "The Ends of Man" also plays on the correspondence between the Hegelian *Aufhebung* and the Greek *telos*, denoting both end and death. Death á la Hegel is an "end of finite man" that relieves (*relève*) him from his finitude. An image of "man" is thereby brought "into relief" by Hegel's definition of proper death. Derrida unravels this consolatory closure for a reflection on human ends:

> The *relève* or *relevance* of man is his *telos* or *eskhaton*. The unity of these two *ends* of man, the unity of his death, his completion, his accomplishment, is enveloped in the Greek thinking of *telos*, in the discourse on *telos*, which is also a discourse on *eidos*, on *ousia*, and on *aletheia*. Such a discourse, in Hegel as in the entirety of metaphysics, indissociably coordinates teleology with an eschatology, a theology, and an ontology. *The thinking of the end of man, therefore, is always already prescribed in metaphysics, in the thinking of the truth of man.* What is difficult to think today is an end of man which would not be organized by a dialectics of truth and negativity, an end of man which would not be teleology in the first person plural. The *we*, which articulates natural and philosophical consciousness with each other in the *Phenomenology of Spirit*, assures the proximity to itself of the fixed and central being for which this circular reappropriation is produced.

The *we* is the unity of absolute knowledge and anthropology, of God and man, of onto-theo-teleology and humanism. "*Being*" and language—the group of languages—that the *we* governs or opens: such is the name of that which assures the transition between metaphysics and humanism via the *we*.[63]

Derrida links the *we* employed in philosophical discourse as exemplified by Hegel with the idealization of death as *Aufhebung*, translated into French as the *relève* and *relevé* of life. Narrated as the relief/supersession that is "proper" to the human experience of mortality, this ideal is imbricated in a metaphysical discourse wherein the *we* tacitly grounds the "truth" and being of "man." For Derrida, this *we* is, thus, the proper expression of an improper complicity between metaphysics and humanism.[64] He rejects the ideal of the human proper, because the *we* that it presupposes is dangerously exclusive.

Derrida's critique of a metaphysical construct of mortality as the essence of the properly human exposes the tacitly Western *we* of humanity. Lyotard draws on this passage in linking *telos* with the Latin *percifere* (accomplishment) and with *tax payment* in light of Adorno's figuration of "Auschwitz" as the scene of the death of the beautiful death. Accordingly, telos might signify "the price for the passage to citizenship," while the "passage" enacted by the beautiful death becomes the aim that completes the (tax-paying) citizen. In Lyotard's words, "what passes away is finitude and what comes to pass is the recognition of the citizen's infinitude as legislator."[65] A beautiful death is the *property* of a citizen who exchanges his finitude as an individual for the infinity of the civic *we*; reciprocally, a dignified death is an *entitlement* of citizenship as the ultimate parameter of the human.

I have connected the ideal of a beautiful death with the redemptive meaning proper to a classical tragic ending. At the same time, I have traced a series of convergences between Derrida's deconstruction of the humanist subject endemic to existentialism and phenomenology, Adorno's repudiation of *Sinnstiftung*, and the extinguished possibility of tragic magnitude and cathartic closure for those living in the aftermath of the death camps. This series opens up the confluence between a narration of experience predicated on the beautiful death and Lyotard's rejection, following Adorno, of phenomenological notions of experience for philosophy "after Auschwitz." The implication is that since speculative conceptions of experience presuppose a beautiful death as a redemptive completion of existence, the world of "Auschwitz" cannot be represented in experiential terms. Conversely, insofar as everyday notions of experience outside the death camps anticipate this synthetic "result" in the image of a uniquely mourned death, experience in general adheres to the conventions of the speculative genre.

A *subgenre* of speculative logic is brought into play here through Lyotard's repudiation, after Adorno, of phenomenological experience as the cumulative dynamic of a dialectical synthesis. This is a subgenre that fulfills the conventions of positive reason by producing a result—namely, the beautiful death as the privilege accorded to an individual who might be redeemed as a member of a community through mourning. Yet Lyotard configures this subgenre in the course of employing Adorno to undo it: the death camps realized a negative model of experience that disabled the speculative and heroic emplotments culminating in a beautiful death.[66] Adorno's annulment of metaphysics "after Auschwitz" helps Lyotard to dissolve this tragic-heroic subgenre while linking post-Hegelianism and posthumanism. Adorno's own predilection for modernist literature and music thus presages Lyotard's "postmodernist" genre of anti-identitarian art and philosophy.[67]

This configuration implicitly parallels a negative historical teleology put forward by Max Horkheimer and Adorno in the *Dialectic of Enlightenment*,[68] which identifes the instrumental reason that orchestrated the mass murders as an Enlightenment inheritance. Lyotard contends that "Auschwitz" represents the nominal site wherein the danger of this inheritance can no longer be deferred. The industrialized barbarism of the death camps was, in appearance, a negation of history conceived in the humanist spirit of the Enlightenment as a "metanarrative" of progress through reason; however, to the extent that the policy authorizing the "Final Solution" was the fruition of bureaucratic instrumentality, it enacted the perniciously "rational" ends of the Enlightenment. Such a topos informs Lyotard's repudiation of modern metanarratives while reinforcing "Auschwitz" as a metonym for the wounding impact of skepticism upon Western philosophy.

In this manner, Lyotard's analysis of the exteriority of the death camps is overdetermined by the assumption that experience is *necessarily* synthetic (and specifically, Hegelian) and that the unification of identity predicated by this understanding both is and should be impossible. In "Discussions," Lyotard never proposes an alternative to the speculative-Hegelian model of experience. His reading of Adorno seems to compel him to regard it as a hegemonically definitive model that he rejects *tout court*. "Auschwitz" is not, properly speaking, an "experience, since it would have no [speculative] result."[69] Rather it indicates a "para-experience" that derealizes narratives of experience and thereby becomes the model of critical philosophy proper.

The generic aim orienting Lyotard's argument in "Discussions" is to testify to a suspicion that the wound or breach Adorno has identified with Auschwitz may already be covering over a fracture.[70] It is a fracture that the Derridean deconstruction of Western metaphysics intentionally inhabits and deepens. In bringing Derridean deconstruction to bear on Adorno's destruction of metaphysics after Auschwitz, Lyotard's "Discussions" figures the death camps as an experience of language rather than an experience of an event. It thereby fulfills Adorno's agenda to set them apart from speculative emplotments of experience while at the same time responding to Derrida's displacements of the humanist subject.

Lyotard's reading of Adorno in light of Derrida implies that the synthetic tendency of positive reason is simultaneously improper and unavoidable after "Auschwitz." Dialectical negation is, for Lyotard, a point of conjuncture between deconstruction and "Auschwitz" as the name of a difference that exceeds speculative thought. Adorno's "Auschwitz" thus provides a quintessentially aporetic figure for Lyotard's opposition to speculative reason. At the same time, even as Adorno's moral agenda qualifies Derrida's emphasis on undecidability, negative dialectics comes into its own as an anticipation of deconstruction. In this valence, "Auschwitz" might now figure as the scene of an *Aufhebung* of two post-Hegelian philosophical strategies. It is, of course, ironic that Lyotard involves Adorno's and Derrida's names in the process of synthesizing this "result."

Expropriating the *We*

> Genocide is the absolute integration. It is on its way wherever men are leveled off—"polished off," (*geschliffen*) as the German military called it—until one exterminates them literally, as deviations from the concept of their total nullity. Auschwitz confirmed the philosopheme of pure identity as death.

—Adorno

It will be helpful to recall from my summary of Jürgen Habermas's intervention in the 1986 Historians' Debate that his figuration of Auschwitz is, like Lyotard's, informed by Adorno's prohibition against employing the death camps as an occasion for a redemptive and identitarian closure of meaning; however, while Habermas tries to endow Adorno's repudiation of identitarian affirmations after Auschwitz with a normative power, Lyotard prefers to dwell on its aporetic dimension. Indeed, to the extent that Lyotard challenges the legitimacy of the discourse of legitimation, his reading of Adorno also preempts Habermas's critique of the *Dialectic of Enlightenment* and his theory of communicative rationality.[71] In Lyotard's view, such a theory implies a plural subject—a preceding *we* who purportedly achieved consensus on the status of a referent. The imagined *we* of consensus functions as a regulative ideal that determines who belongs to a community as well as the criteria for membership; this *we* is tautological to the extent that it functions at once as the premise and as the goal of judgments that reproduce a social order.

Given his long-standing concern with problems of legitimation, it is not surprising that Lyotard devotes sections V–VII of "Discussions" to an analysis of the *we* as an implicit ground and "end" of the consensually-based judgment refuted by "Auschwitz." This reflection not only rearticulates Adorno's prohibition of *Sinnstiftung* in pragmatist terms, but interrogates the normativity of civic obligation as the foundation of justice.

To foreground the potential for violence inherent in the ideal of consensus, Lyotard insists on the untranslatablity of phrase regimes, and the rhetoricity of phrase linkages and of the rules governing proper and improper linkages. His aim is to expose the power relations involved in judgments of historical events. In Lyotard's terms, the phrasing of laws in the form of commands adheres to the regime of *prescriptives* as phrases that enjoin certain beliefs and/or actions. The asymmetry between the addressor who issues the command and the addressee who obeys it threatens to break down the abstract homogeneity of the *we* as the foundation of a command's power. This fault must be covered over if the command is to retain its legitimacy.

The command is particularly problematic, according to Lyotard, because it has no referent that can be mutually validated by its addressor and addressee. Its legitimacy consequently derives from its normative value, which is to say, from its power to refer both parties back to a prior consensus that unites them. Lyotard observes that this normative *we* provides the "supreme argument of authority," or rather authorization insofar as it legitimates the codes, court rulings, laws, decrees, ordinances and commandments that comprise the social order.[72] It consequently establishes an abstract universality among citizens who are defined as such by their willingness to forgo particular interests by obeying the law.

In "Discussions," the injunction to die by execution is represented as an extreme instance of the pressure that the command exerts on a justice that depends on commutability before the law. In this instance, the command's end is fundamentally at odds with the goal of the *we* that authorizes it insofar as death by execution materially removes its addressee from his or her community. In submitting to it, he or she relinquishes commutability as the power to adopt the addressor's position of inclusion in the social order. Lyotard remarks that the historical effect of this sacrifice is that the proper name of the executed "will no longer be able to figure among the instances of addressor and addressee in ulterior unmediated phrases." Instead, his or her name will be restricted to the "referential instance"—which is to say, to a passive existence in citations, chronicles, and historical accounts.[73] But not all is lost for the addressee of the executioner's phrase. Lyotard identifies an "exit clause" that permits the condemned to avoid reduction to "exclusive referentiality" by identifying with a *we* "capable, as the instance of addressor and addressee, of legitimizing all possible commands, starting with the one ordering him to die." In validating the social order that issued the command, "he eludes the death sentence and is able, for that very reason, to die."[74]

Lyotard's "escape clause" is paradoxical insofar as the addressee ostensibly eludes the situation of exclusive referentiality only by exchanging "his particular name for a collective pronoun,"[75] thus dissolving his identity within the abstract homogeneity of the *we*. A lawful execution in this instance would, ironically, be defined by an expropriation of the proper name itself as a designator of the individual. For it is only in confirming an individual's membership in a social order that execution obtains any legal validity as the lawful death of a citizen.

Lyotard's analysis of the death sentence furthers his explanation of the second Adorno chain from *Negative Dialectics* in the opening section of "Discussions."[76] This second chain highlights Adorno's figuration of "Auschwitz" as the scene of the "death of the beautiful death." Extrapolating from Plato, Lyotard has defined a beautiful death as an end of the finite and a revelation of the infinite. In the previous section, I have already elaborated on the ways in which this revelation conforms to the structure of a tragic catharsis and a logic of *Sinnstiftung* prohibited by Adorno in the aftermath of the "extermination" camps. In the classical paradigm, the heroic ideal of beautiful death is presumed to permit the possibility of an honorable ending that completes the individual's life and affirms the continuity of the community that mourns it. In a related vein, Lyotard also cites Hegel's figuration of death as the *Aufhebung* of experience and consciousness.

The logic of beautiful death equates "humanity" with citizenship. It suggests that individual death does not happen outside a community to mourn it as the passing of a citizen; in other words, the reality of individual death is an effect of its social and juridical meaning.[77] This connection is key to Lyotard's reading of Adorno's remarks on the meaning of death "after Auschwitz." For if "fearing death means fearing worse than death" after the "Final Solution," this is because the anonymity of mass death does not permit human death to be properly validated as such. The "exterminated" did not die; they ceased to exist as if they had never existed:

> In 'Auschwitz,' it is not the [command] *Die* which remains nameless and leaves no result but the fact that the reconciliation of the name in the prescription and the pronoun in the norm, of the finitude of death and the infinity of law, is prohibited. The one who commands the death is exclusively other than the one to whom the command is addressed. The former does not have to account to the latter, and the latter does not have to legitimize the former. The two phrase universes have no common application. What the prescriptive phrase presents (the command to die), the normative phrase does not (whence the "We knew nothing about it" of the so-called legislators); what the normative phrase presents (*So says the law*) remains unknown in the universe of the prescriptive phrase *Die* (whence the "Why do they do it? This cannot be" of the victims).[78]

Lyotard represents the Nazi death sentence as a paradigmatic abuse of the presumed consensus that founds civil obedience. A defining characteristic of this abuse was the expropriation of the "escape clause" whereby the Jews might avoid the finitude of exclusive referentiality. Indeed, when the Nazis commanded the Jews to die, they had already revoked the commutability that is the condition of law. The Nuremberg laws deprived German Jews of citizenship, *Kristallnacht* demonstrated that violence against them could be perpetrated with impunity, and a steady stream of venal propaganda foreclosed Jewish membership in the *we* of civil society before the mass deportations began to take place and the Wannsee Conference made official the policy of liquidating Europe's Jews. The Nazis also destroyed many of the records of their crimes that listed the names of the murdered and thereby deprived them of a postmortem referential status as well.

The Nazis' persecution and murder of the Jews illuminate how the anonymity of mass death is partly prefigured by the abstract homogeneity of the juridical subject. Lyotard's argument emphasizes how this abstract homogeneity is a function of the presumed universality of laws themselves. Lyotard cites Hegel to the effect that it is "proper to man to *know* his law" insofar as knowledge is the condition of obedience.[79] To remain just, laws depend on the willingness of their addressees to maintain the social order by obeying the rules upon which it is predicated. This willingness is therefore a condition of their freedom as citizens to know and to accept the law.

For Hegel, what is proper to "man" is "his" *we*, as a right to belong to civil society and to know its laws. This right derives from the individual's absorption into a collective whose identity is bound by law and assumes an implicit social contract. The ideal of a beautiful death affirms this right by requiring a community to mourn the individual's death as the death of a citizen. In the death camps, however, there was not even an illusion of prior consent. The Jews did not belong to a *we* who could authorize commands as laws; nor were they free to reject the commands issued by a National Socialist state. Since the Jews could not willingly recognize the legal authority of the command to die, they could not properly obey it. It is for this reason, then, that the Nazi command to die represents such an extreme negation of justice that it would be impossible to phrase as law: " 'Auschwitz' would be the name of this impossible phrase wherein the law is not known, wherein it cannot be just, wherein the command cannot obligate, wherein man loses what is proper to him, namely, his *we*. At Auschwitz and afterwards, one does not 'know' how to die. . . . One administers (*On administre*)."[80]

The "Final Solution" exposed the abstract *we* of civic membership as the deception that compelled some Jews to obey on faith in what turned out to be the nonexistent universality and commutability of the Nazi legal and moral universe. In commanding the Jews to cooperate, to leave their houses, to enter ghettos, to ride in cattle cars, to undress for the gas chambers, and to believe that these chambers were showers, the Nazis played on the Jews' intuitive faith in a *we* of humanity that was, in the Nazis' perspective, strictly applicable only to themselves as Aryan citizens of a *Judenfrei* Reich. Henceforth "Auschwitz" is the name of this deception that sanctioned a sovereign *we* who delimited civic and human membership to command and execute those whom it excludes.

It is, of course, this equation between citizenship and humanity that Hannah Arendt pinpointed so forcefully in her analysis of Nazi ideology and in her observations about the fate of displaced persons in *The Origins of Totalitarianism.*[81] "Common sense protests desperately that the masses are submissive and that all this gigantic apparatus of terror is therefore superfluous," she writes, yet "if they were capable of telling the truth, the totalitarian rulers would reply: The apparatus seems superfluous to you only because it serves to make men superfluous."[82] According to Arendt, "The law of killing by which totalitarian movements seize and exercise power would remain a law of the movement even if they ever succeeded in making all of humanity subject to their rule."[83]

It is worth remarking even briefly that when Agamben takes up Arendt in his *Homo Sacer* trilogy, he is also following Lyotard's lead fifteen years prior. Lyotard's elaboration on the asymmetry of the command "to die" anticipates Agamben's citations of Carl Schmitt on the "state of exception" to demarcate the government's use of a rhetoric of national emergency and necessity to appropriate absolute sovereignty.[84] Agamben's reconceptualization of Schmitt's "state of exception" allows him in the *Homo Sacer* trilogy to interface Arendt's understanding of totalitarian ideology with Foucault's theses on biopolitics. Hence, the mechanism of the totalitarian state is to establish absolute sovereignty by proclaiming its goal of transforming human nature an emergency. The "urgency" of this goal then rationalizes an expropriation of various constituencies on the basis of racial or ideological "impurity" among the populations the state administers. The Nazi death camp is paradigmatic as a site wherein the pure mechanism of power is exposed in the arbitrary logic that reduces anyone at any moment into a shameful minimum of bare life—into "a kind of absolute biopolitical substance" that Agamben, borrowing from Primo Levi, calls the *Muselmann* (Muslim). Agamben employs this term to refer to inmates who subsisted on the brink of death, retaining a merely biological urge to persist after losing their will to live. As "remnants" of existence more inhuman than human, their emaciated bodies document the complete victory of power over the body. Agamben figures their extreme degradation as the touchstone for a new ethics of witnessing in the age of biopower.[85]

For Agamben, then, the National Socialist death sentence folds an older model of territorial sovereignty into what Foucault calls biopower. Thus a sovereign power, which "defines itself essentially as the right over life and death" that it exerts asymmetrically "above all from the side of death," intersects with a biopower "which can be expressed by the formula *to make live and to let die.*"[86] "In Hitler's Germany," Agamben asserts, "an unprecedented absolutization of the biopower to *make live* intersects with an equally absolute generalization of the sovereign power to *make die,* such that biopolitics coincides immediately with thanatopolitics."[87] The modernization of the ancient power to take life or let live proves Arendt's critique of the "Rights of Man" that laid the groundwork for a situation in which de facto biological existence remains possible only through de jure citizenship. This facilitates precariousness, since citizenship can always be taken away and, in any case, it remains inextricably bound up with bioeconomic safety nets—work, health, shelter, and mobility—that can suddenly drop out.[88] This is why, for Agamben, "Auschwitz marks the end and the ruin of every ethics of dignity and conformity to a norm. The bare life to which human beings were reduced neither demands nor conforms to anything. It itself is the only norm; it is absolutely immanent. And 'the ultimate sentiment of belonging to the species' cannot in any sense be a kind of dignity."[89]

Lyotard and Agamben intersect in their recognition that the blind spot of humanist notions of dignity is made manifest by the Nationalist Socialist eradication of the Jews' citizenship as a precondition of their species-belonging. The juridical subject codifies a belief in the ideal of fair and equal treatment before the law that, in practice, applies exclusively to citizens who can claim the right to protection by the state. Since the *we* who make this claim also determine the criteria for membership, the possibility of justice is tautologically restricted *avant la lettre*. The idea of universal justice is thus complicit with a disavowed selection that predesignates and produces a disembodied collective identity for the subjects under jurisdiction by negating others.[90]

Lyotard's analysis pinpoints the slippery border between the *we* presupposed by the concept of civil society and the arbitrary totalitarian logic that abusively exploits the ambiguity of this presupposition. Yet it is unclear whether Lyotard's repudiation of this "property" of the social-juridical subject does not posit an alternative human proper with its concurrent, albeit negated, first-person-plural pronoun that would never be "stabilized in a name for *we*," but would always be "undone before being constituted." By his own admission, Lyotard's new *we* would be "founded upon the ruins of positive reason and its attendant humanism."[91] It would not only negate the possibility of philosophical prescriptions (and moral judgments); the postmodernist *we* would also disassemble the conditions of obligation to civil or moral laws.

Yet if crisis is a symptom of the impossibility of guaranteeing consensus on the status of an object, then Lyotard's *we* points to a still more vexing inconsistency in his thinking about the conditions and limits of judgment, which has implications for the constitution of the Holocaust as an object of postmodernist philosophy. In keeping with the discourse of impasse that Lyotard favors, his reflection on the death camps precipitates a crisis of legitimation that cannot be resolved. This discourse converts the fracturing effects of a traumatic event into an ineluctable problem for philosophy. Henceforth the traumatic incommensurability of the death camps is universalized as a condition of skeptical thought and "Auschwitz" is emptied of its specificity.

"After Lyotard," so to speak, it becomes difficult to validate survivor testimony as a narration of persecution, murder, and bereavement. The narrative tendency of testimony is potentially troubling for Lyotard after Adorno because conventional emplotments of experience reify the death camps while mobilizing their speculative trace.[92] Lyotard's expropriation of experience would ostensibly save testimony from this pitfall, since it is not only consistent with Adorno's aesthetics, but also with the French postmodernist's repudiation of the humanist subject along with the hegemonic grand narratives to which that subject has given rise.

To summarize, in the first section I focused on the ways in which Adorno's periodization, "after Auschwitz," enables Lyotard to link the death camps with the philosophical "trauma" of skepticism. Hence the negative reason proper to skepticism is the precursor of the representational negativity proper to "Auschwitz" as a historical sign. Such a configuration cements the connection between "Auschwitz" and the other European nations that bore witness to and collaborated with the Nazis' genocidal policies and "implicitly reinforces contemporary culture's identity and history as exclusively Western and European."[93] An additional problem is that Adorno's meditations "after Auschwitz" and Lyotard's citation of them periodize Western thought into the "before" and "after" of a traumatic chasm, which spatializes time by cutting out and freezing a span of events. On an institutional level, periodizations wield the power of generic categories to regulate interpretation by demarcating related phenomena from unrelated phenomena as the contents of an object of inquiry. Adorno's "after Auschwitz" is no exception: it marks a moral and metaphysical dividing line that stipulates negative generic conventions for conducting a "properly" critical philosophy after the death camps.

In his response to "Discussions" at the "Les fins de l'homme" colloquium in 1980,[94] Derrida cautions against inadvertently reconstituting the *we* of the Western humanist standpoint that bears witness to the traumatic rupture that "Auschwitz" names as an offense to human dignity. He identifies two dangers inherent in Lyotard's speculations in that name. First, if Lyotard's reflection on "Auschwitz" is, to some extent, vulnerable to the logic of self-sameness, it is because it "risks reconstituting a kind of centrality" in the implicit *we* that Western Europeans assume in privileging "Auschwitz" as the center and negation of "their" reason. This *we* is troublesome to Derrida because it bears the potential to "consign to oblivion" or ignore "proper names other than that of 'Auschwitz' and which are just as abhorrent as it."[95] The second danger stems from seeing in the event or in the other the site of an absolute and, therefore, unrepresentable difference that would foreclose subsequent discussion. Derrida insists that it is precisely because of this absolute difference that one has "to make links historically, politically and ethically with the name, with that which absolutely refuses linkage."[96]

To fail to do so would be to naturalize the narcissism of the West that sacralizes the Holocaust as its cardinal trauma.

In fairness to Lyotard, Derrida's second criticism reiterates Lyotard's self-proclaimed agenda in *The Postmodern Condition* as well as his repeated insistence on the ineluctable demand to make such linkages. In addition, Lyotard's strategy of citing Derrida broaches the very dangers Derrida identifies. Yet there is also a strong sense in which "Discussions" "sublates" Derrida's warning by setting up Adorno's periodization as an anticipation of Derrida's posthumanist critique of metaphysics. In light of Adorno's "Meditations on Metaphysics," Derrida's deconstruction obtains a historicity as a mode of nonidentitarian thought that could only happen as a result of "Auschwitz" or, at the very least, as a result of Lyotard's dialectic. This ironic strategy does not secure Lyotard's argument against the dangers that Derrida identifies; indeed, as I will demonstrate in my analysis of *The Differend* below, Lyotard's negative apotheosis of "Auschwitz" fails to heed Adorno's warning (echoed by Derrida) against conceiving metaphysics "after the model of an absolute otherness terribly defying thought."[97]

By elevating the Jewish genocide's moral impact above experience, Lyotard treats it as an "absolute otherness" that transcends imagination, but nevertheless functions as a regulative ideal for critical philosophy as whole. Yet his failure to heed Adorno's warning may be attributed in part to the role model himself, who opens this trap when he subjects "Auschwitz" to an image prohibition that would stave off conciliatory representations of the mass murders.[98] A potential for sacralization is compounded by Adorno's revision of the aesthetic of the sublime. As I suggested in the previous chapter, Kant's emplotment of the sublime in the *Critique of Judgment* initially begins with a failure of the faculty of imagination. The individual viewer apprehends a scene whose magnitude and/or power exceeds his or her ability to synthesize a unified intuition (*Anschauung*) of the whole. The faculty of reason supersedes this deficiency in reflecting on the limits of comprehension, and the subject's recognition of reason's power compensates for the initial sense of inadequacy.[99] In Kant's conception, the sublime motivates a reflection on limits that allows the individual to affirm his or her ability to realize and transcend a negative intuition. A failure of imagination ultimately provides the occasion for a *Sinnstiftung* of and by means of reason. Adorno wants to sustain the negativity of this experience of limits without the elevation of reason that the Kantian emplotment of the sublime permits. This distinction is crucial both to an understanding of Adorno's *Aesthetic Theory* as well as Lyotard's investment in the critical and political potential of a negative sublime.

Kant's critical philosophy typically provides Lyotard with a systematic means of radicalizing the splits in the subject brought about by skepticism. If skepticism represents the "free aspect" of all philosophy, it also permits the kinds of negative judgments that transpire in the absence of criteria. For Lyotard, the contemplation of "Auschwitz" as a sublime sign of history indicates the oblique situation of a deregulated judgment when the limits of moral determination become intelligible only through a negative aesthetic response. His project thus reframes Kant's aesthetic of the sublime to open up the freedom that conditions an impossible yet unavoidable judgment.

In this section, I have focused on Lyotard's pragmatist employment of "Auschwitz" to expose the illusion of civic consensus that supports any delimitation of the human proper. By this account, the *we* that commanded the mass death of the Jews had already excluded them from the National Socialist criteria for the human. The *we* of "humanity" was consequently revealed as a tautological and deadly social abstraction. While he shares Derrida's wariness of the *we*, Lyotard's incorporation of Adorno's figuration of "Auschwitz" as the scene of the death of the beautiful death nevertheless capitulates to its seduction in the avatar of a posthumanist consensus. This is the case insofar as Lyotard's reading of Adorno does not contest a melancholic view of beautiful death that consecrates the essential dignity of humans as a "no longer" rather than a "not yet." Lyotard nevertheless seems to recognize the inescapable ambiguities that trouble his position as a posthumanist reinscription of Adorno's periodization. First, the negation of the ideal of a beautiful death does not necessarily signify the impossibility of a result; indeed, the silent, awkward consternation that the readers and witnesses of this history often evince certainly suggests another kind of result, albeit one that both Lyotard and Adorno would repudiate.[100] Second, Lyotard negates the speculative structure of experience, yet this strategy cannot avoid a reciprocal affirmation of certain post-Hegelian and presumably nontotalizing notions of experience and, specifically, those that point to the incommensurability of the death camp universe. Surely, if the "experience" of anonymous death is excluded from analogous structures of experience, then it would not be possible to discuss this "para-empiricism," "Auschwitz," without recourse, by way of negation, to the language of experience. Third, to read "Auschwitz" as a model of negative dialectics is to constitute it as the object of philosophical praxis that reflects a dialectical synthesis between philosophy and history. Logically speaking, if "Auschwitz" "realizes" a trauma to the speculative inflicted on it by skepticism, then the death camps are merely an aftereffect of philosophy's more originary "wound of nihilism."

In contrast with *The Differend*, which provides a thorough critique of the proper name, the problem of reference receives comparatively cursory attention in "Discussions," where Lyotard stresses the ways in which the anonymity of mass death defies Hegel's view of names as place-markers that anchor memories. In opposition to the Hegelian view and in keeping with Adorno, Lyotard constructs "Auschwitz" in the era of its 'after' thought as a determinately negative figure for the anonymous, bureaucratic, and instrumental erasure of proper names that took place in the camps. This construction respects Adorno's sensitivity about protecting the particular against a thematizing usurpation. Figured negatively as an "anonym," "Auschwitz" cannot be incorporated into the unity of a universal. It must, therefore, remain unintelligible for an aggrandizing positive reason.

The danger of this abstraction raises the question of how to outmaneuver Faurisson's negation of the gas chambers. For if the normative structure of moral judgment presupposes consensus on the status of a referent, Lyotard's challenge will then be to defend survivor testimony without reconstituting a univocal *we*. Lyotard directly counters Faurisson's denial of the gas chambers in *The Differend*, which might be read as an attempt to address Derrida's caution about the danger of reconstituting a humanist *we* through a politicized aesthetics.

Faurisson's disbelief is, for Lyotard, a sign that the exteriority of the event of anonymous mass death precludes it from being understood or validated on the basis of empirical and ontological concepts of experience. Lyotard consequently reflects on the conditions for defending the validity of testimony about mass murder in the gas chambers when the language of experience is inadequate to represent it. This critique is taken up from the vantage point of his analysis of reference and, specifically, *designation* as the affiliation between names and referents. The chapter entitled "The Referent, the Name" is devoted to exploring the problematic character of designation as it bears on the authority of survivor testimony and knowledge about the gas chambers. Since the experiences of death camp survivors comprise the implicit referent of testimony, this chapter is a crucial extension of the critique of experience launched in "Discussions."

In turning now to that chapter, I want to focus on Lyotard's use of aesthetics as a response to the question of how knowledge about the death camps is and will continue to be possible. As I have already begun to argue above, his debts to the critical aesthetics of Kant and Adorno incline Lyotard to seek the answer to this question in the subject rather than in the object of testimony—that is to say, in the reception rather than in the referent of accounts about mass death. Following my analysis of Lyotard's discussion of reference, I will consider how Lyotard "disciplines" the Holocaust by formalizing the conditions of its moral and aesthetic reception. Even if the experience of the death camps is "unrepresentable," Lyotard must nevertheless assume an audience that is able to attest to this limit.

Affective Evidence

In *The Differend*, Lyotard dwells on the problems that the experiential referent of testimony poses for historical verification in pragmatist terms. The perceived "truth value" of testimony is a function of the competition among different aims and their respective genres. This competition suggests that the judgment of testimony cannot be reduced to a quest for a "proper" approach to the true, and, accordingly, not in terms of a "correct" mimesis of the historical referent as such.[101] Rather, Lyotard does away with the prospect of judging the empirical and ontological status of testimony by foregrounding its rhetorical stakes and aesthetic effects.

To a certain extent, Lyotard's general preference for aporias of judgment reflects a traditionally modernist recalcitrance against the rhetoric of clarity and its positivistic progeny, a sensibility that also permeates Adorno's and Derrida's writings. One might say that Derrida has made it his particular forte to disarticulate intelligibility as a function of the referent's presumed unity and stasis. In this vein, his formulation of *différance* to stress the historicity and variability of meaning subverts the metaphysical desire for a designation that would be ontologically stable. It is interesting to consider this malleable dimension of intelligibility in relation to Hegel's provision in the *Science of Logic* that the synthesis produced by positive reason is the condition of understanding. This provision suggests that positive reason translates into a process of fixing a nexus of fluctuating aspects so that they might assume intelligibility as a determinate referent; it therefore presages disciplinary invocations of the object proper that are intended to curtail the range of references to it.

In the introduction, I remarked that Faurisson disavows, on naively positivistic grounds, the validity of survivor testimony as evidence for the existence of the death camps. On the other side of the coin, it is worth exploring how negationist views such as Faurisson's may compel disciplinary moves among Holocaust scholars to shore up their object of inquiry against morally offensive revisions. The object proper is at work here as an idealized composite of facts, images, and ideas that functions as the imaginary locus of a field of inquiry to orient and regulate interpretation. Disciplinary mimesis comprises attempts to approximate the nexus of concepts and images that "belong to" an object's historically sedimented field. Of course, these differentiations do not simply transpire *within* a field, insofar as the "field" itself must be "cut out" from the flux of possible, virtual, and intersecting fields. For this reason, the delimitation of objects of inquiry virtually spatializes their contents, which nevertheless change over time.

Lyotard's consideration of designation is explicitly informed not only by Wittgenstein's conception of language games, but also by Saul Kripke's examination of the proper name's *rigidity* or relative invariability across multiple contexts.[102] Kripke provides Lyotard with a basis for arguing that the relation between names and referents is not necessary in the logical sense; it therefore cannot establish a stable foundation for truth and understanding. Among Kripke's significant contributions to twentieth-century philosophy is his critique of essentialism as a view of identity that posits the properties of objects as essential—in other words, as necessary predicates. For Kripke, a property cannot "meaningfully be held to be essential or accidental to an object independently of its description."[103] Proper names do not mark referents understood as stable, invariable contents, but instead "rigidly designate" a certain object wherever it exists.[104]

Lyotard's analysis of reference in the context of testimony extends the analytic critique of essentialism to ontological views of designation that associate the rigidity of proper names with the stability of their referents and, in the process, posit the "truth" of an object as a stable and extractable "substance." "Truth" is figured as a "property" of objects rather than a provisionally attributed value; it would therefore not be affected by resituating the referent in an alternate universe of phrases. From an essentialist standpoint, granting the reality of the gas chambers would simply be a matter of recognizing the "property rights" of Holocaust survivors as eyewitnesses whose sentences "contain" a "truth value" that is exchangeable like goods and is analogous to a private possession that "belongs to" that survivor.[105] Lyotard's Marxist leanings compel him to draw on Kripke's examination of rigidity to deconstruct this proprietary ideology that ontologizes the essential properties of referents.

The analysis carried out in "The Referent, the Name" deconstructs this proprietary figure by interrogating the conditions of possibility for perceiving a necessary filiation between referents and names and by stressing the formal and rhetorical contingencies of historical denomination. For Lyotard, there is no necessary ontological or logical link between the various phrases at play in designation. Instead, it must be assumed that these phrases (ostensive, descriptive, and nominative) are heterogeneous and that the rules for their association are subject to the context and generic goals by which they are provisionally framed.

Kripke speaks of clusters of descriptions that comprise the content of a referent associated with a given name. This content is, by implication, variable insofar as descriptions foreground certain aspects of objects above and against others. Disciplinary reason defends the fiction of an object proper based on the presupposition that stable referents are the condition of understanding and communication. Lyotard opposes this mimetic presupposition by repudiating correspondence theories of truth that adopt the verisimilitude between the referent and its respective description as the determining criterion of the referent's reality. According to Lyotard, designation "is not, nor can it be, the adequation of the *logos* to the being of the existent."[106] The "properness" of a name does not derive from any ontological basis in its referent. Indeed, the ontological argument is false, according to Lyotard, since "nothing can be said about reality that does not presuppose it."[107]

Lyotard's disavowal of the ontological argument echoes Pierre Vidal-Naquet's "A Paper Eichmann," where the historian responds to Faurisson's denial.[108] Vidal-Naquet has observed that Holocaust revisionists such as Faurisson, "use a 'non-ontological' proof in their inquiry into the question of the gas chambers."[109] Their arguments are, in contrast, manifestly empiricist in assuming that seeing is a sufficient condition for verification. This belief is shared by those who value survivor testimony as an authoritative source of "eyewitness" evidence. For Lyotard, neither empiricist nor ontological perspectives offer viable approaches to the problem of verifying history.

His dialogue with Vidal-Naquet provides Lyotard with a pivotal thesis. He suggests that the negationist repudiation of the gas chambers' reality "conforms to the annihilation of the referent's reality during verification procedures."[110] By this account, Faurisson's denial of the gas chambers presumes that death is a reality that can be seen and named. Citing Kripke, Lyotard emphasizes that this stance supposes that reality has a proper name, an assumption that undermines the authority of eyewitness verification insofar as proper names cannot, themselves, be "seen." The name is not an object of cognition (that is, a sensory event to be described). What is more, a cognitive phrase that describes an object would not be sufficient to establish the "properness" of a name as a measure of its referent's reality. Descriptions cannot be validated in the absence of ostensive phrases that show or display the object at stake. The "properness" of designation is intelligible only by virtue of the name's exclusivity and invariability in marking itself from one phrase to the next.

Extrapolating from Kripke, Lyotard speaks of the proper name's *quasi-deictic rigidity* across a variety of signifying chains. A *deictic* is a marker for an ostensive phrase that shows the object at stake. In Lyotard's words, deictics relate "the instances of the universe presented by the phrase in which they are placed back to a 'current' spatio-temporal origin so named 'I-here-now.' " So defined, deictics serve to designate reality, inasmuch as they "designate their object as an extra-linguistic permanence, as a 'given.' " However, they cannot attest to the permanence of this object conceived as an "origin" of a phrase universe. This "origin" would be tied to the universe of a particular phrase that deictics mark, which appears and disappears with the phrase to which it belongs.[111]

By extension, a name functions *like* a deictic in that it situates the referent, the addressor, and the addressee of any phrase in relation to an "as-if-here." Insofar as the name "remains fixed throughout a sequence of phrases," it should be distinguished from "full" deictics that change from phrase to phrase.[112] Hence, if description cannot "free itself from denomination" and "reference cannot be reduced to sense," this is because the name is "a linchpin between an ostensive phrase with its deictics and any given phrase with its sense or senses."[113]

In remarking the name's twin capacity to designate and be signified, Lyotard is also careful to note the implications of its function as a rigid designator. This function suggests an independence from the ostensives and other phrases that situate its referent. Ultimately, however, the name's capacity to endow its referent with reality remains contingent, since "phrases belonging to heterogeneous families can affect the referent of a single proper name by situating it upon different instances in the universes they present."[114] This is to suggest that the referent of a name changes from phrase to phrase; a name's rigidity therefore has no intrinsic relation to the referent's qualities:

> There is no question of validating the truth of name: a name is
> not a property attributed to a referent by means of a description
> (a cognitive phrase). It is merely an index which, in the case of
> the anthroponym, for example, designates one and only one human
> being. The properties attributed to the human being designated by
> this name could be validated, but not his or her name. The name
> adds no property to him or her. Even if initially many names have
> a signification they lose it, and they must lose it.[115]

The name's status as a rigid designator suggests that it cannot be determined by its sense; but neither is this sense furnished by the name. Instead, designation, as Lyotard understands it, is the *effect* of a learned association between a name and various phrases comprising its contents. He contends that learning names involves situating or perceiving them "in relation to other names by means of phrases."[116] Because learning involves perception, this claim raises the question of how Lyotard will theorize denomination without resorting to the category of experience.

As I have already indicated, Lyotard views experience as problematic insofar as it "can be described only by means of a phenomenological dialectic"[117] that negates what it does not synthesize. In the negationists' eyes, it is precisely these negated aspects that controvert the truth of survivor testimony, since an "incomplete" account is partial and thus "false" according to a naively positivistic logic; it may even be contradicted by those aspects that the "finitude" of any witness's perspective prevents him or her from perceiving. His or her testimony's authority will therefore depend on the rigidity of the proper names that anchor his or her account and situate it in relation to other testimonies.

Lyotard observes that the referent of a proper name is strongly determined "in terms of its location among networks of names and of relations between names (worlds)." At the same time, the sense of a name is weakly determined, because it appears in multiple, heterogeneous contexts.[118] This paradox follows from two distinctions that inform Lyotard's approach to the problem of historical verification. Following Frege, Lyotard distinguishes between sense (*Sinn*) and reference (*Bedeutung*) in order to stress the difference between logic and cognition. In the logical genre, sense is presented by well-formed expressions (propositions) that occupy places in "logical space." These places are determined by means of truth tables that map possible relations between elementary propositions. By virtue of their formal necessity, Lyotard observes that logical propositions delimit what is possible, but they cannot determine what is real. Only the cognitive genre has a bearing on whether a knowable reality corresponds to a given proposition that is a logical expression. This is to assert that sense is merely a formally necessary *possibility* that is not to be conflated with reality. Ultimately, a referent can only be verified through a cognition that presupposes the referent's logical possibility.[119]

The distinction between sense and reference informs the relation between *objects of history* and *objects of perception* that organizes Lyotard's understanding of historical denomination. The object of history is the referent of the proper name arising from a world "which is a fairly stable complex of nominatives." The object of perception, on the other hand, is determined by "a field of loose complexes of ostensives and deictics."[120] Stated differently, the perceptual object is the referent of an ostensive phrase, while the historical object is the referent of a nominative phrase. Yet this distinction is not absolute: to learn a historical name is to situate it in relation to other names by means of phrases that constitute a system of cross-references. It is this system of interrelated references that presents a "world" wherein other names have senses attached to them that can be fixed and verified through ostensive phrases. Hence, ostensives and their respective perceptual objects also ground the networks of names that make up history.

This insight formally elaborates the commonplace that perception conditions history. It is, nevertheless, crucial to Lyotard's argument about the problem of validating the experience of a witness as a historical referent. In dialogue with Wittgenstein, Lyotard emphasizes that the ostensive is the "showing of the case" that also alludes to what is not the case. The negative dimension of ostensives is, thus, a feature of the partiality and finitude of perception that prevents a witness from seeing and attesting to "everything." The reality to which he or she bears witness is, instead, "shadowed" by those negated aspects, those senses which he or she cannot show, but which, nevertheless, remain (logically) possible. Lyotard observes that the perceptive field and the historical world are both "hollowed out" by the negation that "is entailed respectively (and differently) by the shown and the named."[121]

Wittgenstein figures the modality of logical possibility as a *Spielraum* (the room or range that a proposition leaves open) bordered by tautology on one side and contradiction on the other. He thereby establishes a metaphoric space for the "swarm of possible senses of indeterminate quantity and quality" that inhabit the "hollow" between the named and shown referent. Insofar as this modality is "axed on the future," Wittgenstein's hollow becomes Lyotard's figure for "time considered as the condition of modalizations."[122] In the sensible field, changes of meaning "happen" over time as alternating aspects of an object are differentially manifest, recognized, and negated in successive moments of perception.

Wittgenstein's *Spielraum* and *hollow* provide spatial figures for the flux of simultaneous and successive interpretations that affect the contours of a referent. In this manner, he "half-opens the door of logic onto phenomenology" insofar as he transfers "into the logical order the 'hollow' which, in the (sensible) field, envelops the referents of ostensives."[123] Both history and perception are negatively determined by this hollow that also affects the integrity of the witnessing "I." Language, space, and time displace and attenuate the content of this "I" as a marker of positionality.

Lyotard's reflections on the "I" owe their impetus to his critical reading of Hegel's *Phenomenology of Spirit* wherein the metaphysical split between substance and appearance is dialectically resolved. The resulting synthesis is the mediation of the negated by the posited and vice versa. Indeed, if "[d]ialectical logic maintains the experience and the subject of the experience within the relative," as Lyotard claims, then it is abetting this structural negation.[124] Such relativity yields a potential basis for critical reflection; however, it is a potential that is undermined by the structure of progressive synthesis with which Hegel's phenomenology of consciousness and self-consciousness is inextricably bound. In this respect, then, the phenomenological concept of experience "presupposes that of an I which forms itself (*Bildung*) by gathering in the properties of things that come up (events) and which constitutes reality by effectuating their temporal synthesis." It consequently endows experiences "with the property of accumulation (*Resultat, Erinnerung*) and places them in a continuity with the final absolute."[125]

Lyotard's perspective on Hegel rehearses the principal tenets of the symptomatic amalgam of phenomenology, existentialism, and humanism that Derrida identifies with a post-Hegelian critique of the transcendental subject.[126] Although Hegel was himself a critic of Kantian idealism, his narrative about the synthetic development of consciousness in the *Phenomenology* nevertheless spectralizes the ideal of a sovereign subject who orchestrates a totality of negations and supersessions. By limiting the perceptual agency of the witness, Lyotard attests to his desire to distance himself from this specter. For Lyotard, the notion of the "absolute witness" facilitates the impossible ideal of a fully present sovereign consciousness capable of representing perceptions as a unified totality. His objection to the phenomenological discourse of experience is that it presupposes the self-identity of an "I" for whom events would be (mere) phenomena. This self-identical presence is, then, the condition permitting "the subordination of the question of truth to the doctrine of evidence," which requires that an object first be verified before it can exist — in other words, that seeing is believing.[127]

To counteract this fallacy, Lyotard asserts that the "I" and the idea of experience attached to it are not philosophically "necessary for the description of reality."[128] Hegel's *Phenomenology of Spirit* demonstrates how the "I" at the center of experience is itself merely a deictic that "has no import outside the phrase universe that it currently designates."[129] From one moment or phrase to the next, there is "no guarantee that I am the same," because the contingency of phrasing enjoins that a subject is "not the unity of 'his' or 'her' experience."[130] In other words, experience is not a stable referent that can be agreed upon or verified, and, as Lyotard concludes, "reality does not result from an experience."[131]

This last point furthers a line of argument introduced in "Discussions" where Lyotard objected to the totalizing and synthetic character of the "speculative" formulation of experience. In keeping with his prejudice against this configuration, Lyotard claims that an experience-based description does not have "a *philosophical value* because it does not question its presuppositions (the I or the self, the rules of speculative logic)."[132] The implication is that the category of experience is insufficiently critical to fulfill Lyotard's standards of philosophical rigor. Such an argument raises the question as to whether Lyotard also holds witnesses accountable to philosophical criteria that would require them to acknowledge the finitude of their descriptions.

Lyotard has already demonstrated that empirical presuppositions "are not necessary for the assertion that a referent is real."[133] Moreover, attempts to represent an experience are necessarily partial and inconsistent (i.e., subject to the ephemerality of deictic markers and the relativity of the possible). The survivor as a witness is consequently caught in a double bind that enjoins him or her to admit this partiality and at the same time attest to the credibility of his or her account. The only option left is for the witness to establish credibility by associating the various, transitional deictics of his or her experience with the quasi-deictic rigidity of the name in accordance with the rules of denomination, but insofar as perception is the condition of such associations, his or her experiences as an eyewitness are always subject to the contingency of future perceptions and interpretations.

To the extent that the witness anticipates this future, he or she confronts the negation inherent in the modality of the possible. Yet Lyotard cautions that "we" must not metaphorize the negation "at the heart of testimony" "into the experience of a subject, but rather as a linking of phrases" regulated by genres.[134] These genres provide the rules for linkage in keeping with particular aims. The evaluation of testimony presents particular problems for this process, according to Lyotard, insofar as the rules for verifying it are incommensurable with the rules of justice. This incommensurability enunciates the empirical derivation of testimony that, paradoxically, cannot be empirically verified by others. By arguing that testimony narrates an experience that cannot be fixed, displayed, or validated as a referent, Lyotard subtends commonsense notions of evidence. Moreover, he suggests that it would be impossible to validate an experience of events on moral grounds that require consensus about its status as a referent in relation to the law.

The implication of Lyotard's analysis of designation is that the empirical referent of testimony cannot be presupposed by any paradigm of justice or validity. Neither should "truth" be viewed as an ontologically predicated "property" of the witness who testifies, since his or her identity is subject to the flux of interpretations and the heterogeneity of phrasing, and there is no means of confirming the experience from which his or her testimony derives. By revealing the sociopolitical indeterminacy of testimonial referents, Lyotard demonstrates the impossibility of judging experience.

Ultimately, then, Lyotard disarticulates ontological and empirical views of experience in order to stress that the interpretation of testimony is subject to a vacillating horizon of recognition and negation. He consequently opens an aporia not only for historical verification, but also for judgments of reality in general. This aporia troubles (albeit abstractly) the litigation of crimes whose representation is fraught with "disputed phrases." Lyotard calls this situation of dispute a *differend* (*différend*), defined as "the case where the plaintiff is divested of the means to argue and becomes for that reason a victim. If the addressor, the addressee, and the sense of the testimony are neutralized," Lyotard writes, "then everything takes place as if there were no damages." In sum, "a case of differend between two parties takes place when the 'regulation' of the conflict that opposes them is done in the idiom of one of the parties while the wrong suffered by the other is not signified in that idiom."[135] Justice is held in abeyance when a plaintiff's inability to prove a wrong is the product of an asymmetrical power relation whereby the empowered party disavows or is too incompetent to recognize the intelligibility of a victim's claim. By failing to understand and validate the plaintiff's testimony, the judge silences his or her complaint and thereby redoubles his or her victimization.[136] For Lyotard, this silence is a sign of the injustice which results from a judgment that expropriates the victim's authority.

Naomi Mandel distinguishes between "the inability of language to adequately convey experience—an inability which pertains to any experience, but which is rendered exceptionally poignant when 'experience' is suffering, horror, trauma, and pain—and the rhetorical evocation of that inability. . . ."[137] Lyotard's analysis of designation capitalizes on this poignancy in linking the negativity and flux of experience with the finitude of the witness as a subject of knowledge whose pained silence represents a withdrawal from the demand of speech that requires him or her to find an appropriate expression for an indeterminate and perhaps disavowed knowledge.

Lyotard responds to Faurisson's denial of the gas chambers by enumerating the silences of survivors who feel prevented, unable, or incompetent to speak. In these cases,

[s]ilence does not indicate which instance is denied, it signals the denial of one or more of the instances. The survivors remain silent, and it can be understood 1) that the situation in question (the case) is not the addressee's business (he or she lacks the competence, or he or she is not worthy of being spoken to about it, etc.); or 2) that it never took place (this is what Faurisson understands); or 3) that there is nothing to say about it (the situation is senseless,

inexpressible); or 4) that it is not the survivors' business to be talking about it (they are not worthy, etc.). Or, several of these negations together.[138]

For Lyotard, though silence is an index that one or more of the addressor, addressee, signification, and referent instances of a phrase have been neutralized or denied, it does not necessarily negate the reality of the event as Faurisson has supposed; it might, instead, point to the limits or "fragility" of empathy, as Carolyn J. Dean has labeled it,[139] because addressees cannot competently hear, understand, or respond to the testimony. Silence may also signal a witness's sense of the inadequacy of language to transmit the inexhaustible depth of horror attending a disaster that destroyed communities and devastated conventional frameworks. Ultimately, then, it may indicate a survivor's guilt about living in the aftermath of murdered relatives, friends, neighbors, and even bunker mates in the camps whose bread or shoes were stolen in the night.

Lyotard employs the term *differend* to mark "the unstable state and instant of language wherein something which must be able to be put into phrases cannot yet be. This state includes silence, which is a negative phrase, but it also calls upon phrases which are in principle possible."[140] The sign of the differend is a feeling, one that arises from the negativity or "indetermination of meanings left in abeyance (*en souffrance*)."[141] This feeling is the index of "our" recognition "that what remains to be phrased exceeds what [existing idioms] can presently phrase." It subsequently becomes "our" task by way of literature, philosophy, and politics "to bear witness to differends by finding idioms for them."[142]

Lyotard asserts that a differend is disclosed by "what one ordinarily calls a feeling," yet this feeling "does not arise from an experience felt by a subject. It can, moreover, not be felt."[143] As Ron Katwan observes, this characterization renders incoherent "the idea that affects are private mental experiences taking place within the mental space of the subject" or, indeed, that "such feelings are *our* experiences."[144] Instead, the "alarm" of painful feeling must be witnessed as a sign that "something 'asks' to be put into phrases, and suffers from the wrong of not being able to be put into phrases right away."[145] It is significant that Lyotard employs scare quotes around *asks* (*demande*) to indicate his distance from this verb, though not around *suffers* (*souffre*), since both personify the silence that results from injustice—silence cannot literally "ask" or "suffer." This personification is symptomatic of the performative contradiction produced by Lyotard's evacuation of the subject of experience in the context of an aesthetic argument, for if the sign of a differend is a feeling, then the question becomes how this feeling can become intelligible in the absence of experience.[146] Lyotard himself poses the question, "[H]ow can it be established that [this feeling] is or is not felt?"[147]

His answer to this question is evasive: the feeling arises from a silence and this silence is "not a state of mind," but a sign.[148] This explanation deflects the problem of how he can posit this sign *as such* without presupposing a subject capable of (or historically prone to) certain aesthetic responses, since signs are perceived and interpreted by definition.[149] Lyotard's segregation of feeling from experience puts into play a potential differend, which evolves from his overly strict adherence to the generic aims of antifoundationalist discourse that he delimits and then imposes on survivors as well as on those who hear or read Holocaust testimony. As I argue above, this genre is defined by a post-Hegelian and posthumanist distaste for acritical formulations of experience that revolve around a voluntaristic, sovereign, or unified consciousness. His skeptical positioning leads Lyotard to reduce experience to a speculative, synthetic logic, which then propels him to reject it *tout court*.

In addition, Lyotard has suggested that the negativity of Auschwitz produces "a feeling that does not arise from an experience," but from a silence indicating that "phrases are in abeyance of their becoming event."[150] This feeling is, then, "the suffering of this abeyance." It announces the wrong committed against the victims (both the survivors and the dead) that preempts their knowledge of the gas chambers. Silence is, consequently, a measure of a veridical default to satisfy the positivist's "cognitive rules for the establishment of historical reality and for the validation of its sense."[151]

This anticipated "failure" of testimony resonates in a milieu that deploys "Auschwitz" to literalize the poststructuralist figure of a "lost" or "missing" referent: "[W]ith Auschwitz, something new has happened in history (which can only be a sign and not a fact), which is that the facts, the testimonies which bore the traces of *here*'s and *now*'s, the documents which indicated the sense or senses of the facts, and the names, finally the possibility of various kinds of phrases whose conjunction makes reality, all this has been destroyed as much as possible."[152] The Nazis' destruction of the evidence of their crimes thus succeeds in imposing (still another) silence on knowledge. Despite this imposition, Lyotard contends that "our" silence in response to the "Final Solution" is not the same as a forgetting; it is, instead, a sign that language is not "our" instrument and that "our" understanding founders over an "indetermination of meaning left in abeyance."[153]

It is worth contemplating whether Lyotard's posthumanist position disallows for the prospect of agency altogether. In the case of survivors, for example, Lyotard argues that what "is subject to threats is not an identifiable individual, but the ability to speak or to keep quiet";[154] however, this abstract "ability" to speak or not to speak is meaningless apart from its contrast to some minimal notion of agency that distinguishes speakers in general from silenced victims. Here I assume that threats to communication are only intelligible for speakers who must face them. Otherwise, as Ewa Ziarek proposes, it will also be impossible to begin to theorize the displacement from the abject "non-position of the differend to the accusative position of the obligated subject."[155] For this reason, while I appreciate his attention to aesthetic experience as a venue for the moral affect that conditions (sympathetic) belief and spurs a desire for justice, Lyotard's posthumanist stance is too stringent. The agenda to circumvent the fallacious ideal of a sovereign subject who controls his or her memories does not logically require Lyotard to jettison all conceptions of experience as a basis for giving or hearing testimony, as if antifoundationalist skepticism is the final court of any appeal to belief.

Such a figuration is counteracted by Lyotard's desire to bear witness to all differends and not only those attached to the proper name *Auschwitz*. Lyotard's politicization of Adorno's negative aesthetics requires a subject who remains critically and imaginatively attuned to the imminence of injustice and therefore believes in it without seeing it. He rightly urges us to validate the effects of traumatic latency and dissociation upon the representation of devastating events along with the gaps that typically mark perception and memory in general. Borrowing his terms, the "manifold senses" attaching to historical names cannot be represented as a totality. I would nevertheless ask whether recognizing the witness's finitude entails the assumption that such experience is, *intrinsically and necessarily*, unrepresentable. More to the point, what is the rhetorical value of insisting that the immediate experience of violent events always exceeds their representations in contexts that do not involve arguing with a real or imagined historian, judge, scientist, or bureaucrat who promulgates a naively positivist standard of completeness and consistency for affirming the veridical status of testimony?

Lyotard's "unrepresentability" thesis performs two rhetorical functions: first, it enables Lyotard to protect the traumatic specificity of the gas chambers against a positivistic and empiricist will toward presence; second, it provides him with an opportunity to theorize the aesthetic conditions of the Holocaust's reception as a trauma to and of language. In the final analysis, it remains obscure how theorizing this aesthetic as a "para-experience" does not ultimately concede a negative ontological dimension to the silence surrounding "Auschwitz." This concession is implicit in Lyotard's citation of Plato who endows silence with an ontological status: "Language is the sign that one does not know the being of the existent. When one knows it, one is the existent, and that's silence."[156] The Platonic opposition between language and being compels mimesis as a "compromise." Plato finds that mimesis is deceitful when it takes the form of idolatry, yet as simulacrum, it "is also a signpost on the path to the true, to the 'proper.'" For this reason, mimesis as verisimilitude should be regulated, according to Plato, for whom "[t]here needs to be good *typoi*, good print keys that give appropriate simulacra."[157]

Lyotard presumably models these typoi in his response to Faurisson's denial of the gas chambers. Lyotard's negative aesthetic is intended to inspire the addressees of testimony to acknowledge the silences undermining our powers to judge and verify traumatic events. Yet it is doubtful that such an aesthetic could mitigate the injustice that failures in language bring to pass, for if, as Lyotard states, silence "does not indicate which instance is denied, it signals the denial of one or more of the instances,"[158] then he must propose a method for determining which instance to reinstate in order to reverse the differend in question.

Derrida observes that "by privileging the example of Auschwitz and the debate about revisionism" in *The Differend*, Lyotard "problematizes the idea of God as absolute witness."[159] Derrida's remark raises the question as to whether, for Lyotard, the discipline of skeptical philosophy takes the place of God on whose behalf the philosopher himself attests. This problem emerges in Lyotard's stylized endeavor to circumvent the resurgence of a unified author-subject. His recourse to an epigrammatic format of numbered paragraphs cites and potentially parodies the genre of philosophical discourse that appears to expunge traces of its author's subjectivity while offsetting the image of a fluid argument. Ironically, however, it is precisely through this asubjective stylistic device that the absent, judging, and navigating subject reemerges in the echo among formally similar instances of paradox that culminate in "The Sign of History." Regarding this final chapter of *The Differend*, my suspicion is that Lyotard's return to Kant by way of the sublime historical sign might permit a veiled return of the Hegelian result as the philosophical *we* of authorship that tacitly realizes the evacuated seat of judgment.

This performative contradiction reflects the fraught synthesis of Kant and Wittgenstein that organizes Lyotard's aporetics of judgment. Richard Beardsworth notes that Lyotard repudiates the subject implied by Kant's division between the domains of cognition, description, and prescription, because it anticipates the analogical finalization of the differences figured in this partition.[160] While Lyotard wants to retain the implications of Kant's critical philosophy, he must struggle to avoid slipping into an idealist nostalgia for a subject whose faculties could be reunified in aesthetic experience. Lyotard sidesteps the danger of resurrecting the subject of transcendental idealism by translating the Kantian faculties into a Wittgensteinian vocabulary of incommensurable phrase regimens. Yet this strategy also permits him surreptitiously to occupy the empty place of the judging subject who "navigates" their respective domains and thus maps the very splits in knowledge that Derrida, in contrast, might blur.

Lyotard observes that the only way one could "make a 'beautiful death' out of "Auschwitz" death . . . is by means of a rhetoric."[161] His own rhetoric nevertheless translates Adorno's stance on Auschwitz as the ultimate denunciation of a reifying culture into a sacralization of the absent referent. Despite his investment in Wittgensteinian notions of language, Lyotard's response to Faurisson paradoxically betrays a hint of the "unknowable" *Ding an sich*, the thing in itself, whose contents cannot, by Kant's definition, be empirically verified (which is to say, Lyotard escapes the Hegelian frying pan by returning to the Kantian fire). In stressing the "inadequacy" of language to represent the gas chambers and the experience of surviving the death camps as a critical reproof to (Faurisson's) naive positivism, Lyotard figures the event of mass death, not as a phenomenon, but as a noumenon that marks the limits of sensible knowing and signification. Following Adorno, Lyotard assumes that the mass murders in the gas chambers subtend conventional emplotments of experience and therefore remain "unrepresentable" above and beyond any other nontraumatic historical events (that also do not have witnesses or leave behind ostensible traces). Adorno thus provides Lyotard with a new genre for converting the moral shock aroused by the gas chambers into an aesthetic form that preserves the traumatic aura of the death camps as a philosophical-historical sign. "Auschwitz" is a figure for the effacement of those shot or gassed millions who cannot be brought back. Though this figuration is intended to expose the limits of representation and judgment, it renders the meaning of the "Final Solution" paradigmatic for Western moral crisis in general and thereby veils the victims' suffering in a negative aura. Adorno's invocation of "Auschwitz" to enunciate the nightmare implications of a totally reified society hereby assumes an immemorial centrality in Lyotard's writings at the risk of being reified in its turn once it is deployed to set the disciplinary protocols of post-Holocaust philosophy.

Lyotard evokes an image of the shades of the exterminated, who "continue to wander in their indeterminacy" after their right to express the wrongs against them was extinguished with their lives.[162] He hears their silence as a summons to recognize and to ameliorate the injustice of (ineluctably?) inadequate communication—to right the wrong committed against the murdered by instituting new addressees, addressors, significations, and referents. Paradoxically, despite the Wittgensteinian claim that "we" do not employ language, according to Lyotard, "we" must nevertheless attempt to answer his summons by reversing differends.[163] Lost in his posthumanist Adorno is Lyotard's stipulation that the name *Auschwitz* forbids a synthesis of a *we* as its result.

This *we* haunts Lyotard's moves to sidestep the normative power of the aesthetics he outlines, which formalizes particular moral feelings for a virtual community of respondents. It is in this respect that Lyotard's post-Hegelian critique of experience cannot forgo the promise of a *sensus communis* as a politicized aesthetic result. For if the emphasis must now be displaced from the ontological and empirical "substance" of "Auschwitz" as a historical experience to its rhetorical and affective impact as a sign, then it will be difficult to account for a shared recognition of this sign without reproducing an as-if *we* of judgment.

To the extent that he converts "Auschwitz" into a paradigmatic case for the fraught future of justice, he normalizes traumatic reactions to historical events as the aporetic effects of failed communication. At the same time, such failures are held up as the impetus for developing a literacy for witnessing historical-moral silences, which seems to take their negative intelligibility for granted. Because he does not name the subject of this literacy, his translation of a moral sensibility into an aesthetic "para-experience" inadvertently enacts in an inverted form the very tendency that he criticizes in the work of his nemesis, Habermas. Specifically, Lyotard finds fault with what he perceives as Habermas's resolution of the crisis of legitimacy through recourse to an ideal of democratically achieved consensus.[164] First, Habermas is naive to assume that "it is possible for all speakers to come to agreement on which rules or metaprescriptions are universally valid for language games, when it is clear that language games are heteromorphous, subject to heterogeneous sets of pragmatic rules." In the second place, Habermas's perspective presupposes that "the goal of dialogue is consensus," which Lyotard perceives as a "particular state of discussion, not its end."[165] As Ziarek keenly observes, the question of justice for Lyotard "does not disappear in the aftermath of the crisis of legitimation, but remains more urgent than ever because its criteria cannot be established on the basis of either knowledge or the emancipation of the universal subject." In this respect, Lyotard, like Derrida, embraces futurity in refusing "the final determination of the social" in order to open "a horizon of justice as the incessant necessity of judging without fixed criteria or law, where the outcome of this judgment provokes further contestation."[166]

Despite Lyotard's dispute with his nemesis, it remains questionable whether, by dwelling on the exteriority of "Auschwitz" as a sign of history and an impetus for continuing vigilance, he does not merely posthumanize Habermas's normative foundation of communication. As I argued in the previous chapter, when Habermas promotes Adorno's concept of critical remembrance, he institutes the Jewish victims' perspective as the horizon of German historical-moral judgment and consensus. The victims' suffering thus serves as a regulative image for German postnational consciousness and the writing of history. Without reference to Lyotard, Habermas inadvertently reinforces the French philosopher's view of "Auschwitz" as a moral-historical sign. Lyotard's "after Auschwitz" leads him to a different paradox. For if he rejects the ontological presuppositions of experience, then Lyotard must find another way to fulfill his "postmodern" agenda to "save the honor of the name" from the totalitarian fantasy of seizing reality.[167]

Survivor Memory and the Limits of Empathy

The fact that nothing has been left intact does not mean that nothing has been left.

—Michael Rothberg

Lyotard's considerations of Auschwitz illuminate a postwar philosophy hemmed in by the clashing rocks of European fascism, Stalinism, and capitalist hegemony. On the one hand, there is a Marxist-inflected ethos that repudiates bourgeois-humanist notions of self; on the other hand, there is an impetus to respect the singularity of individuals (and their vulnerability) while forsaking the comfort of a normative system that recapitulates the hypocrisies of humanism or the dangerous utopian impulses that drove Nazism and Stalinism. A sense of moral propriety demands that outsiders to the event struggle against their own banality by remaining sensitive to the survivors' suffering and by remembering those who did not survive; yet it is still not clear how Lyotard's antifoundationalist rhetoric might provide a way of compassionately acknowledging the specificity of this suffering and its posttraumatic effects.

Despite the complexity of his dialogue with philosophy, it is difficult to defend Lyotard from the accusation that he has posited "Auschwitz" as "a priori incomprehensible," a move that Mandel rejects. She points to the tendency to construct this name as a metonymic substitution for a "vast network of destruction, involving the active and tacit participation of millions" over a significant period of time; such a substitution wrenches it "from its specific historical and political context."[168] The metonym "Auschwitz" thus defers what it purports to name—"the immense, cumulative" and "disturbingly banal process" that reduced "living people to smoke and ash." It both evokes and effaces "the spectral presence of the people who died there" as well as "the accusing presence of those who survived it"—which is to say, "our own relationship to history and to an especially painful past."[169]

As I suggested in the previous chapter on the Memorial to the Murdered Jews of Europe, Lyotard is not the only theorist to invoke the unrepresentability of mass murder as a venue for a broader philosophical agenda. Alongside Lyotard, Maurice Blanchot, George Steiner, Claude Lanzmann, and Shoshana Felman have variously contributed to the institutionalization of this rhetoric as the de rigueur gesture of Holocaust and trauma studies. Felman, a prominent literary critic and theorist of testimony, has capitulated to a tendency, highlighted by Mandel, to render the Holocaust paradigmatic for trauma, a move that ethnocentrically assumes that "what happened in Europe reverberates globally."[170] In the early 1990s, Felman helped to entrench the rhetoric of unrepresentability when she drew on Lyotard to claim that the principal sign of the Holocaust is the proliferation of silences, since such an event not only drastically wounds those witnesses it did not physically destroy, but also remains in abeyance—in spaces where inadequate response, disbelief, or prurient fascination exacerbate the isolating experience of traumatic degradation and loss.

The problem is that empathy, as Dean suggests, may always be lacking, may always be inadequate in instances where people living in relative comfort grow numb in the face of their own failure (a kind of betrayal) to stop atrocities from taking place. Dean observes, "Because numbness may also be a necessary dimension of our ability to absorb mass atrocity, it paradoxically confirms ideas about our common humanity—we can only respond numbly to what we feel in excess—while also rendering humanitarian practice increasingly vexed."[171] The invocation of the sublime as the aesthetic most suited to the unrepresentable clearly serves a need to underscore a sense of excess as a sign of our humanity, a symptom that "we" still relish fantasies about the human proper. This premise infects historiography as much as philosophy, since, as Dean remarks, Nazi-period historians have typically "reaffirmed the power of dignity and empathy particularly embedded in one redemptive strain of historical analysis driven by a vision of 'humanity triumphant.' " She adds, "[T]hey have done so in spite of an increasingly large (mostly literary and philosophical) literature which insists that the Nazi extermination of European Jewry has called the universality of humanist concepts like dignity into question." The problem for Dean with such humanist commitments is that they serve to animate a kind of historical narrative with emotional power and force, a raison d'être, which is "difficult to locate in any specific source because dignity and empathy have become nothing less than synecdoches for the properly human."[172] As I have suggested by drawing on Lyotard and Agamben, this construction of the human proper is dangerous in its complicity with a biopolitical "relation of exception" that institutes social and juridical membership as the basis of survival. Those who belong to the proper group introject a sense of dignity and entitlement to empathy through their exclusion of other groups. The challenge that my analysis of "Discussions" and *The Differend* has permitted me to rephrase entails moving beyond definitions of the human proper in order to discern the limits of (my) empathy as an aesthetic and political problem—to interrogate (my) failure to respond adequately to unbearable events, to react to them as *truly unbearable*, in other words. This is to say that numbness is not a sign of the inhuman but rather the imaginative dimension of what Dean identifies as "the limits of the ideally expansive liberal 'we' . . . whose very self-constitution has always depended on both animal and human 'others.' "[173]

Mandel's and Dean's critiques propel me to pose a new question here that will carry over to the fourth and fifth chapters: How do the limits of empathy figured by the rhetoric of unrepresentability relate to the disciplinary imaginary as I have conceptualized it? More to the point, how do my imaginary identifications with various groups enhance or undermine empathetic awareness, numbness, or indifference in the face of testimonies about traumatic history? How does my contemporary milieu—my training in institutions influenced by posthumanist theories of signification—shape such identifications as layers in my formation as a subject of knowledge?

While my empathy with survivors may lead me to take the authenticity of firsthand accounts for granted, Lyotard, in contrast, argues that the name *Auschwitz* enjoins a distinction between testimony and evidence. Following Adorno's lead, Lyotard's writings about "Auschwitz" assume that the gas chambers permanently scarred Western faith in an intuitive moral consensus. "Auschwitz" is, thus, the name of a wound that exposed the hypocrisy of humanist universalism. It is, for Lyotard, a sign of history as a radical failure of community. Yet Western history is punctuated by such moral-historical wounds and the silences that attend them. It becomes the task that defines thought "after Auschwitz" to bear witness to these silences as signs of injustice.

In dialectically conjoining Adorno's and Derrida's anti-identitarian critiques of positive reason and the humanist subject, Lyotard repudiates metaphysical experience as a "return to the same" and as an anticipation of a beautiful death that bestows redemptive closure on an individual's life. This reading anticipates his rejection of ontological and empirical understandings of experience as a basis for granting the historical authority of victim testimony in *The Differend*. Unfortunately, this rejection also belies a theoretical violence to the extent that it inadvertently expropriates a survivor's mourning for a precatastrophic self not yet devastated by a global betrayal of his or her own desire to live. I wonder whether the confluence of Lacanian psychoanalysis and poststructuralism has made theorists too cynical. Certainly, I have become anxious about employing words such as *self* that expose my critical lack in failing to leap à la Lacan into a properly post-Cartesian understanding of the split subject.

It would be unfair to blame either Lacan or Derrida for this anxiety that arises out of an academic tendency to exaggerate the ideas of thinkers who become persuasive at various moments. Derrida does not contest the validity of the experiences out of which survivor testimonies derive and could even be read as defending it against the more radical implications of his own philosophy.[174] In his reflections on Paul Celan, for example, he decries the contamination of testimony by the notion of proof. "Whoever bears witness [in English in the original] does not provide proof," Derrida writes. He "is someone whose experience, in principle singular and irreplaceable (even if it can be cross-checked with others in order to become proof, in order to become probative in a verification process) attests, precisely, that some 'thing' has been present to him."[175] To bear witness is to attest to a onetime presence in an experience that is no longer present. Derrida calls this transpired presence a "secret," because the witness is "the only one to know what he has seen, lived, felt . . ."[176] This secret is inaccessible as knowledge to the addressee of the testimony, who is left with the choice either to believe or not—an "act of faith." It is this act that is therefore implied, according to Derrida, "everywhere one participates in what are called scenes of bearing witness."[177]

This preoccupation with the inaccessible secret at the core of the witness's irreplaceability in acts of testimony connects Derrida's reading of

Celan with Emmanuel Lévinas's insistence on "my" unsubstitutionability before the other's irreducible vulnerability to violence (and his or her experience in senescence, in mortality). This singularity in the face-to-face encounter is the inauguration of "my" infinite responsibility. "[T]he other is secret," Derrida writes: "I cannot be in the other's place, in the head of the other. I will never be equal to the secret of otherness. The secret is the very essence of otherness."[178] Derrida links this secret to the other's embodiment, which comes to the fore in the poet's idioms and spacing that resist translation.

Derrida's emphasis on the other's nonthematizable vulnerability abides with Lévinas's objections to existentialisms (such as Heidegger's and Sartre's) that reconvene the conceit of a "properly" human consciousness under the auspices of staging encounters between the I and others. As Ziarek keenly observes, Lyotard consistently deploys Lévinas's ethics with and against Kant's understanding of the moral law and his attendant acknowledgment in the *Critique of Practical Reason* that the "prescriptive force of categorical obligation cannot be deduced from cognition or from the political calculation of stakes." According to Ziarek, this failure of deduction suggests to Lyotard that "obligation happens like an event," which "precedes commentary and cognition" and thus "remains anarchic and unlegitimated." Nevertheless, Kant "curtails the anarchic force of the categorical obligation by maintaining the interchangeability between obligation and freedom, on the one hand, and obligation and norm, on the other."[179] Serving as a corrective to Kant, Lévinas permits Lyotard to argue that "neither the symmetry between the self and the other nor the reversibility between the obligated self and the subject of enunciation can be maintained."[180]

In the interests of taking some critical distance from this ethics, it is important to acknowledge that a survivor may, at moments, actively or unconsciously crave a "return to the same," a phrase that "anti-identitarian" theorists modeling themselves after "Adorno," "Lévinas," "Lyotard," or "Derrida" identify with a proprietary and violent will to self-mastery. Because I have also been prone to such anti-identitarian dogmatism, I would like to consider how this disciplinary mantra negates potential dimensions of posttraumatic experience.

In the case of survivors, the idea of "lost" self-presence might figure for the humiliation and betrayal that the Nazis inflicted. In reality, there cannot be a "return to the same" for Holocaust survivors whose families, friends, and communities were murdered and for whom the "impossibility of closure is simply ineluctable."[181] As the memoirs of Ruth Klüger and Cordelia Edvardson attest, bereaved memory remains elsewhere with respect to the daily rituals of post-Holocaust existence. Even as new families, neighbors, and colleagues demand a smooth and affable sociality, former modes of relating with absent parents, siblings, spouses, and children are freighted with their murders. A onetime complacency is irremediably violated by deportation and sustained periods of starvation, hopelessness, and the constant threat of death while others watched and did nothing.[182]

In *The Ruins of Memory*, Lawrence Langer identifies "unheroic" memory as an attribute of the damage inflicted on the survivor's impromptu sense of self. The self that persists is diminished by the memories of the desperation and humiliation of victimization that bear witness to lost possibilities of intention and self-narration.[183] The survivor may therefore yearn for a complacency that can never be regained. A "ruined" memory circles around the idealized self that was destroyed by the Nazi persecution and murder of the Jews, and was thereafter cut off from the present. An irreparably scarred dignity haunts his or her memories of the events that preceded the catastrophe, while the traumatic irrevocability of bereavement preempts his or her ability to be fully invested in the present.

Though I find Langer's description of unheroic memory compelling, I side with Rothberg and Gary Weissman in rejecting his hierarchy of survivor testimony based on a prioritization of the extreme immediacy of the "Holocaust experience," which, as Rothberg notes, excludes "the impingement of normal social relations . . . on the Nazi's construct."[184] Langer not only asserts "the interpreter's authority over the witness in deciding how to weigh the balance of experience," but also "projects his own 'verbal fences' onto his unnamed opponents."[185] "Such a restricted methodology," Rothberg writes, "produces results purified of the contingency and complexity of historical processes and representational practices."[186] Weissman criticizes Langer for stubbornly holding survivors to a standard of consciousness that is most authentic in its despairing confrontation with the harshest truths of persecuted existence. He cites the survivor and literary critic Ruth Klüger, who, in a review of Langer's *Versions of Survival* (1982),[187] lambasts him for disparaging "survivor reports whenever they attempt to put some order into their experience or draw any conclusions from it, no matter how tentative." Thus, even "though Langer himself points out correctly that everyone's camp experience was different, he nevertheless casts doubt on the authenticity of any account that doesn't conform to his own 'version of survival,' and that is essentially one that diminishes the individual and obliterates all differences between inmates."[188] Lyotard, I would argue, falls into a similar trap in "The Survivor," an essay dedicated to Hannah Arendt.[189]

In this essay, Lyotard softens his prior repudiation of phenomenological and ontological notions of experience in the course of contemplating the specific temporality of life after the death camps. Lyotard notes that the very meaning of the word *survivor* "implies that an entity that is dead or ought to be is still alive."[190] For Lyotard, survival is thus defined by the "desolate contingency" of living after probable death. The survivor subsists in the hollow of a past that is simultaneously lost and betrayed—he or she hovers between memories of a life that the Third Reich destroyed and memories of the camps that have faded with time and distance:

One question, however, is whether something is not forgotten in this turning back on the no longer, something that therefore does not survive, a remainder that does not remain. What seems as though it must necessarily be lost is the presence then of what is now past. . . .There is a mortal sadness of the very thing that is retained and transmitted; the sadness of Minerva's owl, of what is bound. The tradition of what was then experienced in the present is its betrayal. The past is betrayed by the simple fact that the present it was is made absent. It lacks a certain mode, the tone of the quick, the lively, even as it is recalled.[191]

Lyotard once again affirms his antifoundationalist alignment here through the imagery of gaps, negated remnants, and failed returns. The survivor's memory is hereby constructed as an uncrossable impasse that does not allow him or her to resuscitate the presence of the past nor the "quickness" and "liveliness" of what Langer calls the "impromptu self" that could spontaneously defend against danger. Lyotard broaches the crucial issue of betrayal, but in terms that undermine its specificity for survivors of extreme persecution. In "Discussions," Lyotard anticipates Agamben in recognizing the tautology of sovereign power upon which this betrayal was based: the command "to die" issued to "the Jews" exposes not only the arbitrariness of Nazi ideology that expropriates their humanity with their juridical subjecthood, but a more profound failure of the local and international communities to protect the vulnerable from the excesses of state power. Unfortunately, in this comment on survival, Lyotard poeticizes the "impasse" of a genocidal betrayal when he writes that "every entity is a survivor" insofar as "the authentic mode of presence"—of resolutely being in time without a nagging sense of lack—is unimaginable.[192] This conclusion suggests that a survivor's inability to "return to the same"—that is, to reactivate the affective force of the past in the present—does not differ from the freighted endeavor to achieve self-certainty by any decentered subject who dwells in the fragile "house of language." A survivor's posttraumatic anxiety following a culture's widespread refusal to protect and preserve life is dispossessed of its specificity to become another paradigmatic illustration, albeit a mournful one, of the subject as a sign under siege.

With this criticism, I do not want to suggest that the experience of surviving and living after the Shoah lies somehow beyond the "errancy" of the signifier, but I want to remain mindful of how the influence of psychoanalysis and deconstruction on cultural critics interested in trauma vexes their discussions with clinicians. I surmise that the disciplinary influence of poststructuralist criticism blocks a few earnest trauma theorists from validating a desire among some (not all) survivors as one constituency of the traumatized to recover a "lost" sense of intact identity. This idealization of intactness might serve as a touchstone for myriad concrete losses, including murdered family and friends, that wound the experience of identity. Furthermore, in societies that demand that self-certainty be performed as evidence of a worker's reliability, reinscriptions of this ideal in Western philosophy, ego psychology, and popular culture are an index that a form of what Lacan called misrecognition abides in beliefs about individual identity as an enduring personal essence.

Though I would not presume to present this standpoint as practical advice for psychoanalytically inclined clinicians, it is important for poststructuralist trauma theorists to make room for the prospect that those who survive episodes of profound biopolitical betrayal might remain unconsciously embroiled in the urge to recuperate "lost presence" as a capacity for composure and self-determination. This urge partly spurs the compulsive repetition of painful scenes displaying the subject as abjectly vulnerable, the anxious pivots upon which a notion of agency disintegrates into a deadly arbitrariness. The longing to resurrect a pretraumatic ideal of agency and to defuse the anxiety that surrounds its destruction resists a post-Cartesian insistence on fluctuating identity, which those of us schooled in Lacanian psychoanalysis and poststructuralism religiously presuppose as if it were the most advanced science of our day.

Derrida provocatively introduces a Freudian vitalism into his reading of Celan's poetry when he contends that texts are narcissistically and libidinally charged[193]—they are acts of declaring the body so as to resurrect a dying language, to rescue it from reification. What antifoundationalist critiques of experience might offer to a psychoanalytic theory of traumatic memory is a formal, linguistically turned enunciation of the nonvoluntary dimensions of cathexis (affective investment) and decathexis (divestment), which Freud understands as libidinal and thus psychobiological. The fourth chapter extrapolates from Freud and Derrida to propose a heuristic for understanding the affective economy of traumatic memory treated as a sign that differentiates as a function of fluctuating investments in shifting contexts of iteration. This heuristic adopts Freudian psychoanalysis to theorize working through as a process of desacralization through desensitization. In the traumatic imaginary, a fragment of the past assumes a sacred aura as "the origin" of posttraumatic anxiety—its core or decisive moment. The compulsive symbolization of this fragment in thought, dreams, or speech is an unconsciously propelled process that gradually loosens a subject's resistance against divesting a narcissistic identification with it as the anxious locus of a rupture between pre- and posttraumatic existence. The structure of this divestiture is partly mimetic to the extent that it revolves around an idealized image of the traumatic wound that produced posttraumatic anxiety. Ultimately, then, compulsive repetition is a symptom of an economic need to reproduce the affective plenitude of a traumatic experience in order to diffuse it. The aim of repetition is therefore gradual desensitization rather than catharsis conceived as an instantaneous and conscious transcendence of memory images that paralyze interpretations of the present.

Derrida's formulation of *différance* as a reproof to the metaphysics of presence, essence, and origin in theories of signification is crucial to this thesis, which hinges on the economic force of compulsive repetition. *Différance* is a dynamic of changing contexts of interpretation that suggests that the contingencies of personal and historical events and their shifting social relevance for us and others propel unconscious slippages in signification. On the one hand, the alienation that results from failures of empathy may foster a traumatized subject's sense of detachment from a particular memory. On the other hand, empathetic responses also play a role in relieving the anxiety that charges episodes of biosocial and political negation. In the rote performance of requisite poststructuralist gestures, we unwittingly circumscribe intellectual openness about and empathy for poststructurally "incorrect" modes of integrating wounding events into individual and collective narratives. While the melancholic ideal of "lost" intactness might be considered naive, critics fall prey to an equally naive dogmatism when they discount the appeal of such familiar metaphors of subject formation, as indicated by their ubiquity in classical and popular culture.[194] It is time to forsake theoretical correctness to account for the repercussions of this disciplinary fantasy of self-mastery for the study of trauma rather than simply decrying it as the veil of an ontological illusion.

4

"Working through" the Holocaust?
Toward a Psychoanalysis of Critical Reflection

Drunken August, the darling of Viennese legend, spent a besotted night in a ditch full of dead bodies and awoke with only a hangover. He staggered out of the ditch, left it behind him, and continued to play his bagpipe. We are different. We don't get off so cheaply; the ghosts cling to us. Do we expect that our unsolved questions will be answered if we hang on to what's left: the place, the stones, the ashes? We don't honor the dead with these unattractive remnants of past crimes; we collect and keep them for the satisfaction of our own necrophilic desires. Violated taboos, such as child murder and mass murder, turn their victims into spirits, whom we offer a kind of home that they may haunt at will. Perhaps we are afraid they may leave the camps, and we insist that their deaths were unique and must not be compared to any other losses or atrocities. Never again shall there be such a crime.

   The same thing doesn't happen twice anyway. Every event, like every human being and even every dog, is unique. We would be condemned to be isolated monads if we didn't compare and generalize, for comparisons are the bridges from one unique life to another. In our hearts we all know that some aspects of the Shoah have been repeated elsewhere, today and yesterday, and will return in a new guise tomorrow; and the camps, too, were only imitations (unique imitations, to be sure) of what had occurred the day before yesterday.

—Ruth Klüger, *Landscapes of Memory*

Ruth Klüger laments that the ghosts of the Holocaust never let her relax.[1] She gathers and preserves these "unattractive remnants of past crimes," not because she honors the dead, but to satisfy "necrophilic" desires. The traces left behind by the violation of taboos against mass murder, including the murder of children, metamorphose into spirits to whom she grants a kind of home in her mind "that they may haunt at will."

Klüger's memoir offers an occasion to remark a few compelling differences between the original, published in 1994, and her own translation of it nine years later from German into English. In 2003, a declarative becomes a question: "Do we expect that our unsolved questions will be answered if we hang on to what's left: the place, the stones, the ashes?"[2] In both versions, this series of images evokes a qualitative egress of memory into the fragile cinders of what has been burnt beyond recognition, which anticipates, in the English version, a "necrophilic" desire to collect and hold on to the memories because "we somehow need them" (*"wir sammeln und bewahren sie, weil wir sie irgendwie brauchen"*). Klüger's incorporation of *necrophilic* into her translation is extraordinary, since it connects the compulsive force of bereaved memory with perversion: a violation of the taboo against intercourse with the dead.

Klüger's memoir and its translation invite us to pose a delicate question. What are we to make of a survivor's avowedly perverse need to revisit ghastly images of her traumatic past? Dominick LaCapra has observed, "Those traumatized by extreme events, as well as those empathizing with them, may resist working through because of what might almost be termed a fidelity to trauma, a feeling that one must somehow keep faith with it. Part of this feeling," he adds, "may be the melancholic sentiment that, in working through the past in a manner that enables survival or a reengagement in life, one is betraying those who were overwhelmed and consumed by that traumatic past." Then, as though he speaks for himself as well as for survivors, LaCapra suggests, "*One's* bond with the dead, especially with dead intimates, may invest trauma with value and make its reliving a painful but necessary commemoration or memorial to which one remains dedicated or at least bound" (my emphasis).[3] In the passage above, Klüger denies that her hauntings serve to honor those friends, neighbors, and relatives who shared her life before the genocide, even as her written testimony confirms again and again the brutality that took them away from her. What seems to be at stake for Klüger is the way in which the dead and the violence of their murders exert a strangely morbid magnetism for her, which she attributes to need and not to will.[4]

The writings of survivors attest that their experiences in the death camps were dominated by the urgent necessity of remaining hypervigilant against imminent starvation, a potentially fatal weakness, and selection for "extermination." A humiliated self-preservative anxiety continues to goad some survivors as they confront the prospect of living after bereavement on a genocidal scale and face the insensitivity of outsiders, who fail to empathize or even to believe. The silences Jean-François Lyotard enumerates in *The Differend* could partly be understood as a historical symptom of a "wound culture," as Mark Seltzer has called it,[5] wherein disbelief is merely the flip side of a salacious fascination with the horror of mass murder. In the face of disbelief, failed sympathy, and intrusive fascination, a survivor's traumatic memory becomes charged anew with anxiety as a "manifestation of the ego's self-preservative instincts." Such anxiety is partly "realistic" yet "inexpedient" according to Freud, since it does not fend off an actual danger.[6] On a bioeconomic level, what Freud refers to as an *Angstaffekt* (anxiety affect) is the psychosomatic force behind a survivor's compulsive reconstructions of the murdered and his or her own experiences of persecution.[7] On an imaginary level, when traumatic images are saturated with belated self-preservative anxiety, they may become overvalued. In this idealized form, the traumatically charged memory orients an impossible desire to reconvene and thereby master the affective presence of the past.

In the second chapter, I reviewed Theodor W. Adorno's understanding of *durcharbeiten* (working through) as *verarbeiten*, which is motivated by a genuine commitment to the process of coming to terms with the past through critical reflection. He distinguishes this conscious critical reflection from a bureaucratic *Erledigung* (dispatching) of an unpleasant obligation spurred by a longing for easy transcendence and narcissistic redemption. However, when scholars reiterate Adorno's injunction to postwar Germans to reflect critically on their role in mass murder, do they consider the prospect that the Holocaust might itself become a "libidinally invested" object in a strongly psychoanalytic sense? It would seem that "after Adorno," appropriate reflection about the Holocaust is only imaginable as a self-conscious integration of those instincts that motivate humans to pursue violent, quasi-sacrificial outlets for aggression. Indeed, insofar as it is identified as a corrective to repressed barbarism, the implication is that reflection could never itself serve as a vehicle for the primal urges that underlie Freud's theory of the drives.[8]

Analysts of German post-Holocaust discourse such as LaCapra and Eric Santner have drawn on Freud's theory of trauma to evaluate the extent to which various representations on the "perpetrator" side work through the Nazi crimes. I have often turned to LaCapra and Santer because I find their conceptions of working through and mourning, both informed by Freud, very persuasive on a critical level; however, their prioritization of the conscious aims of remembrance and mourning "disciplines" psychoanalysis by suppressing the agency of the unconscious in Freud's framework.

Freud's emphasis on the role of sexual tensions and other somatic forces in the formation of unconscious patterns is typically the first victim of any morally earnest scholarly approach that selectively borrows psychoanalytic terminology. Even in his early work, Freud hints at an intimate collaboration between the libidinal economy and the activity of working through traumatic memories. His subsequent attention to this collaboration differentiates a specifically psychoanalytic formulation of working through from a more voluntaristic understanding that affirms the integrity of individual will as a basis of responsibility. A closer look at the relationship between Freud's theory of the drives and compulsive repetition will expose the limits of exclusively focusing on the conscious ends of working through traumatic history.

Since it is the psychoanalytic attention to the unconscious that concerns me in this chapter, I will return to Freud's speculations on its role in repetition in *Beyond the Pleasure Principle*. My aim is to counteract an over-emphasis on free will that comes to the fore whenever scholars equate working through with critical reflection. Freud offers various overlapping, but not altogether consistent theses on the drives, and this requires his readers to extrapolate from shifts in his thinking over time. By reading between the lines, I will outline the *economic* and *imaginary* valences of working through trauma delimited by Freud as a process of making what is pathogenetically unconscious conscious, which enables the analysand to detach from the persisting influence of past experiences. This process is economic to the extent that repetition diffuses a trauma's libidinal charge and thereby attenuates its hold on the analysand. It is imaginary, because remembering trauma is an act of symbolization that is mediated by narcissistic identifications and fantasies. By foregrounding the economic and imaginary dimensions of compulsive repetition as a posttraumatic symptom, I will also demonstrate how the aims of working through depend on unconscious and social forces as well as the structural registers of language in order ultimately to illuminate the disciplinary stakes of a psychoanalytic definition of critical reflection.

Libidinal Reflections

In previous chapters, I have touched on Adorno's polemics on education and working through "after Auschwitz" where he prioritizes critical reflection as the only prospect, albeit limited, for counteracting the internalized effects of domination. In my analysis of the reception of Goldhagen's *Hitler's Willing Executioners* in the first chapter, I introduced LaCapra's adaptation of Freud's term *working through* to describe the process of critically reflecting on the Holocaust as a mode of heightened self-consciousness that combats primal urges without mobilizing them.[9] In this respect, LaCapra shares Adorno's desire to identify a genuinely critical mode of reflecting on Third Reich history. LaCapra's analysis of Holocaust historiography illuminates the ways historians and other scholars enact transferential relations with their object of study that express their investment in or disavowal of a particular subject position. He therefore stresses the importance of taking a historian's subject position into consideration in judgments of scientific and moral propriety.

In his introductory lecture "Transference," Freud discusses situations in which "feelings derived from elsewhere," are "already prepared in the patient and, upon the opportunity offered by the analytic treatment, are transferred on to the person of the doctor."[10] These misdirected feelings indicate that the analysand is actually repeating a prior experience in the therapeutic context. *Transference* as such is the analysand's narcissistic idealization of the analyst upon whom his or her fantasies have conferred the status of an infantile prototype. This idealization leads him or her to reexperience infantile object relations and to "act out" unconscious wishes and behavior patterns. When an analysand acts out in the therapeutic context, he or she dramatizes overdetermined patterns of substitution and resistance. Transferential acting out potentially makes the logic of such substitutions available to the analyst for interpretation. The analyst uses the authority granted to him or her in the transference to oblige the analysand to transform repetition into memory by providing the latter with incontrovertible evidence of his or her narcissistic resistance to abandoning destructive patterns of behavior.[11]

LaCapra is more concerned about making psychoanalytic terms useful to a symptomatic critique of Holocaust historiography than he is about fleshing out their theoretical density and the problems that attend their application. This step would entail a consideration of the psychoanalytic emphasis on the relation between the drives and the unconscious as a dynamic structuring principle for the repressed. Freud's etiology of neuroses suggests that among the contents of the repressed are unprocessed childhood experiences that predate subsequent traumas and that establish the libidinal "substructure" of the neurotic character. The disposition that results from such early experiences is the latent springboard for the onset of neurotic behavior. Freud understands this disposition as an ontogenetic susceptibility, which will be aggravated and thereby activated by a distressful accident or experience. Neurotic symptoms are defensive resurgences of this susceptibility at the base of an individual's development. In short, childhood experiences establish a foundation in the past for a subject's neurotic future.

Freud's etiology of neuroses suggests that their onset is preconditioned by overwhelming or frustrating early childhood experiences, but triggered by a later trauma.[12] A crucial point here is that the affect attending an anterior unprocessed experience is associated with a subsequent event. As a result of this displacement, a memory of the later episode comes to stand-in for the previous experience and its latent effects are belatedly activated by the second, which thereafter bears a double burden of cathected content. This logic does not diminish the import of particular traumas, but it does suggest that their anxious aftereffects will be difficult to distinguish from neurotic symptoms expressing a prior *and* supplemental susceptibility that determines the force and character of future cathexes. By extension, the process of working through cannot be restricted to the "second" more localized trauma; rather, the cathected contents of early childhood events will be symbolized in the process of working through later wounding events.[13]

LaCapra refers to the disposition for traumatic neuroses as "structural" in order to distinguish it from "historical" or "empirical" traumas such as the

Holocaust. One difference is that while historical traumas are potentially preventable, structural trauma is too profoundly ontological and ubiquitous to stave off or work through. However, Freud's etiology of neurosis indicates that working through will necessarily engage both "structural" and "empirical" traumas since patterns of resistance and cathexis resurface and combine with the effects of discrete events. This understanding challenges the efficacy of LaCapra's distinction and, as LaCapra himself admits, "[T]he two do interact in complex ways in any concrete situation."[14]

One of the hallmarks of Freudian psychoanalysis is the premise that instinctual forces are involved in symbolizations of the past. Freud's speculations on the unconscious often refer to repressed instincts, which are simultaneously pre- and suprahistorical in manifesting the inherent tendencies of all animal life. Freud's work repeatedly draws attention to their role in shaping conscious psychic processes as well as less conscious responses to traumas and other phenomena.

While LaCapra's distinction between structural and empirical traumas is intended to protect the historical and moral specificity of the latter, this strategy detaches them from the libidinal infrastructure that mediates our imaginary and our reception of events. Hence, even as I subscribe to LaCapra's commitment to encouraging historians to recognize and examine their investments,[15] his selective adoption of Freudian terminology tends to treat academic discourse as either a properly or improperly sublimated response to the traumatic impact of the Holocaust. He thereby avoids a risky theorization of scholarship's libidinal economy, which he relegates to the inchoate realm of the repressed. This deflection allows the Holocaust to retain its moral purity and thus remain an appropriate object of contemplation.[16] I will broach this "moral purity" problem again later in this chapter and in the last, where I turn to the pivotal role that fantasy plays in sympathy conceived as an ethical act. For now, I want to highlight the psychoanalytic specificity of the "impurity" that LaCapra has banished to the less critically urgent category of structural trauma.

Over the years, the perceived impropriety of Freud's emphasis on the sexual dimension of the unconscious has, in the United States at least, sometimes led to a complete negation of the value of his thought. The controversy in 1995–96 over the planning of a national exhibit devoted to Freud's work and influence is a telling instance of this suppression in the public sphere both within and beyond academia. To be sure, Freud himself sometimes felt compelled to qualify some of the more scandalous aspects of his own thinking on sexuality, including his initial belief in his patients' statements that they had been seduced into sexual acts as children by adults, including family members. As is well known, he later relinquished this hypothesis in favor of the theory that these confessions reflected fantasies about incest and seduction.[17] In addition, his 1914 rejoinder to C. G.

Jung in "Introduction: On Narcissism" awkwardly guards an increasingly untenable distinction between the "nonsexual" ego drives and the sexual drives in an attempt to separate his theory of the libido from his former disciple's more generalized understanding of it as the primal energy invested in all drives as an "original unity."[18] It is, of course, significant that despite his various protests to the contrary, Freud's subsequent descriptions of the libidinal economy in 1915, 1920, and 1923 will tend to confirm rather than undermine Jung's concept.

Jean Laplanche notes that "the most frequent model used by Freud to account for the relation between the somatic and the psychical forces employs the metaphor of a kind of 'delegation' provided with a mandate that need not be absolutely imperative. Thus a local biological stimulus finds its delegation, its 'representation' in psychical life as a drive."[19] Freud proposes various versions of the libidinal economy in his oppositions between ego or narcissistic drives and sexual or object drives before arriving at the duality of the life and death drives in *Beyond the Pleasure Principle* in 1920.[20] Prior to 1920, Freud's "[Drives] and Their Vicissitudes" (1915) maps the dynamics destinies (*Schicksale*) of the drives (*Triebe*) in relation to the configuration of four essential components. According to this map, each drive is differentially determined by its respective source (*Quelle*) as the "region or zone of the body from which it derives." In addition, every drive is theoretically distinguishable on the basis of its pressure (*Drang*), aim (*Ziel*), and object (*Objekt*).

In his reading of Freud's *Three Essays on the Theory of Sexuality* (1905), Laplanche delineates variant definitions for the source (*Quelle*) in Freud's work. In its concrete, local, and "strictly physiological" sense, the source is an "erotogenic zone" understood as a privileged site of sexual stimulation. The implication here is that sexual tension is exclusively a property of the oral, anal, urethral, and genital loci. In a broader sense, however, the source may refer to any organ or body part that becomes the vehicle of stimulation. This is to suggest that the term *erotogenic* may alternately describe corporeal tension in general.[21]

In the last instance, Laplanche identifies the instinct as the ultimate source of the drive that "mimics, displaces, and denatures it."[22] The instinct itself is a trace of primal forces that originate with the first organism. The source of the drive so conceived exceeds psychology insofar as it incorporates the history of organic life.[23] It therefore comprises the phylogenetic substrate of the human's psychophysical system.

Freud confirms this reading in *Beyond the Pleasure Principle*, where he defines a drive as a derivative of a repressed instinctual urge (*Drang*) that has been refracted through socializing constraints. In that context, he argues that drives are essentially "conservative" in nature because they aim to return the organism to a "prior" state. In Freud's words: "*[a drive] is an urge inherent in organic life to restore an earlier state of things* which the living entity has been obliged to abandon under the pressure of external disturbing forces; that is, it is a kind of organic elasticity, or, to put it another way, the expression of the inertia inherent in organic life."[24] This prior state expresses itself in the so-called return of the repressed as an uncanny resurgence of earlier phases of organic and psychic development—those repudiated primal instincts and infantile beliefs or fears that could be said to lie at the root of "irrational" behaviors and that seem mechanical in their nonvoluntary relentlessness when they reemerge in a "rational" and thus unhomelike space.

Laplanche's progressively general definition of the source is valuable for a reading of the economic valence of Freud's theory of the psychic apparatus. For it suggests that the source "is nothing but the transcription of the sexual repercussions of anything occurring in the body beyond a certain quantitative threshold."[25] This is to attribute a polymorphous autoeroticism to the body and its organs, a condition that the genital stage of sexuality both inhibits and aggravates. In addition, because such tensions pass through the whole body, this understanding of the source suggests an abstraction of sexual energy that would precede object orientations.[26]

This abstraction allows Laplanche to revise Freud's definition of the libidinal object, which is hereafter conceivable as a condensation or displacement of autoerotic stimulation deriving from the tension exerted by repressed instincts. One important implication is that the object will actually be constituted by the drive as a vehicle of residual instinctual energies that pressure the psyche to seek a locus of investiture and release. Fantasies offer an obvious forum for this constitutive investiture whereby an object is bestowed with its focal status. Laplanche also identifies intense intellectual activity as a potential impetus and venue for sexual stimulation.[27] This identification bears crucially on the constitution of objects of inquiry as socially acceptable loci for the drives.

Laplanche's reading of the source of the drives invites us to understand autoeroticism in Freud's work as both a dynamic nexus of tensions and as an impetus of libidinal investiture. Libidinal investiture, or cathexis (*Besetzung*), is a term that would then describe a subject's charged captivation with an object that provides an orientation for generalized somatic tensions. To the extent that the quantity of tension determines the intensity of investiture, the libidinal economy configures a systematic interrelation among differential degrees of cathexis along with shifts in the measure of stimulation or affect that must be regulated by the psychic apparatus.

From Laplanche I also take the lesson that to ignore the drives is to diminish and obscure the specificity of Freudian psychoanalysis. The drive is a delegate for an affect-charged compulsion to obtain satisfaction in relation to an object. This object is a figure in its own right insofar as it is a metonym or condensation of psychophysical tensions. Drives are therefore inextricably bound up with fantasy, which dramatizes the otherwise obscure trajectory and motility of unbound affective energy by providing it with an imaginary object and an aim.

I will turn to Freud's theorization of the relation between affect and anxiety in the next section on compulsive repetition. For now, I want to stress that Freud's recurrent speculations about the status of sexuality for his theory of the unconscious demonstrate that the overdetermined functioning of the libido remains a focal object of Freudian psychoanalysis. According to Freud's 1923 essay on the subject, *libido* "is a term used in the theory of the [drives] for describing the dynamic manifestation of sexuality."[28] Freud places the emergence of the libido with the discovery of hysteria and obsessional neuroses. He notes that the symptoms of these "transference neuroses" result from the ego's rejection or repression of sexual urges that "then [find] circuitous paths through the unconscious."[29] The concept of *sublimation* allows Freud to account for aims that preserve the drive as libido, but do not appear to be sexual.

Freud's conception of sublimation is generated by his need to theorize the division between sexual and nonsexual aims in his theory of the drives. His derivation of this concept nevertheless reinforces the importance of libidinal energy as the impetus of the scholarship (or other culturally acceptable aims) that reroutes and domesticates it. As Laplanche has reminded us, Freud's concept of sublimation is complicated by a shift from an opposition between sexuality and self-preservation to Eros and the death drive, which highlights two completely different forms of the sexual and the nonsexual. The "discovery of narcissism" indicates a moment when the libido "sexually invests the ego" and then "takes over theoretically the ego's task of maintaining the self-preservative functions."[30] Self-preservation is hereby co-opted by sexuality "in the guise of the sexual investment of the ego, narcissism."[31] Accordingly, humans "take sustenance and fight one another, ultimately, not for survival but out of love for the ego, or more precisely out of hatred of any alien ego."[32] When the death drive has made its official appearance, Laplanche observes, Eros has colonized self-preservation under the dominance of binding. It thereby introduces a distinction between bound and unbound forms of sexuality, whereas Thanatos assumes the irreconcilable status of the "unbridled sexual drive."[33] The implication, as John Fletcher observes, is that "the death drive is not opposed to sexuality but is the return of the earlier conception of a fragmented and fragmenting sexual drive."[34] Henceforth, the ego is the "foremost agent of Eros, that takes charge of vital interests." Sublimation understood as the "mutation of the drive as regards its aims and its object" must be reconceived as "the transference or transposition of the sexual energy of the death drive to the life drive, the taming or binding of a drive that was originally anarchic and destructive."[35] The idea that sublimation might replace "sexual" objects with socially acceptable "nonsexual" ones therefore denies what is common to both: the binding of affect through acts of imagination that transpire at the intersection of the drives and fantasy and the narcissistic and social registers of identification. Social valorization, Laplanche argues, is *intrinsic* rather than supplemental to the process of binding.[36]

I have cited LaCapra's prioritization of historical over structural trauma, a distinction he reinforces through a related opposition between losses "situated on a historical level" and "transhistorical" absences that he links to ontological lack—an absence of self-certainty experienced as if it were a loss. LaCapra is targeting a tendency that he attributes to Slavoj Žižek and Cathy Caruth: the tendency to avoid addressing losses "in sufficiently specific terms or to enshroud, perhaps even to etherealize, them in a generalized discourse of absence." He contends that in "an obvious and restricted sense, losses may entail absences, but the converse need not be the case."[37] "In terms of absence," LaCapra insists, "one may recognize that one cannot lose what one never had."[38]

LaCapra's alignment between historical trauma and actual loss, on the one hand, and structural trauma and transhistorical absence, on the other, is consonant with a heuristic that Santner develops by drawing on Freud's "Mourning and Melancholia." In *Stranded Objects: Mourning, Memory, and Film in Postwar Germany* (1990), Santner traces the vicissitudes of inherited repression, mourning, and melancholia in West German representations of postwar memory.[39] His analysis revises and extends the principal observations of Alexander and Margarete Mitscherlich's famous 1967 study of prevailing West German attitudes and behavior in the first two decades following the fall of the Third Reich. *The Inability to Mourn* offers a critical egopsychology of German postwar repression.[40] Here the Mitscherlichs observe that Third Reich Germans identified with the *Führer* as an ideational anchor for their investment in a unified, self-contained German *Volk*. After the war, however, Germans repressed their complicity with the mass deportation, internment, and murder of European Jews and other groups. This repression disabled critical reflection about crimes against these groups while blocking mass depression over Germany's defeat and Hitler's suicide. What is crucial in the Mitscherlichs' and Santner's analysis is their shared insight into the narcissistic impetus of a widespread German failure, following the war, to register the moral significance of the "Final Solution." In this respect, their diagnosis keeps faith with Adorno's excoriation of postwar German attempts to draw a line between themselves and the past in the interests of national ego redemption.[41]

In "History beyond the Pleasure Principle: Some Thoughts on the Representation of Trauma," Santner adopts Adorno's hierarchical opposition between "short-circuited" and "critical" modalities of remembering for the purpose of evaluating German representations of their wartime past. Santner coins the term *narrative fetishism* to describe "the way an inability or refusal to mourn emplots traumatic events."[42] *Emplotment*, in this instance, refers to "the construction and deployment of a narrative consciously or unconsciously designed to expunge the traces of the trauma or loss that called that narrative into being in the first place." Like mourning, narrative fetishism responds to a loss "that refuses to go away due to its traumatic impact"; however, it bypasses "proper" mourning "by simulating a condition of intactness."[43]

The psychoanalytic antecedent of Santner's distinction between bereavement and narrative fetishism is Freud's opposition between mourning and melancholia. In that essay, Freud identifies the object of mourning as a conscious and actual loss in contrast to the unconscious object or "loss of a more ideal kind" that orients melancholia. A melancholic who undergoes some form of bereavement "knows *whom* he has lost, but not *what* he has lost in him." Freud therefore suggests that melancholia "is in some way related to an object-loss which is withdrawn from consciousness, in contradistinction to mourning, in which there is nothing about the loss that is unconscious."[44]

The problem with this opposition is that it implies that mourning is somehow an exception in relation to Freud's own considerations of the role of fantasy and censorship in mediating memories of empirical loss, which may come to serve as the ideational object of an unconscious investment. Laplanche cites a lengthy passage from a letter to Wilhelm Fliess dated September 21, 1897, where Freud identifies his reasons for abandoning the infamous "seduction hypothesis" that shaped "The Aetiology of Hysteria" (1896).[45] In the third of four objections to the seduction theory, Freud notes that "there are no indications of reality in the unconscious so that one cannot distinguish between truth and fiction that has been cathected with affect."[46] For Laplanche, this observation represents one of the "cornerstones" of Freudian theory—namely, that "there is no 'indication of reality' allowing one to distinguish a 'real' memory from pure and simple imagination." In the unconscious, he insists, "it is impossible to distinguish between truth and emotionally-charged fiction."[47] As Janet Walker suggests, citing Laplanche and Pontalis, fantasy "is both 'a distorted derivative of the memory of actual fortuitous events' and 'an imaginary expression designed to conceal the reality of the instinctual dynamic.'" It might therefore be understood as "a nonveridical construction that is nevertheless 'propped on' a real event. To be sure, the real event is 'fortuitous,' meaning that it is not the origin of the fantasy but rather the grain of sand around which the pearl of fantasy is deposited, but it plays a role nonetheless."[48]

Freud's early recognition in 1897 that the unconscious has the power to transpose fantasy with reality was reinforced a quarter century later by his observations on sublimation in the context of his essay "The Libido Theory" of 1923. There he asserts that the "aim is always discharge accompanied by satisfaction." However, this aim "is capable of being changed from activity to passivity." In addition, an external object can be "turned around upon the subject's own self" or be combined with another object so that the cathexis of one is transferred to the other as the basis of satisfaction. Significantly, sexual objects can also be displaced and exchanged through a process of sublimation that allows a sexual drive to be discharged through a morally or socially valued achievement. Freud also hints that all the achievements of Western civilization are essentially sublimations that convert "improper" into "proper" objects for the sake of maintaining the social order.[49]

The narcissistic reluctance to relinquish psychic objects indicates another explanation for the "improper" form of mourning that Santner calls narrative fetishism. In these instances, a particular memory assumes a charged aura because it has been invested with libidinal forces: the autoerotic and self-preservative tensions in the body that Laplanche identifies as the "source" of the drives and that require an object to orient them. When a memory image of loss or pain becomes the focus of a libidinal investment, it spurs repetitions that would capture and economically defuse the force of belated traumatic anxiety. Such repetition is mimetic as much as it is fetishistic; at the level of the "metaphysically naive" imaginary, it involves an urge to master the experiential plenitude of an "originary" event.

Drawing primarily on *Beyond the Pleasure Principle*, in dialogue with Santner, my reading of Freud's theory of trauma stresses the economic role of compulsive repetition as a nonvoluntary process of decathecting from a charged memory of a wounding event. My reading will propose that a mimetic captivation with this impossible-to-replicate ideal may be a component in the economy of compulsive repetition, which aims to diffuse the self-preservative anxiety that retroactively saturates trauma as a pivot of posttraumatic identity. A poststructuralist standpoint assumes that adequation as such is impossible because of the social contingencies of signification that inflect the valuation or force of a remembered event in various contexts. The spatiotemporal alterity of a moving body along with the vacillating demands of the subject's shifting social position generate a corresponding variability in the form and psychic value of memory as a sign. This flux exacerbates and controverts an anxious mimetic capitivation with a wounding event, since it prevents the subject from reproducing the affective plenitude, the tension of the event that precipitated wounding memories. It is then the successive failure to recapture this "presence" that may play a structural role in derealizing and thereby dispersing the anxiety that saturates images of a traumatic experience in the very act of (re)constituting it.

Against Catharsis

In the section entitled "Models" in *Negative Dialectics*, Adorno insists that there can be no redemptive transcendence of anonymous mass murder. Indeed, his repudiation of identitarian affirmation implicitly rejects the possibility that Germans might enjoy the "higher meaning" of a cathartic release from the shame of anonymous mass murder. Auschwitz can never become the material for a tragic accumulation of pathos that precipitates a sense of relief or closure. The "Final Solution" must remain the negative object of open-ended reflection.

Among the many popular misconceptions about psychoanalysis is that a therapeutic encounter instantly "cures" patients merely by reactivating a repressed trauma, thereby permitting them to achieve catharsis.[50] Of course, the very notion of a cure is clouded with fantasies about a "happy ending" for the neurotic afflicted by traumatic pathos. The concept of a cure is idealistic insofar as it anticipates the prospect of bringing to a close what is, by Freud's own account, an interminable process. In addition, this ideal is naively hermeneutical in assuming that the secret "origin" of neuroses can be located, recognized, and "processed" once and for all as the latent spur of symptomatic behavior. In a Freudian framework, the ideal of a cure also revolves around the economic goal of breaking up libidinal investments that mobilize a nexus of anxieties and repressions.

The reductive conflation between catharsis and cure has, of course, a historical lineage in Freud's own work. The goal of the so-called cathartic method, which explicitly governed Freud's hypotheses in the late nine-teenth-century, was to bring about a *purgation* or *discharge* of pathogenic affects that are bound to a latent trauma. In keeping with this goal, therapy would aim to loosen the patient's repression, and thereby allow him or her to neutralize or "abreact" a traumatically charged memory in the course of "reliving" it. The economic goal of abreaction governed Freud's early experimental work with Josef Breuer in the period between 1880 and 1895. This work largely comprised attempts to reproduce the results of J.-M. Charcot's experiments with hypnosis as a technique for approaching nervous illnesses, including those that Freud sometimes encountered in his treatment of "hysterical" patients.[51] Freud became increasingly disaffected with hypnosis as a technique for lifting the repression of what he subsequently identified as unconscious or primary investments. His early work was nevertheless crucial in directing him to view repression as the central concern of his budding psychoanalytic science.

In the early period, before his "discovery" of the unconscious, physicalist assumptions heavily informed Freud's commitment to the hypnotic method, and he principally viewed nervous disorders as the effects of biochemical dysfunctions and imbalances. Despite his eventual disillusion with Charcot's techniques, Freud continued to embrace physicalist principles, which spurred him to apply thermodynamic and mechanical metaphors to the goals of working through. Freud came to view treatment as a means of aiding the analysand to work through his or her unconscious narcissistic resistance to divesting destructive modes of libidinal organization by bringing them into the domain of consciousness. Nevertheless, in keeping with an economic emphasis, the process of making unconscious contents conscious would also treat excess tensions. For this reason, while Freud's praxis did not remain captive to the false simplicity of the cathartic method, it also cannot be said that his subsequent speculations were ever completely purged of the biological, economic, and metaphysical assumptions underpinning the ideal of catharsis.

The physicalist principles he employed in early works such as the *Project for a Scientific Psychology* (1895) return in the short yet densely speculative *Beyond the Pleasure Principle*, which represents Freud's most developed attempt to account for the dynamics of compulsive repetition as one of the chief symptoms of trauma. In perhaps the most cited passage from this text, Freud describes a game played by his one-and-a-half-year-old grandson as a case of compulsive repetition:

> The child had a wooden reel with a piece of string tied round it. It never occurred to him to pull it along the floor behind him, for instance, and play at its being a carriage. What he did was to hold the reel by the string and very skilfully throw it over the edge of his curtained cot, so that it disappeared into it, at the same time uttering his expressive "o-o-o-o." He then pulled the reel out of the cot again by the string and hailed its reappearance with a joyful "*da*" ["there"]. This, then, was the complete game—disappearance and return. As a rule one only witnessed its first act, which was repeated untiringly as a game in itself, though there is no doubt that the greater pleasure was attached to the second act.[52]

In Freud's reading, the *fort/da* game clearly symbolizes his grandchild's anxiety about the disappearance of his mother. Because this prospect cannot be pleasurable for an infant, it strikes Freud as peculiar that his grandson would be compelled to restage an event that causes him pain. More precisely, it is the child's tireless repetition of the *fort* more than the *da* part of the game that fascinates Freud, for it indicates an infantile desire to master the vicissitudes of his maternal "referent." He subsequently interprets his grandson's pleasure in this ritual as a "great cultural achievement" insofar as it compensates the child for his "instinctual renunciation" (*Triebverzicht*) in allowing his mother to leave without protesting.[53]

In keeping with the delight Freud takes in the success of his grandson's sublimation, Santner reads the *fort/da* game as a staging of the threat of maternal bereavement through a process of symbolic substitution. This substitution allows the child to experience the anxious idea of mother loss in a controlled and muted form. The infant's symbolic mastery of this threat renews his sense of empowerment, which permits the pleasure that he derives from his repetition of this game:

Bereft by the mother's absence, and more generally by the dawning of awareness that the interval between himself and his mother opens up a whole range of unpredictable and potentially treacherous possibilities, he reenacts the opening of that abysmal interval within the controlled space of a primitive ritual. The child is translating, as it were, his fragmented narcissism (which might otherwise pose a psychotic risk—the risk of psychological disintegration) into the formalized rhythms of symbolic behavior; thanks to this procedure, *he is able to administer in controlled doses* the absence he is mourning. The capacity to dose out and to represent absence by means of substitutive figures at a remove from what one might call their "transcendental signifier," is what allows the child to avoid psychotic breakdown and transform his lost sense of omnipotence into a chastened form of empowerment.[54] (My emphasis)

Santner's reading of the *fort/da* game shapes his hierarchical opposition between narrative fetishism and mourning conceived as a homeopathic strategy "of elaborating and integrating the reality of loss or traumatic shock by remembering and repeating it in symbolically and dialogically mediated doses." According to Santner, homeopathic mourning "empowers" the bereaved to "master" the negative element through its gradual and diluted administration in small amounts. In short, it heals the individual through a "controlled" introduction of the very pain that "poisons" him:

> The dosing out of a certain negative—a thanatonic—element as a strategy of mastering a real and traumatic loss is a fundamentally homeopathic procedure. In a homeopathic procedure the *controlled* introduction of a negative element—a symbolic or, in medical contexts, real poison—helps to heal a system infected by a similar poisonous substance. The poison becomes a cure by *empowering* the individual to master the potentially traumatic effects of large doses of the morphologically related poison. In the *fort/da* game it is the rhythmic manipulation of signifiers and figures, objects and syllables instituting an absence, that serves as the poison that cures. These signifiers are *controlled symbolic doses* of absence and renunciation that help the child to survive and (ideally) be empowered by the negativity of the mother's absence.[55]

Santner's model of homeopathic mourning proposes an incremental succession of symbolizations that gradually introduce and diffuse the painful impact of the loss at the crux of bereavement. These symbolizations comprise the "solution" that dilutes a trauma's "poisonous" effects and thereby harnesses its potency as a "homeopathic" remedy. Though he draws on Freud's configuration of the *fort/da* game, Santner's model of healthy homeopathic mourning flirts with voluntarism in sidestepping the question of who or what "administers" or "dilutes" the poison. This model privileges a conscious desire to symbolize and master traumatic pain and casts aside the economic determinism that informs Freud's theorization of compulsive repetition.

Though I am partially persuaded by Santner's homeopathic metaphor, I want to qualify its voluntarism by emphasizing the economic, imaginary, and structural dimension of repetition for working through. In *Beyond the Pleasure Principle*, compulsive repetition is, by definition, not consciously controlled or motivated. Indeed, Freud connects it with the death drive as a systemic, primal, and potentially destructive urge to neutralize unbound tensions. In the instance of trauma, compulsive repetition promotes a gradual desensitization of the anxiety that permeates memories of the wounding event. The impetus of this desensitization is economic and thus nonvoluntary; it is also an unconscious condition for any prospective sense of renewed control.

As the title suggests, the manifest aim of *Beyond the Pleasure Principle* is to account for the ways in which the psychic apparatus both is and is not captive to the thermodynamics of the pleasure principle (*das Lustprinzip*). Freud derives this principle in part from G. T. Fechner's 1873 theses in *Einige Ideen zur Schöpfungs- und Entwicklungsgeschichte der Organismen* concerning the interrelations between pleasure, unpleasure, and the conditions of systemic stability. From these theses, Freud extrapolates his reformulation of the goal of homeostatic constancy. The pleasure principle is a systemic urge to maintain a psychophysical balance by regulating the quantity and force of unbound energies. According to this hypothesis, any psychophysical motion "rising above the threshold of consciousness" produces "pleasure" when it approximates homeostatic stability and "unpleasure" to the extent that it deviates from this ideal. In this respect, the pleasure principle trans-figures a physicalist hypothesis that the mental apparatus "endeavours to keep the quantity of excitation present in it as low as possible or at least to keep it constant."[56]

Freud's analysis of the pleasure principle implies that an important economic operation of the mental system is to convert freely mobile cathectic energy into mainly quiescent (or "tonic") cathexis. This principle indicates a strong systemic tendency to maintain constancy by regulating the degree and force of tensions, a task that falls to the death drive. In its moderate valence, the death drive converges with the work of the pleasure principle to regulate systemic pressures by neutralizing "excess" stimuli; in a more radical register, however, the death drive exceeds this function in its impetus to neutralize *all tensions* and thereby yield a state of nirvana-like calm.

Borrowing from Barbara Low, Freud adopts the term *Nirvana principle* to describe this primary self-aggressivity as the dominant action of the mental apparatus "to reduce, keep constant or to remove internal tension."[57] Freud's invocation of the Nirvana principle thus points to a primal and potentially destructive register of the death drive that emerges from this slippage between zero tension and constancy in the systemic regulation of vital energies.[58] The death drive is Freud's metapsychological figure for fundamentally conservative instincts that pressure the psychic organism to return to an inorganic (i.e., deathlike) state. This derivation suggests that the very forces animating living bodies also incite a destructive urge to extinguish them. In the throes of this aim to quell all corporeal tensions, the psyche seeks to neutralize both the basis and effects of staying alive.

To understand this paradox, it is worth revisiting Freud's phylogenetic allegory revolving around the adaptive transformation of a basic unicellular organism that develops a functionally differentiated psychic economy, which Freud then translates into the division between the perceptual-conscious and unconscious systems. This allegory posits a homology between the perceptual-conscious as a system that selectively processes sensory inputs and a "deadened" cortical layer that protects the unicellular organism's vulnerable "vital substance" from a barrage of external stimuli. Freud writes that this "little fragment of living substance" would be killed by the stimulation emanating from the outer world "if it were not provided with a protective shield" against stimuli. This shield is acquired when the organism's "outermost surface ceases to have the structure proper to living matter, becomes to some degree inorganic and thence forward functions as a special envelop or membrane resistant to stimuli." By virtue of this shield, external forces "are able to pass into the next underlying layers, which have remained living, with only a fragment of their original intensity." This deadening enables these layers to "devote themselves, behind the protective shield, to the reception of the amounts of stimulus which have been allowed through it."[59]

It is significant that death itself is integrated into this organism in the form of a "deadened" protective barrier when the outer skin is "baked through" (*durchgebrannt*) by external stress. It is by this death, Freud claims, that "the outer layer has saved all the deeper ones from a similar fate"; however, a crisis develops when internal pressure burdens the system. Freud remarks that while the perceptual-conscious buffers external sources of stimulation, the interior substance has no shield to protect it from internal excitations. His speculations about this interior vulnerability deepen Freud's need to conceptualize a death-driven repetition compulsion, which rises from the primal depths of the psyche to "deaden" the impact of a breach.

Freud's speculations about unicellular organisms lead him to view trauma as an economic and a structural crisis for the psyche.[60] Trauma generates excessive tensions—affect, in short—that pressure the system from within and interfere with its maintenance. Here, *affect* might be understood in keeping with Freud's definition from his introductory lecture entitled "Anxiety." In the first place, Freud asserts, "it compromises particular motor innervations or discharges and secondly certain feelings." These feelings might be further broken down into two kinds: "perceptions (*Wahrnehmungen*) of the motor actions that have occurred and the direct feelings of pleasure and unpleasure which, as we say, give the affect its keynote."[61] Yet this definition does not go far enough, as Freud admits. The "essence" of an affect comes to the fore in the repetition of a particular significant experience, which follows the model of general or individual hysteria that emanates from either the subject's phylogenetic or ontogenetic heritage (*Erbschaft*).[62]

In the "Anxiety" lecture, Freud admits to his conviction that "the problem of anxiety occupies a place in the question of the psychology of the neuroses which may rightly be described as central."[63] From this lecture it thus becomes clear that anxiety is inextricably linked to the vicissitudes of the libido and to affect more generally speaking. When "we have a hysterical anxiety-state before us," Freud notes, "its unconscious correlate may be an impulse of a similar character—anxiety, shame, embarrassment—or, just as easily, a positive libidinal excitation or a hostile aggressive one, such as rage or anger."[64] Ultimately, anxiety is, as Freud proposes, the "universally current coinage for which *any* affective impulse is or can be exchanged if the ideational content attached to it is subjected to repression." The problem remains, however, both to distinguish between and also to connect "neurotic anxiety, which is libido put to an abnormal employment, and realistic anxiety, which corresponds to a reaction to danger."[65] The connection between them is, perhaps, less murky than Freud surmises here. As his etiology of neurosis suggests, a prior latent traumatic event establishes the precondition for the development of a neurotic disposition, which is marked above all by the formation of symptoms that "bind" neurotic anxiety. This form of anxiety is a defensive excrescence of the narcissistic libido, which mobilizes around an unconscious wound to the ego. The difficulty thus remains of distinguishing self-preservative from neurotic anxiety.

In his introductory lecture "Fixation to Traumas—the Unconscious," Freud remarks that the "traumatic neuroses give a clear indication that a fixation to the moment of the traumatic accident lies at their root" and that neurotic patients "regularly repeat the traumatic situation in their dreams. . . . It is as though these patients had not finished with the traumatic situation, as though they were still faced by it as an immediate task which has not been dealt with." For Freud, this observation underscores his thesis that "the term 'traumatic' can have no other sense than an *economic* one." It applies to an experience that "within a short period of time presents the mind with an increase of stimulus too powerful to be dealt with or worked off in the normal way, and this must result in permanent disturbances of the manner in which the energy operates."[66]

A different conception emerges when we return to the thermodynamics of trauma elaborated in *Beyond the Pleasure Principle* in light of Freud's earlier formulation of *Angstaffekt* from the *Introductory Lectures*. Now, it appears that a wounding event inaugurates a painful overload of self-preservative anxiety, which mobilizes the inner world to converge on this surplus tension at the expense of other processing functions. In the psyche conceived as a thermodynamic economy, posttraumatic anxiety must be defused in pursuit of homeostasis. Generally speaking, *anxiety* is the psychosomatic effect of an instinctual "fight or flight" mechanism. In the second chapter of *Beyond the Pleasure Principle*, Freud speculates that a traumatic break occurs because of an absence of anxiety that would have prepared the individual for the impact of the wounding event. The intense anxiety that follows a traumatic event is thus inversely related to its absence beforehand, whereas its presence afterward is belated and therefore excessive.

The posttraumatic anxiety that permeates a cluster of memory images constitutes the "active ingredient" in working through conceived on Santner's model of mourning as a homeopathic strategy. In this model, the poisonous element would be diluted and administered through controlled doses in the interests of critical consciousness. Yet Santner's prioritization of this conscious dimension disengages the prospect that the bereaved might not be able to regulate the repeated return of the ghosts who haunt them against their will. In contrast, I insist on recognizing the unconscious impetus of compulsive repetition that, by definition, cannot be "strategically administered," since the economic aim of diffusing adrenalized affect lies beyond conscious intention.

I have reiterated Freud's emphasis on the economic dimension of traumatic fixation as an overcharged relation to a particular memory. This memory may come to operate as an *imaginary regulative ideal* when self-preservative anxiety invests it with the status of a vital key to the rupture between pretraumatized and traumatized self-concepts. Here it might be recalled that in his narcissism essay, the category of the ego drives already implied the ontological mediation of the biological self-preservative instincts that he remarks in 1920; however, his 1915 essay "[Drives] and Their Vicissitudes" revises this opposition in demarcating the ego drives from the sexual or object drives that Freud associated with reproductive urges. In *Beyond the Pleasure Principle*, he proposes still another distinction between the life and death drives. The shift in 1920 from the object to the life drives permits Freud to link the urge to survive with the sexual urge to reproduce. It also suggests that the ego drives might be conceived as an ontogenetic avatar of the more phylogenetic life and death drives. When I refer to the libidinal dimension of traumatic fixation, I am alluding to an ontological and instinctual convergence in the lineage of the drives.

The imaginary dimension of memory suggests that the traumatized might become unconsciously and narcissistically invested in his or her trauma as the anxious crux of a posttraumatic identity. This self-preservative dimension of posttraumatic anxiety points to a view of working through as a process whereby individuals divest affectively saturated memories as the focal point for self-understanding. Though symbolizations of traumatic experiences can involve tremendous suffering, they also yield images of the self that work over various aspects of the event. Memories are specularized and revised as a component of a subject's narcissistic captivation with the vicissitudes of his or her self-image. I want to stress the role of this imaginary captivation in motivating critical assessments of the past's meaning in the present. Memory images are never merely "reactivations" of transpired events; insofar as they are triggered by present contexts and perceptions, their contents are also differentially determined by unconscious patterns of censorship that extend the rules for retaining membership in various groups. Memory might therefore be seen as both a source and a product of symbolic processes that specularize personal and collective experiences as well as received ideas about the past. This repertoire of images mediates memory and fantasy; its influence is not always conscious or even intelligible, since it is a variable by-product of the shifting demands of cultural and social assimilation.

Freud offers an ego-psychological account of the subject's imaginary in his 1914 "On Narcissism: An Introduction,"[67] where he rejects a definition of the term that restricts it to a perverse form of sexualized self-absorption. Instead, normal narcissism is, for Freud, both primary and generalized: it is "the libidinal complement to the egoism of the instinct of self-preservation, a measure of which may justifiably be attributed to every living creature."[68] What distinguishes a narcissist is the focus of his or her cathexis, which is withdrawn from the external world and is instead directed toward the ego as an ideational object.

The subject delimited in this account experiences himself or herself as split between the drives that motivate his or her desires and the social constraints that discipline them. His or her narcissistic longing for acceptance renders this subject responsive to constraints and the ideologies they convey. To the extent that social conventions and expectations regulate behavior and desire, they acquire a capacity to shape the memories and fantasies that provide the ideational content of self-evaluations.

When Freud is writing the 1914 "Introduction," he has not yet arrived at the opposition between life drives and death drives that he develops in conjunction with his observations about the economic function of compulsive repetition in *Beyond the Pleasure Principle*. Moreover, the "Introduction" was published before "[Drives] and their Vicissitudes" (1915), which proposes a general theory for the drives. In the absence of a broader framework, Freud finds himself in the narcissism essay wrestling with the contradictory implications of an opposition between the ego and sexual drives. Although he refers to an ego and an object libido, it would seem that he is not yet ready to pursue the thesis that a generalized form of "sexual" or "erotogenic" energy might motivate both ego- and object-cathexes. He continues to separate self-preservative instincts from libido by referring to an "ego interest," even though the generality of both narcissism and libido vexes this distinction.[69]

In *Beyond the Pleasure Principle*, Freud comes around to the thesis that the narcissistic libido "had necessarily to be identified with the 'self-preservative instincts.' "[70] This revision abandons the opposition between ego drives and object drives and replaces it with a new opposition between life drives and death drives (Eros and Thanatos). Given the trajectory of the 1920 text, which identifies a primary masochism that lies beyond the pleasure principle, it is compelling to see a convergence between narcissism and the death drive in the aggressivity and paranoia of a narcissistic ego that jealously guards the conditions for continuing self-love against the threat of social devaluation. I would like to suggest that in instances of traumatic fixation, this defensiveness extends to memory images as "vital pieces" of self that must be protected from external and imagined attempts to diminish them. At the same time, however, the interdependent relation between a primary narcissistic self-love and a secondary narcissistic desire for social acceptance perpetuates an unconscious screening of memory images in keeping with changing societal norms and values. This screening is a mode of internalized surveillance that mirrors anticipated condemnations of the subject for his or her imagined "lapses" into selfishness, lust, aggression, passivity, and abjection.

It is worth exploring Freud's reasoning for hanging on to this distinction between ego and sexual drives in 1914 in the face of the contradictions it poses to his thesis respecting the "primordiality" of autoeroticism as a precursor to the narcissistic libido. This reasoning does not solve these contradictions, but it is suggestive because it anticipates an understanding of the ego as the object of a fantasy of unity. Freud acknowledges that "we are bound to suppose that a unity comparable to the ego cannot exist in the individual from the very start" insofar as the ego as such "has to be developed."[71] In the third section of the "Introduction," Freud turns to the imaginary as the stage of narcissistic identifications that yield an idealized image of the ego as an object of self-love. The resulting *ideal ego* is an image of perfection against which the subject feels compelled to measure his or her so-called actual ego. Initially, Freud identifies this ideal as a source of self-love and respect. To a certain extent, then, it is the subject's desire to maintain self-respect, which compels him or her to renounce those impulses and desires that come into conflict with sociocultural morals; however, Freud will ultimately locate the repressive influence of these moral ideas in parental criticism, public opinion, and the admonishing judgments of a host of others. He subsequently proposes the companion term *ego-ideal* to designate the introjected confluence of external judgments whose power over the subject derives from their role in revealing his or her failure to measure up.[72] Significantly, Freud links the formation of an ego-ideal with the activities of conscience as an internalized disciplinary system that measures the ego and feeds the paranoid delusion of being "*watched.*"[73] It will be useful to think about how this ego-ideal is at stake in transferential identifications with an object of inquiry, but also in the internalization of surveillance that scripts memory as a content of self-contemplation.

Freud's formulation of the imaginary dimensions of narcissistic identification yields potentially rich insights pertaining to the role of memory in subjectification.[74] Judith Butler reminds us that in *Discipline and Punish*, Foucault (following Nietzsche) has called the soul "the prison of the body."[75] While the soul serves as the cornerstone of "scientific techniques and discourses, and the moral claims of humanism,"[76] the body, for Foucault, is "that for which materialization and investiture are coextensive."[77] Moreover, in Butler's reading, its coextensivity would be formed entirely by the symbolic at the expense of the body it destroys. This destruction is "preserved (in the sense of sustained and embalmed) *in* normalization," which frames, regulates, and subordinates the body. We might therefore think of the soul as "a normative and normalizing ideal according to which the body is trained, shaped, cultivated, and invested; it is a historically specific imaginary ideal (*idéal speculatif*) under which the body is materialized."[78]

Arnold I. Davidson remarks on Foucault's commitment to constructing a history (and a politics) "without human nature," which is not altogether inconsonant with his archaeological approach designed "to bring to light a *positive unconscious* of knowledge." It is an unconscious, as Davidson notes, "that is precisely the site of those rules of formation that make possible the objects, concepts, and theories of scientific discourse. . . ."[79] Yet one problem with Foucault's model of subjection is that it does away with interiority, and, more precisely, with an imaginary that would not be entirely the effect of power. For Butler, in contrast, it is important to rethink the value of Lacan's concept of the imaginary, which "signifies the impossibility of the discursive—that is, symbolic—constitution of identity." "Identity can never be fully totalized by the symbolic," Butler writes, "for what it fails to order will emerge within the imaginary as a disorder, a site where identity is contested."[80]

Though I am less hopeful than Butler about the value of such unconscious contestation, my understanding of the disciplinary imaginary pivots on her elaboration of the "psychic life of power." Butler emphasizes the manner in which a modern subject's interiority is already an inverted exteriority that records the changing influences of social identification and domination—"the unconscious of power itself, in its traumatic and productive iterability."[81] Remembering belongs to this imaginary as a mode of symbolization: it entails the imaginative production of images that stand in for absent persons and objects, transpired events, and other phenomena. These symbolizations draw upon personal and collective image repertoires as well as the metaphoric, idiomatic, and spatiotemporal registers of language. To a certain extent, signs themselves are memory images that stand in for absent objects. Memories operate as magnets of the ego-drives when they are mourned as the stage of possible selves destroyed by a traumatic episode, and/or guarded as the sacred justification of present attitudes, including symptomatic forms of enjoyment. Yet because memories are also signs, even when they are narcissistically invested and idealized, they are nevertheless susceptible to shifting contexts of enunciation.

Maurice Halbwachs observes that memories fluctuate in response to the changing qualities of membership in particular groups with their attendant expectations. Memory images may be reinforced, attenuated, or displaced by the ebbs and flows of collective identifications that produce an individual's selective valuation of his or her past for imagined others whose acceptance or empathy is desired. This is to say, with Kelly Oliver, that identity "need not be the result of expelling or excluding difference," since it is "constantly renegotiated through interpretation." The "performative aspect of signification will yield new forms of relationships, both with one's self and with others."[82] "To conceive of oneself as a subject," Oliver contends, "is to have the ability to address oneself to another, real or imaginary, actual or potential."[83] Hence the self-awareness that is presumed to result from self-reflection "cannot mean the reflection of a self-contained, unified self. Instead, self-reflection must be the reflection of otherness that constitutes the self as a subject."[84]

Oliver hereby alludes to the prospect that memories are "sociographic" (to borrow John Mowitt's term) to the extent that their activation anticipates their virtual or real communication. This anticipation may objectify and estrange a memory in the imagined eyes and ears of others whose introjected gaze has the power to divide memories against themselves and, more precisely, to divide affect from itself. "Each encounter with memory," Michael Bernard-Donals writes, "repeats the trauma, but by other means— narrative means— which are constantly interrupted by a gap of memory and of experience."[85] Such gaps, I would suggest, refract an anxious relation to the internalized gaze defined as a superegoic composite of conventions and constraints that orchestrates memories as scenarios of self-surveillance. The danger of failed empathy may also fracture the trauma's aura by introducing a sense of self-alienation into painful memories or it might intensify their charge of guilt and shame. If remembering is subject to internalized surveillance as an effect of different collective identifications, then working through must be rethought as a socially mediated interpretative movement between collective identifications and narcissistic desires.

It is this sociographic dimension of working through that speaks to the value of Derrida's elaboration on dissemination to highlight the intimate relationship between memory and writing. Santner's conception of the homeopathic metaphor is explicitly indebted to Derrida's "Plato's Pharmacy," a chapter in *Dissemination* that deconstructs the spiritualization of memory as a reigning trope in an ontotheological hierarchy invested in the metaphysical ideal of unmediated truth.[86] "Plato's Pharmacy" and *Dissemination* as a whole furthers his ongoing deconstruction of the Western subordination of writing to speech as an avatar of the metaphysics of presence.[87] In Derrida's reading, part of the legacy of Plato's suspicion of the "artifice" of rhetoric is a subordination of writing to memory as the spirit and locus of true knowledge. Throughout his early works, Derrida exposes the metaphysical premises in different disciplinary canons that oppose the spiritual immediacy of speech and memory to the material "corruption" of writing as the artificial aid of a sophist. In *Of Grammatology* and *Dissemination*, Derrida foregrounds writing's supplemental relationship to speech and thus undermines their discrete identities. The agency of writing as a supplement implies that speech is not "primary" or unmediated, since its consistency as an intelligible venue of communication depends upon and anticipates its own inscription. The same might be said of the relation between writing and memory as a mode of symbolization.

In "Plato's Pharmacy," Derrida deconstructs the subordination of writing to memory in the course of tracing ambivalent valences of the terms that structure the Platonic dialogues. Derrida's discussion unfolds between various versions of a myth recorded in *Phaedrus* that revolves around the god Theuth, known as the "master of arts." In Derrida's retelling, Theuth originally presents writing as a remedy for memory to Ammon, the king of Egypt and the god/father of speech (*Logos*). The king rejects this gift, seeing in it memory's displacement and contamination rather than its remedy. Playing on other nuances of writing deriving from its identification with *pharmakon* in the *Dialogues*, Derrida reinforces writing's ambivalent associations with *poison* and *cure*.[88] This play suggests a "homeopathic" potential for writing as a *pharmakon* that has the power to restore the "health" of memory if introduced in minuscule, diluted amounts; however, large doses threaten to denature memory's eidetic purity.

Derrida's insights about the interrelations among writing, memory, and speech illuminate memory's destiny as a sign that bears the traces of its graphic supplement—the signifier that circulates through shifting contexts. The influence of these shifts differentiates and defers memory's status as a misrecognized "origin" of subjective truth. Memory has no identity "before" this differentiation. It only comes to exist through the contexts and interests that mobilize it.[89]

In "Tropics of Desire: Freud and Derrida," Cynthia Willett bridges the economics of repetition between Derrida and Freud by interpreting deconstruction as a "tropic movement" aligned with Freud's equivocation about the death drive.[90] In his reading of Freud's analysis of the *fort/da* game in *The Post Card*, Derrida locates a "more originary force" than pleasure-seeking desire [that] does not simply oppose desire as would a drive towards death." Rather, this force "precedes and renders possible the opposition between dismembering death and the unifying urges of desire." This is the fundamental force Derrida names *life death*, which "disperses desire from its first conception and deprives it of a proper object or orientation. Consequently, desire forever drifts after anonymous chains of substitute objects that can never satisfy."[91]

According to Willett, "Derrida insists, the rhythm of Freud's writing alludes to a force that precedes any subjective drive"; he also "infers that Freud's text mimes not only the origin of desire but also the beginnings of language." In this respect, "the movement of Freud's text traces an originary force of dissemination."[92] Willett refers to Derrida's speculation on Freud as "tropic" because it "moves to the rhythm of a force that produces and dislocates language and desire. But if this absolute other is at the origin of language and desire, and if what is sometimes called the death drive, sometimes more originally life death, does not oppose desire but divides desire at its origin," then, as Willett discerns, "nothing in human experience could exceed the morbid cycles of reversal and repetition of the same."[93]

Willett's reading demonstrates how Derrida's dissemination of Freud's model of "fundamental repetition" performs a deconstruction of desire that "borrows heavily from this vehicle of death"[94] while paradoxically forwarding the conclusion that "philosophy today can no longer claim that its primary task is to argue for or against statements of a thesis."[95] Derrida's "antithetical" performance plays on the fear expressed by Freud himself about the prospect of establishing a budding science that rests on increasingly outdated research. The survival of this science must therefore presuppose "a force of repetition that is more originary than the power to repeat that defines scientific mastery." Thus, "[L]ife death entangles every attempt at scientific mastery in a movement of repetition that is absurd."[96] And, as if to mobilize this absurdity, deconstructive strategies undo systems of mastery "by contextualizing or, better, 'textualizing' any system in a scene of writing that it cannot control."[97]

Though his recourse to the homeopathy metaphor is clearly indebted to Derrida's deconstructive invocation of writing as *pharmakon*, Santner reinstates an ontotheological figuration of mourning when he distinguishes it from narrative fetishism. In Santner's theorization, Thanatos is the negative element, the "poison" that cures if introduced gradually in "diluted" doses. This configuration of Thanatos is confusing in light of Freud's figuration of the death drive as a primal urge to revert to an originary state of inorganic calm. In addition, the very metaphor of dilution endows the death drive with an ontological status as an elemental substance (rather than a motility) that exists prior to its dissolution. This substance would be poisonous if pure, but in "controlled" doses that dissolve its danger, it obtains a "medicinal" value.

What is more, Santner completely ignores the unconscious impetus of Thanatos, or the death drive, that informs Derrida's elaboration on the relation between writing and memory. By delimiting mourning proper as a practice of "controlled" homeopathic symbolization, Santner deflects the nonintentional dispersive-affirmative agency of dissemination that insinuates itself into the sociographic scene of memory and functions to diffuse the painful impact of a traumatic event over time. The structural logic of compulsive repetition may make it more theoretically viable to view posttraumatic fixation as a narcissistic-libidinal cathexis that resists the spatiotemporal dynamic of *différance*. Working through (including mourning) would then depend on the prospect that an anxious investment in a particular cluster of traumatic memory fragments could be progressively diffracted by their travels through different contexts of enunciation. This qualification of Santner's model assumes that the "substance" to be diluted by working through is posttraumatic affect and not a literal registration of the loss in its preinterpretative "poisonous" purity. A poststructuralist standpoint suggests that such diffusion might be carried out by language itself, by Derrida's "life death" agency of *différance* or the "inhuman" errancy of the signifier, as Paul de Man once characterized it, which inhabits and disperses a trauma's "originary" aura.

In *Stranded Objects*, Santner identifies a poetic and structural kinship between mourning and de Man's analysis of translation in " 'Conclusions': Walter Benjamin's 'The Task of the Translator.' "[98] De Man's analysis reflects on Benjamin's notion of an original work linked to its translation through the medium of a prelapsarian "pure" language. De Man deconstructs this ideal by demonstrating how it displaces and alienates the language of translation. Translation canonizes this disjunction in the place of an original that is, paradoxically, the effect of translation rather than its source. What is important for de Man is how this "originary" disjunction illuminates a fracture at the heart of every interpretative activity that is vulnerable to the violence of the signifier.[99]

De Man's deconstruction of the ideal of a pure and transparent language targets the ideological investment in a stable, extralinguistic, and originary meaning—an abiding referent prior to or beyond rhetorical contamination. The signifier enacts this deconstructive principle as a nonphenomenal and nonvolitional "errancy"—what de Man characterizes as an "inhuman" movement within the structure of language itself. The unconscious dimension of history is partly a function of this "errancy of language which never reaches the mark."[100] It is an "inhuman" slippage of signifiers because it transpires independently of cognition or will.

Santner cites this thesis in the course of remarking the elegiac dimension of de Man's own writings as a form of *Trauerarbeit* that formalizes mourning by converting it into a paradigm or heuristic for translation, reading, and speaking.[101] In Santner's view, this formalization reduces mourning to an abstract linguistic operation that disassociates its affective and social specificity and reifies history by distilling it to "a series of structural operations depleted of affect."[102] The "loss" that is mourned is neither "human" nor intentional, since it reflects a structural "death" of the referent. Santner is committed to retaining a sense of the historical victim as a thinking and feeling agent who suffers because of a "moral shortcoming or failure in the realm of empirical decisions and politics."[103] He therefore criticizes de Man's structural abstraction of mourning, because it "precludes the possibility of distinguishing one victim from any other" while derealizing empirical losses.[104] According to Santner, de Man adumbrates this sense in converting bereavement into a melancholic poetics that attenuates the specificity of the victims' experiences. Instead, he mourns the structural catastrophes "that are inseparable from being-in-language."[105] The responsibility for producing or mitigating historical suffering is hereby "overshadowed by an impersonal and apathetic 'dismemberment' at the violent hands of the signifier." To be a victim of history is, for de Man, to be the victim of a purely " 'linguistic complication.' "[106]

According to Santner, much theory in the 1980s and 1990s follows de Man's lead by privileging the structures of signification at the expense of its ethical and subjective dimensions. In this respect, de Man's work is exemplary of a contemporary strain of theory that treats "the appeal to human subjectivity" as evidence of a "lack of rigor."[107] Santner's objection is presumably directed at a posthumanist repudiation of this appeal as a regressive, nostalgic, and sentimental indulgence in hypocritical Western notions of a universal human dignity. Santner, like LaCapra, is committed to recovering the role of individual and collective agents, who can be held accountable for their actions or offer empathetic solidarity with the traumatized and the bereaved by bearing witness to the reality of their suffering. In the absence of this solidarity, Santner argues, "suffering will no doubt always be felt to be unreal, even inhuman, dissociated from the drama of human subjectivity."[108]

In *Witnessing Beyond Recognition*, Oliver likewise argues that "working through is possible only when there is a social space and symbols available with which to articulate the trauma of oppression in a way that binds affect to words."[109] An empathetic environment is therefore necessary to the integration of trauma. Though I appreciate the concerns that animate this emphasis on empathy, I worry that these very same concerns also sometimes lead trauma theorists to impose a hierarchy on varying experiences of post-traumatic anxiety.[110] In their categorizations of "authentic" versus "inauthentic" working through, LaCapra and Santer seem to hold preconscious and unconscious investments responsible to a consciousness-raising rhetoric that sequesters trauma in zones of purity or impurity, proper or improper aims. It is more realistic to recognize how the distinction between acting out and working through unravels once we acknowledge the economic and structural import of compulsive repetition. To clarify this importance, I want to draw on de Man's attention to the signifier as an "impersonal" force in the dismemberment of a particular meaning to rethink the process of what Oliver, citing Santner and Julia Kristeva, calls "binding affect to words."[111]

As Santner acknowledges, the play of a disarticulating signifier is the principal trope of "linguistically turned" endeavors among philosophers and social theorists to rethink the constitution of identity and meaning in the wake of structuralism and Lacanian psychoanalysis. This post-Cartesian and posthumanist discourse favors a radically decentered subject as a corrective to the voluntarism presupposed by notions of a "sovereign" individual who unilaterally decides his beliefs and actions. In keeping with this milieu, the inhuman indicates de Man's turn toward the immanence of structure in order to divest signification and history of their ontological and moral connotations as properties of transcendentally unified intentions. He therefore identifies the inhuman with "linguistic structures, the play of linguistic tensions, linguistic events that occur, possibilities which are inherent in language—independently of any intent or any drive or any wish or any desire we might have."[112]

Notably, by emphasizing the "impersonal" structure of language, de Man nevertheless brackets the value of psychoanalytic accounts that acknowledge a relationship between unconscious mechanisms and the slippage of signifiers as an important dynamic of subject formation.[113] However, Freud's configuration of the drives as metapsychological figures for repressed instincts qualifies de Man's formal delimitation of the inhuman. For Freud, the drives are at once economic, structural, and *automatic* in character. Their uncanny relentlessness produces the effect of the *inhuman within the human*—the machine, structure, system, or apparatus that subtends the possibility of a unified intention and vexes primary and secondary narcissistic investments in a coherent ego as the ideational centrifuge of self-love and social acceptance. Like traumatically charged memory, de Man's dislocated original is a *transcendental fault*, a structural lack that spurs successive failed attempts to secure an adequate foundation against the "errancy" of the signifier. Insofar as this errancy is, at once, systemic and unintentional, it may be likened to the unconscious operations of the death drive. To return to trauma by way of de Man is to suggest that a cathexis with an idealized traumatic origin enjoins an alienating confrontation with this structural default, which could function to dissolve the suturing impetus of repetition. The question I would like to introduce here is how this structural effect of repetition may also serve an economic aim to break up a traumatic fixation by *failing* to reproduce the affective plenitude of an event.

Earlier in this section, I spoke of compulsive repetition as the symptom of a traumatic fixation that develops when the climax of a wounding experience is retroactively charged with anxiety. In that context, I cited Freud's observation respecting repetition among traumatically fixated patients: "It is as though these patients had not finished with the traumatic situation, as though they were still faced by it as an immediate task which has not been dealt with."[114] In extending this thesis, Caruth has argued that compulsive repetition reflects an urge to redress the shock of a traumatic accident, a dangerous "missed encounter" with the real. According to Caruth, when Freud's traumatized World War I veterans dream about the events that physically and mentally wounded them, they are *re-creating* the conditions for anxiously anticipating the threatening event. She therefore interprets posttraumatic nightmares as expressions of a wish to master the shock of a traumatic event after the fact.[115]

Ruth Leys castigates Caruth for eliding the distinction between the veridical and the literal in maintaining that massive trauma leaves behind a material registration of the event that is "dissociated from normal mental processes of cognition" and that returns belatedly in flashbacks, even as Caruth insists that trauma symptoms stand "outside representation" altogether.[116] Though I follow Leys in dismissing the idea of a "literal" registration, which she associates with a mimetic conception of trauma, I would nevertheless argue that fixation results in part from a mimetic interest in freezing the event in time and space as an anxious content that can be known and prepared for only after the shock that occasioned it. On an epistemological level, as Caruth suggests, compulsive repetitions of the event in the form of acting out and nightmares comprise various attempts to replace posttraumatic anxiety with knowledge as the foundation for retroactive preparedness and mastery. This mimetic urge cannot be fulfilled, since compulsive repetition involves symbolizing or performing responses to remembered signs of the threat that "should have" produced anxiety.

This thesis bypasses Leys's valuable critical intervention when she draws on Mikkel Borch-Jacobsen to problematize the "mimetic" and "anti-mimetic" models that regulate trauma studies.[117] Leys notes that in the beginning, when it was theorized via hypnosis, "trauma was understood as an experience that immersed the victim in the traumatic scene so profoundly that it precluded the kind of specular distance necessary for cognitive knowledge of what had happened."[118] Proponents of the "anti-mimetic" model, on the other hand, tend "to regard trauma as if it were a purely external event coming to a sovereign if passive victim."[119] Leys touches on Borch-Jacobsen's substitution of the term *mimesis* for imitation in his critique of Freudian and Lacanian psychoanalysis for a tautological tendency to "interpret narcissistic desire along the same lines as desire; they subscribe to a certain autointerpretation of desire, whereas desire is precisely a *desire to be a subject*, a desire to be oneself for oneself within an unalienated identity and an unalienated autonomy." By submitting to the paradigm of the subject, Borch-Jacobsen argues, "psychoanalysis in its essence is deeply narcissistic," and "it reinstates, sometimes in the form of a caricature, the old but always new question of the subject."[120]

My own conception of traumatic fixation could be accused of capitulating to this narcissistic circularity. My justification is that I am attempting to negotiate the straits between two theoretical dogmatisms: on the one hand, there is the standpoint that prioritizes moral consciousness over and against a postmetaphysical emphasis on logics of disintegration; on the other hand, there are the exaggerated recitations of these logics by poststructurally brainwashed scholars (myself included). Despite the moral relativism that is attributed to poststructurally inclined theorists, an inflexible renunciation of idealized notions of unified self-presence converts us into disciplinarians who, on behalf of all subjects, expropriate identitarian desires. The qualification that I would like to offer is that the deconstruction of the metaphysics of presence should not preclude the prospect that the traumatized themselves might remain ideologically governed by naive self-concepts, including a longing for cohesive agency. A savvy critique of psychoanalytic theories does not obviate persistent narcissism or an attendant ideology of subjective mastery among individuals who invest in it as a basis for self-love and social acceptance.

In acknowledging a desire for a stable sense of identity, I align myself with Butler's theses on performativity that foreground the impossibility that vexes a subject's attempts to simulate an internalized ideal. Butler has proposed that "a subject only remains a subject through a reiteration or rearticulation of itself as a subject"; however, the subject's dependency on such reiteration for coherence may actually "constitute that subject's incoherence, its incomplete character."[121] The subject "is precisely the possibility of a repetition which does not consolidate that dissociated unity, the subject, but which proliferates effects which undermine the force of normalization."[122]

In extending the implications of Butler's theses about the performativity of identity, I want to read a passionate attachment to a wounding memory as a refraction of the subject's "shamefully clumsy failure" to fulfill the normative ideal of self-mastery. Perpetual crises sustain certain bodies more than others in an overwhelming vulnerability, a condition that Butler, after Emmanuel Lévinas, has recently highlighted as "precariousness."[123] According to Butler, Lévinas presumes that if "the first impulse towards the other's vulnerability is the desire to kill, the ethical injunction is precisely to militate against that first impulse. In psychoanalytic terms, that would mean marshalling the desire to kill in the service of an internal desire to kill one's own aggression and sense of priority."[124] The dilemma that Lévinas poses, in Butler's reading, is "constitutive of the ethical anxiety" that stems from "a constant tension between the fear of undergoing violence and the fear of inflicting violence."[125] This dilemma radicalizes an intuitive recognition of the other's vulnerability and the implied power of my own self-defensive actions to reduce him or her to that "biological minimum" Giorgio Agamben calls "bare life."[126]

Drawing on this reading, I would like to rethink the return of the real as the aftereffect of a missed encounter with precariousness—a dire reduction of the social and ontological human to a mere biological organism that can suddenly cease to exist. There is reason to be anxious in a social Darwinist society, where this "disgraceful" precariousness is the isolating fate of homeless derelicts and others who have somehow "botched" their own survival and whom the state deigns to let die rather than make live. A persistent attachment to a remembered wound may therefore register this general state of biosocial anxiety that goads the subject's success in reproducing the evidence of his or her proper socialization. This performance is key to inclusion, yet it always "fails," because the subject at some level cannot or does not want to be adequate to disciplinary codes. This is why, for Jacqueline Rose, " '[f]ailure' is not a moment to be regretted in a process of adaptation, or development into normality, . . . Instead, 'failure' is something endlessly repeated and relived moment by moment throughout our individual histories."[127]

It is also important to remember that the Freudian standpoint does not assume that a narcissistic fixation on an anxious memory is necessarily conscious. The compulsive return of traumatic images is nonvoluntary even if it is fueled by an ontological vicissitude of self-preservative anxiety. This unconscious aspect is pivotal because it may *force* a gradual decathexis from an idealized memory as successive failures to reproduce it break up an affective investment in it. In its emphasis on the economic and nonvoluntary aspects of the drives as evinced in the language of dreams and symptoms, Freudian psychoanalysis, as Lacan and Derrida have apprised us, undercuts a metaphysics of the intentional subject targeted by their own critiques.

From this economic, imaginary, and structural conjuncture in traumatic fixation, another view of compulsive repetition emerges. On an imaginary level, the longing to recuperate and protect an original experience feeds a subject's mimetic investment in the event as ontological property. Traumatic repetition ensues, in part, from this mimetic urge to convene and fix once and for all images of an original wound. As my reading of Derrida and de Man stipulates, the "presence" of the traumatic "origin" can never be reactivated or secured against the slippage of signifiers and the flux of social relations; nevertheless, it is the very impossibility of recuperation that spurs a death-driven economy of successively failed realizations, which disintegrate the trauma's aura as a wound that could be closed through an "adequation" of a missed experience. Imagined returns to a traumatic event therefore serve a contradictory purpose: they reactivate and sediment it for the present (thereby keeping it "alive") while incrementally derealizing its status as a source of posttraumatic stress.

The economic motivation behind desensitization troubles the tendency to prioritize conscious reflection as a means of redeeming the traumatized from narrative fetishism. Indeed, rather than propelling a critical integration of experiences, the "entropical" economy of compulsive repetition suggests that the subject will gradually become bored of his or her trauma. The question remains as to whether the repetition compulsion may, nevertheless, prepare the way for a healing distance insofar as it succeeds in propelling an affective divestiture, for if a critical consciousness is at all possible for the traumatized, then it is both limited and enabled by unconscious mechanisms.

Sadomasochism and the Disciplinary Imaginary

The "discovery" of the unconscious was a product of Freud's insight that the mechanisms affecting dreams also affect waking life. Through the heuristic that Freudian psychoanalysis offers, those inexplicable parapraxes and lapses of memory formerly believed to be the product of chance became thereafter intelligible as the expressions of a fundamental determinism. The idea of a prior episode whereby the libidinal disposition of a subject is fixed will thus allow Freud to place irrational manifestations within a causal chain. In *Beyond the Pleasure Principle*, this determinism is not only implied by Freud's thesis that the psychical and somatic tensions affected by repressed instinctual urges are the ultimate source of all object investments. It is also explicit in Freud's phylogenetic narrative about an originary antagonism between life drives and death drives. On a metacritical level, this antagonism is a *mise en abyme* of Freud's investment in the dream of science that inspired him to seek a rational and physical explanation for the irrational that would one day establish the basis for a *truly* causal psychoanalytic science.

Freudian psychoanalysis enjoins its disciples to recognize what its neurotic analysands disavow: the myriad unconscious forces that produce or curtail decisions and actions. In the fields of Holocaust and trauma studies, however, the earnest commitment to an ethical standpoint that does not diminish the genocide and its victims has sometimes led scholars to exclude the unconscious from psychoanalytically directed evaluations of discourse about traumatic history.

I have already discussed LaCapra's and Santner's adaptation of Freudian terminology to evaluate the extent to which perpetrators, victims, and their descendents work through the Holocaust. These theorizations promote the commonplace that responsibility depends on self-awareness. Santner's distinction between "proper" and "improper" mourning (as homeopathic mourning and narrative fetishism, respectively) is consistent with this standpoint. He is committed to understanding the dilemma that Germans face in attempting to rebuild their national identity without disavowing the Nazi-period crimes. In a similar vein, LaCapra is invested in identifying the symptoms of a blindness that compels some German historians to disavow their implication in persecution and genocide and, conversely, some scholars such as Daniel Jonah Goldhagen who, in their identification with the Jewish victims, act out the past as if it were still present. LaCapra praises Santner's formulation of homeopathic mourning as a conscious mode of coming to terms with loss. Ultimately, then, for LaCapra, Santner's model is valuable because it permits the prospect that a socialization of the repetition compulsion might "turn it against the 'death drive.' "[128]

My disagreement with these critics lies in their tendency to discipline psychoanalysis by expropriating its emphasis on the unconscious. The concept of the unconscious subverts a tacit equation between moral consciousness and freedom, which is presumed to be possible only when agents can recognize and change their actions. I suspect that this equation is at the root of a tendency to avoid the notorious oedipal, biologistic, and metaphysical commitments that nettle a contemporary use of Freud's framework. Yet by identifying working through with conscious critical reflection, these critics not only bracket out the libidinal determinisms that are pivotal to Freudian theory; they also preempt a consideration of how such dynamics might contribute to an explanation for why mass violence takes place and why "we" continue to be so compulsively fascinated by it.

A theory of working through that deflects the unconscious is ill equipped to explain Klüger's acknowledged compulsion to reconstruct her father's murder in the gas chambers: "I see my father as an authority figure in the life of a small girl. That he ended in a cramped room, naked, swallowing poison gas, most likely struggling for an exit, makes all these [girlhood] memories singularly insignificant. Which doesn't solve the problem that I can't replace them or erase them. There is a gap between knowledge and memory, and I can't bridge it."[129]

Klüger claims the priority of childhood memories of her father over what she invents in the absence of recall; yet she hints that this more honorable priority is attenuated by the decidedly unheroic resurgence of morbid inventions of her father's fate—naked, swallowing poisoned gas in a "cramped room," his struggle in vain for an exit. She laments that such fantasies not only persist, but also render all actual childhood memories of her father meaningless. Yet she can neither replace nor extinguish them: an unbridgeable gap (*"da klafft etwas"*) remains open between knowledge and memory. Thus, it is in defiance of her own *conscious* inclinations that Krüger finds herself *needing* to imagine her father's murder. She observes that the affect invested in such memories stems from nothing "higher" than self-love (*Eigenliebe*), "love of one's own roots."[130]

Klüger's reflections seem to confirm Freud's thesis concerning a masochistic tendency that forces the traumatized to return to painful scenes. Not surprisingly, the scope of LaCapra's and Santner's ethically minded expropriation of unconscious determinisms extends to a primal masochism that Freud identifies in his speculations on the economic implications of compulsive repetition for a theory of traumatic memory. In contrast to Santner and LaCapra, my agenda in this chapter has been to retrieve the speculative density of Freudian psychoanalysis in order to understand its efficacy and limits for the study of traumatic history. Thus far, my reading of Freud has foregrounded the economic, imaginary, social, and structural valences of traumatic repetition. In this section, I will focus on the preliminary understanding of masochism that Freud develops in the aftermath of *Beyond the Pleasure Principle* as an overdetermined self-destructive tendency that simultaneously conditions and transcends the secondary processes. His theses about a death-driven masochism disarticulate a prioritization of critical reflection that presupposes freedom of will as the condition of an authentic moral consciousness about historical trauma. Insofar as the death drive is involved in compulsive repetition as well as the structures of imaginary identification that inform fantasy and memory, it would necessarily shape critical reflection as a mode of symbolization.

An "amoral" reading of *Beyond the Pleasure Principle* suggests that compulsive repetition progressively "kills" the anxiety that generates a memory's traumatic charge. The eventual "death" or neutralization of this self-preservative tension provides the closest libidinal homology to the tragic ideal of catharsis as the systematic purging of accumulated pathos. The clichéd parallel between catharsis and orgasm is also relevant here. Given Freud's generalized theory of sexuality, there is no theoretical reason to separate the goal of catharsis from the biochemical and thermodynamic metaphors that organize his theory of the pleasure principle and the libidinal economy. Yet it is the deterministic tenor of this theory that has disturbed many of Freud's readers, who are reluctant to accept his thesis that sexual tensions constitute the psychophysical foundation of all neurotic behavior. Perhaps more disturbing is the related idea that all conscious human activity is, at best, a sublimation of primal tendencies.

The overdetermined character of the psychophysical apparatus may explain Freud's recognition of the impossibility of "curing" an analysand, which ultimately leads him to doubt the ideal of a terminable analysis. Indeed, the very goal of "abreaction" that inspired his early delineation of the goals of psychoanalytic treatment presumes an absolute termination that only death is suited to fulfill. It is perhaps not surprising, then, that death and self-destructive forces come to play pivotal roles in Freud's speculations on trauma and the libidinal economy.

In *Beyond the Pleasure Principle*, Freud finds evidence for a destructive tendency in the traumatic neuroses suffered by soldiers who fought in the First World War. He remarks that while their dreams compel them to return to the scene of their traumatic experiences, their conscious life remains, in contrast, relatively free of these intrusions. In Freud's view, this observation challenges the commonly held assumption that such dreams provide evidence of the "strength" of the impression left on these soldiers by their experiences. Rather it suggests that traumatic repetition is neither voluntary nor intentional, but belongs instead to the domain of the repressed; it therefore cannot be viewed as a vehicle of resistance. More problematically, however, these nightmares would also seem to undermine Freud's earlier thesis that unconscious wishes are the key to dreams. Surely, the repeated return to violent scenes of wounding, killing, and terror could not possibly reflect any wish, unconscious or otherwise, to endure the imminence of death. Yet it is precisely this unsettling paradox that confronts a Freud unwilling to relinquish his principal insight from *The Interpretation of Dreams*. For if the veterans' nightmares symbolize unconscious desires as Freud's *Traumdeutung* suggests, then "we may be driven to reflect on the mysterious masochistic trends of the ego."[131] Freud writes: "It is clear that the greater part of what is re-experienced under the compulsion to repeat must cause the ego unpleasure, since it brings to light activities of repressed instinctual impulses. . . . But we come now to a new and remarkable fact, namely that the compulsion to repeat also recalls from the past experiences which include no possibility of pleasure, and which can never, even long ago, have brought satisfaction even to instinctual impulses (*Triebregungen*) which have since been repressed."[132]

Freud's observations about World War I veterans lead him to identify a potentially masochistic component in the traumatic nightmares that compel them to relive scenes of injury and devastation. These traumatic dreams seem destructive and thus masochistic because they appear to counteract the aims of the pleasure principle as a systemic urge to reduce the pressure of excessive or unbound tensions in a psychic economy governed by the goal of constancy; as I mentioned, they also trouble Freud's wish fulfillment thesis. He must therefore consider the prospect that posttraumatic repetition might nevertheless respond to a systemic wish that reflects the economic aims of the pleasure principle.

Dreams and memories provide a means of symbolizing the anxiety belatedly triggered by a traumatic experience. Notably, however, this *Angstaffekt* may be less clearly motivated insofar as it is intermixed with indefinite unbound tensions, including self-preservative instincts and a general quantity of free-floating energy produced by the body and its organs, which Laplanche, it might be recalled, has identified as the source of the drive. As I have already pointed out, this autoaffective source is of particular interest for Laplanche because it indicates "the point of articulation between instinct and drive."[133] This definition sheds light on a slippage in Freud's understanding of *pleasure*, which oscillates between a regulative valence and a radical one. In the regulative form, pleasure is systemic relief from excess tensions, or what Freud refers to as *unpleasure*; alternatively, in the radical form, he associates pleasure with a totally tension-free state.

Freud's thesis about a primary masochism is affected by his ambivalence about the death drive as it relates to these two valences of systemic pleasure. The modus operandi of the death drive is compulsive repetition, which through successive reactivations dissipates the pressure of strong cathexes as well as the posttraumatic anxiety that is the dominant psychosomatic aftereffect of an unanticipated threat. In this valence, the death drive pursues the homeostatic aims of the pleasure principle; in its radical valence, however, this drive also expresses a primal urge to defuse *all* internal tensions, even vital levels of stimulation—which is to say, the very animus of psychophysical existence. The radical variant is Freud's figure for a primordial destructive urge to quell the very vitality of the "psychic organism," what he describes as "the most universal endeavor of all living substance—namely to return to the quiescence of the inorganic world."[134] So defined, the death drive expresses a "nostalgia for origins" at the roots of organic life. It is, thus, a force of nature *and* a vehicle of self-aggression in the related processes of acting out and working through traumatic affect.

This radical figuration of the death drive creates an "economic problem" for Freud insofar as it suggests that subjects are phylogenetically determined to destroy themselves and that this determinism is merely the primal flip side of a functionally differentiated homeostatic system. This paradox troubles any move based on moral grounds to reduce working through to a process of critical reflection that would aim to bring unconscious contents into the "light" of consciousness. For it implies that the repetition involved in remembering and reflecting on the past may be motivated by an urge, at once before and beyond the pleasure principle, to attain the ultimate economic "pleasure" of death.

Freud extends his speculations on the implications of this "beyond" in "The Economic Problem of Masochism" (1924), where he grounds his delimitation of sadism and masochism in an etiology of aggression and self-aggression as redirected forms of the death drive. In this context, the death drive is, once again, a fundamental destructive tendency that seeks to "disintegrate" the life force of a multicellular being in order to achieve a state of "inorganic stability." The task consequently falls to the sexual libido to fend off this danger to the individual organism by directing the death drive toward "the objects in the external world."[135] As a destructive drive "for mastery, or the will to power," this redirected tendency might assume the form of sadism to the extent that it serves the sexual function; but if not disposed of externally, it will remain, instead, within. This internalization produces self-aggression, which might be libidinally "bound" through sexual excitation and thereby yield the basis for "erotogenic masochism proper."[136] This is Freud's term for the arousal of sexual excitation in the course of suffering pain or identifying with the position of suffering, which underlies two other forms. The second is what Freud refers to as *feminine* masochism to characterize the pleasure of occupying a passive position.[137] The third is *moral* masochism, which is distinguished by a self-punishing guilt that haunts a subject who imagines he or she has committed some typically ineffable crime.

To understand moral masochism, it is important to recognize that redirected aggressions do not simply disappear from a "closed" psychic economy. While they are partially exorcised through sadomasochistic fantasies, internalized aggressions will ultimately be converted into unconscious guilt, self-hatred, or depression. According to Freud, moral masochism is, for this reason, evinced in fantasies of reprisal, victimization, beatings, sickness, suicide, or martyrdom, which provide an ideational venue and narrative structure for guilt. This form of masochism stipulates a subject who lives in the thrall of a disciplinary fantasy wherein the ego is enslaved to a punishing superego.

Lacan's famous denunciations of the excesses of American ego psychology do not detract from the value of Freud's concepts of the conscious ego and unconscious ego. These concepts provide the basis for the Lacanian conception of *méconnaissance*, or misrecognition, to characterize a subject's narcissistic investment in the idealized image of a stable, unified, and masterful self. The issue is not whether such an ideological investment is "correct," but whether it mediates a traumatized subject's desire to regain a firm sense of self-determination. Here it will be helpful to turn to Laplanche again, who has written a critique of the category of *narrativity* in psychoanalytic literature. This category "assigns a primordial importance to the manner in which [a subject] expresses his existence to himself in the form of a more or less coherent narrative." Laplanche suggests that "from the point of view of psychoanalytic practice, the narrative attitude consists in privileging the construction of a coherent, satisfying and integrated story, in preference to a recollection of the past or its accurate reconstruction." Yet Laplanche is critical of authors such as Serge Viderman, Donald Spence, and Roy Schafer who emphasize "the importance of this 'putting-into-narrative' as the driving power of treatment, a work performed by both the analyst and analysand."[138] Laplanche also rejects the prioritization of "narrative truth" over "historical truth," which naively assumes the raw unmediated reality of primary experiences that would not be shaped by memory and fantasy.[139] In contrast, Laplanche insists that such prereflective experience is already a "proto-understanding" coded by ideology that yields no knowledge value, but only a potential for "binding and giving form."[140] Moreover, the "enigmatic" dimension of early experiences—"the fact that the first messages from the adult are compromised by his sexuality"—implies that their belated configuration as narrative will partially fail as a result of repression.[141] According to Laplanche, analysis aims to detranslate, unbind, and question the analysand's investment in old defensive narratives rather than aid him or her in rebuilding such syntheses and the ideas connected to them.[142] The goal of psychoanalytic dialogue would then be to open early patterns that enact "the subject's first primal translations" of caretaking adults' enigmatic messages, their "untranslated, resistant and troubling remainders." Because they do not know what they want from the infant, the adults' own otherness to themselves persists in the child as an unmetabolizable *other thing* in the other" whose by-product is the unconscious.[143]

In a reconsideration of sublimation, Laplanche also cruelly assesses the synthesizing "gestaltist" mode of the ego, which would impose "unity upon the diversity and anarchy of the drive through its own unitary, specular form. Such binding," as Laplanche refers to it, "is eminently narcissistic, and as such crude."[144] Traumatic events would presumably derail the "stupidity of narcissistic-gestaltist binding" by yielding humiliating memory images of the subject as a passive and vulnerable victim. Once translated into a narrative form, however, these images may also paradoxically assume a climactic and therefore foundational status in narcissistically invested self-interpretations. In some cases, traumatic narratives motivate the subject to seek to transcend his or her past; however, in other instances, they may expose a masochistic investment in his or her self-image as a traumatized and suffering victim. Laplanche calls this investment the "sexual death drive," which aggressively reduces any object to a pure index of the subject ("the philosopheme of pure identity as death" in Adorno's words).[145]

To understand the implications of this thesis, it is fruitful to recall that when Freud in 1920 locates "mysterious masochistic trends" in the ego, he is referring to a parallel structure of repression whereby the id (es) is held in check by the ego (ich), which is overseen, in its turn, by the superego (über-ich). Despite the heavily anthropomorphic character of Freudian ego psychology, the ego should not be mistaken for an unmediated conflation between consciousness, perception, and intention; rather, it is the interior projection of an idea of a self that is conceived as an individual agent. The ego is, thus, Freud's metapsychological delegate for a subject's self-image, which establishes an ideational orientation for his or her narcissistic libido.

In Beyond the Pleasure Principle, Freud admits he is forced to recognize that "the self-preservative [drives] too are of a libidinal nature." In the same instance, he also surmises that the "narcissistic libido of the ego" derives "from the stores of libido by means of which the cells of the soma are attached to one another."[146] This is to imply that the narcissistic imago is a deformation of the instinct to survive as an organic unity, which explains a subject's aggressive sensitivity to real and anticipated criticisms. Though the false ideal of ego integrity might owe its strength to bourgeois ideology, it will be jealously guarded as though it was the condition of life itself.

Freud's theory of primary narcissism suggests that subjects are invested in an ideal ego as the locus of puerile self-love; yet this investment will be countered by a competing investment in obtaining and sustaining the recognition and respect of others. The subject internalizes societal constraints through the introjected representatives of these others, whose critical judgments will be experienced as punitive when they impinge on the conditions for continuing self-love. The superego is a self-standard that absorbs and condenses criticisms and expectations. It renders the subject susceptible to the socioeconomic aims of surveillance and containment.

A subject who craves the acceptance and recognition of others endows them with the power to denigrate his or her ego as a worthy love object, a vulnerability aggravated by a puritanical milieu. Such a milieu inclines the subject to view sexual urges and aggression, along with most affective and biological exigencies, as painfully at odds with the norms and values that constrain him or her. Alienation from the social order stems from this split that compels subjects to suppress the "improper" outgrowths of primary narcissism and self-preservative anxiety in the interests of social acceptance. Aggression toward others is the effect of this self-denial when it is experienced as a coerced response to an external demand; however, when such aggression becomes a source of guilt, then it has been turned against the ego. Self-aggression is a means of punishing real or potential lapses in civility; it is the internalized disciplinary rod of a society that enjoins a rigid compartmentalization of anxiety and desire.

When Freud wrestles with the relation between ego drives and self-preservative instincts in 1914 and 1920, respectively, it is because he recognizes the instinctual impetus of the compulsion to defend the "life" of the ego against anticipated threats to its ideational integrity. I am suggesting that this idealized integrity is disciplinary, because it is related to the subject's desire to fulfill the generic conventions of a "properly" restrained and thus civilized social agent. Social discipline is measured by a subject's ability to rein in his or her libidinal impulses and to divert them toward the pursuit of higher aims. Self-discipline thus requires the subject to regulate and repress the splintering effects of the sexual and aggressive drives that impede his or her ability to perform a rational, reliable, and socially desirable self-image.

For Freud, the primal urge of an organic entity to return to an inanimate state is the impetus of a drive to neutralize the energy flowing through the body. This is a body whose energies and anxieties will need to be regulated if it is to enter the realms of civil society and the workplace. The demand for such regulation on a social level consequently becomes conjoined with the anxiety that surrounds the bio-economic exigencies of survival. The continuing reverberating presence of this anxiety threatens to reveal the cracks in a civilizing process that imbues its subjects with a reluctance to expose their vulnerabilities in public. Under the duress of socialization, self-preservative anxiety is experienced as a threat that must be managed, if not put to rest. It therefore mobilizes the "excess" of a death-driven masochism as an internalized regulative mechanism that targets any kind of affect (including anxiety) that tears the veneer of stoic mastery. I am hereby borrowing loosely from Foucault to rethink masochism, not as a primal tendency to return to a deathlike state, nor as "a natural phenomenon, a primordial force that disrupts the polished machinery of culture," as Charles Shepherdson articulates it, but rather as "a peculiar feature of culture itself, an effect of language, which includes its own malfunction. . . ."[147] This is to rethink the death drive (in keeping with Herbert Marcuse) as a modality of "surplus-repression"—which is to say, the "irrational" repression that results from "the restrictions necessitated by social domination."[148] If, as Freud asserts, the organism wishes to die in its own way, then death-driven repetition becomes a venue for the subject to kill off his or her own affect as a means of conforming to the ideal of self-effacing containment enjoined by a disciplinary society. "The radical hypothesis of *Beyond the Pleasure Principle* would stand," as Marcuse writes: "[T]he instincts of self-preservation, self-assertion, and mastery, in so far as they have absorbed this destructiveness, would have the function of assuring the organism's 'own path to death.' "[149]

To view the death drive as a "perverse productivity"[150]—as an aftereffect rather than as a precursor of modern forms of socialization—is to understand it as an expression of a subject's urge to "reify" inner life and thus assume the calcified composure of an inorganic thing. The metaphorical implication is that at the libidinal level, psychophysical life will mirror the external forces of domination. Self-destructive and punishing impulses would then be modern by-products of a civilizing process that sentences the anxious signs of embodiment to death.

In the previous section, I argued that a traumatized subject experiences the actual, anticipated, and internalized judgments of others as an objectifying and potentially deadening influence on his or her memories. This deadening can also be conceptualized as an effect of internalized discipline. On an imaginary level, the subject of discipline experiences his or her ego as a captive to the demands of a punishing superego—an introjected idealization of a merciless socioeconomy. The superego is, thus, a metapsychological representative for internalized norms. It is the imaginary organ of a masochistic self-surveillance mechanism mobilized by the guilt of an unavoidably fractured self-mastery. Needless to say, it is possible neither to fulfill each of the minute behavioral strictures of bourgeois society nor to adhere to any one of them at all times. The impossibility of meeting the goal of absolute discipline therefore produces a subject who feels himself or herself to be perpetually lacking with regard to the rules that determine social acceptance, and he or she might long to be brought (back) into line. It is this overdetermined failure to behave completely in accordance with an ascesis of personality that triggers self-punishing guilt as a regulative mechanism, which is how the masochistic ego comes to be hailed by its superegoic master.

My delineation of death-driven self-aggression as an internalized disciplinary device calls for a revised understanding of Freud's sadomasochistic subject. Under the heading of moral masochism, I would therefore like to identify a guilty disposition affected by the failure to remain absolutely "proper" (and worthy of love) by domesticating libidinal pressures. The influence of this sense of lack would then extend to critical remembrance as a mode of working through traumatic history.

I have already defined memory as a socially mediated symbolization of transpired experience that is produced in the imaginary. In its image form, memory functions as an ideational orientation for narcissistic and collective identifications. Critical reflection about the traumatic past would involve an evaluation of these identifications for the purpose of gauging their distorting effects on historical and moral judgment; however, this process is not autonomous, since it relies on moral criteria that derive from institutional and cultural sources whose explicit or unconscious influence on judgment is a measure of their interpellative power. This power is determined by the subject's differential desire to belong to a particular collective or institution, a desire that encourages self-surveillance as a means of ensuring acceptance.

Freud has broached the possibility of a punishing self-consciousness based on his topology of the *es*, *ich*, and *über-ich*. I have argued that this moral masochism is the precipitate of an ideological desire to emulate the ideal of a socially acceptable self; it should therefore be viewed as an internalized disciplinary regime in the context of a society that enjoins its subjects to take pleasure in the mechanisms of their repression (or to suffer interminably from them). This socially produced masochism points to a systemic perversity that structures the imaginary as a stage for fantasies that play out identifications. While memories contribute material for fantasies, it is important to acknowledge that fantasies also mediate symbolizations of the past. This is to suggest that sadomasochistic fantasies might come to inform the content of critical reflections about historical or personal traumas. In short, the primal masochism Freud identifies in the shadow of the death drive may structure or even motivate a critical engagement with the traumatic past.

If critical reflection about the past involves the evaluation of self as a character in one's memories, then it also entails a form of *autovoyeurism*: the subject "watches" his or her own self-images. Such autovoyeurism provides a venue for a masochistic reflection that compulsively returns a subject to memories that "play back" images of his or her own suffering or passivity for the unconscious purpose of symbolizing self-aggressive impulses. Freud's thesis on moral masochism also implies that once the death drive is "erotogenically" bound, there may be a level at which a subject *enjoys* his or her traumatic memory to the extent that it allows him or her to contemplate passive and punished subject positions in relation to the wounding event.

The prospect of this enjoyment provides an explanation for Freud's observation that "people never willingly abandon a libidinal position, not even, indeed, when a substitute is already beckoning to them."[151] This attachment is evidence of *jouissance*, which, as Shepherdson defines it, "is Lacan's name for Freud's thesis on the death drive, the name for a dimension of unnatural suffering and punishment that inhabits human pleasure, a dimension that is possible only because the body and its satisfaction are constitutively denatured, always already bound to representation."[152] The death-driven disposition of *jouissance* suggests that even though the traumatized suffer, they might also derive unconscious enjoyment from the victim subject positions that memory images of persecution compel them to occupy. Here the superego plays the role of a backstage disciplinarian who polices perverse pleasure by expelling it "beyond the pale" of consciousness. In such instances, the foreclosure of this belated shame of masochistic enjoyment may also banish the memories that occasion it.

I would like to conclude by emphasizing that such a thesis does not disavow the devastatingly intense revulsion and profound sadness that traumatic memories awaken. For to suggest that a traumatized subject may be captivated by the *idea* or fantasy of his or her own suffering is not to assume that he or she enjoys a traumatic experience while it takes place or even that he or she takes pleasure in actual pain. I mainly want to foreground the ways in which remembering trauma will, at the level of the imaginary, reflect the alienation of a subject split between self-love and social restraint.

Of course, the prospect of enjoying trauma is, for those affected, a traumatizing possibility in its own right. Indeed, it may be worth considering the proposition that painful memories become charged in part by virtue of this disturbing potential for sadomasochistic enjoyment, albeit one so shameful that it will be disavowed or repressed.[153] To take this proposition seriously is to rethink the conditions and aims of working through traumatic history. The implication is that a subject's repression of this morally untenable *jouissance* will first need to be lifted before he or she can undo the trauma's domination over his or her thoughts and behavior. The irony is that cause and cure are inextricably bound together to the extent that the death-driven aggression underlying such enjoyment also mobilizes the repetition compulsion to extinguish posttraumatic anxiety. Perhaps, then, the radicality of Freudian psychoanalysis derives from its very circularity—from its power to assume such an economy while simultaneously marking it for extinction.

Earlier in this chapter, I mentioned LaCapra's articulation of historical trauma with loss, on the one hand, and structural trauma with transhistorical absence (or lack), on the other. One of his concerns is that the collapse of this distinction may also elide our sense of the difference between victim trauma and perpetrator trauma. "We" ethical critics need to remain vigilant against misdirecting our sympathies toward criminals in a manner that detracts from our ability to hold them responsible for their atrocities and that encroaches on our respect for the specificity of the victims' suffering. Clearly, there is a disciplinary dimension to such ethical commitments. Another of LaCapra's worries is that structural traumas tend to revolve around unspecified absences or a general sense of lack that animates a potentially limitless search for surrogates rather than actual losses that would presumably direct a finite desire for resolution. He thus betrays a certain anxiety about the "danger" of unbounded desire when he writes, "The problem and the challenge become how to orient and perhaps limit desire, which is inherently indeterminate and possibly limitless."[154]

In Naomi Mandel's discussion of LaCapra's work, she observes that the "alignment of trauma with ethical engagement reestablishes inclusive and exclusive communities, here identified not geopolitically but juridically." "When susceptibility to trauma is legislated in this way," Mandel writes, "access to the ability to be traumatized becomes an index of ethical commitment, whether directly, for the victim . . . or indirectly, for the critic. . . . Access to trauma is," for this reason, "also access to the attractive position of responsibility and empathy." To monitor the determination of who is or is not "historically" traumatized, and thus properly traumatized, is to instrumentalize trauma theory as "both the subject and the object of cultural and ethical surveillance."[155]

Mandel's comments highlight a tendency among scholars to turn to trauma as moral capital that establishes them as responsible and caring critics by eloquently articulating the profound stakes of representation. In previous chapters, I have demonstrated how disciplinary protocols enter into definitions of the proper mode of representing the Holocaust. Disciplinary praxis is oriented by an image of the object as the imaginary locus of the event's rigorous and ethical mimesis. In connecting this discussion to Freud's theory of narcissism, I want to suggest that the "Holocaust proper" be understood as an idealized composite formed of images derived from scholarship, media, personal and collective memory, and fantasy. The varying contents of this composite are shaped by a scholar's secondary narcissistic investment in retaining and controlling the terms of his or her own and others' social acceptance. Hence, self-preservative anxiety and narcissistic desire may explain the earnestness of those scholars most likely to invoke the object proper (or trauma proper) to police the field.

To the extent that I have, after Foucault, come to understand the internalization of surveillance as a venue and effect of discipline, this policing implicates Holocaust studies and trauma theory in contemporary modes of subjection. Foucault focuses on the contexts of discursive enunciations and their material effects in practices that constitute docile yet productive bodies. As Butler, among others, has underscored, this emphasis largely sidesteps the psychoanalytic preoccupation with unconscious motivation and fantasy. Working from Butler's qualification that practices of subject formation cannot be divorced from mimetic identifications and desires, the next chapter reintroduces the concept of the imaginary into a theory of subjectification with and against Foucault in order to address the question of how we fantasize ourselves as scholars and critics with respect to our institutional authorities and objects of inquiry, even in their absence.[156] The challenge is to consider how professional and ethical commitments regulate our imaginative relationship to traumatic history. Such investments sometimes foreclose important questions about potential intersections between trauma and the related senses of *discipline* I have been working with here as a field of knowledge and a nexus of subject-forming technologies. Yet it is precisely a hapless reproduction of our training that renders us complicit with modes of dehumanization that are not unique to fascism but are also shared by the neoliberal democracies where many of us conduct research. If we begin to examine our behavior with the eye of a satirist, then, as Shepherdson proposes, we will recognize how the "normal, liberal individual who has 'natural rights' and a native capacity for moral reflection, is itself already inverted, that it contains the totalitarian authority in its origins, not as its opposite, not as its contradiction, not as its degenerate or perverted form, but as its repressed foundation, its internal 'other.' "[157] For this reason, to borrow Shepherdson's wording, "[i]t is the story we tell ourselves, and not the barbarism of the past, that Foucault wishes to interrogate."[158] What satisfactions does this story contain?

In the course of defining ideology in 1948, Hannah Arendt acknowledged that "[w]hat totalitarian rule needs to guide the behavior of its subjects is a preparation to fit each of them equally well for the role of executioner and the role of victim."[159] To the extent that identifications with these positions would be involved in such preparation, the role of fantasy in self-narration is of paramount importance to my theory of the disciplinary imaginary as a site of cohabitation among critical reflection, scholarly rigor, domination, subordination, and desire. The disciplinary imaginary is where sadomasochistic fantasy binds the depressive-aggressive vicissitudes of the death drive. It is no accident, then, "that most examples of sublimation, in particular those relating to professional matters, involve the integration of aggressiveness," as Laplanche suggests.[160] He thus prods us to rethink professionalization itself as a vehicle of sadomasochistic binding and internalized surveillance.

Our anxiety about being perceived as poorly behaved scholar-subjects impedes us from confronting these and other "gray zones" in our work that psychoanalysis has elsewhere spurred us to enter. Gillian Rose borrows the term *gray zone* from Primo Levi to refer to situations in which complicity with dehumanization can become ineluctable even among victims, thereby clouding comfortable distinctions between evil perpetrators and their innocent prey.[161] In the final chapter, I perform the sympathetic imaginary as a gray zone where fantasies influence our identifications with victims and perpetrators and the not always dignified pleasures we derive thereby. This performance is intended to cast light on the disciplinary formation of sympathy as an imaginative act that permits a transgressive enjoyment forbidden and thus intensified by our inner puritans. A critical understanding of this enjoyment as a refraction of self-discipline is therefore crucial to any ethics that presupposes sympathy.

5

Unspeakable Differences, Obscene Pleasures

The Holocaust as an Object of Desire

The "Departures: New Feminist Perspectives on the Holocaust" conference in the spring of 2001 brought together scholars who shared an interest in moving away from perspectives on the genocide that relied on falsely neutral or essentialist treatments of gender and sexual differences. Midway through the proceedings, we participants were invited to step outside our debates to hear a panel of women survivors recounting scenes of physical violation, bereavement, and, in the interstices, the sheer luck that allowed them to stay alive. We sat in rows in a capacious auditorium at the University of Minnesota, our eyes riveted on the platform below. The survivors on the platform had been encouraged to speak specifically about their experiences as women who had been interned in the concentration camps or who, through resistance and flight, had miraculously evaded the sweeping arm of the "Final Solution."

Like the other members of the audience, I listened sympathetically to the testimonies of the survivors. In the conversations that took place afterward, I agreed with the conference participants that these women had courageously confessed incidents that added a new and important dimension to our understanding of the Holocaust. Yet my sympathy for these women could not foreclose an uneasy awareness that the space of our encounter distanced the scholars from the survivors, and elevated us above them for the purposes of observation. Was this auditorium not, in effect, a theater of what Michel Foucault would call the will to power/knowledge?

To visualize this point, it is worth recalling another auditorium scene, the one depicted in Thomas Eakins's *The Agnew Clinic* (1889). The painting portrays a surgery theater closely packed with male medical students—some are half asleep or dozing while their colleagues keenly observe an operation being performed on a woman's breast. Eakins's reflexive depiction of this scene ironically links the viewer's attention with the perspective of the medical students concentrating on the surgical demonstration in the foreground. Their rapt or sleeping eyes are deepened by shadowy contours. In contrast, the prone white female body covered from the waist down on the surgery table is lit up as though it were onstage.[1] Dark hair swathes a pale face partially shown. One breast is exposed, while the other disappears under the surgeon's hands and their ambiguous instrument. Either the missing breast has been mutilated, or cut away altogether, or the angle prevents us from viewing it.

Yet her nude female body remains, before the "man of science," a nude female body, even under his surgical knife. In its depiction of the drive to penetrate the secrets of a female breast, Eakins's realist painting thus performs a paradoxically clinical analysis of the crudely masculinist ethos of modern scientific progress. The object of desire is an object of knowledge: the quintessential fetish poised for dismemberment.

I conjure up this scene because it illustrates an ominous nexus of corporeal objectification and voyeurism as the conditions of an emerging scientific self-consciousness. The clinical gaze is a product of professional

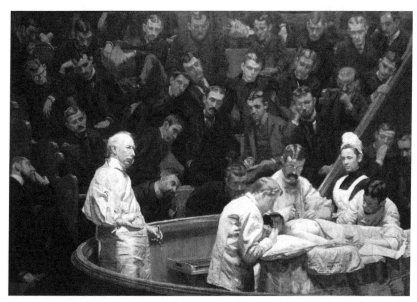

The Agnew Clinic by Thomas Eakins, 1889. Courtesy of the University of Pennsylvania Art Collection, Philadelphia, Pennsylvania.

training and disciplinary rigor that nevertheless cannot be separated from a lust for mastery that establishes the collective identification of medical students as a scientific community in a surgical theater at the end of the nineteenth century. The painting disturbs me because the moral and social sanctioning of this gaze in the name of medical progress does not relieve my suspicion that observers in and beyond the frame nevertheless derive obscene pleasure from this spectacular penetration of naked female flesh.

As a feminist, I could, perhaps, assure myself that I occupied the auditorium in Minneapolis very differently—as a compassionate listener rather than as a clinical voyeur. Yet to the extent that feminist studies has emerged, in the course of the last four decades, as a disciplinary field in its own right, my attempt at self-assurance seems naively self-congratulatory. It takes for granted the institutional trajectory leading up to that moment when women survivors were positioned publicly to confess incidents that shamed them while placing a professionalized me on the observer side of that auditorium (my sympathy notwithstanding) as a vehicle of disciplinary power.

Certainly, the differences between the scenario depicted in *The Agnew Clinic* and the panel of survivors at the "Departures" conference are considerable and will require discussion, but there may also be crucial lessons to be learned from their troubled similarities for feminist scholarship and for progressive agendas as a whole. To bring these lessons to the fore, what follows is a critical speculation on the prospect of a feminist gaze. In keeping with Foucault, I understand the gaze in a disciplinary sense as a locus of external and internal surveillance structured by a confluence of professional training, ethical or scientific protocols, and institutionally shaped scholarly desires. The issue is how I might take responsibility for the ways in which my gaze as a "compassionate feminist" may be inadvertently complicit with what Foucault has critiqued as a will to power/knowledge in his history of the discourse of sexuality: the urge to construct, implant, and locate sexual perversity under the guise of unmasking it, and to isolate, map, and codify its secrets as a means of controlling it. Foucault suggests that the promise of shedding light on this "latent" or "dark" secret animates a psychoanalytic will to secure its scientific self-understanding. The question I invite readers to consider is whether a feminist scholarly agenda calling for attention to the gendered and sexual differentiation of historical experiences colludes with this will in sexualizing the untold and therefore "secret" horrors of the Holocaust. To answer this question, I will find it necessary to depart from Foucault in order to consider the unconscious value of women's Holocaust testimony as an object of feminist inquiry. What would it mean to view this testimony not only as a focus of feminist scholarship, but also as a voyeuristic venue of fantasy and repressed desire?

The Discipline of Compassion between
Testimony and Confession

There is a telling slippage in my introductory remarks when I allude to Holocaust testimony as a form of "confession." Given my references to Foucault, this slippage is obviously not inadvertent. My contention is that the context of giving and hearing testimony in an academic forum mobilizes and reinforces disciplinary categorizations that locate and form subjects while configuring modes of imaginary identification that include sympathy. I will begin by exploring the differences elided by such a slippage that bear on the status of testimony for firsthand witnesses, historians, and psychoanalysts.

One ostensible difference between my relation to the survivors' testimony at the "Departures" conference panel and the clinical gaze of the surgery students in Eakins's *The Agnew Clinic* is the compassion that I felt for the women seated on the platform. This compassion is genuine, but it is also obligatory on an ethical and professional level. A failure to sympathize with testifying survivors would be deemed morally repugnant by Holocaust scholars and feminists alike. In addition, my willingness to permit myself an explicitly affective relation to my object has been historically enabled by feminist critiques of the myth of scientific neutrality. Such critiques affirm the need to retain sympathy in my professional demeanor as a scholar who positions herself precisely against a masculinist and positivistic opposition between "objective" science and feeling. From this perspective, sympathy is no longer simply a "spontaneous," "natural," or "heartfelt" response, since it is also already coded on a professional level as "proper" feminist behavior. In addition, Holocaust scholars who reflect on the processes of giving and hearing testimony foreground the role of compassionate listening in response to survivor testimony and, by implication, testimonies about other traumas. What is sometimes missing from these accounts is a willingness to recognize the structural and regulative effects of the testimonial context upon individual and collective processes of subjective formation.

It is a commonplace that historians see testimony as a prospective source of evidence they can employ to evaluate details and resolve disparities between varying accounts, though one that must itself be evaluated with and against other sources. In contrast, some theoretical and literary considerations of witnessing and testimony, among them Lawrence Langer's *Holocaust Testimony: The Ruins of Memory* (1991), Shoshana Felman's and Dori Laub's *Testimony: Crises of Witnessing in Literature, Psychoanalysis, and History* (1992), Michael Bernard-Donals' and Richard Glejzer's *Between Witness and Testimony: The Holocaust and the Limits of Representation* (2001), and Kelly Oliver's *Witnessing Beyond Recognition* (2001), treat it as a poetic configuration of traumatic history's overwhelming impact on the witness.[2] In foregrounding the performative dimension of Binjamin Wilkomirski's controversial *Fragments*, a fictional "memorial" about the Holocaust, Bernard-

Donals even goes so far as to do away with the importance of the distinction between actual and fictional witnesses. "If a witness's participation in the events of history—particularly in traumatic events—is irrecuperable except through the fragmented and troubled narratives that fail to contain those events," Bernard-Donals writes, "then the connection between the events and the resulting testimony is more tenuous than we would like to think."[3] To the extent that he applies such claims equally to firsthand and fictional Holocaust memorials, Bernard-Donals throws out "the baby of fact with the bathwater of empiricism," to borrow Janet Walker's apt phrasing.[4]

Bernard-Donals' seems to prioritize the literary value of testimony as a "firsthand" description of the genocide in order to enunciate its abiding significance for and above the writing of history and in survivors' own personal trajectories. In the act of bearing witness, the surivivor surpasses the cold information in the written record by enacting, as Bernard-Donals and Glejzer contend, the impasses and incommensurabilities between an experience that remains latent and its telling, between what is recalled and what is said, and between the event and its historical narration, which reveal the "sublimity" of the trauma that exists beyond language.[5] The dissociations and anxious hesitations that fracture memories of persecution are, from this standpoint, no longer an aspect or consequence of the traumatic event, but *intrinsic* to its configuration as a noumenal object. This is how the gaps in a subjective act of witnessing could be translated into an "impossibility" and how a "not all" can signify an absolute negation.[6] It may be too extreme to suggest that such a logic is consonant with the premises underlying the negationist repudiation of testimony's veridical status on the basis of its incompleteness and inconsistency, which would be inadvertently to concede the success of the Nazis' decision to destroy the evidence of their crimes along with the witnesses. Yet surely the repeated emphasis on the "impossibility" of bearing witness to the "Final Solution" ontologizes Auschwitz, in Giorgio Agamben's phrasing, as "a reality absolutely separated from language"?[7]

As I have argued in previous chapters, this poignant rhetoric of impossible witnessing, sublime impasse, and absolute incommensurability in theorizations of trauma and the Holocaust bears the traces of Theodor W. Adorno's, Jean-François Lyotard's, Maurice Blanchot's, and George Steiner's various pronouncements about the "negativity" of anonymous mass death. The power of such pronouncements became still more normative after the publication of Felman's and Laub's stirring 1992 theses on "crises" of witnessing. The psychiatrist Laub's assessment of the incompatibility between historical and psychoanalytic views of Holocaust testimony prioritizes the need to treat all events in the survivor's discourse as valuable in contexts where analysts and other scholars make up the audience. Compassionate listening affirms the truth of the survivor's testimony as an imaginary and poetic venue for understanding the impact of events on frames of reference. This subjective truth takes precedence over and against competing historiographical

protocols, including the demand for facticity, consistency, and logic.[8] Yet
as Gary Weissman argues, Laub goes too far when he claims that "what
precisely made a Holocaust out of the event is the unique way in which
during its historical occurrence, *the event produced no witnesses.*"[9] Weissman
blanches at this "nonsensical" concept, which implies that the traumatic
event was so overwhelming that it happened "outside the parameters of
'normal' reality, such as causality, sequence, place and time. The trauma is
thus an event that has no beginning, no ending, no before, no during and
no after."[10] I share Weissman's concern that Laub's analysis leaves us with a
reductive opposition between factual and psychoanalytic definitions of truth.
I would add that it also ignores Roland Barthes's critical lessons about how
the discipline of history relies on a realist style of narrating events that
poetically and rhetorically consolidates a referential illusion and an account's
attendant authority.[11]

    Ellie Ragland moves beyond this reductive distinction between the
factual and the figurative in recognizing that compassion turns on a *transferential
relation* to the testifying survivor that inspires the listener's belief in the truth
of the testimony within and beyond its imaginary and narrative valences.[12]
This recognition suggests that the good intentions motivating a testimonial
audience do not negate its potentially disciplinary aspects, but may, in effect,
reinforce them. Dominick LaCapra has argued that transferences occur not
just between analysts and analysands in the psychoanalytic session, but also
between scholars and their objects of inquiry. In his analyses of historical
debates, LaCapra defines *transference* in a nontechnical sense to refer to the
ways in which historians are implicated through their affective investments in
the objects they study. Their identification with the object becomes charged
or "cathected" through "processes active in it [that] are repeated with more
or less significant variations in the account of the historian."[13]

    More recently, LaCapra has warned scholars against the danger of
narcissistic identification with the traumatized when he cautions us not
to assume the voice of the victim in our interpretations.[14] His warning
strikes against the myth of scientific neutrality as well as the paradoxical
ideal of disinterested or professional sympathy. My compassion for Shoah
survivors transpires within imaginary structures of individual and collective
identification, which are narcissistic insofar as they shore up a sense of
professional selfhood that is inextricably intertwined with a desire for social
acceptance. It is this desire that sustains academic investments in disciplinary
protocols for protecting the contents and parameters of an object of inquiry.
The implication is that my sympathy, no matter how helpful or sincere,
offers the inadvertent "side benefit" of confirming my membership in a
professional community while simultaneously reinforcing the Holocaust's
value as an object of inquiry.

    There is another structure of imaginary identification that influences
my investment in any field of inquiry, including but not limited to Holocaust

studies. When I speak about the Holocaust as an object of desire, I am acknowledging its regulative power. An idealization of the object of inquiry guides my attempts to do justice to it in my work and thereby affirm my sense of rigor. By virtue of its status as a regulative ideal "in the mind's eye," as it were, the internalized image of the object of inquiry is *disciplinary* in a double sense: it functions as a touchstone for scholars' endeavors to police the boundaries of their fields of study and it thereby reproduces the power of institutional protocols to compose new phenomena.[15]

My conceptualization of the Holocaust as an object of inquiry/desire highlights its configuration as a composite memory image, or perhaps more precisely, as a *memory idealization* based on my imaginative re-creation of historical narratives and testimonies, as well as trace recollections of photographs and films depicting it. This idealized composite shares a permeable border with what Marianne Hirsch calls *postmemory* to designate secondhand identifications with survivors and victims of the Holocaust through the images that memorialize it.[16] Borrowing from Geoffrey Hartman, Hirsch defines postmemory as "*retrospective witnessing by adoption*" that involves taking on the experiences of the Holocaust's victims as if they were one's own and "inscribing them into one's own life story."[17] This vicarious inscription is the condition for a link, postulated by Hirsch, between the belatedness of trauma as an aftereffect of a wounding event and the potentially ethical role of postmemory, which entails a work of formulation and "attempted repair."

Hirsch's analysis echoes Cathy Caruth's standpoint on the traumatic event as an epistemological "missed encounter."[18] The repetition that reveals the impact of trauma thus represents a paradoxical mode of retrospectively seeking to obtain knowledge of a wounding event that could not be anticipated. The lag between the event and its affective reactivation structurally divides the prospect of this knowledge from its origin, which means that the traumatized may not ever succeed in closing the gap between an experience of the past and the present where its impact is relived (to recall Ruth Klüger's words, "Ich bring's nicht zusammen, da klafft etwas"). For this reason, it may, as Hirsch remarks, be left up to subsequent generations to work through a traumatic encounter that they were never in a position to miss.[19]

Hirsch's emphasis on the social and potentially ethical dimensions of postmemory casts a constructive light on the compulsive recycling of certain photographs of the Holocaust that might otherwise indicate the paralysis of traumatic fixation. Yet she is also committed to theorizing the relationship between postmemory and a potentially voyeuristic gaze, which she distinguishes from the look that might interrupt and thus disorient it. Drawing on Jacques Lacan, Hirsch notes that, "while the *gaze* is external to human subjects situating them authoritatively in ideology, constituting them in their subjectivity, the *look* is located at a specific point; it is local and contingent, mutual and reversible, traversed by desire and defined by lack."

Whereas the look is returned, the gaze turns the subject into a spectacle.[20] In sum, the look disrupts the gaze's powers of unilateral objectification by aggravating the subject's sense of being split between imaginary and symbolic identifications.

Hirsch's investment in the ethical potential of postmemory leads her to situate it, not with the gaze, but with the look, which can be shared between the first- and second-generation witnesses of the Holocaust and therefore counteract the distancing effects of the gaze. Yet in an academic forum, such as the one that took place in Minneapolis in an auditorium that separated and elevated the surveyors from the surveyed, the sharing of looks cannot be isolated from the process of mapping the space of an encounter between firsthand and postmemorial witnesses. In this space, the survivor's look temporarily breaks my fascination and unsettles my gaze as a professional listener, but this provisional disruption may actually reinforce disciplinary power rather than dissolve it.

Hirsch's delineation of the gaze underscores its external power over the subject who experiences it as an alienating outside that profoundly determines him or her in the visible realm. Though she relies on Lacan for this definition, it overlaps with Foucault's conception in *Discipline and Punish* of the gaze as a venue for the intersubjective specularity of surveillance.[21] The Foucauldian gaze renders the subject visible, thereby locating him or her in space and time; however, Foucault's concept sidesteps the psychoanalytic focus on conscious and unconscious mechanisms. Instead, he foregrounds the structural and material power of the gaze to exact and reproduce willing subjection. The gaze is the medium and effect of *panopticism* conceived after Jeremy Bentham's eighteenth-century design for a prison as the topos of modern societies: since, at any given moment, the guard in the wide-windowed central tower may or may not be watching the prisoners in the encompassing ring of cells under his purview, they regulate themselves to avoid the punishments that befall those who are inadvertently caught transgressing the prison rules. The panoptic theory of generalized yet partial surveillance suggests that the external and internal valences of the gaze contribute to the formation of subjects as docile bodies. The subject's internalization of the surveillant gaze (of the prison guard, the foreperson, the teacher, the administrator) is the basis of the "success" of societies that depend upon the self-regulative pliancy of citizens and workers, who must be reliable enough to oil the machinery of capitalism without overtly repressive interventions by the state.

What is crucial to this understanding of the gaze is Foucault's thesis that subjectification is a by-product of disciplinary specularity, or what he calls the "trap" of visibility: the gaze marks out its subjects in a field as objects/specimens of information and of institutional, clinical, and/or voyeuristic interest at the same time that the voyeurs in their turn remain sensitive to the prospect that they may also be caught in the act of stooping to peer through the keyhole. This prospect shames them not only in the moment, but also prior to the act to the extent that it compels the subject to anticipate the ever-imminent look that spells humiliation, punishment, and ostracism. In this manner, the present and future contingency of the look subtly spurs the internalization of the gaze that coerces subjects to behave properly both in public and private. Once reexternalized, however, this gaze functions as a camera lens/weapon to study and discipline other subjects.

This collusion between the external and internal force of the gaze has significant implications for professional academic behavior; it suggests that scholarly approaches bear the fruit of behavioral codes that hold social subjects in a superegoic thrall and direct their critical and analytical evaluations of others. The subject is, in this respect, spatiotemporally fractured between the external and internal gaze: beholden to the present and future judgments of his or her prospective critics and colleagues, on the one hand, and, on the other, the protocols modeled by his or her past masters that he or she assimilated through training and professionalization. The external-internal matrix of the disciplinary gaze is important because it organizes the imaginary relations that constitute my sympathetic connection with survivors. It may therefore determine the effect of giving and hearing survivor testimony in the space of power/knowledge. I want to argue that the structure of such spaces is more coercive than we might care to believe insofar as the tacit rules governing them induce the survivor to perform in front of an audience that reciprocally feels authorized and/or obliged to listen.

Lyotard and Felman have observed that Holocaust witnesses are sometimes reluctant to speak out of guilt for having survived when so many others have died, out of fear that their speech will not do justice to the events, or out of fear that it will not be believed.[22] In such instances, the survivor may not wish to revisit agonizing situations or burden others by bringing them into the light of day. In these cases, the attempts of historians, psychoanalysts, interviewers, or even family members to convince a survivor to testify may be experienced as coercive despite any relief it might bring.

While it cannot be extended to all testimonial contexts, it is instructive to consider what I want to call the *confessional effect* to enunciate the ways that sympathy cannot erase the disciplinary structure of a testimonial transmission of traumatic knowledge—the very fact of a distance at once spatial and empirical that separates the survivor testifying before an analyst or audience. This effect is remarkable in certain scenes of Claude Lanzmann's *Shoah*, and particularly those centering on the barber Abraham Bomba, who was forced to cut the hair of women and children in consecutive groups of 70 to 140 people before they entered the gas chambers. Recalling that he also cut the hair of women who had been neighbors and close friends, and that another barber had been compelled to work on his own wife and sister, Bomba begins to weep and does not want to continue. Lanzmann is unrelenting in his insistence that the survivor not only recount the most excruciating details from this incident, but that Bomba also describe his feelings about it while cutting hair in a barber shop. Lanzmann's technique hereby confronts the spectator with the monstrosity of a genocidal system that places Bomba in the position of cutting the hair of women, among them relatives, friends, and neighbors, when he knows that it is in preparation for their murders. The director clearly operates on the assumption that the more personally devastating it is for the witness to recall an incident, the more profound the nature of the evil displayed. Learning this unbearable "lesson" firsthand is important, but it comes to us by means of a confession employed as a disciplinary technology to ferret out a "hidden truth" rendered more valuable by virtue of the painful reluctance that surrounds it and the labor of mining it.

As Gertrud Koch suggests, from Adorno's standpoint, Auschwitz radically exposes the emptiness of moral claims based on a "bad metaphysics" that presumes an individual's "'inner' potential" for resistance in "situations that eliminate every human measure of freedom."[23] Koch's argument is that no art or representation can claim to redeem freedom as a measure of dignity even if it is "engaged," following Sartre's model, in reflecting on boundary situations that reveal human authenticity.[24] In cajoling his witness-characters into "doing and saying things which would have otherwise remained silenced and hidden," Lanzmann is, as Koch observes, a "loyal Sartrean," committed to *expressing* rather than communicating the "presence of an absence which is located outside the spatiotemporal continuum of the image."[25]

In her analysis of Lanzmann's impact on the debate about *Schindler's List*, Yosefa Loshitzky notes that Lanzmann himself defined his film as a "fiction of reality" in opposition to Steven Spielberg's effort, which was based on a "real story," but "simulated many documentary traditions (including cinema verité features) in order to make the events of his film look more real."[26] In this respect, Lanzmann, as Loshitzky observes, echoes Godard's definition of cinema as "the fiction of reality and the reality of fiction." Lanzmann shares Godard's distrust of "verisimilitude as a means of rendering reality." His modus operandi is not to pursue "a crude transformation of reality into cinematography, but rather a presentation of representation. It is a documentation of the process of producing events in front of a camera." The witnesses are "characters" whose testimony Lanzmann aggressively elicited and assiduously edited. It is a style that assumes the value of the camera as a "catalytic agent, a revealer of inner truth." This approach is historically marked by the events of 1968, which cemented the existentialist valuation of cinema verité as a mode of "engaged art."[27]

It might be objected that Lanzmann is purposefully coercive in contrast to a scholarly conference in which survivors are invited to say what they wish on their own behalf rather than cringe before a camera that eternalizes their spontaneous expressions of anguish as they face an inescapable barrage of questions. The problem with this view is that it sets Lanzmann's technique apart from less explicitly coercive testimonial modes; it consequently leaves no room for a consideration of the nonvoluntary and even involuntary aspects of speaking about mass murder and persecution before an audience. In public forums, the Holocaust survivor's status as a firsthand witness places a particular onus on him or her as a bearer of historical and moral lessons and as the immediate "presence" of an event's "truth." The premise that obligates his or her consent is that offering up his or her truth will benefit humankind by teaching us "what went wrong" in Germany in the first half of the twentieth century and/or by giving us "important insights into the nature of evil" and the experience of victimization. From this standpoint, a survivor's testimony begins to resemble confession in the Foucauldian sense of a disciplinary technology.

It is in the context of the first volume of *The History of Sexuality* that Foucault introduces the confession as a technology of modern power that has been deployed with varying degrees of sadism by an array of state-sponsored authorities from the premodern to the early modern and modern periods.[28] According to Foucault, it is when the confession is separated from torture and becomes voluntary that its coercive powers become subtler and therefore more effective. In a voluntary confession, belief and action reciprocally affirm while consolidating a subject's identity as an individual and as an accepted member of a collectivity. The voluntary confession thus derives its power by serving a fourfold purpose: it elicits information that may further a particular social, progressive, or scientific agenda; it produces the status of the confessing individual as a particular subject; it affirms this subject's compliance with the rules and values of a civil society; and it consolidates the authority and respectability of the interests that enjoin or enable the confession.

Once connected to Foucault's argument about the discursive construction of sex, the disturbing dynamics of this fourfold power become unmistakable. Here we will do well to remember that his departure point in the introduction to *The History of Sexuality* is a critical challenge to the so-called repressive hypothesis, which reductively assumes that power functions only negatively as a function of norms, social policy, and laws that systemically impose prohibitions and constraints. If followed through historically, this hypothesis would purport to explain the alleged silencing of sex, treated as the essence and origin of transgression, and a pathological "excess" as such. Yet Foucault dismisses this narrative, focusing instead on the proliferation throughout the modern period of juridical, institutional, and medical strategies for isolating and regulating sex as an emerging object of knowledge. The evidence for this multiplication reverses the repressive hypothesis in demonstrating that discourse about sex was hardly suppressed. Indeed, it was becoming omnipresent and omnivalent as the impetus and end of technologies of power aimed at "discovering"—which is to say, producing, implanting, and regulating—the "essence" of human life and death. Sex would become this "essence" to the extent that it had been constructed through interweaving discourses as the covert motivation of human activity, which, by virtue of its innate impropriety, lies buried "in the depths." Bringing this secret to light thereby becomes the modus operandi of a rational bourgeois science caught in a paradox of its own making: its practitioners naturalize its class-specific norms and anxieties in the same moment that they hold these self-same norms up to methodical scrutiny as "repressive," "neurotic," or "primitive" superstitions, a judgment that their own detached public airing of the issue at once contravenes and supersedes.

In short, the first volume of *The History of Sexuality* suggests that sex is the incentive and aim of the confession as a technology of modern subjectification. Within this economy, sex assumes the value of power/knowledge capital as the mystery of mysteries, the shameful secret that must be suppressed beyond (and beneath) all others. Its extrication promises wisdom into the "shadowy recesses of human nature"; this bestows still greater authority upon the "surgeon" of souls, the confessor garbed in various professional uniforms. At the same time, the voluntary confession corroborates the commitment of the confessing subject along with his or her confessor to the conventions and ideals of an enlightened civil society. The uniqueness of the disciplined subject is inaugurated in this moment of offering up his or her essential, personal, and ultimate truth, his or her hidden perversions and unspeakable desires. Is it surprising, then, that he or she would come to enjoy confession as a means of shoring up his or her individuality, expressing his or her unique subjectivity, and of guaranteeing the existence of his or her soul? If lyric poetry, autobiographical novels, and pseudotherapeutic talk shows proliferate in the contemporary era, then it is because the pleasures of confession as a technology of subjective constitution have expanded to the domain of public consumption as a whole.

In "Social Bonds and Psychical Order: Testimony," Susannah Radstone highlights the ways in which a narcissistic and confessional culture promotes self-absolution through public acts of self-scrutiny. Her aim is to historicize testimony in light of shifting styles and aims of confession in the modern era. Radstone's reading of the contemporary proliferation of confession suggests that it covers over the nature of postmodern authority, which has become "diffuse, all-pervasive, and unavailable as a point of identification." In such an environment, the public character of testimonies cannot be extricated from the legacy of public confession as a "technology of self" that serves to restructure confused power relations between civil subjects and the social order.[29]

Radstone notes that "at least since the 1980s, the confessional injunction has been countermanded by an injunction, not to self-scrutiny and self-implication, but to bear witness, rather, to the sufferings of others."[30] I would add that this "countermand" is, in part, a product of the recent institutional history of feminism growing out of the early consciousness-raising groups that led up to the women's liberation movement.[31] Once it became coupled with the multiculturalist perspective in the 1980s, academic feminism opened an institutionally sanctioned channel for women of various backgrounds to testify on their own and others' behalf in order to reverse the silences imposed on them by a sexist and racist society and thereby raise critical consciousness among members of dominant groups. It is important to bear in mind that this agenda also instituted subject positions for survivors of persecution and genocide to the extent that it presumed their willingness to fill certain preassigned roles in public forums that were typically organized and attended by white liberal feminists. Because such forums institutionalize a moral inducement to give and to hear testimony, they additionally assume a disciplinary power to constitute the testifying individual as an obedient subject offering up his or her "authentic" firsthand knowledge.

What is paradoxical about this institutional history is that it transpired in tandem with the growing currency of Foucault's work in feminist circles and among cultural critics as a whole. The broader availability of *The History of Sexuality* in English-speaking countries after its translation in 1978 coincided with the rise of feminist perspectives in North American universities where Foucault's emphasis on the discursive construction of bodies and pleasures was perceived as groundbreaking. By demonstrating that discourse is not merely written or spoken, but contingently embodied, Foucault offered a nonessentialist view of the ways subjects are inscribed by categories of gender and sexuality that are produced by historical forces. His consideration of a discourse-power-knowledge matrix was thus a boon for feminist scholars who sought to disarticulate sex and gender while challenging the putative neutrality of male-centered approaches.

Despite their self-conscious embrace of his influence, Foucault's analysis of disciplinarity implicates a feminist critic's preoccupation with sex, gender, and the body in a contemporary will to power/knowledge. For if the repressive hypothesis orients a modern search for truth, then it would compel us to locate the "real" secret of historical existence in its sexual dimensions—those erotic elements that our societies compel subjects to hide or confess. These are the "secrets" that a feminist emphasis on embodied experience is customized not only to expose and dissect, but also to disavow. The issue is how a feminist approach to testimony about the Nazi crimes both thwarts and enables these ambivalent pursuits. What would it mean to "sexualize" the Holocaust?

The Holocaust as a Feminist Object of Desire

In the first part of this chapter I linked the audience of the survivor panel at the "Departures" conference with the specular dynamics of a nineteenth-century surgery theater and the coldness of the male scientific gaze depicted in Eakins's *The Agnew Clinic.* Such a linkage chafes against the ethos of feminists and Holocaust scholars who prioritize compassion and respect in testimonial contexts. It might be objected that the scholars filling the seats of the auditorium at the University of Minnesota were not ponderous nineteenth-century men in black, but feminists who consciously discipline themselves to avoid a masculinist objectification of the female body. In addition, while the institutional dimensions of such a forum undeniably propelled both audience members and survivors to fulfill certain prescribed roles, the women on the platform were neither passive nor prone as they spoke about their experiences. Unlike the woman in the Eakins painting, the panelists were not precisely abject: they had survived persecution, genocide, and devastating bereavements—the losses of parents, siblings, children, and spouses who were sometimes murdered right before their eyes.

Indeed, what I learned from their testimony is that these women suffered forms of objectification that surpassed the uncanny and alienating spectacles of early surgical exploration captured in *The Agnew Clinic*. One woman testified that she had not only been forced to strip before being subjected to a vaginal search, but was also compelled to watch as her mother and others endured this humiliation. Mother and daughter were enjoined in turn to undergo and to witness each other's degradation. It is, of course, significant that my memory of the panel lingers on this testimony. What needs to be considered is how this evidence of my own fascination troubles the ethics of my position as a sympathetic witness in ways that bear on the very different experiences of giving and hearing this testimony at a scholarly conference.

I will begin by noting that the survivor who recounted this episode seemed both surprised by and grateful for the safe and respectful space that had been opened for her to articulate what she had never before revealed: the humiliations that she endured in the camps. The mortification and shame that had prevented her from previously mentioning this situation involving a hostile stranger probing her body against her will potentially returned in the course of her reconstruction. "Along with the pain of remembering physical abuse and torture," Oliver stresses, there is a "special pain involved" in recalling degradation—the *shame* of being "made into an object."[32] For my part, I could, perhaps, pride myself for belonging to a community of scholars who were opening up this officially sympathetic space in which the survivor might break a burdensome silence to share a humiliating episode from an unbearable history.

I employ the word *break* here to emphasize the potentially problematic nature of my well-intentioned sympathy in these contexts. Such sympathy is vexed because it entails a fantasy-prone mode of transferential identification with the other whereby I introject myself into a reconstruction of her experience. In previous chapters, I cited Wilhelm Dilthey's definition of historical *Verstehen* as "the rediscovery of the I in the Thou" whereby "the mind rediscovers itself at ever higher levels of connectedness." This definition might be considered identitarian if it is viewed as promoting a neutralization of differences, as when Dilthey stresses that "this sameness of the mind in the I and the Thou and in every subject of a community, in every system of culture and, finally, in the totality of mind and universal history, makes the working together of the different processes in the human studies possible." This definition structures *Verstehen* as a self-confirming fantasy: "[T]he knowing subject is one with its object, which is the same at all stages of its objectification."[33]

Radstone takes up the social dimensions of this problematic in a reflection on September 11 in which she contends that there is always a fantasy at stake in the way that we narrate and make sense of the trauma.[34] She observes that an "event may prove traumatic, indeed, not because of its inherently shocking nature but due to the unbearable or forbidden fantasies that it prompts." She consequently argues for the value of a psychoanalytic perspective with its emphasis on the ways in which "the world of fantasy is inextricably connected with sexual difference and with desire."[35]

In "Social Bonds and Psychical Order," Radstone analyzes the prospective staging of such fantasies in the testimonial context. While she reaffirms the distinction between perpetrators and victims, Radstone argues that testimony's audience may cross that line on an imaginative level, thus creating what she calls, after Primo Levi, a "gray zone" between good and evil.[36] In *Remnants of Auschwitz*, Giorgio Agamben cites Levi to define it as a zone of irresponsibility in which "'the long chain of conjunction between victim and executioner comes loose, where the oppressed becomes oppressor and the executioner in turn appears as victim. A gray, incessant alchemy in which good and evil and, along with them, all the metals of traditional ethics reach their point of fusion."[37] Agamben situates this gray zone *before* rather than *beyond* good and evil, a topology that affirms Radstone's conceptualization of it as a site of fantasized identifications with victims and perpetrators. In her view, identifications with victims and perpetrators may serve to override "'an absence of internalised personal authority'" while structuring and compensating for amorphous modes of surveillance and control in contemporary society.[38]

Radstone's observations about the destructuring of contemporary authority and surveillance suggest that what I have referred to as the external gaze cannot be localized. By extension, the internal gaze may respond to an imaginary need to *invent* a unified locus for surveillant judgment through self-regulative and punishing fantasies that symbolize, reproduce, and work through the guilty residues of failed self-mastery.[39] In calling for a recognition of the ways in which fantasy structures the reception of events, Radstone's thesis about the psychosocial value of traumatic testimony acknowledges the function of sadomasochistic identifications that symbolize the prospects of omnipotence and coherent control. Even if these prospects are presumed to be lacking on a psychosocial level, they must nevertheless be disavowed on a moral one to the extent that they involve identification with the perpetrators. Following Gillian Rose, Radstone urges us to abandon a certain "Holocaust piety" that leaves room for an untroubled absolutism of morally acceptable identifications with the victims, but not with the perpetrators. Instead, she asks us to consider the "hidden *violence* that subtends identification solely with victimhood, since it is only from a position of absolute power that the predatory capacity of others can cease to be a point of identification."[40]

Radstone's argument resonates in several notes with Laura Frost's study of the cultural fascination with fascism and the eroticized figure of the Nazi as an icon of sadistic violence.[41] Frost's *Sex Drives* draws out the implications of Foucault's comments in the 1970s about Nazism as the "ultimate symbol of eroticism," a fixation he attributes to a general desire for power.[42] Frost also extends Susan Sontag's speculations on a "natural link" between sadomasochism and the exotic lure of fascist transgression for a sexually repressive society.[43] Never before was "the relation of masters and slaves so consciously aestheticized" as in the "master scenario" that Nazism offers, in which the "color is black, the material is leather, the seduction is beauty, the justification is honesty, the aim is ecstasy, the fantasy is death."[44]

Frost's reading of modernist literature leads up to an analysis of the fantasies and foreclosures that haunt feminist constructions of Nazism as a radical embodiment of patriarchal evil. According to Frost, a strategic conflation between patriarchal oppression and Nazi brutality is not as pure as the political and moral conscience of feminism requires. In various references to Nazis, she pinpoints stirrings of transgressive fascination with shiny boots of leather, steel-eyed ruthlessness, and impenetrable indifference coded as phallic potency and strength. The Nazi thus serves as a highly libidinalized venue for the fantasy interplay of sexualized aggression and submission scenarios both inside and outside women's writing. The question is whether feminists could extirpate such sadomasochistic fantasies, given a liberatory agenda, which is opposed to persecution and forced passivity. For if "every woman loves a fascist," as a literal reading of Sylvia Plath's "Daddy" suggests, then feminists must stop being "women" by killing their "inner Hitlers" along with their "inner fathers," not to mention the sadomasochistic inclinations that resurrect their ghosts.

To take Frost's argument in *Sex Drives* seriously is to reconceptualize the feminist gaze as the effect of a constitutive foreclosure that is, at once, disciplinary, libidinal, and potentially traumatic.[45] For if sadomasochistic fantasies about the hard and cruel Nazi master suggest a particularly vexed set of identifications for feminists, then the feminist gaze is overdetermined by such a repression. That is to say, feminist sadomasochism may actually be a by-product of progressive or democratic politics to the extent that the very taboo against morally forbidden identifications with Nazi violence might unconsciously mobilize the very desire it aims to contain.

Frost observes that feminists have bypassed the implications of the cultural fascination with fascism. Consequently, they have not fully taken into consideration the erotic allure that transgressive identifications with Nazi perpetrators retain, which might commit them to own up to their fantasies and libidinal investments.[46] The eroticized figure of the Nazi may creep into my memories by means of my mass-culturally permeated fantasy life, both despite *and because of* my earnest and high-minded ethics. For this reason, while the commitment to acknowledge such fantasies may seem controversial when we are talking about the reception of survivor testimony, it is essential to any consideration of the ethics of this encounter. But what possible erotic fantasy could be functioning in the instance of the survivor panel at the "Departures" conference and, more crucially, perhaps, how do I take responsibility for it? Must I admit what I most fear morally and politically—which is to say, my pleasurable complicity with violence?

Radstone and Frost invite me to take responsibility for my "post-memorial" fantasies as a preliminary step in thinking through what I earlier referred to as the compassionate imaginary to designate the image content and creative operations involved in "adoptive witnessing." My fantasy-building mechanisms were set into play in that moment I identified with the testifying survivor by imagining how I would have felt in her place. Obviously, I cannot "screen" her memory images like a film. Instead, I must re-create her memory in my own mind by drawing on stores of personal memory and mass-produced images from movies, television, textbooks, and magazines. Fantasy and sympathy are modes of visual symbolization that borrow from this repertoire of images—that is to say, the compassionate imaginary shares a permeable border with unconscious wishes, including aggressive and/or sadomasochistic urges that may be further specified through Nazi iconography.

The sharing of images between fantasy and sympathy conditioned my response to the survivor's testimony at the "Departures" panel in giving rise to my speculation that the men strip searching women prisoners for hidden valuables may have derived sadistic enjoyment from this otherwise "banal" task. It is crucial to recognize that this sadistic pleasure is *imagined*. Whether or not the survivor's testimony concretizes it, I *attributed* this enjoyment to the Nazis who conducted these searches. My moral repugnance thus stems from the *idea* of this enjoyment, which I subsequently shun as "obscene." For it is in the specter of this sickening enjoyment that my own visceral disgust and unspeakable fascination with Nazi barbarism lurks.

My inner puritan is responding, in part, to a moralizing dichotomy that conjoins sympathy with a bourgeois sense of tastefulness in opposition to those scrofulous emotional excrescences such as Goldhagen's "pornographic" rage, which evidently subtended the protocols of restrained scholarship. I would like to broaden the implications of this line of argument by reiterating the obvious—namely, that it is the largescale repression of a variety of aggressively self-preservative and erotic impulses that, generally speaking, determines "successful" membership in societies dominated by a secularized "Protestant work ethic" and Christian stoicism. The assumption is that property rights are sacrosanct and that the personal should be subordinated to social relations, which must themselves be serviceable to free-market principles of exchange. These societies require their constituents to control or conceal the symptoms of their desires as the "private property" of the individual soul. "Proper" subjects are willing to bring themselves into line with bourgeois norms and virtues: dependability, consistency, Christian-stoic self-mastery, respect for private property (including the nuclear family), and heterosexual monogamy. "Health" and "happiness" in such societies is measured by the ability to acquire and enjoy the fruits of subjection through a secondary narcissistic cathexis with the socioeconomic protocols of emotional and corporeal containment.[47]

I suspect that Adorno might have viewed these norms as another manifestation of the coldness required for survival—"the basic principle of bourgeois subjectivity, without which there could have been no Auschwitz. . . ."[48] He does not stop short of implicating himself in this "basic principle" in referring to those living after Auschwitz "who escaped by accident," including exiles like himself and Horkheimer. Yet as Adorno also admits, the "inhuman part of it, the ability to keep one's distance as a spectator and to rise above things, is in the final analysis the human part, the very part resisted by its ideologists."[49] The politics of purity establishes a moral high ground for a restrained (and thus politely neutral) sympathy at the expense of new and potentially unsettling knowledge about the pervasiveness of complicity that "we, heirs to the horrors of the twentieth century, cannot afford to ignore," as Naomi Mandel argues.[50] "When sympathy is aligned with knowledge, and the lack of one is wielded to demonstrate the absence of the other," she writes, "evoking the unspeakable takes the form not of knowledge's abnegation but of its legislation: an unacceptable truth that, sympathy dictates, cannot be uttered."[51]

In *Against Unspeakability*, Mandel has identified the rhetorical and disciplinary valences of the unspeakable as a term imbued with "an ethical imperative which presumes that to translate another's experience into language is to perform some sort of violence, and which advocates that the limits of language be delineated in order to make space for cultural, experiential, or epistemological difference."[52] Such invocations, Mandel contends, allow scholars to claim moral identity capital by policing others, since the implication is that certain people are allowed to speak about certain things and, implicitly, certain people are qualified to decide who "*can speak about not being able to speak.*"[53] Yet the recourse to unspeakability is not only disciplinary but also cowardly: it elides the materiality of the suffering that is assumed to lie beyond speech; it also avoids "an explicit confrontation" with the "inevitable complicity" that speaking about fragile and vulnerable bodies in pain would perform.[54] It is this unbearable sense of precariousness—others' and our own—that deepens the sting of Adorno's pronouncement that "[e]ven in his formal freedom, the individual is as fungible and replaceable as he will be under the liquidators' boots."[55] It is an insight that Agamben retheorizes when, in *Remnants of Auschwitz,* he makes the concentration camp the emblematic locus of biopolitics: "I" am always imminently one whom a sovereign power can reduce to vital signs, to a skeletal minimum of bare life.

In Holocaust studies, the trope of unspeakability functions as a means of declaring the radical moral otherness of the atrocities committed by the Nazis and the "unrepresentable" enormity of the suffering they caused. Such rhetoric is empty in view of the manifold conferences, articles, edited volumes, book-length studies, dramatic films, documentaries, and memorials devoted to the Holocaust, not to mention the frequency of debates and scandals about National Socialism over the last quarter century.[56] Already in 1967, Emmanuel Lévinas worried that the "acuity of the apocalyptic experience lived between 1933 and 1945 is dulled in memory. . . . There have been too many novels, too much suffering transformed on paper, too many sociological explanations and too many new worries."[57] Mandel quips, "The more we speak about Auschwitz, it seems, the more prevalent and compelling the gestures toward the limits of speech, thought, knowledge, and world."[58] This is to call attention to the Holocaust as a vehicle for producing poignancy capital for those of us who "speak the unspeakable" and "represent the unrepresentable," all the while congratulating ourselves on our bravery for taking on these impossible yet morally urgent tasks. At the same time, the heavy circulation of this trope in the discourse of Holocaust studies enacts the oxymoron of a verbose silence, a symptom of the weakness of the repressive hypothesis as Foucault has defined it.

On a substantive level, of course, the two logics are very different. The repressive hypothesis would narrate the history of sexuality as a suppression and prohibition of discourse about sex treated as a concealed and potentially "pathological excess" or as an "origin" of personality. Once again, Foucault overturns this hypothesis by revealing that references to sex were not suppressed in authoritative discourse. Rather, the multiplication of such references and their effects raised this hypothesis to the level of a pseudoepidemiology animated by the assumption that to discover a sexual source for a symptom or a personality trait was to cure a perversion conceived as a disease. In this manner, the constructed ubiquity of sex and perversion as diagnostic targets medically sanctioned efforts to induce submission to the authorities in question.

Foucault's critique of the repressive hypothesis spurs a certain cynicism regarding repeated references to the unspeakability of Nazi torture and genocide that unmask an ambivalent motive: to inoculate authoritative discourse against the pathological perversity of the phenomena it investigates.

The aim would then be to "root out" this pathology—to expose this evil for all the world to see—and thereby rid ourselves of genocidal xenophobia. Foucault's critique of the repressive hypothesis thus invites a consideration of the perverse pleasure-in-power that motivates such an exposure, whereby a "pathological origin" must first be implanted—which is to say, invented in discourse—before it can be properly "discovered" and "extracted."

Thomas Trezise has analyzed the normative assumptions that enter into the logic of the unspeakable in the context of Holocaust studies.[59] In that context, the unspeakable typically refers to the magnitude of the evil perpetrated by the Nazis, which exposes the limit of the moral imagination and thereby evokes an experience of the sublime. Trezise explains this experience in Kantian terms: "[N]either a single representation nor even a totality of all possible representations could make of the Holocaust the object of a comprehensive 'view from nowhere.' "[60] In effect, one *must* not speak of "it" (these crimes, this suffering), because one *cannot* do so without profaning a morally transcendent event. The genocide thereby assumes a sacred stature, beyond human powers of representation, for which the experience of the sublime is an aesthetic analogue.[61]

In his scathing rebuke of Steven Spielberg for the impropriety of *Schindler's List*, Lanzmann invoked a "circle of fire" that burns around the atrocities perpetrated by Germans and in their name.[62] His example highlights the ethical injunction at stake in the unspeakable as a speech-act version of this protective circle of fire that allows a morally righteous "us" to align ourselves with the "innocent" Jewish victims while distancing ourselves from a guilty German "them." For this reason, Mandel is right to stress that when we say *unspeakable*, we are not just referring to an "experiential shortcoming" or the inadequacy of language to do justice to the extremity of the "Final Solution," but are also identifying the victims as "human" (as long as they are innocent?) and the perpetrators as "inhuman," which is why their mentality would transcend our "properly human" modes of understanding.[63] It also suggests that "we" refuse to contemplate those life-forms that we still hold in common with past perpetrators and with the new ones who thrive among us now.

"The negation performed by the 'un' in 'unspeakable,' " Mandel observes, "can be more accurately described as a prohibition, a kind of taboo, itself untouchable, around which discourse and culture are structured but which also embodies the disturbing potential of violence and contamination."[64] It is precisely this unbearable prospect of contamination—which, following Mandel, I link to a disavowal of complicity—that spurs a compulsive recourse to this term. The unspeakable is, thus, a rhetorical shorthand for that which is tacitly acknowledged, but kept under wraps for the sake of propriety. It applies to those phenomena that "cannot" or "should not" be made public. Against the backdrop of an increasingly voluble discourse about the Holocaust, the "cannot" and the "must not" upon which the unspeakable turns appear to be gestures of disavowal. What is disavowed is that which "cannot" and "must not" be admitted (for the sake of maintaining the distinctiveness of civil society and its moral order). This speculation leads me to suspect that what is most unspeakable are not the crimes themselves or the pain that they caused, but rather the shameful fascination with transgression that compels us to dwell on them. Such transgression is "unspeakable" because it violates deeply held bourgeois social codes; it "cannot" be spoken because to speak it is to imagine it and to imagine it is to share it.

When the survivor testified about vaginal-cavity searches, she remarked that she had never mentioned this incident during years of public appearances. Somehow the prospect of speaking at this conference before receptive women scholars eroded the reluctance that had prevented her from recounting these humiliating searches on prior occasions. It is, of course, relevant that a feminist conference elicited precisely this kind of testimony. It is also important that her testimony ostensibly fulfills a desire for new knowledge about the Shoah as a radical instance of state mandated violence that affected men and women in different ways. Nevertheless, given the proliferation of discussions and institutional forums devoted to the Holocaust over the past quarter century, we should ask ourselves what was precisely "new" about this knowledge? What did it "contribute" to our understanding of human suffering?

By communicating this degrading experience, the survivor did not merely expose another facet of Nazi brutality. Her testimony also illuminated the ambiguously sexual and thus sinister character of the putatively "medicinal" and instrumental strip searches endured by women prisoners. I insist on this ambiguity because the silence that formerly buried this episode implies a sense of shame, which I connect to the sociocultural coding of sexual violence with its roots in a disavowed eroticization of power and of Nazism in particular. By implication, my sympathetic visualization of the survivor's testimony confirms and augments a culturally mediated repertoire of erotically charged scenarios involving Nazis sadistically enjoying their crimes against the Jews. In the grand scheme, however, it is an abhorrent image that will join the host of similarly abhorrent images that already fill my personal vision of the nauseating mechanics of the "Final Solution." This is to admit that my imaginary is also a posthistorical repository of violent imagery that I have absorbed over the years from movies and televised news reports alongside my studious encounters with historical and documentary depictions of the Holocaust.

As I have noted above, Hirsch suggests that postmemorial repetition is ethical if motivated by a sympathetic identification with the survivors and a vicarious effort to work through their trauma.[65] Yet Hirsch also complicates this claim when she cites Barbie Zelizer's anxieties about certain Holocaust photographs that "have become no more than decontextualized memory cues, energized by an already coded memory, no longer the vehicles that can themselves energize memory."[66] For Hirsch, in contrast, the obsessive recirculation of these images reveals their function as charged icons of Holocaust memory that stand in for the postmemorial witness's affective relation to the present by means of the historical past.[67]

The fixity of my own memory makes me hesitate to affirm the virtue of my sympathy for the survivors. When I think about the "Final Solution," my mind sifts through historically detached memory traces drawn from images of impending doom and extreme dehumanization: the photographs of human experimentation; the shooting of infants, children, and the elderly at point-blank range; the tracks leading up to the entrance to Auschwitz-Birkenau; the gates emblazoned with *Arbeit macht frei*; the bulldozers clearing bodies following the liberation of Bergen-Belsen; the cremation of corpses in stacks. My imagination gags on these images, which seem at once to crystallize and seduce my horror; it is nevertheless driven to return to them again and again. This compulsion betrays a shamefully perverse side to my attempts to assimilate the traumatic significance of the Holocaust through its imagery of death and destruction.

These grim images are "scenes of the crime" whose charged aura indicates a different crime scene altogether, one that transpires in the past, present, and future alluded to by the photographic frame and enacted imaginatively offscreen. This offscreen staging memorializes the Nazi atrocities, but also displaces and defers their impact to the realm of fantasy—in other words, to what Radstone has called a gray zone where scenarios of domination and sadistic bloodlust alternate with images of masochistic abjection before the sublime tortures of authoritarian masters. The easy currency of these scenarios is a symptom of my capitulation to the scopic drive that spurs me to visualize violent scenes as a means of appeasing an urge to see what should shame me to enjoy, and to take pleasure (without admitting it) in the transgression of scrutinizing what is ordinarily veiled out of a sense of bourgeois propriety, but also fear (of my own repressed aggression). A sense of moral delicacy makes me inclined to pass over the implications of this perversity for feminist scholarship, but I will nevertheless take the risk of broaching it now.

At the beginning of the chapter, I mentioned that one objective of the conference was to move beyond essentialist understandings of gender and sexual differences in feminist approaches to the Holocaust. Over the last two decades, the feminist critique of essentialism has typically been deployed as a means of unsettling assumptions that gender and sexuality could be conflated or defined as stable determinants of identity that transcend context and elude historical transformation.[68] My claim that perverse fantasies may play a disciplinary role in feminist compassion for women survivors is problematic if my sympathy transpires through a set of identifications that contravene an antiessentialist disarticulation of gender and sex. For if my feminist gaze could be said to "sexualize" the Holocaust, then it is by virtue of its power to elicit testimony that the witness formerly suppressed, not only because it humiliated her as a person and a Jew but also specifically "as a woman." In addition, to the extent that I sympathize with her "as a woman," I become inadvertently guilty, from the standpoint of my own antiessentialist gaze, of acritically rearticulating sex and gender. Indeed, it is this very rearticulation that propels my compassionate imaginary to fasten on to the obscene prospect of the Nazi official's enjoyment while probing her body: it is an "unspeakable secret" lodged in the traumatic heart of the Holocaust that a feminist gaze focused on sex and gender is critically and professionally equipped to "draw out" and "lay bare."

The shadow that cuts across my own act of "laying bare" is deepened by the positions that an empathetic "drawing out" inadvertently produces for the firsthand and secondhand witnesses in the auditorium. In my complicity with an institutional summons to the survivor to serve as an eyewitness to a "different" form of suffering, my compassion as a feminist scholar and as a woman in the space of the auditorium could not dispel her double bind as an informant in a disciplinary society, but rather confirmed it: she bore a secret whose confession would constitute her as a subject, yet would also convert her into an object of the feminist moral imaginary. She thereby serves to further my knowledge by filling out my map of a field. From the standpoint of Foucault's *The History of Sexuality*, what is still more troubling is the implication that this double bind is accompanied by a double pleasure reflected on either side of the scientific speculum: on the one hand, there is the pleasure of the testifying eyewitness in becoming an individualized subject, located in space and time before a gaze that enjoins her confession in the name of progress; on the other hand, there is the pleasure of the scholarly audience in deploying this gaze that marks out a position of mastery. The scholar who occupies this position by eliciting the secret (not to mention emplotting it in a "new" narrative) will confirm her membership in a scientific community to the extent that she demonstrates a properly feminist approach to her object of inquiry.

From a professional standpoint, then, my sympathetic yet fantastic reconstruction of the Nazi's violation of the survivor inadvertently serves to reconstitute, at least provisionally, the survivor's feminist audience as a moral community with whom I identify through our shared sense of outrage. The act of sympathizing as a group also retrieves my sense of the feminist "we" that was subtended by a posthumanist rejection of a human essence alongside multicultural and postcolonial critiques of white liberal solipsism in the 1980s and 1990s. This point compels me to return, briefly, to the question of institutional value. In a contemporary milieu marked in part by backlashes against both feminism and the Holocaust, each orientation stands to benefit from the other: the Holocaust is an object that allows me to recover the concepts of personal and collective experience that I divested as a basis for moral solidarity during the poststructuralist turn in the course of the last quarter century, while Holocaust studies rejuvenates itself through a feminist approach that sheds new light on the subject of xenophobia and the apparatus of genocide. This intersection raises still more troubling questions about what a Jewish feminist such as myself stands to gain by way of "identity capital."

In light of the narcissistic aspects of my relation to any object of inquiry ("One identifies with 'objects' because one lacks innate being," as Ragland attests),[69] I cannot help but wonder whether the evidence that I obtain through a cross-pollination between feminism and Holocaust studies does not also redeem my collective identification, not only with feminists, but also with "my people" by fueling my continuing ressentiment as a member of a long-suffering minority. Wendy Brown's observations about the masochistic stake in identity politics are relevant here: "reliving a certain punishing recognition reassures us not only of our own place (identity) but also of the presence of the order out of which that identity was forged and to which we remain perversely beholden," she writes. "The repetition gratifies an injured love by reaffirming the existence of the order that carried both the love and the injury."[70] Judith Butler underscores the narcissism of this passionate attachment to the persecuted subject position: "[B]ecause a certain narcissism takes hold of any term that confers existence, I am led to embrace the terms that injure me because they constitute me socially."[71] This attachment to subjection is, for Brown and Butler, what raises the question of masochism in the "state-linked" formation of the liberal individual.[72]

Another reason for my peculiar fascination with the strip search scene is that it affirms my belief that sadistic enjoyment comprises the barbaric essence of the Third Reich's "orgy" of murderous violence and permits me to ponder unspeakable images of transgression under the rubric of the Holocaust as an officially sanctioned object of inquiry. Foucault is persuasive when he suggests that alongside the progressive goal of forestalling future violence by exposing its myriad forms and effects lies an inadmissably erotic fascination with power and violence. The Nazi persecution and torture of the Jews is hereby renewed as an inexhaustible object of investigation precisely by virtue of its inexpungeable capacity to shame the very moral imaginary that memorializes it.

The complicity of these positions and their respective pleasures confronts me with an interesting paradox: the survivor on the podium positioned as an "object of inquiry" is active in testifying, while the scholar is, relatively speaking, passive insofar as I look on and listen from the luxurious safety of my empirical distance, from the comfort I take in my ability to scrutinize all phenomena with scientific equanimity and compassion as proof of my fastidious professionalism. The sordid issue that intrudes here stems from the obverse possibility that this scrutiny might itself be sadistic: Does my deployment of a sympathetic feminist gaze not also permit some form of enjoyment in enabling me to capture in my lens an object that is, in fact, a subject, an all too human one, who suffered terribly and, what is worse, consciously?

This question leads me to my ultimate claim. The sympathetic imaginary that establishes professional and moral solidarity among feminist scholars also provides a vehicle for the scopic drive and the perverse compulsion to view the visceral: the inside, the guts, the *sex*, if you will, of psychic and material existence. In consonance with Weissman, I am inclined to see this scopophilic element in sympathy as a means of feeling the horror of the Holocaust—to make it seem more real than its images in the wash of American culture.[73] A woman testifies to a violation that both is and is not sexual. Whether or not the Nazis took pleasure in performing vaginal searches on naked Jewish concentration camp prisoners is a matter of conjecture on my part and, as I have been arguing, fantasy. Certainly, the women prisoners themselves would have suffered these involuntary searches as a kind of rape (violence that leaves no room for erotic pleasure). The sexual dwells, rather, with the graphic imprint left on my imaginary of a hostile invasion of a tender corporeal inside that does not merely arouse a sense of visceral disgust, *but an equally visceral fascination with my own disgust*, which I then feel compelled to work through.

In officiating the survivor's confession as an addition to our knowledge, the institutional setting that placed me voluntarily in that auditorium also made me a vehicle of a disciplinary sympathy. Such sympathy inadvertently collaborates with a bourgeois hermeneutic that presupposes sexual repression; it therefore targets "sex" as a "dark secret" and earmarks my horror as a sign of that forbidden and furtive excess, which "must," for the sake of scientific progress, be disinterred as a truth. When I surgically probe my symptomatic disgust, a process of sympathetic introjection consequently allows me to "discover" that the truth I seek lies in the possibility that the Nazis sexually enjoyed vaginal searches of Jewish prisoners.

It is therefore no coincidence that I have "chosen" to analyze my response to this testimony in particular. The disciplinary value of such testimony is overdetermined as a focus of feminist inquiry in ways that extend beyond the commonplace that feminists are committed to undoing the silences imposed on women as marginalized or forgotten historical agents and victims. The "Final Solution" demands a measure of moral sensitivity and care, which provokes an attendant sense of anxiety about speaking improperly and thereby adding to the injustice and outrage experienced by those who survived and by the bereaved. This anxiety leads me to check the kinds of claims I might skeptically "entertain" in the spirit of open-ended inquiry.

It has been this very anxiety before my own "contamination" at the level of fantasy that I have wanted to explore. I have therefore written this essay in a confessional mode, but without following through on the generic convention to leave readers with a cathartic message of hope that would allow me to suture my unsettling contradictions and redeem myself as an ethical scholar of the Holocaust, a constructive feminist, and a decent human being.

Rather, my aim has been to track a professional and personal unconscious that surely exceeds me and that has spurred me to enact the very symptoms of the problematic at stake even as I analyze their unspeakable implications. In this respect, my performance has mirrored the chain of assumptions targeted by Foucault's critique of psychoanalysis as a technology of disciplinary power that implants the "secret" of sexual perversion into a confessing subject, thereby reproducing her half-willing subjection.[74] This self-scrutiny may be consistent with the honesty required of a rigorously feminist inquiry, but it cannot be entirely divorced from the clinical "male" perspective of Eakins's erotically charged painting of a surgery demonstration on a woman's breast: my critical imagination colludes with the medical students' desire to know what lies inside female flesh (including my own).

Perhaps my frank speculations suggest an explanation for the syndrome whereby controversy has come to be such a predictable feature of Holocaust studies. I have breached my own deeply held sense of propriety in the hope that the import of my analysis will not be limited to a pedestrian increase in self-awareness, but will instead motivate scholars to take responsibility for the fantasies and foreclosures that propel our compulsive repetitions. The commitment to refine our analytical tools cannot be entirely separated from a scientific gaze that objectifies in order to penetrate its object; nor can it be extricated from the narcissistic and erotic dimensions of fantasy that we might otherwise foreclose in the spirit of a crusade for moral legitimacy. To recognize this blind spot in the scholar's speculum is to begin to assume responsibility for the unconscious aspects of our fascination with the Holocaust—to break down unacknowledged obsessions, end a cycle of ritualized scandals, and thereby discover a different way of counting ourselves among the accountable, to become more accountable still. At stake is the future of a critical approach that could allow for a genuine departure from these vicious circles of righteous self-selection.

Notes

Introduction

1. Norman G. Finkelstein, "Daniel Jonah Goldhagen's 'Crazy' Thesis: A Critique of *Hitler's Willing Executioners*," *New Left Review* 224 (July/August 1997): 39–87.

2. See Norman G. Finkelstein, *The Holocaust Industry: Reflections on the Exploitation of Jewish Suffering*, 2nd ed. (New York: Verso, 2000); and idem, *Beyond Chutzpah: On the Misuse of Anti-Semitism and the Abuse of History* (Berkeley and Los Angeles: University of California Press, 2005).

3. James Berger attributes this climate to the "overriding anticolonialist politics of New Historicism. Attitudes toward Nazism intersected with attitudes toward Zionism and Middle East politics." He suggests that "[c]ontemporary postcolonial politics and theory seem to have difficulty accounting for the intra-European racism and genocide of the Second World War." See James Berger, *After the End: Representations of Post-Apocalypse* (Minneapolis: University of Minnesota Press, 1999), 232 n. 4. If Berger's assessment of this "difficulty" in anti- and postcolonial theory is correct, then Paul Gilroy's analysis of the conjunctions between fascism, aesthetic politics, and the historical lineage of the category of race in modernity is an admirable exception. See Paul Gilroy, *Against Race: Imagining Political Culture Beyond the Color Line* (Cambridge, MA: Harvard University Press, 2000).

4. Norman G. Finkelstein and Ruth Bettina Birn, *A Nation on Trial: The Goldhagen Thesis and Historical Truth* (New York: Henry Holt & Company, 1998). Birn's essay appears on pages 103–8.

5. Ibid., 147.

6. Ibid., 126, 133.

7. Robert Eaglestone, *Postmodernism and Holocaust Denial* (Cambridge, England: Icon Books, 2001). Eaglestone rejects the historical status of revisionist and negationist claims in his analysis of David Irving's libel suit against Deborah Lipstadt from January to April 2000. Irving's case against Lipstadt was based on his accusation that she had maligned his "legitimacy as a historian." In her 1994 book, *Denying the Holocaust: The Growing Assault on Truth and Memory*, Lipstadt repudiates Irving as a "Nazi apologist who distorted facts and manipulated documents." One of Eaglestone's aims in analyzing this trial is to respond to critics such as Lipstadt who have denounced the "constructivist

relativism" of the postmodernist framework for supporting negationist and revisionist arguments (4). See, in this connection, Deborah Lipstadt, *Denying the Holocaust: The Growing Assault on Truth and Memory* (London: Penguin, 1994).

8. Eaglestone follows Hayden White in repudiating constructions of the historian as a passive vehicle unaffected by his or her location in the world who simply "marshals the evidence," as encapsulated by Ranke's well-known dictum that the historian's task is to "re-create" the past *"wie es eigentlich gewesen war"* (as it actually was) (Eaglestone, 2001, 23). Eaglestone also shares White's deep suspicion of claims that history is a science by virtue of its mastery of the truth of the past as a measure of correspondence between the account and its object. Robert Eaglestone, *The Holocaust and the Postmodern* (Oxford: Oxford University Press, 2004), 170–71. Postmodernist skepticism subtends this pretension in reminding us that no account of a period or situation can ever be absolutely complete. Furthermore, since history is at once representational and retrospective, its accuracy cannot be gauged in relation to an actual and shown referent, but only in comparison with other historians' accounts that serve as provisional standards (Eaglestone, *Postmodernism and Holocaust Denial*, 23–26).

9. Hayden White, "Historical Emplotment and the Problem of Truth in Historical Representation," *Figural Realism: Studies in the Mimesis Effect* (Baltimore: Johns Hopkins University Press, 1999), 27. I am borrowing Hayden White's term *emplotment* to underscore the ways in which the imposition of various story types on a sequence of events endows them with a particular meaning. White warns against a tendency to misconstrue certain familiar tragic, comic, or farcical topoi as causal explanations: "[I]t would have to be recognized," he writes, "that the generalizations that serve the function of universals in any version of a nomological-deductive argument are the *topoi* of literary plots, rather than the causal laws of science." White, *The Content of the Form: Narrative Discourse and Historical Representation* (Baltimore: Johns Hopkins University Press, 1987), 44. By emphasizing that particular plots are not intrinsic to events, but must be imposed on them to give history structure and, by extension, meaning (its very status as history), White highlights the fallacy of a naively positivist standpoint that separates content from form while striving to simulate a transparent and neutral methodology to convey a "scientific" effect. He thus demonstrates the value of a rhetorical standpoint for shedding light on the poetic and moral configuration of events.

10. Eaglestone, *Postmodernism and Holocaust Denial*, 50.

11. Wilhelm Dilthey, *Pattern and Meaning in History: Thoughts on History and Society*, ed. H. P. Rickman (London: George Allen & Unwin, 1961), 67–68.

12. Michel Foucault, "The Order of Discourse," in *Untying the Text: A Post-Structuralist Reader*, ed. Robert J. C. Young (Boston: Routledge & Kegan Paul, 1982), 48–77.

13. Ibid., 59.

14. Ibid., 61.

15. Ibid., 59.

16. John Mowitt, *Text: The Genealogy of an Antidisciplinary Object* (Durham, NC: Duke University Press, 1992), 30.

17. Michel Foucault, "Truth and Power" (interview conducted in June 1976), in *Michel Foucault: Power*, ed. James D. Faubion, vol. 3 of *Essential Works of Foucault, 1954–1984* (New York: New Press, 2000), 120.

18. Michel Foucault, *Discipline and Punish: The Birth of the Prison*, trans. Alan Sheridan (New York: Vintage Books, 1979), 200.

19. I am admittedly uncomfortable with the way that the term *postmodernism* is used, because it elides the complex differences between thinkers as diverse as Jacques Derrida, Paul de Man, Michel Foucault, Jean-François Lyotard, Gilles Deleuze, Hayden White, Donna Haraway, and Judith Butler, among many others. Foucault is obviously not antifoundationalist in the same way as Derrida, since their interpretative strategies reflect very distinct notions of the archive.

20. Cited by Eaglestone, *Holocaust and the Postmodern*, 191. See Cathy Caruth, *Unclaimed Experience: Trauma, Narrative and History* (Baltimore: Johns Hopkins University Press, 1996), 74. Caruth is citing Paul de Man's "The Resistance to Theory," in *The Resistance to Theory* (Minneapolis: University of Minnesota Press, 1986).

21. Roland Barthes, "Myth Today," *Mythologies*, trans. Annette Lavers (New York: Hill and Wang, 1972), 109–59.

22. Ibid., 109.

23. Ibid., 129, 131. Significantly, even though he acknowledges that motivation is crucial to the mythic equation ("there is no myth without motivated form"), Barthes is, by no means, reinstituting Husserl's transcendental consciousness unified by intention. Nor is he projecting a paranoid image of Ideology as a totalizing conspiratorial system. Mythic motivation is, for Barthes, simultaneously ineluctable and fragmentary. It is not natural, since history "supplies its analogies to the form." Moreover, "the analogy between the meaning and the concept is never anything but partial: the form drops many features and keeps only a few." Indeed, "a *complete* image would exclude myth," which generally "prefers to work with poor, incomplete images, where the meaning is already relieved of its fat, and ready for a signification..." (126–27).

24. Barthes' description of the mythic concept thus applies to the object proper: "[I]t is a kind of nebula, the condensation, more or less hazy, of a certain knowledge ... its mode of presence is *memorial*" (ibid., 122; my emphasis). Barthes raises the problem of the discursive constitution of the object of inquiry in his 1971 comment on "Myth Today," entitled "Change the Object Itself: *Mythology Today*," in *Image, Music, Text*, trans. Stephen Heath (New York: Hill and Wang, 1977), 165–169.

25. Daniel Jonah Goldhagen, *Hitler's Willing Executioners: Ordinary Germans and the Holocaust* (New York: Alfred A. Knopf, 1996).

26. Jane Caplan, "Reflections on the Reception of Goldhagen in the United States," in *The "Goldhagen Effect": History, Memory, Nazism—Facing the German Past*, ed. Geoff Eley (Ann Arbor: University of Michigan Press, 2000), 154. While processes of identification are decisive here, as Caplan argues, it is nevertheless difficult without recourse to a theory of masochism to understand why a younger generation of nonacademic Germans would vicariously take on Goldhagen's enraged gaze. Perhaps, as Ulrich Herbert suggests, identifying with the victim offers a way out for Germans striving "to circumvent the discomforting demands of post-Holocaust society" while "satisfying an understandable desire: By applauding his book, they need no longer be lumped in with the vilified but can stand on the side of the vilifiers." Ulrich Herbert, "Extermination Policy: New Answers and Questions about the History of the 'Holocaust' in German Historiography," in *National Socialist Extermination Policies: Contemporary German Perspectives and Controversies*, ed. Ulrich Herbert (Oxford: Bergahn Books, 2000), 3.

27. Geoff Eley, "Ordinary Germans, Nazism, and Judeocide," in *The "Goldhagen Effect": History, Memory, Nazism—Facing the German Past*, ed. Geoff Eley (Ann Arbor: University of Michigan Press, 2000), 30–1. Eley points out that the nonacademic public's enthusiasm was "not 'about' the substantive historical and historiographical arguments at all." Rather, the demonstrative reactions should be seen as "the latest installment in a long-running public struggle to ground the ethics of democratic citizenship in a country where fascism seemed to have successfully claimed—and disqualified—the national past as a source of inspiration" (30).

28. Theodor W. Adorno, *Prisms*, trans. Samuel Weber and Shierry Weber (London: Spearman, 1967), 34. In the German, Adorno writes: "Nach Auschwitz ein Gedicht zu schreiben, ist barbarisch, und das frißt auch die Erkenntnis an, die ausspricht, warum es unmöglich ward, heute Gedichte zu schreiben." Adorno, "Kulturkritik und Gesellschaft," in *Prismen* (Munich: Deutscher Taschenbuch Verlag, 1963), 26, cited by Klaus Laermann, "Nach Auschwitz ein Gedicht zu schreiben, ist barbarisch': Überlegungen zu einem Darstellungsverbot," in *Kunst und Literatur nach Auschwitz*, ed. Manuel Köppen (Berlin: Erich Schmidt Verlag, 1993), 11. This statement first appeared in *Soziologische Forschung in unserer Zeit: Leopold von Wiese zum 75. Geburtstag* (1951) and subsequently in the 1955 edition of *Prismen* (Frankfurt am Main: Suhrkamp), 31. Adorno later confirmed the so-called *Lyrikverbot* in "Commitment" (1962) where he writes: "Den Satz, nach Auschwitz noch Lyrik zu schreiben, sei barbarisch, möchte ich nicht mildern; negativ ist darin der Impuls ausgesprochen, der die engagierte Dichtung beseelt." Adorno, *Noten zur Literatur: Band 3* (Frankfurt: Suhrkamp, 1962), 125. See also Detlev Claussen, "Nach Auschwitz: Über die Aktualität Adornos," in *Kunst und Literatur nach Auschwitz*, ed. Manuel Köppen (Berlin: Erich Schmidt Verlag, 1993), 16–22.

29. Theodor W. Adorno, *Negative Dialectics*, trans. E. B. Ashton (New York: Continuum, 1995), 367. In the original German, Adorno writes: "Alle Kultur nach Auschwitz, samt der dringlichen Kritik daran, ist Müll." *Negativ Dialektik* (Frankfurt am Main: Suhrkamp, 1966), 359.

30. See Paul Petzel, " '. . . kein Bildnis machen!' beim Erinnern? Theologische Überlegungen zur ästhetischen Repräsentationskritik" in *Verbot der Bilder—Gebot der Erinnerung: Mediale Repräsentationen der Schoah*, ed. Bettina Bannasch, and Almuth Hammer (Frankfurt am Main: Campus, 2004), 359–80. Petzel's analysis explores the contested history of the Second Commandment inside and outside of the Talmudic tradition. This contestation is mostly elided in discussions about the Holocaust. For a valuable article on the importance of the *Bilderverbot* (image prohibition) for Adorno's aesthetic theory, see Gertrud Koch's "Mimesis und *Bilderverbot* in Adornos Ästhetik," in *Die Einstellung ist die Einstellung* (Frankfurt: Suhrkamp Verlag, 1992), 16–29; and Klaus Laermann's discussion of this connection in "Nach Auschwitz ein Gedicht zu schreiben" (cited above). See also Michael Rothberg, "After Adorno: Culture in the Wake of Catastrophe," in *Traumatic Realism: The Demands of Holocaust Representation* (Minneapolis: University of Minnesota Press, 2000), 25–58. Rothberg's chapter, previously published in *New German Critique* 72 (Fall 1997): 45–81, provides an excellent assessment of the nuances that differentiate Adorno's various statements about art, culture, lyric poetry, metaphysics, and education that cite the chronotrope "after Auschwitz." On this line of inquiry, see also Klaus Hofmann, "Poetry After Auschwitz—Adorno's Dictum," *German Life and Letters* 58, no. 2 (April 2005): 182–94.

31. Theodor W. Adorno, "On Lyric Poetry and Society," in *Notes to Literature Volume One*, ed. Rolf Tiedemann, trans. Shierry Weber Nicholsen (New York: Columbia University Press, 1991), 37–54. Hayden White, "Figural Realism in Witness Literature," *Parallax* 30 (2004): 123.

32. Rothberg, "After Adorno," 39.

33. Theordor W. Adorno, "Commitment," *Notes to Literature Volume Two*, ed. Rolf Tiedemann, trans. Shierry Weber Nicholsen (New York: Columbia University Press, 1992), 91.

34. Theodor W. Adorno, *Aesthetic Theory*, trans. Robert Hullot-Kentor (Minneapolis: University of Minnesota Press, 1997), 294.

35. Adorno, "Commitment," 88.

36. Ibid., 88.

37. See Jean-François Lyotard, "Discussions, or Phrasing 'after Auschwitz,' " in *The Lyotard Reader*, ed. Andrew Benjamin (Cambridge: Blackwell, 1989), 360–92 and Maurice Blanchot, *Vicious Circles*, trans. Paul Auster (Barrytown, NY: Station Hill Press, 1985). See also Michael Rothberg's analysis in "Before Auschwitz: Maurice Blanchot, From Now On" in *Traumatic Realism: The Demand of Holocaust Representation* (Minneapolis: Univeristy of Minnesota Press, 2000), 59–96.

38. See George Steiner, *Language and Silence: Essays on Language, Literature, and the Inhuman* (New Haven, CT: Yale University Press, 1998); and idem, *The Death of Tragedy* (New Haven, CT: Yale University Press, 1996).

39. James Young, "Germany's Memorial Question: Memory, Counter-Memory, and the End of the Monument," *South Atlantic Quarterly* 96, no. 4 (Fall 1997): 856. See also the chapter with this title in *At Memory's Edge: After-Images of the Holocaust in Contemporary Art and Architecture* (New Haven, CT: Yale University Press, 2000), 90–119.

40. Naomi Mandel, *Against the Unspeakable: Complicity, the Holocaust, and Slavery in America* (Charlottesville: University of Virginia Press, 2006), 8.

41. Young, "Germany's Memorial Question," 855–56.

42. Karen E. Till, "Staging the Past: Landscape Designs, Cultural Identity and *Erinnerungspolitik* at Berlin's *Neue Wache*," *Ecumene* 6, no. 3 (1999): 254.

43. M. C. Boyer, *The City of Collective Memory: Its Historical Imagery and Architectural Entertainments* (Cambridge, MA: MIT Press), 21. Cited by Till, "Staging the Past," 254.

44. Till, "Staging the Past," 254.

45. Ibid.

46. Giorgio Agamben, *Remnants of Auschwitz: The Witness and the Archive*, trans. Daniel Heller-Roazen (Cambridge: Zone Books, 1999). In this connection, see also idem, *State of Exception*, trans. Kevin Attell (Chicago: University of Chicago Press, 2005); and idem, *Homo Sacer: Sovereign Power and Bare Life*, trans. Daniel Heller-Roazen (Stanford, CA: Stanford University Press, 1998).

47. Michel Foucault, "Right of Death and Power over Life," in *The History of Sexuality: An Introduction Volume I*, trans. Robert Hurley (New York: Vintage, 1990), 143. See also idem, "Security, Territory, and Population" and "The Birth of Biopolitics," in *Michel Foucault: Ethics, Subjectivity and Truth*, ed. Paul Rabinow, trans. Robert Hurley et al. (New York: New Press, 1997), 67–72 and 73–80, respectively.

48. Foucault, "Birth of Biopolitics," 74.

49. More crucial, perhaps, is Foucault's qualification of this observation: "Instead of making the distinction between state and civil society into a historical universal that allows us to examine all the concrete systems, we can try to see it as a form of schematization characteristic of a particular technology of government" (ibid., 75). This "technology" shifts to accommodate a symbiosis between neoliberalism and transnational capitalism that breaks down the liberal conception of society as an agency that could stave off governmental overreach.

50. Carolyn J. Dean, *The Fragility of Empathy after the Holocaust* (Ithaca, NY: Cornell University Press, 2004), 83.

51. This contention supports Tony Kushner's argument that the Holocaust exposed the limits of the liberal imagination. See Tony Kushner, *The Holocaust and the Liberal Imagination: A Social and Cultural History* (Oxford: Blackwell, 1994).

52. John Mowitt, "Trauma Envy," *Cultural Critique* 46 (2000): 293.

53. "It is almost as if, starting from a certain point, every decisive political event were double-sided," Agamben writes: "[T]he spaces, the liberties, and the rights won by individuals in their conflicts with central powers always simultaneously prepared a tacit but increasing inscription of individuals' lives within the state order, thus offering a new and more dreadful foundation for the very sovereign power from which they wanted to liberate themselves" (Agamben, *Homo Sacer*, 121).

54. Agamben, *Remnants of Auschwitz*, 157, 13, 157.

55. Jacques Derrida, "The Ends of Man," in *Margins of Philosophy*, trans. Alan Bass (Chicago: University of Chicago Press, 1982), 109–36.

56. For Lyotard's identification of the negative sublime with the postmodern, see his "Answering the Question: What is Postmodernism?" trans. Régis Durand, in *The Postmodern Condition: A Report on Knowledge*, trans. Geoff Bennington and Brian Massumi (Minneapolis: University of Minnesota Press, 1984), 71–82. In that context, Lyotard's call for the death of grand narratives headlines his celebration of a postmodern aesthetic of the negative sublime.

57. Dorota Glowacka, "Lending an Ear to the Silence of the Phrase," in *Minima Moralia: In the Wake of Jean-François Lyotard*, ed. Claire Nouvet, Zrinka Stahuljak, and Kent Still (Stanford, CA: Stanford University Press, 2007), 51.

58. Ibid., 62.

59. Claire Nouvet, "The Inarticulate Affect: Lyotard and Psychoanalytic Testimony," in *Minima Moralia: In the Wake of Jean-François Lyotard*, ed. Claire Nouvet, Zrinka Stahuljak, and Kent Still (Stanford, CA: Stanford University Press, 2007), 110, 111.

60. Ibid., 112, 113.

61. Ibid., 106.

62. See Jean-François Lyotard, *Libidinal Economy*, trans. Ian Hamilton Grant (Bloomington: Indiana University Press, 1993). First published in France in 1974. See also Lyotard's "Emma: Between Philosophy and Psychoanalysis," trans. Michael Saunders et al., in *Lyotard: Philosophy, Politics and the Sublime*, ed. Hugh J. Silverman (New York: Routledge, 2002), 23–45. First published in French in 1989.

63. Judith Butler, *The Psychic Life of Power: Theories in Subjection* (Stanford, CA: Stanford University Press, 1997).

64. See Wendy Brown, *States of Injury: Power and Freedom in Late Modernity* (Princeton, NJ: Princeton University Press, 1995).

65. Tim Cole, *Selling the Holocaust: From Auschwitz to Schindler; How History Is Bought, Packaged, and Sold* (New York: Routlege, 2000), 172, 185.

66. Jacques Lacan, "The Function and Field of Speech and Language in Psychoanalysis," in *Écrits*, trans. Bruce Fink (New York: W. W. Norton & Company, 2002), 42.

67. Nietzsche famously writes: "Ah, reason, seriousness, mastery over the affects, the whole somber thing called reflection, all these perogatives and showpieces of man: how dearly they have been bought! How much blood and cruelty lie at the bottom of all 'good things'!" Friedrich Nietzsche, "Second Essay: On 'Guilt,' 'Bad Conscience,' and the Like," in *"On the Genealogy of Morals" and "Ecce Homo*, trans. Walter Kaufmann (New York: Vintage Books, 1967), 62 (section 3).

68. Adorno, *Negative Dialectics*, 363.

Chapter One

This chapter is a revised and expanded version of an essay with the same title, which appeared in *Cultural Critique* 46 (Fall 2000): 124–52.

1. Daniel Goldhagen, *Hitler's Willing Executioners: Ordinary Germans and the Holocaust* (New York: Alfred A. Knopf, 1996).

2. Hans Mommsen, "Die Dünne Patina der Zivilisation: Der Anti-Semitismus war eine notwendige, aber keineswegs hinreichende Bedingung für den Holocaust," *Die Zeit* (August 30, 1996). I happened to be living in Berlin during the period preceding and following the book's translation and publication in Germany in the summer of 1996, and therefore had access to the responses of the critics and historians as they appeared in *Die Zeit* in 1996–97 as well as other newspapers and magazines. I principally relied on these sources for my initial analysis of the Goldhagen controversy. For a collection of reviews that excludes Mommsen's article cited above, see Julius H. Schoeps, ed., *Ein Volk von Mördern? Die Dokumentation zur Goldhagen-Kontroverse um die Rolle der Deutschen im Holocaust* (Hamburg: Hoffman & Campe Verlag, 1996). For the English translations of many of the historians' reviews as well as significant additional material, consult Robert Shandley, ed., *Unwilling Germans? The Goldhagen Debate*, trans. Jeremiah Riemer (Minneapolis: University of Minnesota Press, 1998), here p. 195 (translation modified).

3. Hans Mommsen, "The Thin Patina of Civilization: Anti-Semitism Was a Necessary, But by No Means a Sufficient, Condition for the Holocaust," in Shandley, *Unwilling Germans?* 183.

4. Geoff Eley, "Ordinary Germans, Nazism, and Judeocide," in *The "Goldhagen Effect": History, Memory, Nazism—Facing the German Past*, ed. Geoff Eley (Ann Arbor: University of Michigan Press, 2000), 7.

5. Jane Caplan, "Reflections on the Reception of Goldhagen in the United States," in *The "Goldhagen Effect": History, Memory, Nazism—Facing the German Past*, ed. Geoff Eley (Ann Arbor: Univeristy of Michigan Press, 2000), 156.

6. I am relying on Omer Bartov's translation of Ilana Hammermann, "The Shoah and Best-Sellers," *Ha'aretz*, December 26, 1997. See Bartov, "Reception and Perception: Goldhagen's Holocaust and the World," in *The "Goldhagen Effect": History,*

Memory, Nazism—Facing the German Past, ed. Geoff Eley (Ann Arbor: Univeristy of Michigan Press, 2000), 74 n. 91.

7. Bartov, "Reception and Perception," 76.

8. Caplan, "Reflections," 160–62.

9. Among the mass media, this traumatic anger animates what Goldhagen calls a "misrecognition" of the book as a reopening of the debate over the "collective guilt" thesis (see, for example, the cover article that appeared in *Der Spiegel* 21 (May 20, 1996), 48–77. Of course, it was rather naive of Goldhagen to deny that a book that makes a point of referring to the perpetrators as "the Germans" does not raise the collective guilt issue. Whether he acknowledges it or not, his book reinstigated this debate.

10. Grossmann observes, "The romance with the tragically lost legacy of German Jewry—a considerable portion of whom survived in exile—facilitated a recognition of Nazi anti-Semitism and its cost but in no way forced the visceral confrontation with the reality of the genocide that a book like Goldhagen's would demand." Atina Grossmann, " 'The Goldhagen Effect': Memory, Fixation, and Responsibility in the New Germany," in *The "Goldhagen Effect": History, Memory, Nazism—Facing the German Past*, ed. Geoff Eley (Ann Arbor: University of Michigan Press, 2000), 101. Likewise, Dominick LaCapra acknowledges that Goldhagen "may formulate and give what seems to be scholarly legitimation to the visceral response or 'gut reaction' of some (certainly not all) Jewish victims and those who identify with them in an unmediated form." LaCapra, *Writing History, Writing Trauma* (Baltimore: Johns Hopkins University Press, 2001), 122.

11. Robert Eaglestone, *The Holocaust and the Postmodern* (Oxford: Oxford University Press, 2004), 159.

12. As Eaglestone observes, historians typically take a belief in truth for granted; thus, when they debate the status of history as an "art" or a "science," they are actually struggling over "the sort of truth to which history aspires" (ibid., 160).

13. Hayden White, "The Burden of History," *History and Theory* 5 (1966): 130. Cited by Eaglestone, *Holocaust and the Postmodern*, 167.

14. Hayden White, *The Content of the Form* (Baltimore: Johns Hopkins University Press, 1987), 14.

15. Eley, "Ordinary Germans, Nazism, and Judeocide," 4.

16. Ibid., 6.

17. Anson Rabinbach, " 'The Abyss that Opened Up Before Us': Thinking About Auschwitz and Modernity," in *Catastrophe and Meaning: The Holocaust and the Twentieth Century*, ed. Moishe Postone and Eric Santner (Chicago: University of Chicago Press, 2003), 53. Rabinbach's essay historicizes the German émigrés' views of the relationship between the Third Reich and modernity. He notes that Jewish-German exiles such as Max Horkheimer and Theodor W. Adorno "most emphatically saw the Holocaust in the context of a much larger picture of destructive modernity spun out of control" or at least recognized that "the crimes of Nazism as well as those perpetrated by the Soviet Union during the 1930s required a certain level of modernity or even of 'progress.' " In many respects, as Rabinbach suggests, "the discourse of the modernity of the Holocaust was a counterdiscourse to the thesis of a German *Sonderweg*;" it was a Eurocentric response of the German Jewish *Bildungsbürgertum* to preserve the image of "Germany's better self," as George

Mosse phrased it, against an "excessively Germanophobic discourse." Rabinbach, "Abyss," 55, citing George L. Mosse, *German Jews beyond Judaism* (Bloomington: Indiana University Press, 1983), 82. As Rabinbach keenly observes, this trope of a negative modernity has played a decisive role in the last half century since the catastrophe; nevertheless, the concept of a specifically European cultural trajectory of secularization and rationalization propagated by Marx, Weber, and Durkheim, and, more recently, Zygmunt Bauman, seems increasingly out of date now that scholars have recognized the need to speak of "multiple modernities" (52). See also, in this connection, Zygmunt Bauman, *Modernity and the Holocaust* (Ithaca, NY: Cornell University Press, 1989 and 1991).

18. Michael Brennan, "Some Sociological Contemplations on Daniel J. Goldhagen's *Hitler's Willing Executioner's*," *Theory, Culture & Society* 18 (2001): 93.

19. Caplan, "Reflections," 157, and Eley, "Ordinary Germans, Nazism, and Judeocide," 24. For an incisive and detailed critique of the *Sonderweg* thesis, see David Blackbourn and Geoff Eley, *The Peculiarities of German History: Bourgeois Society and Politics in Nineteenth-Century Germany* (Oxford: Oxford University Press, 1984). See also Rabinbach, "Abyss."

20. Brennan, "Some Sociological Contemplations," 97, 95–96.

21. In his chapter entitled "The Deadly Way" (*Hitler's Willing Executioners*, 327–54), Goldhagen cites the attempts of German civilians in Ahornberg to offer food to the starving Jews on the death marches at the end of the war (348). Since Goldhagen's general aim in this project is to expose the cruelty of the guards, his report on this incident is intended to emphasize their mercilessness in forbidding the townspeople from giving the Jewish prisoners food and water and in threatening to shoot one woman for attempting to do so. In the course of his reiteration of this incident, however, he fails to remark the significance of these efforts on the part of the bystanders who wanted to help the suffering Jews. Were these altruistic bystanders in Ahornberg not also "ordinary" Germans?

22. Eley, "Ordinary Germans, Nazism, and Judeocide," 22; and Bartov, "Reception and Perception," 41.

23. For Goldhagen, this is clearly the case even in the absence of a comparative analysis that would illuminate the distinctiveness of German anti-Semitism under the Third Reich in the context of European anti-Semitism as a whole. The intensity of French anti-Semitism before, during, and after the German Occupation is well known. Certainly, the Ukrainians, Lithuanians, Latvians, and Romanians were, by most accounts, eager to collaborate with the Nazi murders. But the pogroms perpetrated in Central and Eastern Europe in the nineteenth and twentieth centuries were not bureaucratically orchestrated. Nor was it imaginable in the areas where pogroms were likely to occur to gas Jews en masse and cremate their bodies. In light of the bureaucratic and industrial aspects of the "Final Solution," Mommsen's articulation of the key question is not sufficiently precise. More to the point is the issue of how German xenophobia and anti-Semitism were unique within the European context in culminating in the systematic murder of Jews, Roma, and Sinti on a continental scale. It is, in any case, naive to ask how such barbarity became possible in a civilized country. Over the course of the last six centuries the governments, armies, and police of self-styled "civilized" countries have frequently committed massive violence against indigenous peoples, often under the banner of "updating" their moral and cultural standards.

24. As Brennan points out, however, Goldhagen still does not "attempt to explain how the Germans' deeply held animus towards Jews should have translated into the loathsome and barbaric actions" that he outlines—"how views could so easily be transposed into deeds" (Brennan, "Some Sociological Contemplations," 95).

25. Hans Mommsen in Shandley, *Unwilling Germans?* 194.

26. Goldhagen, *Hitler's Willing Executioners*, 189–90.

27. Brennan, "Some Sociological Contemplations," 88, 99, quoting Finkelstein and Ruth Bettina Birn, *Nation on Trial: The Goldhagen Thesis and Historical Truth* (New York: Henry Holt, 1998), 90, 143. See also Carolyn J. Dean, *The Fragility of Empathy after the Holocaust* (Ithaca, NY: Cornell University Press, 2004), 49. Norman Finkelstein is by far the most hostile of Goldhagen's critics. It was the commercial success of his graphic style that presumably incited Finkelstein to credit Goldhagen with the invention of a new "subgenre" the former calls "Holoporn." His neologism *Holoporn* acidically targets the way in which *Hitler's Willing Executioners* blurs the boundaries between Holocaust scholarship and literature. In Finkelstein's view, such a blurring foments the "Disneyfication" of the Holocaust and a burgeoning market in Holocaust kitsch. Goldhagen's obscene "subgenre" is yet another crass contribution to the mushrooming of Holocaust studies as a "veritable industry" that abuses victim memory to consolidate the legitimacy of the Zionist project and specifically Israel's illegal occupation of Palestinian territory.

28. Eberhard Jäckel remarks, "Goldhagen always refers to 'the Germans' (the term occurs on practically every page, sometimes eight times" (Shandley 89). Jäckel, "Einfach ein schlechtes Buch," *Die Zeit*, May 17, 1996, repeated in Schoeps, *Ein Volk von Mördern?* 187–92. Except where otherwise noted, page references to Jäckel's essay cite Jeremiah Riemer's translation, "Simply a Bad Book," in Shandley, *Unwilling Germans?* 87–91.

29. Eley, "Ordinary Germans, Nazism, and Judeocide," 7.

30. Josef Joffe " 'The Killers Were Ordinary Germans, Ergo the Ordinary Germans Were Killers': The Logic, the Language, and the Meaning of a Book that Conquered Germany," in Shandley, *Unwilling Germans?* 224. The piece originally appeared in the *New York Review of Books*, November 8, 1996. Joffe does not provide dates for the sources of the critics' comments he cites, except to note that Dan Diner's remark appeared in the fall 1996 issue of the *Frankfurter Jüdische Nachrichten* and Y. Michal Bodemann's in the Berlin *Tageszeitung*. The excerpt, "Die Killer waren normalen Deutsche, also waren die normalen Deutschen Killer," that appears in Schoeps, *Ein Volk von Mördern?* 160–70, excludes this part of his comments.

31. Franklin H. Littell, ed., Introduction to *Hyping the Holocaust: Scholars Answer Goldhagen* (Merion Station, Philadelphia, PA: Merion Westfield Press International, 1997), x.

32. Mary Nolan speculates that the book's "appealing shock effect" stemmed not from its putative originality, but rather from Goldhagen's "single-minded concentration on groups that had been neglected," its "appealingly simplistic argument about causality," and his deployment of "a level of detail that some critics regarded as almost pornographic," to describe "exactly what SS guards and reserve police did in roundups, on the forced marches back to Germany, and in the camps." Yet Goldhagen "has his own silences and containments," as Nolan remarks, "and these enhanced the appealing shock effect of his work." See Mary Nolan, "The Politics of Memory in the Berlin Republic," *Radical History Review* 81 (Fall 2001): 117, 118.

33. Josef Joffe in Shandley, *Unwilling Germans?* 224.

34. Grossmann, "Goldhagen Effect," 117.

35. Dean, *Fragility of Empathy*, 50.

36. Ibid., 45.

37. Ibid., 47.

38. Bartov, "Reception and Perception," 74, n. 91, quoting and translating Hammermann, "The Shoah and Best-Sellers."

39. Bartov, "Perception and Reception," 77.

40. Dean, *Fragility of Empathy*, 49.

41. Ibid., 54.

42. Ibid., 55.

43. Bartov speculates, "This kind of prose may have appeared innovative, or even morbidly fascinating, to certain American and German readers who were dissatisfied with the drier, more detached depictions and interpretations of conventional Holocaust scholarship." "Reception and Perception," 77.

44. Dean, *Fragility of Empathy*, 45.

45. Bartov, "Reception and Perception," 77, Caplan 158, 159.

46. Bartov, "Reception and Perception," 77, Grossmann, "Goldhagen Effect," 120. On "negative nationalism," see Heinrich August Winkler's "Lesearten der Sühne," *Der Spiegel*, August 24, 1998, 180–81 cited by Nolan, "Politics of Memory," 117, 120 n. 20.

47. Christopher Browning, *Ordinary Men: Reserve Police Battalion 101 and the Final Solution in Poland* (New York: HarperPerennial, 1993), 12.

48. Eley, "Ordinary Germans, Nazism, and Judeocide," 14.

49. Moishe Postone, "The Holocaust and the Trajectory of the Twentieth Century," in *Catastrophe and Meaning: The Holocaust and the Twentieth Century*, ed. Moishe Postone and Eric Santner (Chicago: University of Chicago Press, 2003), 85.

50. LaCapra, *Writing History, Writing Trauma*, 126–27.

51. Brennan, "Some Sociological Contemplations," 93 citing Raul Hilberg, *The Destruction of the European Jews*, vol. 3 (New York: Holmes and Meier, 1985) and Zygmunt Bauman, *Modernity and the Holocaust* (Cambridge: Polity Press, 1989).

52. Bartov, "Reception and Perception," 40. As Yehuda Bauer observes, "People don't like complicated explanations, they don't want differentiated analyses, they want simplicity. Goldhagen gave it to them." Bauer, "Daniel J. Goldhagen's View of the Holocaust," in *Hyping the Holocaust: Scholars Answer Goldhagen* (Merion Station, Philadelphia, PA: Merion Westfield Press International, 1997), 71.

53. Dean, *Fragility of Empathy*, 45. Dean is paraphrasing the standpoint of those critics who found the book important.

54. Nolan observes that by detailing the gruesome actions of the perpetrators beyond Hitler and high-ranking officials, Goldhagen "found a middle ground between structural/functional arguments that seemed to leave out the moral responsibility of perpetrators by focusing on abstract processes and macroinstitutions and an intentionalism that blamed Hitler while exonerating most Germans" ("Politics of Memory," 117).

55. Eberhard Jäckel in Shandley, *Unwilling Germans?* 89 (translation modified); Schoeps, *Ein Volk von Mördern?* 190.

56. Jäckel in Shandley, *Unwilling Germans?* 89.

57. Jäckel in Shandley, *Unwilling Germans?* 88.

58. Jäckel in Shandley, *Unwilling Germans?* 90. Jäckel concludes by condescendingly lauding this "capable young man" for getting himself "into the headlines," while nevertheless robbing "himself of any scholarly prestige" (90).

59. Jäckel in Shandley, *Unwilling Germans?* 87 (translation modified); Schoeps, *Ein Volk von Mördern?* 187.

60. Eley, "Ordinary Germans, Nazism, and Judeocide," 4. At the very least, as Goldhagen observes, his considerable research on the background and behavior of the *Einsatzgruppe* and guards of the death marches is important in compelling historians to rethink certain predominant clichés of Holocaust scholarship generated by the focus on the death "factories" as prime instances of the antiseptic and industrial character of the murders. As he puts it in a reply to his critics that appeared in the December 23, 1996, issue of the *New Republic*, the focus on "industrial killing" to describe the use of gas chambers and gas wagons is "a reduction of complexity and all of the comparative features that need to be explained" and, thus, "one of the principal clichés of the period." In this connection, he points out that the perpetrators killed "over 40 percent of their victims by means other than 'industrial killing'" and emphasizes that it was "the will and the motivation to exterminate European Jewry . . . that is the crucial issue." "Motives, Causes, and Alibis: A Reply to My Critics," *New Republic* (December 23, 1996), 45.

Goldhagen rightly reminds scholars that the gas chambers and wagons were not the only means of mass murder; however, I question the dichotomy his criticism implies between the industrial "death factories" and the presumably nonindustrial shootings. One might argue that, both in scale and intent, these shootings were also industrial, if not always smooth at the level of their implementation. Of course, to acknowledge the industrial scale and structure of these killings does not preclude Goldhagen's major thesis: that the perpetrators of these shootings were not mindless drones who carried out their "work" in a mechanical manner, but instead inflicted countless cruelties on their victims before annihilating them. Dean is nevertheless justified in criticizing his intensive focus on anti-Semitic ideas, which has the effect of stripping "the Nazi genocide of European Jewry of its socioeconomic and political context" while neglecting the role of the state (Dean, *Fragility of Empathy*, 48).

61. Littell, introduction, xi.

62. See Bartov, "Reception and Perception," 33, Grossmann, "Goldhagen Effect," 91.

63. See Eley, "Ordinary Germans, Nazism, and Judeocide," and also Grossmann, "Goldenhagen Effect," 113.

64. Grossmann, "Goldenhagen Effect," 113.

65. Caplan, "Reflections," 153.

66. Eley, "Ordinary Germans, Nazism, and Judeocide," 29; and Debra Bradley Ruder, "Goldhagen Wins German Prize for Holocaust Book," *Harvard University Gazette*, January 9, 1997, *Harvard Gazette Archives*, http://www.hno.harvard.edu/gazette/1997/01.09/GoldhagenWinsGe.html.

67. Grossmann, "Goldenhagen Effect," 118.

68. Jürgen Habermas, "Goldhagen and the Public Use of History: Why a Democracy Prize for Goldhagen?" in Shandley, *Unwilling German?* 263.

69. Ibid., 271.

70. Eley, "Ordinary Germans, Nazism, and Judeocide," 30.

71. As the intellectual historian Gopal Balakrishnan caustically observes, "[I]t was in this capacity too that Habermas, in an extraordinary display of indifference to historical accuracy that took even close friends on the liberal Left aback, hailed Daniel Goldhagen's grotesque distillation of modern German national identity prior to occupation into a psychotic anti-Semitism. The trashiness of this American best-seller was apparently less important to him than its serviceability as political grist to his mill." It would seem that even to praise Goldhagen for heightening German consciousness is to condone his methodological impropriety and it is this guilt by association that renders Habermas politically incorrect from the standpoint of the New Left.

Balakrishnan's criticism of Habermas is presented in the course of a review of Martin Beck Matustík's *Jürgen Habermas: A Philosophical-Political Profile*. Balakrishnan writes: "Despite his respect for the philosopher, [Matustík] could not follow [Habermas] in endorsing America's wars in the Gulf and the Balkans. Most painful of all, in this association with 'cluster-bomb liberals,' was the glaring contrast between Habermas's intemperate denunciation of the unarmed student protests of '68 and his complaisance towards the raining down of high-tech military violence by the most powerful state machine in the world—'his fear of student street activism and revolutionary aspirations,' on the one hand, and his 'support for extreme levels of the state monopoly of violence and killing,' on the other." See Gopal Balakrishnan, "Overcoming Emancipation," *New Left Review* 19 (January–February 2003) http:// newleftrev.vm.bytemark.co.uk/A2435.

72. Habermas, "Goldhagen," 271.

73. Eaglestone, *Holocaust and the Postmodern*, 222 n. 67.

74. Ibid., 240.

75. Eley, "Ordinary Germans, Nazism, and Judeocide," 6.

76. Brennan, "Some Sociological Contemplations," 100 paraphrasing Birn in Finkelstein and Birn, *Nation on Trial*, 114.

77. Jacob Neusner, "Hype, Hysteria, and Hate the Hun: The Latest Pseudo-Scholarship from Harvard" in Littell, *Hyping the Holocaust*, 147, 151.

78. For these definitions of the Lacanian imaginary, symbolic, and the real, I consulted *The Four Fundamental Concepts of Psycho-Analysis*, ed. Jacques-Alain Miller, trans. Alan Sheridan (New York: W. W. Norton & Company, 1981). Because Lacan's understanding of the real changes over time, it would be impossible to offer a concise identification of the term that would be accurate for all the stages of his thinking. Generally speaking, the Lacanian real is not to be confused with reality. It is, instead, the foreclosed element: the refractory, impossible fantasy-residue that escapes and obstructs yet also informs and is structured by the symbolic and imaginary orders. The initial appearance of the real is "unwelcome" and must be symbolically mediated through fantasy before it can be acknowledged. This is why the first encounter (*tuché*) with the real leaves a trace that will be later (re)awakened and misrecognized as an origin. For a breakdown of the changes in Lacan's understanding of the real, see Slavoj Žižek, *The Sublime Object of Ideology* (London: Verso, 1989), particularly chapter 5, "Which Subject of the Real?" 153–99.

79. LaCapra, *Writing History, Writing Trauma*, 114.

80. Hans Ulrich Wehler, "Wie ein Stachel im Fleisch," *Die Zeit*, May 14, 1996. A longer version appears in Schoeps, *Ein Volk von Mördern?* 193–209. See also Shandley, *Unwilling Germans?* 93–104.

81. Wilhelm Dilthey, *Pattern and Meaning in History: Thoughts on History and Society*, ed. H. P. Rickman (London: George Allen & Unwin, 1961), 67.

82. Caplan, "Reflections," 161.

83. Historians have documented the effects of sedimented anger and prejudices circulating among groups in post-Soviet states such as present-day Ukraine, where surprising numbers continue to harbor rabidly anti-Semitic views; and immigrants from there to the United States and Canada vociferously deny or deflect the collaboration of Ukrainian nationalists in the mass murders under the cover of their own victimization. See Per Anders Rudling, "Theory and Practice: Historical Representation of the War Time Accounts of the Activities of OUN-UPA (the Organization of Ukrainian Nationalists—the Ukrainian Insurgent Army)," *East European Jewish Affairs* 36 no. 2 (December 2006): 163–88; idem, "Organized Anti-Semitism in Contemporary Ukraine: Structure, Influence, and Ideology," *Canadian Slavonic Papers/Revue canadienne des slavistes* H8, nos. 1–2 (March–June 2006): 81–119; and idem, "Bogdan Musial and the Question of Jewish Responsibility for the Pogroms in Western Ukraine in the Summer of 1941," *East European Jewish Affairs* 35, no. 1 (June 2005): 69–89. See also John-Paul Himka, "A Central European Diaspora under the Shadow of World War II: The Galician Ukrainians in North America," *Austrian History Yearbook* 37 (2006): 17–31; idem, "Ukrainian Collaboration in the Extermination of the Jews during the Second World War: Sorting Out the Long-Term and Conjunctural Factors," *Studies in Contemporary Jewry: An Annual* 13 (1997): 170–89; idem, "War Criminality: A Blank Spot in the Collective Memory of the Ukrainian Diaspora," *Spaces of Identity* 5, no. 2 (April 2005), http://www.univie.ac.at/spacesofidentity/ _Vol_5_1/HTML/Himka.html; idem, "Dimensions of a Triangle: Polish-Ukrainian-Jewish Relations in Austrian Galicia," *Polin* 12 (1999): 25–48; and idem, "Ukrainian-Jewish Antagonism in the Galician Countryside during the Late Nineteenth Century," in *Ukrainian-Jewish Relations in Historical Perspective*, ed. Peter J. Potichnyj and Howard Aster (Edmonton: Canadian Institute of Ukrainian Studies, 1988), 111–58. It is also worth noting that my colleague John-Paul Himka has been attacked, sometimes savagely, by members of the Ukrainian community in Alberta for his research about the Ukrainian role in the Nazi mass murders.

84. Dominick LaCapra, *Representing the Holocaust: History, Theory, Trauma* (Ithaca, NY: Cornell University Press, 1994). LaCapra has revisited the problem of traumatic history in *History and Memory after Auschwitz* (Ithaca, NY: Cornell University Press, 1998), *Writing History, Writing Trauma* (Baltimore: The Johns Hopkins University Press, 2001), and, most recently, in *History in Transit: Experience, Identity, Critical Theory* (Ithaca, NY: Cornell University Press, 2004). Though he subtly refines his theory of trauma in these subsequent books, my own treatment of disciplinary issues in the historiography of trauma was inspired by his presentation of the paper "Reflections on the Historians' Debate" in 1990 at the U.C.L.A. conference, "Probing the Limits of Representation: Nazism and the 'Final Solution'" organized by Saul Friedlander, who edited and published the collected proceedings under the same title with Harvard University Press, 1992. See LaCapra, *Representing the Holocaust*, 43–67 and in Friedlander, ed., *Probing the Limits of Representation: Nazism and the "Final Solution"* (Cambridge, MA: Harvard University Press, 1992), 108–27.

85. LaCapra, *History in Transit*, 61.

86. LaCapra, *Writing History, Writing Trauma*, 120.

87. Ibid., 121.

88. LaCapra, *Representing the Holocaust*, 12. Brennan writes that "Goldhagen's *HWE* appears to continue an endless cycle of compulsively repeating the past" ("Some Sociological Contemplations," 101).

89. LaCapra, *History and Memory after Auschwitz*, 206.

90. LaCapra, *Representing the Holocaust*, 30, n. 4.

91. Ibid., 46, and idem, *History in Transit*, 74.

92. LaCapra, *Representing the Holocaust*, 46.

93. Ibid., 30, n. 4.

94. Ibid., 48, n. 6. LaCapra notes that while the therapeutic goal in Freudian analysis is "to further the movement from denial and 'acting-out' to 'working-through,'" the term *working through* receives little theoretical elaboration in Freud's own published work.

95. LaCapra, *Representing the Holocaust*, 174; and idem, *History in Transit*, 119. Such critical self-consciousness may, nevertheless, elude scholars like Goldhagen with strong personal and moral investments in the representation of the Nazi crimes against the Jews.

96. For an historicization of the splits and shifts in East and West German memory, see Elizabeth Domansky, "Die Gespaltene Erinnerung," in *Kunst und Literatur nach Auschwitz*, ed. Manuel Köppen (Berlin: Erich Schmidt Verlag, 1993), 178–96. See also Jeffrey Herf's *Divided Memory: The Nazi Past in the Two Germanys* (Cambridge, MA: Harvard University Press, 1997).

97. Maurice Halbwachs, *The Collective Memory*, trans. Francis J. Ditter, Jr. and Vida Yazdi Ditter (New York: Harper & Row, 1980).

98. One might also speak of an *aphanisis* of identity as a socially mediated idea in relation to changing or fading investments in a particular vision of the object of inquiry. I am employing the term *aphanisis* in consonance with Jacques Lacan's use of it to refer to the fading of the subject as a function of the dialectic between meaning and being, language, and desire, in *Four Fundamental Concepts of Psycho-Analysis*, 207–8.

99. See LaCapra, "Canons, Texts, and Contexts," in *Representing the Holocaust*, 19–41. Here, LaCapra, *Representing the Holocaust*, 25.

100. LaCapra extrapolates from Hans Blumenberg's "more psychoanalytically acute theory of secularization" in *The Legitimacy of the Modern Age*, trans. Robert M. Wallace (Cambridge, MA: MIT Press, 1983). In LaCapra's words, this theory views secularization as a form of *reoccupation* whereby "an older, typically religious or theological cultural territory or set of concerns is reoccupied or reinvested ('recathected' in Freud's sense) by contemporary modes of thought and practice, which may in the process be deformed or disfigured in unconscious ways. In this sense, the very notion of anachronism, while having certain obvious but significant uses, may be superficial insofar as it diverts attention from the intricate process in which older forms are regenerated or reaffirmed with more or less significant differences over time. One might even venture to say that old problems never die, or even fade away. They tend to return as the repressed. Coming to terms with them requires a process of working-through that is cognizant of their role and the possibilities or difficulties it creates for interpretation and for life" (LaCapra, *Representing the Holocaust*, 37–38).

101. LaCapra, *Representing the Holocaust*, 27.

102. Ibid., 14, n. 10. LaCapra is well aware that history only assumes its intelligibility as such in discourse, which stages and thereby produces the return of the repressed; however, his decision to employ *historiography* to refer to the writing of history in apparent opposition to history raises other problems, as history implicitly becomes the "analysand" of a properly critical historiography. Indeed, in assuming that historical understanding is delayed or belated, LaCapra's concept of repetitive temporality implies that repression is a condition that might be surpassed rather than inherited and embedded. Presumably, it is the potential to overcome repression that distinguishes critical from uncritical historiography. This logic suggests that traumatic events are not the only phenomena that require working through. All pasts are potential "patients" of a critical historicization that would free them of repressed and/or ideological elements.

103. LaCapra, *History in Transit*, 80.

104. LaCapra, *Representing the Holocaust*, 220; and Postone, "Holocaust," 87, 111, n. 35.

105. Sigmund Freud, "On Narcissism: An Introduction," *The Standard Edition of the Complete Psychological Works of Sigmund Freud*, trans. and ed. James Strachey in collaboration with Anna Freud (London: Vintage, 2001), Volume 14: 73–102, here 73–74.

106. John Mowitt, "Textuality and the Critique of Disciplinary Reason," in *Text: The Genealogy of an Antidisciplinary Object* (Durham, NC: Duke University Press, 1992), 23–47.

107. Ibid., 26, citing Thomas Kuhn's *Structure of Scientific Revolutions* (Chicago: University of Chicago Press, 1969) and "Second Thoughts on Paradigms," in *The Essential Tension* (Chicago: University of Chicago Press, 1977).

108. René Girard, "From Mimetic Desire to the Monstrous Double," in *Violence and the Sacred*, trans. Paul Gregory (Baltimore: Johns Hopkins University Press, 1977), 143–68.

109. Brennan, "Some Sociological Contemplations," 101.

110. Mowitt, "Textuality," 40. Mowitt also cites Samuel Weber, who shares an interest in the significance of academic ostracism and exclusion as formal, institutionalized principles of interpretation that produce and guarantee the identity and autonomy of a community and its object. For Weber, that which is excluded is not simply externalized, but exists at some level internally as the negated trace of the community's praxis. See his "Texts/Contexts: Closure and Exclusion," in *Institution and Interpretation* (Minneapolis: University of Minnesota Press, 1986), 3–17.

111. Mowitt, "Textuality," 39.

112. Bauer writes that he "cannot recollect that any of the historians who deal with the Holocaust approached their colleagues, never mind their subject, with an overbearing attitude" (Bauer 71–72).

113. Max Horkheimer and Theodor W. Adorno, *Dialectic of Enlightenment: Philosophical Fragments*, ed. Gunzelin Schmid Noer, trans. Edmund Jephcott (Stanford, CA: Stanford University Press, 2002), 162.

114. Ibid., 149.

115. Max Weber, *The Protestant Work Ethic and the Spirit of Capitalism, and Other Works*, ed. and tran. Peter Baehr and Gordon C. Wells (New York: Penguin, 2002), 104 (Weber's emphasis).

116. Mowitt, "Textuality," 27.

117. As LaCapra suggests, "The feeling of trust betrayed or fidelity broken (however unjustified the feeling may in fact be) is one of the greatest impediments to working through problems" (LaCapra, *History in Transit*, 104). The persistent memory of Jewish pain will only be valid for certain people under particular circumstances, such as for Jäckel, who employed his position as a historian to insist that the Memorial to the Murdered Jews of Europe be dedicated exclusively to Jewish victims. In effect, Jäckel abrogated Goldhagen's unshakable insistence upon the singular trajectory of German anti-Semitism while seeming nevertheless to officiate it as part of his definition of what Germans should remember and say by way of apology to the world.

118. Hans Mommsen, "The Thin Patina of Civilization," in Shandley, *Unwilling Germans?* 183.

119. Caplan notes that whenever Goldhagen spoke at the public symposium that took place at the Washington Holocaust Museum attended by senior specialists from Germany, the United States, and Israel, he received "enthusiastic applause, but when the other historians criticized him, the audience was silent or emitted murmurs of dissent. This was partly because the sound of junior knuckles being rapped by elder statesmen was especially audible and patently offensive to the audience, which rallied to defend the younger man under attack." She adds that she does not think they would have done this "unless they had also had some real sympathy for his views" ("Reflections," 154, n. 5).

120. Dean, *Fragility of Empathy*, 55.

121. Horkheimer and Adorno, *Dialectic of Enlightenment*, 144. Horkheimer and Adorno write: "The Jews were the trauma of the knights of industry, who have to masquerade as productive creators. In the Jewish jargon they detect what they secretly despise in themselves: their anti-Semitism is self-hate, the bad conscience of the parasite."

122. Dean encourages suspicion "of works that make us too comfortable" and calls us to explore "in more depth our responses to works that make us squirm" (*Fragility of Empathy*, 75).

Chapter Two

1. Atina Grossmann, "The 'Goldhagen Effect': Memory, Repetition, and Responsibility in the New Germany," in *The "Goldhagen Effect": History, Memory, Nazism—Facing the German Past*, ed. Geoff Eley (Ann Arbor: University of Michigan Press, 2000), 92. Grossmann is citing Charles S. Maier, "A Surfeit of Memory? Reflections on History, Melancholy, and Denial," *History and Memory* 5 (Fall/Winter 1993): 136–52.

2. Grossmann, "Goldhagen Effect," 93 citing Dan Diner, "On Guilt Discourse and Other Narratives: Epistemological Observations regarding the Holocaust," *History and Memory* 9 (Fall 1997): 301–20.

3. Geoff Eley, "Ordinary Germans, Nazism, and Judeocide" in *The "Goldhagen Effect": History, Memory, Nazism—Facing the German Past*, ed. Geoff Eley (Ann Arbor: University of Michigan Press, 2000), 26.

4. Mary Nolan, "The Politics of Memory in the Berlin Republic," *Radical History Review* 81 (Fall 2001): 115.

5. Anson Rabinbach, "From Explosion to Erosion: Holocaust Memorialization in America since Bitburg," *History and Memory*, 9 nos. 1 and 2 (1997): 232.

6. Eley, "Ordinary Germans, Nazism, and Judeocide," 26.

7. Grossmann, "Goldhagen Effect," 97.

8. Ibid., 93 citing Cilly Kugelmann (coeditor of the German-Jewish journal *Babylon*), " 'Tell Them in America We're Still Alive!' The Jewish Community in the Federal Republic," *New German Critique* 46 (Winter 1989): 136, special issue on minorities in German culture.

9. Nolan, "Politics of Memory," 113.

10. Not all the architects featured in this exhibit embraced this label or a direct connection to deconstruction—only Tschumi and Eisenman. The exhibit was curated by the architect, Philip Johnson, in collaboration with the architecture theorist Mark Wigley, who is now dean of Columbia University's Graduate School of Architecture, Planning, and Preservation. As Wigley acknowledges: "Deconstruction itself . . . is often misunderstood as the taking apart of constructions. Consequently, any provocative architectural design which appears to take structure apart—whether it be the simple breaking of an object or the complex dissimulation of an object into a collage of traces—has been hailed as deconstructive. . . . On the contrary, deconstruction gains all its force by challenging the very values of harmony, unity, and stability, and proposing instead a different view of structure: the view that flaws are intrinsic to the structure. A deconstructive architect is therefore not one who dismantles buildings, but one who locates the inherent dilemmas within buildings." Mark Wigley, "Deconstructivist Architecture," in *Deconstructivist Architecture*, Philip Johnson and Mark Wigley (New York: Museum of Modern Art, 1988), 11, cited by Brooke Hodge, "Deconstruction and Architecture: Conflicting Interpretations," in *Skin and Bones: Parallel Practices in Fashion and Architecture* (New York: Thames & Hudson, 2006), 39.

11. See the first transcript of a conversation between Jacques Derrida and Peter Eisenman in *Chora L Works*, ed. Jeffrey Kipnis and Thomas Leeser (New York: Monacelli Press, 1997), 7–13.

12. On the difference between Adorno's and Lanzmann's adaptations of the image prohibition, see Gertrud Koch, "The Aesthetic Transformation of the Image of the Unimaginable: Notes on Claude Lanzmann's *Shoah*," trans. Jamie Owen Daniel and Miriam Hansen, *October* 48 (Spring 1989): 15–24. See also Michael Rothberg, " 'Touch an Event to Begin': Americanizing the Holocaust," *Traumatic Realism: The Demands of Holocaust Representation* (Minneapolis: University of Minnesota Press, 2000), 221–64; and Yosefa Loshitzky, "Holocaust Others: Spielberg's *Schindler's List* versus Lanzmann's *Shoah*," in *Spielberg's Holocaust: Critical Perspectives on Schindler's List*," ed. Yosefa Loshitzky (Bloomington: Indiana University Press, 1997), 104–18.

13. See Karyn Ball, "For and Against the *Bilderverbot*: The Rhetoric of 'Unrepresentability' and Remediated 'Authenticity' in the German Reception of Steven Spielberg's *Schindler's List*" in David Bathrick, Brad Prager, and Michael D. Richardson, eds. *Visualizing the Holocaust: Aesthetics, Documents, Memory* (Rochester: Camden House, 2008).

14. In his catalogue essay for the "Deconstructivist Architecture" exhibit, Mark Wigley writes that the works in the MOMA exhibition "irritate modernism from within, distorting it with its own genealogy." See Wigley, "Deconstructivist Architecture," 16 cited by Hodge, "Deconstruction and Architecture," 42.

15. Eisenman has expressed distaste for self-righteous leftist grandstanding and sees himself as an unsettling figure for those who would align him against conservative interests since, as he readily admits, his expensive projects depend on accumulated capital and most of his clients are Republicans or right-leaning. He is contemptuous of young left-identified architects who worry about himself or Rem Koolhaas appearing to be radical when they are believed to be conservative. See Peter Eisenman, "Liberal Views Have Never Built Anything of Any Value," interview by Robert Locke (July 27, 2004). http://archinect.com/features/article.php?id=4618_0_23_24_M.

16. James E. Young, *At Memory's Edge: After-Images of the Holocaust in Contemporary Art and Architecture* (New Haven, CT: Yale University Press, 2000), 163.

17. Grossmann, "Goldhagen Effect," 94.

18. Ibid., 91.

19. Ibid., 89. Though I share Grossmann's mixed sense of irritation, resignation, and intrigue, I perceive this compulsive public scrutiny as a hopeful sign for continuing German-Jewish discussions even as they founder between antithetical memories and generational interests. Certainly, it is hopeful in light of the relative dearth of such reflection in Austria, where historiography in the 1980s and 1990s did not entertain the kinds of questions that instigated the 1986 Historians' Debate and the Goldhagen controversy, both of which provoked reevaluations of intentionalist and functionalist approaches as well as the *Sonderweg* and collective guilt theses. Instead, as Pieter Judson asserts, the Austrian debates were concerned about whether to address the question of the Holocaust at all. See Judson, "Austrian Non-Reception of a Reluctant Goldhagen," in Eley *The "Goldhagen Effect: History, Memory, Nazism—Facing the German Past*, ed. Geoff Eley (Ann Arbor: University of Michigan Press, 2000), 146.

20. Grossmann, "Goldhagen Effect," 89.

21. Jürgen Habermas's "A Kind of Settlement of Damages (Apologetic Tendencies)," originally appeared in the July 11th, 1986 issue of *Die Zeit*. My discussion cites Habermas, "A Kind of Settlement of Damages (Apologetic Tendencies)," trans. Jeremy Leaman, *New German Critique* 44 (1988): 25–39. For English translations of the collected documents pertaining to the *Historikerstreit*, see *Forever in the Shadow of Hitler? Original Documents of the* Historikerstreit, *the Controversy concerning the Singularity of the Holocaust*, trans. James Knowlton and Truett Cates (New Jersey: Humanities Press, 1993): 18–23. For the articles in their original German, I have consulted *Historiker"streit": Die Dokumentation der Kontroverse um die Einzigartigkeit der nationalsozialistischen Judenvernichtung* (Munich: Piper, 1987).

22. Charles Maier, *The Unmasterable Past: History, Holocaust, and German National Identity* (Cambridge, MA: Harvard University Press, 1988), 139.

23. Ibid., 139.

24. Ibid.

25. Eley, "Ordinary Germans, Nazism, and Judeocide," 30.

26. Jürgen Habermas's "Concerning the Public Use of History" [trans. Jeremy Leaman, *New German Critique* 44 (1988): 40–50] was originally published in the November 7th, 1986 issue of *Die Zeit*. This essay and "A Kind of Settlement of Damages (Apologetic Tendencies)" (cited above) are included in *Eine Art Schadensabwicklung* (Frankfurt am Main: Suhrkamp, 1987). See also Habermas, *The New Conservatism: Cultural Criticism and the Historians' Debate*, ed. and trans. Shierry Weber Nicholsen (Cambridge, MA: MIT Press, 1994). The Bonn historian, Klaus Hildebrand is mainly alluded to as a member of a supporting cast to the revisionists' antics. Following his

discussion of Hillgruber, Habermas denounces Hildebrand for praising Nolte's *Fascism in its Epoch* (1963) as "pioneering" because "it has the merit of removing the 'seemingly unique character' from the history of the 'Third Reich' and of classifying historically 'the destructive capacity of the worldview and the regime' within the overall development of totalitarianism." Habermas citing *Historische Zeitschrift* 242 (1986): 456ff; Habermas, "Kind of Settlement of Damages," 33.

27. Habermas cites Alfred Dregger's "Nicht in Opfer und Täter einteilen," *Das Parlament*, May 17–24, 1986, 21. In Habermas's words: "Whoever still insists on mourning collective fates, without distinguishing between culprits and victims, obviously has something else up his sleeve" ("Kind of Settlement of Damages," 27).

28. Dregger's language provides a perfect example of the kind of incidents to which Adorno critically alludes in "What Does Coming to Terms with the Past Mean?": "The attitude that it would be proper for everything to be forgiven and forgotten by those who were wronged is expressed by the party that committed the injustice." Adorno, "What Does Coming to Terms with the Past Mean? *Bitburg in Moral and Political Perspective*, ed. Geoffrey Hartman (Bloomington: Indiana University Press, 1986), 115.

29. Theodor W. Adorno, *Negative Dialectics*, trans. E. B. Ashton (New York: Continuum, 1973), 361.

30. My distinction between these two understandings of *working through* is indebted to the notes provided by Henry W. Pickford to accompany his translation of Theodor W. Adorno, "The Meaning of Working Through the Past" in *Critical Models: Interventions and Catchwords*, trans. Henry W. Pickford (New York: Columbia University Press, 1998), 89–103 nn. 337–43.

31. Theodor W. Adorno, "Education after Auschwitz," in *Critical Models: Interventions and Catchwords*, trans. Henry W. Pickford (New York: Columbia University Press, 1998), 194.

32. Ibid., 193.

33. Michael Stürmer writes, "In the reality of a divided Germany, the Germans must find their identity, an identity which can no longer be found in the nation state but can also not be found without a nation." Michael Stürmer, "Kein Eigentum der Deutschen: Die deutsche Frage," in *Die Identität der Deutschen*, ed. Werner Weidenfeld (Bonn: Goldmann, 1983), 98, quoted by Habermas, "Kind of Settlement of Damages," 36.

34. In Habermas's words, "Stürmer pleads for a *unified* picture of history, which can secure both identity and social integration in place of the religious powers of belief which have drifted off into the private sphere" ("Kind of Settlement of Damages," 38).

35. Although he was writing in the 1960s, he seemingly anticipates Stürmer's 1980s rhetoric when in *Negative Dialectics*, Adorno observes, "The substance of the lament about lack of ties is a condition of society that simulates freedom without realizing it" (285).

36. Habermas, "Kind of Settlement of Damages," 25–26.

37. Ibid., 26.

38. As Reagan stated it, "we" can now mourn "the German war dead today as human beings, crushed by a vicious ideology." And a bit further on: "The moral measure of our two nations will be found in the resolve we show to preserve liberty, to protect life, and to honor and cherish all God's children. That is why the free,

democratic Federal Republic of Germany is such a profound and hopeful testament to the human spirit. . . . On this 40th anniversary of World War II, we mark the day when the hate, the evil and the obscenity is ended and we commemorate the rekindling of the democratic spirit in Germany." "Remarks of President Reagan at Bitburg Air Base, May 5, 1985," in *Bitburg in Moral and Political Perspective*, ed. Geoffrey Hartman (Bloomington: Indiana University Press, 1986), 259, 261.

39. Habermas writes: "To start with, the memory of recent periods of history which is a predominantly negative one and which inhibits identification must be bulldozed clear; then, under the sign of freedom or totalitarianism, the always virulent fear of Bolshevism must be used to keep alive the correct image of the enemy. The scenario at Bitburg contained precisely these three elements. The aura of the military cemetery in Bitburg served to mobilize historical consciousness through national sentiment. The juxtaposition of Bitburg and Bergen-Belsen, of SS-graves and the mass graves in a concentration camp took away from the singularity of Nazi crimes. And finally the handshake of the veteran generals in the presence of the American president could confirm that we Germans had always been on the right side in the struggle against the Bolshevist enemy" ("Kind of Settlement of Damages," 27–28).

40. Writing in the 1980s, Habermas is referring to plans for the German Historical Museum in Berlin and the House of the History of the Federal Republic in Bonn. For a fuller discussion of the issues and conflicts surrounding this planning, see Charles Maier, "A Usable Past? Museums, Memory, and Identity," in *Unmasterable Past*, 121–59. See also Andreas Huyssen, "Escape from Amnesia: The Museum as Mass Medium," in *Twilight Memories: Marking Time in a Culture of Amnesia* (New York: Routledge, 1995), 13–35.

41. Habermas, "Kind of Settlement of Damages," 28, 27.

42. Huyssen. "Escape from Amnesia," 22.

43. Maier, *Unmasterable Past*, 136.

44. Habermas refers to Nietzsche (along with the Marquis de Sade) as one of the " 'black' writers of the bourgeoisie" in the opening of "The Entwinement of Myth and Rationalism: Max Horkheimer and Theodor Adorno," in *The Philosophical Discourse of Modernity* (Cambridge, MA: MIT Press, 1987), 106. See also idem, "Die Moderne—ein unvollendetes Projekt," in *Die Moderne—ein unvollendetes Projekt: Philosophisch-politische Aufsätze, 1977–1990* (Leipzig: Reclam, 1990), 32–54. See additionally Peter Uwe Hohendahl's insightful reconsideration of Habermas's critique of Horkheimer and Adorno in "The Dialectic of Enlightenment Revisited: Habermas's Critique of the Frankfurt School," *New German Critique* 35 (1985): 3–26.

45. Habermas, "Entwinement," 114.

46. Ibid., 119.

47. Ibid., 129.

48. John Torpey, "Introduction: Habermas and the Historians," *New German Critique* 44 (1988): 12.

49. Habermas, "Kind of Settlement of Damages," 26–27.

50. Ibid.; idem, "Public Use of History," 47.

51. Habermas, "Public Use of History," 43–44. Survivors living in Germany do, indeed, find it "difficult to breath," as it were. In 1995, one survivor explained his silence to me this way: "I don't even bother to try to talk to them about it anymore; their excuses are too tiresome."

52. Jürgen Habermas, "Historical Consciousness and Post-Traditional Identity: The Federal Republic's Orientation to the West," in *New Conservatism*, 252.

53. Habermas, "Kind of Settlement of Damages," 39.

54. Ibid.

55. As Habermas puts it in the revised version of his Sonning Prize acceptance speech in Copenhagen (May 14, 1987): "That through which we Germans disassociated ourselves from Western civilization, and indeed from any and every civilization, set off a shock-wave; and though many citizens of the Federal Republic fended off this shock at first, they remained under its influence as they gradually abandoned their reservations about the political culture and social forms of the West. A mentality changed" ("Historical Consciousness and Post-Traditional Identity," 250).

56. While Habermas's understanding of postnationalist critical remembrance does not repeat Kant's circumscription of public reason to scholars, as his criticisms of Horkheimer and Adorno suggest, he remains committed to redeeming the "rational potential of bourgeois culture" repudiated by self-destructing pessimists. It is telling that Nietzsche is one of Habermas's prime examples of such antibourgeois pessimism along with de Sade, since the interconnection among responsibilities, promises, and debts infuses Habermas's ethics. Without investing too literally in Nietzsche's standpoint, it is hard to resist the judgment that Habermas's rhetoric about "indebted memory" reenthrones the very debtor-creditor relationship that the nineteenth-century philosopher excoriated in the "Second Essay" in *On the Genealogy of Morals* as the paradigm of bourgeois Western morality and justice. Nietzsche goes on to identify the source of this "ineradicable idea" as the "contractual relationship between *creditor and debtor*, which is as old as the idea of 'legal subjects' and in turn points back to the fundamental forms of buying, selling, barter, trade, and traffic." Friedrich Nietzsche, "Second Essay: 'Guilt,' 'Bad Conscience,' and the Like," in "*On the Genealogy of Morals*" and "*Ecce Homo*," trans. Walter Kaufmann (New York: Vintage, 1967), section 4, p. 63. Morality and responsibility are linked by Nietzsche to memory by way of the ability to remember and therefore fulfill a promise, which entails that "[m]an himself must first of all have become *calculable, regular, necessary*, even in his own image of himself, if he is to be able to stand security for *his own future*, which is what one who promises does!" (section 1, p. 58). Hence the "oldest psychology" is a mode of "*mnemotechnics*: 'If something is to stay in the memory it must be burned in: only that which never ceases to *hurt* stays in memory' " (section 3, p. 61). Nietzsche proclaims: "Throughout the greater part of human history punishment was *not* imposed *because* one held the wrong-doer responsible for his deed, thus *not* on the presupposition that only the guilty one should be punished: rather as parents still punish their children, from anger at some harm or injury, vented on the one who caused it—but this anger is held in check and modified by the idea that every injury has its *equivalent* and can actually be paid back, even if only through the *pain* of the culprit" (section 4, p. 63).

57. Karen E. Till, "Staging the Past: Landscape Designs, Cultural Identity and *Erinnerungspolitik* at Berlin's *Neue Wache*," *Ecumene* 6, no. 3 (1999): 269.

58. Elke Grenzer, "The Topographies of Memory in Berlin: The Neue Wache and the Memorial for the Murdered Jews of Europe," *Canadian Journal of Urban Research* 11, no. 1 (2002): 101.

59. Ibid.

60. Ibid., 100; and Till, "Staging the Past," 258.

61. Grenzer, "Topographies of Memory," 100.

62. Till, "Staging the Past," 273. Weizäcker's speech is also quoted by Grenzer, "Topographies of Memory," 98–99, and with admiration by Joachim Schlör, *Memorial to the Murdered Jews of Berlin*, with photographs by Jürgen Hohmuth (Munich: Prestel, 2005), 28.

63. See in particular, Habermas, "A Kind of Settlement of Damages (Apologetic Tendencies)" cited above. See also his "Historical Consciousness and Post-Traditional Identity: The Federal Republic's Orientation to the West," in *The New Conservatism: Cultural Criticism and the Historians' Debate*, ed. and trans. Shierry Weber Nicholsen (Cambridge, MA: MIT Press, 1994), 249–67.

64. Till, "Staging the Past," 265.

65. Nolan, "Politics of Memory," 121 n. 4.

66. Grossmann, "Goldhagen Effect," 90 n. 1.

67. Nolan, "Politics of Memory," 119.

68. Ibid., 121.

69. Ibid., 119.

70. Till, "Staging the Past," 253, 265 n. 58.

71. Nolan, "Politics of Memory," 129 n. 6.

72. Grenzer, "Topographies of Memory," 94.

73. Till, "Staging the Past," 266.

74. Kirsten Harjes, "Stumbling Stones: Holocaust Memorials, National Identity, and Democratic Inclusion in Berlin," *German Politics and Society*, issue 74, vol. 23, no. 1 (Spring 2005): 139–40.

75. Ibid., 141.

76. "Bürgerinitiative Perspective Berlin 1995 e.V., ed., *Ein Denkmal für die ermordeten Juden Europas: Dokumentation 1988–1995* (Berlin: Bürgerinitiative Perspektive Berlin eV, 1995), 14, cited by Gerd Knischewski and Ulla Spittler, "Remembering in the Berlin Republic: The Debate about the Central Holocaust Memorial in Berlin," *Debatte* 13, no. 1 (April 2005): 25.

77. James E. Young, "Germany's Holocaust Memorial Problem—and Mine," in "Justice and the Politics of Memory," special issue of *Religion and Public Life* 33 (2003): 56.

78. Lea Rosh (writing as the president of the Society for the Promotion of the Memorial to the Murdered Jews of Europe), "From Three to Four Years to Seventeen," in *Materials on the Memorial* (Berlin: Nicolai, 2005), 9. In a chapter on the memorial in Karen Till's *The New Berlin*, she observes that, "Rosh typified her mission to establish the memorial as a difficult battle and often took hard-line 'fighting' positions to make sure the project would be realized, sometimes ostracizing people in the process." Till, *The New Berlin: Memory, Politics, Place* (Minneapolis: University of Minnesota Press, 2005), 164. While I will not be pursuing one here, it would be worth undertaking a feminist analysis of varying reactions to the well-meaning Rosh, who was sometimes characterized as egotistical and vain in the course of pursuing a seventeen-year commitment. Salomon Korn, for example, suspects her of a "compensatory overidentification" with the actual victims. See Salomon Korn, "Der Tragödie letzter Teil—das Spiel mit der Zeit," in *Das Holocaust-Mahnmal: Documentation einer Debatte*, ed. Michael S. Cullen (Zurich: Pendo, 1999), 72, originally appearing in the *Frankfurter Rundschau*, September 13, 1996.

79. Knischewski and Spittler, "Remembering," 26.

80. Young, "Germany's Holocaust Memorial Problem," 56.

81. Sibylle Quack, "Das Bewahren des Grauens: Zur Diskussion um Mahnwachen, Denkmale und KZ-Gedenkstätten," *Vorgänge* 1 (1994): 45, cited by Knischewski and Spittler, "Remembering," 39, 36.

82. Knischewski and Spittler, "Remembering," 36. See also Peter Hayes, *Die Degussa im Dritten Reich: Von der Zusammenarbiet zur Mittäterschaft* (Munich: Beck, 2004).

83. Knischewski and Spittler, "Remembering," 36.

84. Günter Schlusche, "A Memorial Is Built," in *Materials on the Memorial* (Berlin: Nicolai, 2005), 28.

85. Rosh, "From Three to Four Years," 9. As Young observes, this exclusive dedication was the first of "five aims" that she stipulated as inviolable: "(1) this would be a memorial only to Europe's murdered Jews; (2) ground would be broken for it on 27 January 1999, Germany's newly designated 'Holocaust Remembrance Day' marked to coincide with the 1945 liberation of Auschwitz; (3) its location would be the 20,000 square meter site of the Ministers Gardens, between the Brandenburg Gate and Potsdamer Platz; (4) the nine finalists' teams from the 1995 competition would be invited to revise their designs and concepts after incorporating suggestions and criticism from the present colloquia; and (5) the winning design would be chosen from the revised designs of the original nine finalists" (Young, "Germany's Holocaust Memorial Problem," 58). See also Young's longer version of this essay in *At Memory's Edge*, 184–223.

86. Eberhard Jäckel, "An alle und jeden erinnern? Der Plan für ein Berliner Mahnmal zum Gedenken an den Judenmord darf nicht zerredet werden" (*Die Zeit*, 7 April 1989, p. 12), cited by Knischewski and Spittler, "Remembering," 26. See also Jäckel, "Kernstück," *Tagesspiegel*, August 3, 1991.

87. As Henryk Broder in "'Auf der Höhe der Zeit,'" *Der Spiegel*, December 11, 1997, sarcastically observed: "The Jews deserved recognition for their contributions to German culture, and from Heinrich Heine to Albert Einstein, they had enriched Germany as the 'culture nation' while the Gypsies at best could produce a couple of merry musicians." See Broder, *Das Holocaust-Mahnmal*, ed. Cullen (Zurich: Pendo, 1999), 188. I am grateful to Ole Gram for helping me with this translation. Jäckel's stubborn insistence upon this hierarchy is paradoxical, given his repudiation of Goldhagen's "simply bad" book in 1996; it is almost as if he has appropriated Goldhagen's outrage about German anti-Semitism in particular (as opposed to racial hygiene policies in general) as the proper affect for the memorial while denying it to a Jewish scholar and survivor's son. This is to suggest that Jäckel deems affective identification with Jewish suffering valid in relation to the memorial, but not in a historiographical context.

88. Claus Leggewie and Erik Meyer, *Ein Ort, an den Mann gerne geht: Das Holocaust-Mahnmal und die Deutsche Geschichtspolitik nach 1989* (Munich: Carl Hanser, 2005), 69. My translation.

89. Henryk Broder, "Wer ein Menschenleben rettet, rettet die Welt," *Tagesspiegel*, August 22, 1997, cited by Leggewie and Meyer, *Ein Ort*, 69. See also Broder, "Wer ein Menschenleben rettet, rettet die Welt" in *Das Holocaust-Mahnmal*, ed. Cullen (Zurich: Pendo, 1999), 166. My translation.

90. Salomon Korn, "Mit falschem Etikett," *Frankfurter Rundschau*, September 4, 1997, cited by Wolfgang Benz, "A Memorial for Whom? The Debate about the

Memorial to the Murdered Jews of Europe, about Victims of Persecution under National Socialism, and about Memorial Sites," in *Materials on the Memorial* (Berlin: Nicolai, 2005), 31.

91. Korn, "Der Tragödie letzter Teil," 82.

92. Reinhart Koselleck, "Vier Minuten für die Ewigkeit," *Frankfurter Allgemeine Zeitung*, January 9, 1997, cited by Benz, "Memorial for Whom?" 32. Koselleck is quite caustic in moments. In "Vier Minuten," he writes: "The obliquely raised graves in the Christian tradition at one time indicated the promise of the Resurrection. After we Germans beat to death, shot or gassed, then dissolved in ashes, air and water five to six million Jews, we presume at this point to be able to offer symbolically these very same Jews a resurrection. Here one has to ask oneself if there should not nevertheless be a debate about political taste." Koselleck, "Vier Minuten," in *Das Holocaust-Mahnmal*, ed. Michael S. Cullen (Zurich: Pendo, 1999), 88. I am grateful to Clemens Ruthner for his advice about this translation.

93. Benz, "Memorial for Whom?" 33.

94. Knischewski and Spittler, "Remembering," 33, 34, citing *Chronik* in *Das Holocaust-Mahnmal*, ed. Cullen (Zurich: Pendo, 1999), 291.

95. Knischewski and Spittler, "Remembering," 26, citing Romani Rose, "Ein Mahnmal für alle Opfer: Im NS-Regime gab es keine Verfolgung erster oder zweiter Klasse," *Die Zeit*, April 28, 1989; and Heinz Galinski, "Presserklärung des Vorsitzenden des Zentralrates der Juden in Deutschland und der Jüdische Gemeinde zu Berlin" (March 15, 1992), reprinted in the Bürgerinitiative, *Ein Denkmal*, 113, 107.

96. Schlusche, "A Memorial Is Built," 24.

97. Ibid., 23–24.

98. With the Information Center, Wolfgang Benz writes, the memorial "becomes a cite for cognitive experience that includes all victim groups" while acting as "a portal for memorials at authentic sites." This function further distinguishes it from the Jewish Museum, "which endeavors to present Jews to the public not as victims, but as a culture" (Benz, "Memorial for Whom?" 39). Curated by Sibylle Quack and Dagmar von Wilcken, the subterranean Information Center consists of five rooms that are structured to resonate spatially with the stelae. The first hall offers an overview of the incremental escalation of the Nazi policies against the Jews from 1933 to 1945 that culminates in a wall with six photographs of individual victims, which are intended to provoke an encounter with individual destinies. This aim also structures the "room of dimensions," where the number of Jewish victims from each occupied country is written on the walls. In this second room, fifteen personal documents, letters, and desperately scribbled messages from men, women, and children who faced imminent murder have been set into the floor. The stelae motif from above is transmitted below in the layout and form of the informational displays. This arrangement, as von Wilcken suggests, should create the effect of the stelae pressing downward into the room from above, thereby becoming information vehicles (Schlör, *Memorial to the Murdered Jews of Berlin*, 61). In their contribution to *Materials on the Memorial*, the curators von Wilcken and Quack comment on the "tension between 'above' and 'below' [that] derives from the fact that the memorial, as an abstract work of art, is experienced by the visitor both physically and emotionally, while the exhibition presents the context of and background to the Holocaust." Dagmar von Wilcken and Sibylle Quack, "Creating an Exhibition about the Murder of European Jewry: Conflicts of Subject, Concept and Design in the 'Information Centre,' " in *Materials on the Memorial* (Berlin: Nicolai, 2005), 45. In the

"room of families," visitors view assemblages of documents and photographs that detail the histories and fates as well as the "cultural diversity" of Jewish families throughout Europe before the Holocaust. The "room of names and pages of testimony from Yad Vashem" is blank except for the name, year of birth, and year of death of each of eight hundred individuals projected onto the four walls. It is the only room containing sound. Since the board of trustees decided in their third meeting (February 24, 2000) that the main function of the center would be " 'to personalize and individualize the Holocaust' " (Wilcken and Quack, "Creating an Exhibition," 40), Jäckel writes, this room "is, in a sense, the heart of the memorial. One can interpret it as a blank gravestone, a cenotaph" (Eberhard Jäckel, "The Importance of Names," in *Materials on the Memorial* [Berlin: Nicolai, 2005], 123). The Information Center's pamphlet notes that reading all the names in German and English "would take approximately six years, seven months and 27 days," yet as the guidebook reminds viewers, "Even now, not all the names of those murdered are known." The final room offers visitors an opportunity to enter information about undocumented victims. The "room of sites" is devoted to the geographic spread of the genocide and employs maps, photographs, and films depicting places of persecution, mass murder, concentration camps, ghettos, deportation routes, and death marches. The visitor can also listen to testimony about Auschwitz-Birkinau, Chelmno, Treblinka, Belzec, and Sobibor, as well as Baba Yar. The visitor's tour ends at the memorial's database, which provides access to information about historical and research institutions in Europe.

99. Knischewski and Spittler, "Remembering," 33. Knischewski and Spittler cite Martin Walser, "Dankrede beim Empfang des Friedenpreises des Deutschen Buchhandels in der Frankfurter Paulskirche am 11. Oktober 1998" (extracts), *Blätter für deutsche und internationale Politik* 1 (1999): 119ff. See also Johannes Klotz and Gerd Weigel, eds., *Geistige Brandstiftung? Die Walser-Bubis Debatte* (Köln: PapyRossa, 1999).

100. Salomon Korn remarks that Bubis is overtaxed in his role as the Jewish arbiter of German-Jewish issues: he not only speaks on behalf of all Jews, but also relieves Germans from the risk of making judgments and decisions on their own behalf (Salomon Korn, "Monströse Platte: Zur Debatte um des Holocaust-Menkmal," in Cullen, *Das Holocaust-Mahnmal* (Zurich: Pendo, 1999), 40. This article originally appeared in the *Frankfurter Allgemeine Zeitung*, July 3, 1995.

101. Grossmann, "Goldhagen Effect," 104.

102. In Young's words, "The Holocaust, after all was not merely the annihilation of nearly 6 million Jews, among them 1.5 million children, but also the extirpation of a thousand-year-old civilization from the heart of Europe. Any conception of the Holocaust that reduces it to the horror of destruction alone, ignores the stupendous loss and void left behind" (Young, "Germany's Holocaust Memorial Problem," 62–63).

103. This statistic was cited in "Ein Antisemit im Kabinett? Israel boykottiert den neuen polnischen Vizepremier," *Jüdische Allgemeine*, June 15, 2006. The article reports on Israel's reaction to the appointment of former vice premier and minister of education, Roman Giertych, who is affiliated with the League of Polish Families, a shamelessly anti-Semitic and homophobic right-wing party.

104. I would have strongly preferred to see the Sinti and Roma and other victimized groups included in the dedication, but admittedly, in view of the ongoing persecution of the Sinti and Roma, the most desirable memorial may not be a site at all, but rather a commitment among state and local governments to create policies

that protect them along with guest workers and immigrants from oppression. As Henryk Broder observes, "[T]here is no reward in the present" and, for this reason, we would do better to help living victims remain alive rather than honor the dead victims of the Nazis. See Henryk Broder, "Wer ein Menschenleben rettet" (Cullen, 169, 170).

105. Hanno Rauterberg, Holocaust Memorial Berlin Eisenman Architects, text by Hanno Rauterberg, photo essay by Hélène Binet, photo impressions by Lukas Wassmann (Baden Switzerland: Lars Müller Publishers, 2005).

106. Habermas, "Der Zeigefinger. Die Deutschen und ihr Denkmal," *Die Zeit Feuilleton* (1999) http://www.zeit.de/archiv/1999/14/199914.denkmal.2_.xml (downloaded July, 2006 [8 pages]), here p. 2 of 8. I am grateful to Patricia Ehrkamp and Ole Gram for their revision of my translation of this quotation. See also "The Finger of Blame: The Germans and Their Memorial," in Habermas, *Time of Transitions,* trans. Max Pensky (Cambridge, England: Polity, 2006), 38–50.

107. Ibid., cited by Benz in *Materials on the Memorial,* 32.

108. The use of the word *branded* (*eingebrannt*) with *persistently* (*persistierende*) is redundant and thus symptomatic of the force of Habermas's investment in disciplining German national consciousness. Such diction also seems ironic, given his criticisms of Foucault, among others, in *The Philosophical Discourse of Modernity,* since the latter took seriously Nietzsche's claim that memory is a venue of a punishing "bad conscience." Nietzsche defined bad conscience as the masochistic supplement of a history in which "the oldest 'state' thus appeared as a fearful tyranny, as an oppressive and remorseless machine, and went on working until this raw material of people and semi-animals was at last not only thoroughly kneaded and pliant but also *formed*" (Nietzsche, *"Second Essay,"* section 17, p. 86; Nietzsche's emphasis). In this respect, Habermas's rhetoric resonates with Salomon's Korn's conclusion that "The Memorial for the Murdered Jews of Europe may, indeed, it should, remain a public outrage—a thorn in the flesh of memory." See Korn, "Monströse Platte," 41.

109. Heinrich August Winkler, "Lesarten der Sühne," in *Das Holocaust-Mahnmal,* ed. Michael S. Cullen (Zurich: Pendo, 1999), 245. This article originally appeared in *Der Spiegel,* August 24, 1998.

110. Young, "Germany's Holocaust Memorial Problem," 60.

111. Ibid.

112. Till, *New Berlin,* 179.

113. Rauterberg, *Holocaust Memorial Berlin,* no page numbers provided in text.

114. Young, "Germany's Holocaust Memorial Problem," 56.

115. In commenting on Hoheisel's proposition to blow up the Brandenburg Gate, Young remarks: "How better to remember a destroyed people than by a destroyed monument? Rather than commemorating the destruction of a people with yet another constructed edifice, Hoheisel would mark destruction with destruction. Rather than filling in the void left by a murdered people with a positive form, the artist would carve out an empty space in Berlin by which to recall a now absent people." He adds: "[P]erhaps no single emblem better represents the conflicted, self-abnegating motives for memory in Germany today than the vanishing monument." Young, "Germany's Memorial Question: Memory, Counter-Memory, and the End of the Monument," *South Atlantic Quarterly* 96, no. 4 (Fall 1997): 853, 854. Hoheisel's

proposal is highlighted among other rejected entries in a volume devoted to the
documentation on Rudolf Herz and Reinhard Matz's proposals entitled "Leerstelle"
(1995) and "Überschrieben" (1997) along with accompanying texts by James Young,
Aleida Assmann, Jochen Geerz, Klaus Theweleit, and others. See Rudolf Herz
and Reinhard Matz, *Zwei Entwürfe zum Holocaust-Denkmal*, ed. Matthias Reichelt
(Nürnberg: Verlag für moderne Kunst, 2001).

116. Korn, "Der Tragödie letzter Teil," 75.

117. Young, "Germany's Holocaust Memorial Problem," 57.

118. Ibid.

119. Ibid., 56–57.

120. Ibid., 61.

121. Ibid., 58.

122. Harjes, "Stumbling Stones," 140–41.

123. Young, "Germany's Holocaust Memorial Problem," 61.

124. Derrida and Eisenman, *Chora L Works*, 8. Dalibor Vesely observes that
because "architects are not usually much concerned with the sources and the nature
of the knowledge received from other fields, tending to view it either uncritically or
as a pragmatic tool, they are very often victims of deep confusion." Whether he is
deeply confused or not, Eisenman's characterization of Hebraic thought smacks of
such intellectual dilettantism. See Dalibor Vesely, *Architecture in the Age of Divided
Representation: The Question of Creativity in the Shadow of Production* (Cambridge,
MA: MIT Press, 2004), 23.

125. Derrida and Eisenman, *Chora L Works*, 7.

126. J. Hillis Miller, "Beginning from the Ground Up," and Jacques Derrida,
"Letter to Peter Eisenman," in *Critical Architecture and Contemporary Theory*, ed.
William Lillyman, Marilyn F. Morariarty, and David J. Neuman (New York: Oxford
University Press, 1994), 13–19 and 20–28, respectively.

127. Peter Eisenman, "Moving Arrows, Eros and Other Errors," *Précis* 6 (Spring
1987): 138–43; and idem, *Arquitectura* 69, no. 270 (January–February 1988): 66–81.
See also idem, *Moving Arrows, Eros and Other Errors: An Architecture of Absence*
(London: Architectural Association, 1986).

128. Derrida, "Letter to Peter Eisenman," 21 n. 126.

129. Ibid., 28, citing an Eisenman interview published in *Arquitectura* 69, no.
270 (January–February 1988).

130. Peter Eisenman, "Post/El Cards: A Reply to Jacques Derrida," in *Critical
Architecture and Contemporary Theory*, ed. William Lillyman, Marilyn Moriarity, and
David J. Neuman (New York: Oxford University Press, 1994), 41.

131. Ibid., 41, 42.

132. Derrida, "Letter to Peter Eisenman," 27.

133. Ibid.

134. Andreas Huyssen, "The Voids of Berlin," *Critical Inquiry* (Autumn 1997):
57–81 here p. 80, n. 14 paraphrasing Derrida, "Jacques Derrida zu 'Between the
Lines,' " (1991), in Daniel Libeskind, *Radix-Matrix: Architecture and Writings*, trans.
Peter Green (Munich: Prestel Verlag, 1997), 115–17. Young cites Derrida's critical
queries about the literal and figurative valences of the void that bears witness to
the "haunting" present absence of murdered Jewish citizens in Berlin, but does not
attempt to pressure or consider the horizon of his own enunciations (rather than
ever more eloquently rephrasing them). Young, *At Memory's Edge*, 178, citing Der-

rida, "Response to Libeskind," in *Radix-Matrix: Architecture and Writings*, by Daniel Libeskind, trans. Peter Green (Munich: Prestel Verlag, 1997), 111.

135. See Jacques Derrida, "Response to Libeskind" and Libeskind's response to Derrida in the "Discussion" following it in *Research in Phenomenology* 22, (1992): 98.

136. Noah Isenberg, "Reading 'Between the Lines': Daniel Libeskind's Berlin Jewish Museum and the Shattered Symbiosis," *Unlikely History: The Changing Jewish-German Symbiosis, 1945–2000*, ed. Leslie Morris and Jack Zipes (New York: Palgrave Macmillan, 2002), 171.

137. Daniel Libeskind, *Daniel Libeskind: The Space of Encounter* (New York: Universe, 2000), 25; and Young, *At Memory's Edge*, 163.

138. Young, "Germany's Memorial Question," 857. On the post-Holocaust vicissitudes of German-Jewish relations, see Jack Zipes and Anson Rabinbach, eds., *Germans and Jews since the Holocaust: The Changing Situation* (New York: Holmes and Meier, 1986); and Anson Rabinbach, "The Jewish Question in the German Question," and Dan Diner, "Negative Symbiosis: Germans and Jews after Auschwitz," in *Reworking the Past: Hitler the Holocaust, and the Historians' Debate*, ed. Peter Baldwin (Boston: Beacon Press, 1990), 45–73 and 251–61, respectively. See also Leslie Morris and Jack Zipes, eds., *Unlikely History* (cited above).

139. Young, "Germany's Memorial Question," 855–58.

140. Ibid., 858.

141. Ibid.

142. Mark Wigley, *Derrida's Haunt: The Architecture of Deconstruction* (Cambridge, MA: MIT Press, 1993), 73.

143. Ibid., 71.

144. Ibid., 107. Wigley asks us to think how "the politics of the institution involves placing into question the traditional sense of building, not to simply dismantle any building, but rather to identify the strange ruses by which it assumes authority and to thereby disturb traditional relationships to that authority." Yet he also acknowledges in keeping with a deconstructive standpoint that "the mechanisms of authority are not simply discredited or destroyed. On the contrary, they become more formidable" (49).

145. Daniel Libeskind, *End Space: An Exhibition at the Architectural Association* (London: Association, 1980), 12, 22, cited by Vesely, *Architecture*, 21.

146. Vesely, *Architecture*, 21.

147. Stanley Allen, "Libeskind's Practice of Laughter: An Introduction," *Assemblage* 12 (1990): 21.

148. In *End Space*, (1970–1980), Libeskind remarks, "An architectural drawing is as much a prospective unfolding of future possibilities as it is a recovery of a particular history to whose intentions it testifies and whose limits it always challenges." Cited by David Farrell Krell in " 'I Made It on the Verge': A Letter from David Farrell Krell," in Daniel Libeskind, "Between the Lines," *Assemblage* 12 (1990): 56.

149. Libeskind, "Between the Lines," *Assemblage* 12 (1990): 50.

150. Young, *At Memory's Edge*, 165, 163.

151. Isenberg, "Reading 'Between the Lines,' " 158.

152. Libeskind, "Between the Lines," 48.

153. Bernhard Schneider and Daniel Libeskind, *Daniel Libeskind: Jewish Museum Berlin; Between the Lines* (New York and Munich: Prestel, 1999), 36, 40.

154. Ibid., 58.

155. Libeskind, "Between the Lines," in *Space of Encounter*, 26–27. In his introduction to Libeskind's "Between the Lines" in *Assemblage* cited above, Stanley Allen notes an echo between Libeskind's description of "an architecture where the unnamed remains in the name that keeps still" and Moses's lines from Schönberg's unfinished opera: "Then I have fashioned an image, too, false as an image must be. / Thus I am defeated! Thus all was but madness that I believed before, / and can and must not be given voice." *Assemblage* 12 (1990): 48 and 24.

156. Libeskind, *Space of Encounter*, 27 and 26.

157. Libeskind, *Space of Encounter*, 26.

158. Writing in the early 1990s, Wigley could not yet have visited the Holocaust Tower, but he nevertheless offers a prescient theorization of its effect in his reading of Derrida's critique of Nicolas Abraham's and Maria Torok's psychoanalysis of the refusal to mourn, which hinges on their definition of the *crypt*: It is "constructed by the libidinal forces of the traumatic scene, which, as Derrida argues, 'through their contradiction, through their very opposition, support the internal resistance of the vault like pillars, beams, studs. And retaining walls, leaning the powers of intolerable pain against an ineffable, forbidden pleasure.' " Wigley, *Derrida's Haunt*, 144, citing Derrida, "Fors: The Anguish Words of Nicolas Abraham and Maria Torok," trans. Barbara Johnson, foreword to Nicolas Abraham and Maria Torok, *The Wolf Man's Magic Word*, trans. Nicholas Rand (Minneapolis: University of Minnesota Press, 1986), xxxviii. In *Derrida's Haunt*, Wigley elaborates on the systemic significance of architectural figures for Derrida's method. This emphasis inflects Wigley's paraphrasing of Abraham's and Torok's conception of the refusal to mourn as a fantasy of *incorporation*: "of taking into the body the lost object itself, literally consuming the object but doing so precisely to preserve it, to deny its loss" (143). Hence, "The forbidden object is thrown up into some folds in the body's limit, hidden in a space that is neither inside or outside" (144). The topology of this fantasy of incorporation preserves the traumatic memory "in the body's limit," which captures the effect of the Holocaust Tower. Like the crypt described by Abraham and Torok, it is folded into the building's outer line, yet because it is freestanding and unheated, it is, at the same time, external to the museum.

159. Isenberg, "Reading 'Between the Lines,' " 167.

160. Ibid., 168, citing Philip Noble, "The Mystic of Lindenstrasse," *Metropolis*, January 1999, 85.

161. Libeskind, *Space of Encounter*, 23.

162. Libeskind, "Between the Lines" (1990), 49.

163. Huyssen, "Voids of Berlin," 80.

164. Ibid., 59–60. Derrida echoes this sentiment in his "Response to Daniel Libeskind": "Why is Berlin exemplary? It is a city, has been a city, because of its split, which symbolizes all the division of the world, all the divided cities of the world—think of Jerusalem, for instance—and because the inner difference and the void precisely follow the line or the cut of this difference. Berlin could be considered a noncity city, a city whose identity or unity is split along an interrupted line" (91).

165. Huyssen, "Voids of Berlin," 62, 64.

166. Ibid., 6, 73.

167. Libeskind, "Between the Lines," *Assemblage* 12 (1990): 49.

168. Young, *At Memory's Edge*, 165, 163–64.

169. Ibid., 165.

170. Ibid.

171. Isenberg. "Reading 'Between the Lines,' " 174.

172. Ibid., 170, 173, citing Dan Diner, "Negative Symbiose: Deutsche und Juden nach Auschwitz," *Babylon* 1 (1986): 9–20. As Isenberg explains, Diner defines "negative symbiosis" as a German self-understanding that starts in the aftermath of the Holocaust.

173. Isenberg, "Reading 'Between the Lines,' " 173.

174. Wigley, *Derrida's Haunt*, 108. Wigley is citing Derrida's *Dissemination*, trans. Barbara Johnson (Chicago: University of Chicago Press, 1981), 220.

175. Derrida, *Dissemination*, 220 n. 32, citing Freud's "The Uncanny," trans. Alix Strachey in *Creativity and the Unconscious* (New York: Harper & Row, 1958), 152.

176. Derrida, *Dissemination*, 220 n. 32, citing Freud's "The Uncanny" (1958), 131.

177. Wigley, *Derrida's Haunt*, 117.

178. Ibid., 108–9, 114.

179. Ibid., 121.

180. Young, *At Memory's Edge*, 154, citing Freud, "The Uncanny," in Volume 17 of *The Standard Edition of the Complete Psychological Works of Sigmund Freud*, trans. James Strachey (London: Hogarth Press, 1955): 219–52, here 241.

181. Young, *At Memory's Edge*, 154, citing Anthony Vidler, *The Architectural Uncanny* (Cambridge, MA: MIT Press, 1996), 7.

182. Young, *At Memory's Edge*, 154, paraphrasing Robin Lydenberg, "Freud's Uncanny Narratives," *PMLA* 112 (October 1997): 1076.

183. Young, *At Memory's Edge*, 154–55. My emphasis.

184. Ibid., 178.

185. Ibid., 179.

186. Ibid.

187. Ibid., 180.

188. Ibid., 154, 155.

189. Wigley, *Derrida's Haunt*, 142, citing Freud, "The Uncanny," in SE (1955) 17: 235.

190. Wigley, *Derrida's Haunt*, 142.

191. Huyssen, "Voids of Berlin," 64.

192. Young, *At Memory's Edge*, 183, citing Theodor W. Adorno, *Aesthetic Theory*, trans. Paul C. Lenhardt (New York: Routledge and Kegan Paul, 1984), 262.

193. Young, *At Memory's Edge*, 183.

194. Schneider and Libeskind, *Daniel Libeskind*, 60.

195. Anthony Vidler, " 'Building Empty Space': Daniel Libeskind's Museum of the Voice," in Libeskind, *The Space of Encounter*, 222.

196. *Judenplatz Wien 1996: Wettbewerb Mahnmal und Gedenkstatte für die jüdischen Opfer des Naziregimes in Osterreich, 1938–1945* (Vienna: Folio, 1996), 109, cited by Young, "Germany's Memorial Question," 869.

197. Wolfgang Thierse, "Preface" to *Materials on the Memorial*, 6.

198. Juli Carson, "On Atrocity and Empathy: Reading Virilio through Eisenman," *ArtUS* 10 (October/November 2005): 49.

199. Schlör, *Memorial to the Murdered Jews of Berlin*, 45.

200. Carson, "On Atrocity and Empathy," 50.

201. Niklas Maak, "Im Stelengang: Peter Eisenman beim Baubeginn des Holocaust-Mahnmals," *Frankfurter Allgemeine Zeitung*, August 16, 2003, 31 cited by Knischewski and Spittler, "Remembering," 39.

202. Schlör, *Memorial to the Murdered Jews of Europe*, 45.

203. Peter Eisenman, "Memorial to the Murdered Jews of Europe," in *Materials on the Memorial* (Berlin: Nicolai, 2005), 11.

204. John Paul Richter, *Horn of Oberon: Jean Paul Richter's School for Aesthetics*, trans. M. R. Hale (Detroit: Wayne State University Press, 1973), 73, cited by Vesely, *Architecture*, 333.

205. Immanuel Kant, *Critique of Judgment*, trans. Werner S. Pluhar (Indianapolis: Hackett, 1987), 106. His emphasis.

206. Vesely, *Architecture*, 333.

207. Kant, *Critique of Judgment*, 101.

208. Eisenman, "Memorial," 10.

209. Ibid., 12.

210. Carson, "On Atrocity and Empathy," 50.

211. Grenzer, "Topographies of Memory," 107 citing Susan Stewart, *On Longing* (Durham, NC: Duke University Press, 1993), 31.

212. Schlusche, "Memorial Is Built," 28.

213. Nicolai Ouroussoff, "A Forest of Pillars, Recalling the Unimaginable," published by the *New York Times* (NYTimes.com May 9, 2005) (http://isurvived.org/InTheNews/Memorial2MurderedJews.html)

214. Young, "Germany's Holocaust Memorial Problem," 68.

215. My emphasis. See Rowan Moore, "The Arts: A Place to Remember the Life Before," *Daily Telegraph*, October 11, 1997, found at http://architectstore.com/news/jewish-museum-berlin.htm. This parallel is made explicitly by Peter Davey in "Field of Memory," *Architectural Review*, July 2005. http://www.findarticles.com/p/articles/mi_m3575/is_1301_218/ai_n14892897/pg_

216. Carson, "On Atrocity and Empathy," 49.

217. Peter Eisenman, www.CNN.com, August 2003.

218. Harjes, "Stumbling Stones," 142.

219. Rauterberg, *Holocaust Memorial Berlin*.

220. Peter Eisenman, "Liberal Views Have Never Built Anything of Any Value," interview by Robert Locke, July 27, 2004. http://archinect.com/features/article.php?id=4618_0_23_24_M.

221. Habermas, "Der Zeigefinger," p. 1 of 8; Young, "Germany's Holocaust Memorial Problem," 62.

222. Jörg Lau, "Nichts gegen Patriotismus: Erstaunlich unbefangen vertritt Charlotte Knoblauch die Juden. Sie will mehr als mahnen und warnen," *Die Zeit*, June 14, 2006, 5.

223. Harjes, "Stumbling Stones," 142.

224. Grenzer, "Topographies of Memory," 95, citing Cees Nooteboom, *All Souls Day*, trans. Susan Massotty (New York: Harcourt, 2001), 23–24.

225. I am thankful to my colleague John-Paul Himka for suggesting this translation.

226. Grenzer, "Topographies of Memory," 101.

227. Isenberg, "Reading 'Between the Lines,' " 172. On this phenomenon of Jewish-American importation, Isenberg cites Leibl Rosenberg's article, "Der Onkel

aus Amerika: Eine Polemik gegen die Einmischung von US-Organisationen in deutschjüdische Angelegenheiten," that appeared in the Berlin-based newspaper *Allgemeine Jüdische Wochenzeitung*, May 25, 2000.

228. Isenberg cites Thomas Lackmann's *Jewrassic Park* to the effect that the "entire Libeskind project thrived on a climate of philosemitism" ("Reading 'Between the Lines,'" 172). See Thomas Lackmann, *Jewrassic Park: Wie baut man (k)ein jüdisches Museum in Berlin?* (Berlin: Philo, 2000).

229. Isenberg, "Reading 'Between the Lines,'" 172, citing Julius Schoeps in Roger Cohen, "A Jewish Museum Struggles to Be Born," *New York Times*, August 15, 2000; Henryk M. Broder, "Nun weiter im Pogrom . . ." posted on www.henryk-broder.de; and Lackmann, *Jewrassic Park*.

230. Grenzer, "Topographies of Memory," 94–95. Grenzer's emphasis.

231. Ibid., 95.

232. Reinhart Koselleck, "War Memorials: Identity Formations of the Survivors," in *The Practice of Conceptual History: Timing History, Spacing Concepts*, trans. Todd Samuel Presner and Others (Stanford, CA: Stanford University Press, 2002), 288.

233. Traudl Junge, Hitler's personal secretary from 1942 to 1945, waited to express regret for her stubborn ignorance about the Nazi mass murders in confessional interviews taped shortly before her death in 2002. Her head-in-the-sand perspective informs Oliver Hirschbiegel's 2004 film *Downfall (Der Untergang)*, which dramatizes Junge's experience of the events in and around Hitler's bunker in the weeks leading up to the fall of Berlin and the dictator's suicide. The dialogue is largely devoid of references to his murderous policies (the Jews are mentioned only in the context of his paranoid rants). Despite, or, perhaps, because of the research that informed it, the film heroicizes Albert Speer as the genteel Nazi with integrity who takes the risk of speaking honestly with his friend, admitting that he disobeyed the dictator's orders, just before the latter's suicide. The nondiegetic music affectively supplements *Downfall*'s recreation of these tension-filled days to seduce the spectator into a tragic sense of pathos in the face of the "hubris" displayed by the Führer's inner circle in (necessarily? admirably?) standing by their man in keeping with their oath of loyalty despite his obvious madness. The German playwright Oliver Reese's *Emmy Göring an der Seite ihres Mannes* [*Emmy Göring Stands by Her Man*], winner of the 1996 Friedrich Luft Prize, provided Germans with a previous occasion to identify with the "pathos" of self-interested ignorance. Hirschbiegel focuses on Hitler, Goebbels, and the latter's cold-blooded wife who manages an uncanny composure as she poisons each of her children rather than let them continue to live on in a world without Hitler. The German film industry thereby holds true to its tradition of leaving the work of dramatizing Jewish suffering up to foreigners—for instance, Steven Spielberg with *Schindler's List* in 1993 and Roman Polanski with *The Pianist* in 2002.

234. Young, "Germany's Holocaust Memorial Problem," 64.

235. Robert Eaglestone, *The Holocaust and the Postmodern* (Oxford: Oxford University Press, 2004), 1.

236. Ibid., 2–3.

237. Ibid., 4.

238. Naomi Mandel, *Against the Unspeakable: Complicity, the Holocaust, and Slavery in America* (Charlottesville: University of Virginia Press, 2006), 5.

239. Ibid., 13.

240. Moishe Postone and Eric Santner, introduction to *Catastrophe and Meaning: The Holocaust and the Twentieth Century*, ed. Postone and Santner (Chicago: University of Chicago Press, 2003), 12.

241. Dan Diner, "The Destruction of Narrativity: The Holocaust in Historical Discourse," in *Catastrophe and Meaning*, ed. Moshe Postone and Eric Santner, 78.

242. Postone and Santner, introduction, 12.

243. In both Germany and France, as Omer Bartov observes, "what has been lacking is an understanding of how a nation turns against a part of its own population." It is "this hiatus in historical knowledge, this national amnesia camouflaged by euphemisms of distance and strangeness," Bartov contends, that "is also at the root of current German and French xenophobia and definitions of national identity." Omer Bartov, "Reception and Perception: Goldhagen's Holocaust and the World," in *The "Goldhagen Effect": History, Memory, Nazism—Facing the German Past*, ed. Geoff Eley (Ann Arbor: University of Michigan Press, 2000), 66.

Chapter Three

I am grateful to María Brewer for her guidance during the initial drafting of this chapter and to Michael O'Driscoll, who generously offered to read a more recent version. A version of section 4 and part of section 5 appeared as a chapter entitled "Expropriating Survivor Experience, or Auschwitz 'after' Lyotard" in *Witness & Memory: The Discourse of Trauma*, ed. Ana Douglass and Tom Vogler (New York and London: Routledge, 2003): 249–73. Tom Vogler also provided helpful comments.

1. See "The Problem of the Gas Chambers or the Rumor of Auschwitz," *Le Monde*, December 29, 1978. This article is included in Faurisson's *Mémoire en défense: Contre ceux qui m'accusent de falsifier l'histoire* (Paris: La Vielle Taupe, 1980), 73–75. On Faurisson and the French negationists, see Pierre Vidal-Naquet, *Assassins of Memory: Essays on the Denial of the Holocaust*, trans. Jeffrey Mehlman (New York: Columbia University Press, 1992).

2. Omer Bartov, "Reception and Perception: Goldhagen's Holocaust and the World," in *The "Goldhagen Effect": History, Memory, Nazism—Facing the German Past*, ed. Geoff Eley (Ann Arbor: University of Michigan Press, 2000), 60.

3. See Bartov's discussion of the French reception of Goldhagen (ibid., 56–67); in this connection, see also François Furet, *Le passé d'une illusion: essai sur l'idée communiste au XXè siècle* (Paris: Robert Laffont, 1995); Stéphane Courtois et al., eds., *Le Livre noir du communisme. Crimes, terreur, répression* (Paris: Robert Laffont, 1997); and Alain Brossat, *L'epreuve du désastre: Le XXe siècle et les camps* (Paris: Albin Michel, 1996).

4. Jacques Derrida, "Différance," in *Margins of Philosophy*, trans. Alan Bass (Chicago: University of Chicago Press, 1982), 9.

5. For a discussion of postmodernism as a response to the Holocaust in the work of Lévinas and Derrida, see Robert Eaglestone's *The Holocaust and the Postmodern* (Oxford: Oxford University Press, 2004).

6. Jean-François Lyotard, *La condition postmoderne: Rapport sur le savoir* (Paris: Les Éditions de Minuit, 1979); idem, *The Postmodern Condition: A Report on Knowledge*, trans. Geoff Bennington and Brian Massumi (Minneapolis: University of Minnesota Press, 1984).

7. In Lyotard's words, "There is nothing to prove that if a statement describing a real situation is true, it follows that a prescriptive statement based upon it (the effect of which will necessarily be a modification of that reality) will be just" (Lyotard, *Postmodern Condition*, 40).

8. Jean-François Lyotard, *The Differend: Phrases in Dispute*, trans. Georges van Den Abbeele (Minneapolis: University of Minnesota Press, 1988), xii. Originally published as *Le Différend* (Paris: Les Éditions de Minuit, 1983).

9. Theodor W. Adorno, *Negative Dialectics*, trans. E. B. Ashton (New York: Continuum, 1973); idem, *Negative Dialektik* (Frankfurt am Main: Suhrkamp, 1966); Jean-François Lyotard, "Discussions, or Phrasing 'after Auschwitz,'" in *The Lyotard Reader*, ed. Andrew Benjamin (Cambridge: Blackwell, 1989), 360–92.

10. Michael Rothberg, "After Adorno: Culture in the Wake of Catastrophe," in *Traumatic Realism: The Demands of Holocaust Representation* (Minneapolis: University of Minnesota Press, 2000), 29. For other valuable readings of the permutations of the lyric prohibition, see Klaus Hofmann, "Poetry After Auschwitz—Adorno's Dictum," *German Life and Letters* 58, no. 2 (April 2005): 182–94; Klaus Laermann, " 'Nach Auschwitz ein Gedicht zu schreiben ist barbarisch': Überlegungen zu einem Darstellungsverbot," and Detlev Claussen, "Nach Auschwitz: Über die Aktualität Adornos," in *Kunst und Literatur nach Auschwitz*, ed. Manuel Köppen (Berlin: Erich Schmidt Verlag, 1993), 11–15 and 16–22, respectively.

11. Adorno, *Negative Dialectics*, 362.

12. Rothberg, "After Adorno," 50. As Rothberg stresses, this Jewish-messianic (and also Benjaminian) dimension of Adorno's understanding of the negative suggests that his figuration of the nonidentical as a "resistance to universality" cannot be conflated with the poststructuralist celebration of difference.

13. Cited above. In keeping with Lyotard's punctuation in this essay, I will employ quotation marks to underscore the status of *Auschwitz* in his argument as a name, a citation, and a sign of history that negates speculative synthesis and narratives of progress.

14. Lyotard, *Differend*, xii.

15. Lyotard, *Postmodern Condition*, 10.

16. Ibid.

17. Anne Barron, "Lyotard and the Problem of Justice," in *Judging Lyotard*, ed. Andrew Benjamin (New York: Routledge, 1992), 32.

18. Georges van den Abbeele provides the following clarification in the Glossary of his English translation of *The Differend*: "Rather than defining a grammatical or semantic unit, a *phrase* designates a particular constellation of instances, which is as contextual as it is textual—if it is not indeed precisely what renders the 'opposition' between text and context impertinent" (Lyotard, *Differend*, 194).

19. Ibid., xii.

20. Lyotard writes that since phrasing entails an endless series, in order for a phrase to be the last one "another one is needed to declare it, and it is then not the last one" (Ibid., 11, section 17).

21. Adorno, *Negative Dialectics*, 361–65; *Negative Dialektik*, 354–58.

22. Ibid., 361; Adorno, *Negative Dialektik* 354. This quotation from *Negative Dialectics* applies to the postwar German rhetoric of *Vergangenheitsbewältigung* (mastery of the past) as a short-circuiting of critical reflection that supersedes a genuine confrontation with the Nazi crimes in the process of moving beyond them. See

Theodor W. Adorno, "The Meaning of Working Through the Past" and "Education after Auschwitz," in *Critical Models: Interventions and Catchwords*, trans. Henry W. Pickford (New York: Columbia University Press, 1998), 89–103 and 190–204, respectively.

23. Lyotard, "Discussions," 378.

24. Ibid., 367.

25. Ibid., 367 citing G. W. F. Hegel, "Verhältnis des Skeptizismus zur Philosophie," *Aufsätze aus dem Kritischen Journal der Philosophie, Werke II* (Frankfurt am Main: Suhrkamp, 1970), 229.

26. Ibid., citing Hegel, ibid.

27. Ibid., 367 citing Hegel, *Hegel's Logic: Being Part One of the ENCYCLO-PAEDIA OF THE PHILOSOPHICAL SCIENCES (1830)*, trans. William Wallace (Oxford: Clarendon Press, 1975), 111–12.

28. Ibid., citing Hegel, *Phänomenologie des Geistes, Werke III* (Frankfurt am Main: Suhrkamp, 1970), 74; *Phenomenology of Mind*, trans. J. B. Baillie (New York: Harper & Row, 1976), 137.

29. G. W. F. Hegel, *Science of Logic*, trans. A. V. Miller (Atlantic Highlands, NJ: Humanities Press International, 1989).

30. Ibid., 28.

31. Lyotard, "Discussions," 368–69.

32. Ibid., 360.

33. See the "Hegel Notice" (Lyotard, *Differend*, 91–97) in the context of the "Result" chapter (Lyotard, *Differend*, 86–106).

34. Lyotard, "Discussions," 364.

35. Geoffrey Bennington, "Lyotard and 'the Jews,' " in *Modernity, Culture and "the Jew,"* ed. Bryan Cheyette and Laura Marcus (Stanford, CA: Stanford University Press, 1998), 194.

36. Adorno, *Negative Dialectics*, xx.

37. Lyotard, "Discussions" 363, citing Adorno, *Negative Dialectics*, xx.

38. Lyotard, "Discussions," 363.

39. I am borrowing John Mowitt's language from *Text: The Genealogy of an Antidisciplinary Object* (Durham, NC: Duke University Press, 1992), where he provides a genealogy of the *text* as the object of critical reading practices influenced by the linguistic turn. Mowitt's use of the term *antidisciplinary* applies to the emergence of *text* as a means of referring to the formal object of reading practices whose travels beyond literature departments brought disciplinary boundaries into question and *interdisciplinary* became *intertextual* as these boundaries collapsed. The still recent institutionalization of cultural studies in the United States attests to the emergence of a hybridized literary, anthropological, and sociological approach to texts as "artifacts."

40. The reading practices I have in mind here are Derrida's performative disarticulation of the opposition between literature and philosophy, along with Roland Barthes' celebration of the text over and against the work and his critique of the poetic devices and aesthetic ideology shared by realist fiction and historical narrative.

41. Lyotard, "Discussions," 361. Lyotard is citing Derrida's "Signature Event Context," in *Margins of Philosophy*, trans. Alan Bass (Chicago: University of Chicago Press, 1982), 329.

42. Lyotard, "Discussions," 361.

43. "Discussions" enacts a series of *paralogisms* as contingent "moves" in the pragmatics of knowledge that expose the complicity of all thought, including Lyotard's own, with the speculative tendency to efface the particular. In *The Postmodern Condition*, Lyotard defines *paralogy* as "a move (the importance of which is often not recognized until later) in the pragmatics of knowledge." He favors paralogy over *innovation*, which falls under the system's command, or is "at least used by it to improve its efficiency," though one might be transformed into the other (*Postmodern Condition*, 61).

It is helpful to understand this distinction in relation to Michel de Certeau's discussion of *strategies* versus *tactics* in *The Practice of Everyday Life*, trans. Steven Rendall (Berkeley and Los Angeles: University of California Press, 1984). *Strategies*, according to de Certeau, privilege spatial relations: they "are actions which, thanks to the establishment of a place of power (the property of a proper), elaborate theoretical places (systems and totalizing discourses) capable of articulating an ensemble of physical places in which forces are distributed." In contrast, *tactics* are temporally determined: they are "procedures that gain validity in relation to the pertinence they lend to time—to the circumstances which the precise instant of an intervention transforms into a favorable situation, to the rapidity of the movements that change the organization of a space, the relations amongst successive moments in an action, to the possible intersections of durations and heterogeneous rhythms, etc." Ultimately, then, the difference between them "corresponds to two historical options regarding action and security (options that moreover have more to do with constraints than with possibilities): strategies pin their hopes on the resistance that the *establishment of a place* offers to the erosion of time; tactics on a clever *utilization of time*, of the opportunities that it presents and also of the play that it introduces into the foundations of power." In sum, while strategies are determined by discourse and uphold its structures, tactics *happen* in reaction to contingently emerging gaps in discourse and the system as such (de Certeau, *Practice of Everyday Life*, 38–39).

44. As Stuart Barnett has pointed out in his introduction to *Hegel after Derrida*, ed. Stuart Barnett (New York: Routledge, 1998), 1–37, Derrida's and Lyotard's engagements with Hegelian dialectics should be read against the background of the French reception of Hegel via the groundbreaking work of Jean Wahl and Alexandre Koyré and the critical interventions of Alexandre Kojève and Jean Hyppolite. In this context, the paramount influence of Kojève's lectures between 1933 and 1939 and his reading of Hegel's *Phenomenology of Spirit* is, in part, attributable to what Barnett calls his "detranscendentalization" of speculative idealism whereby the "discomforting notions of the Absolute and spirit were transformed into more concrete material notions" (Barnett, *Hegel after Derrida*, 19). For Kojève, Hegel's "evolution of spirit becomes the anthropogenetic self-articulation of discourse" while recasting the latter's "constitutive element," the sign, "in a decidedly modern light" (18). The Kojèvian Hegel thus offered academic philosophers a means to move beyond the impasse between "the thoroughly abstract subject of Cartesian rationalism" and "a theory of society and history in the grips of the determinism of orthodox Stalinist Marxism" (19). Kojève not only established the postwar aims for the reading of Hegel in France, but also constituted the parameters for the emergence of post-Hegelianism as a genre of discourse in its own right, as evinced in Lyotard's argument in "Discussions," which demonstrates the aptness of Barnett's claim that "postmodernism is the unconscious but logical culmination of speculative idealism" (5).

45. Lyotard, "Discussions," 363–64, quoting Jacques Derrida's "The Pit and the Pyramid: Introduction to Hegel's Semiology," in *Margins of Philosophy*, trans. Alan Bass (Chicago: University of Chicago Press, 1982), 107.

46. Lyotard, "Discussions," 362, citing Adorno, *Negative Dialectics*, 408.

47. Lyotard, "Discussions," 362.

48. Ibid., 364.

49. Ibid., 365, 364, citing Hegel's *Phenomenology of Mind*, 93.

50. See Derrida's "The Ends of Man," in *Margins of Philosophy*, trans. Alan Bass (Chicago: University of Chicago Press, 1982), 109–36.

51. Derrida introduces the problem of the "form of democracy" as an implicit issue for international philosophical colloquiums such as the one at which he presented "The Ends of Man." After proposing to place the "accent" on form "no less than on *democracy*," he remarks: "Such, in its most general and schematic principle, is the question which put itself to me during the preparations for this encounter, from the invitation and the deliberations that followed, up to acceptance, and then to the writing of this text, which I date quite precisely from the month of April 1968: it will be recalled that these were the weeks of the opening of the Vietnam peace talks and of the assassination of Martin Luther King. A bit later, when I was typing this text, the universities of Paris were invaded by the forces of order—and for the first time at the demand of a rector—and then reoccupied by the students in the upheaval you are familiar with. This historical and political horizon would call for a long analysis. I have simply found it necessary to mark, date, and make known to you the historical circumstances in which I prepared this communication. These circumstances appear to me to belong, by all rights, to the field and the problematic of our colloquium" (ibid., 114).

52. See Lyotard, "The Sign of History," in *The Lyotard Reader*, ed. Andrew Benjamin (Cambridge: Blackwell, 1989), 393–411 and his chapter of the same title in *Differend*, 151–81.

53. I am referring to the presentation or publication dates of the original French versions of these essays.

54. Derrida, "Ends of Man," 116. In this measure, Sartre's existentialism validates Heidegger's proposition that "every humanism remains metaphysical" inasmuch as it seeks to finalize the meaning of Being.

55. Ibid., 118.

56. Ibid.

57. Ibid., 119.

58. See Theodor W. Adorno, *The Jargon of Authenticity* (Evanston, IL: Northwestern University Press, 1973).

59. In Heidegger's view, what is particular to humans in contrast to animals is the way in which death as destiny is at once ontically near, but ontologically far. The paradoxical essence of human mortality is that it remains simultaneously "out there," but never not near. For Heidegger, then, the anticipation of death recalls *Dasein* from out of its distance (*da*) to reflect on existence (*sein*).

60. Hegel's writings on death are explicitly shaped by his reading of Greek tragedy (and Sophocles' *Antigone*, in particular). In *Antigone*, the protagonist must choose to suture the split between the sociopolitical and moral realms by disobeying the king in order to bury her brother, fulfill her obligations to honor her family, and

thereby satisfy divine law. Her act of rebellion is, thus, also an act of devotion that overcomes a dangerous rift between the human and the divine.

61. Aristotle writes in the *Poetics*: "Tragedy is, then, an imitation of a noble and complete action, having the proper magnitude; it employs language that has been artistically enhanced by each of the kinds of linguistic adornment, applied separately in the various parts of the play; it is presented in dramatic, not narrative form, and achieves, through the representation of pitiable and fearful incidents, the catharsis of such pitiable and fearful incidents." *Aristotle's Poetics*, trans. Leon Golden (Tallahassee: University Press of Florida, 1981), 11.

62. In concentrating on the English translation of *relever*, my gloss of its various meanings does not do justice to Derrida's elegant and complex elaboration on this verb as a translation of Hegel's *aufheben*. See Derrida, "The Pit and the Pyramid: Introduction to Hegel's Semiology," in *Margins of Philosophy*, trans. Alan Bass (Chicago: The University of Chicago Press, 1982), 68–108 and particularly the last section, entitled "*Relever*—What Talking Means," 88–108, as well as Alan Bass's note for the English edition at 88.

63. Derrida, "Ends of Man," 121 (Derrida's emphasis).

64. Ibid., 121, 123.

65. Lyotard, "Discussions," 375.

66. In Lyotard's words, "If 'Auschwitz' speaks, it is in order to say not the unintelligible but the intelligible, and it becomes necessary to speculate. If it does not speak, if death is senseless (*insensée*) there, it is because one does not speculate" (ibid., 378). Eighteen years later (in 1998), Agamben locates the authority of the witness "*in his capacity to speak solely in the name of an incapacity to speak—that is, in his or her being a subject.*" *Remnants of Auschwitz: The Witness and the Archive*, trans. Daniel Heller-Roazen (Cambridge, MA: Zone Books, 1999), 158, his emphasis.

67. See Lyotard's essays, "Philosophy and Painting in the Age of Their Experimentation: Contribution to an Idea of Postmodernity" and "The Sublime and the Avant-Garde" in *The Lyotard Reader*, trans. Andrew Benjamin (Cambridge: Blackwell, 1989), 181–95 and 196–211, respectively.

68. Max Horkheimer and Theodor W. Adorno, *Dialectic of Enlightenment: Philosophical Fragments*, ed. Gunzelin Schmid Noerr, trans. Edmund Jephcott (Stanford, CA: Stanford University Press, 2002).

69. Lyotard, "Discussions," 365.

70. Ibid., 370.

71. See Jürgen Habermas, *Philosophical Discourse of Modernity: Twelve Lectures*, trans. Frederick Lawrence (Cambridge, MA: MIT Press, 1987).

72. Lyotard, "Discussions," 370.

73. Ibid., 374.

74. Ibid.

75. Ibid.

76. Ibid., 362–63.

77. Here we have an anticipation of what Agamben has referred to as life that can be killed, but not sacrificed. See *Homo Sacer: Sovereign Power and Bare Life* (Stanford, CA: Stanford University Press, 1998); and idem, *Remnants of Auschwitz*.

78. Lyotard, "Discussions," 375.

79. Ibid., citing Hegel's *Encyclopaedia*.

80. Lyotard, "Discussions," 375.

81. On the fate of the stateless and refugees, Arendt cites John Hope Simpson: "The many and varied efforts of the legal profession to simplify the problem by stating a difference between the stateless person and the refugee—such as maintaining 'that the status of a stateless person is characterized by the fact of his having no nationality, whereas that of a refugee is determined by his having lost diplomatic protection'—were always defeated by the fact that 'all refugees are for practical purposes stateless.'" See Hannah Arendt, *The Origins of Totalitarianism* (San Diego: Harcourt, 1976), 281 n. 28 and John Hope Simpson, *The Refugee Problem* (Oxford: Institute for International Affairs, 1939), 232, 4.

82. Arendt, *Origins of Totalitarianism*, 457.

83. Ibid., 464.

84. See Agamben, *State of Exception*, trans. Kevin Attell (Chicago: University of Chicago Press, 2003).

85. Agamben, *Remnants of Auschwitz*, 156. The term *Muselmann* [Muslim] apparently originated among inmates who perceived a similarity between the prone state of lethargic near-death prisoners and the image of a Muslim prostrating himself on the ground in prayer. I am, admittedly, nervous about Agamben's adaptation of the term *Muselmann* as the limit case of human suffering and the exemplar of bare life because he has not historicized its ideological valences. J. M. Bernstein excoriates Agamben for his synecdochic concentration on the *Muselmann* as the supreme instance of a "body without dignity." According to Bernstein, Agamben idealizes, specularizes, and thus objectifies this figure in a manner that renders his gaze grotesque if not pornographic. See J. M. Bernstein, "Bare Life, Bearing Witness: Auschwitz and the Pornography of Horror," *Parallax* 10, no. 1 (2004): 2–16.

86. Agamben, *Remnants of Auschwitz*, 82.

87. Ibid., 83.

88. See Arendt, *Origins of Totalitarianism*, 279–80; and Giorgio Agamben, "Biopolitics and the Rights of Man" and "The Camp as the Nomos of the Modern" in *Homo Sacer*, 126–43 and 166–80, respectively.

89. Agamben, *Remnants of Auschwitz*, 69 citing Robert Antelme, *The Human Race*, trans. Jeffrey Haight and Annie Mahler (Marlboro, VT: Marlboro Press, 1992), 5–6.

90. Ewa Ziarek's reconsideration of the value of Lyotard's thought for a politics of difference that does not, by definition, transcend conflict or embodiment offers an adept characterization of the stakes of this connection between a biopolitical administration of life and death and citizenship. Ziarek notes that what his essay, "One Thing at Stake in Women's Struggle," "adds to the critique of the normative discourse in *The Differend* is an important insight that the transformation of the particular strategies of winning into norms transcending political conflict occurs at the price of effacing embodiment as the site of historical struggles." The consequence is, as Ziarek contends, that "the 'normative we' is a 'disembodied we,' and those who occupy that position and thus claim its performative power know how, in good Hegelian fashion, to make use of death, how to risk life in order to gain mastery, the ultimate expression of which is the capacity of thinking death itself." Ewa Ziarek, "Toward a Feminist Ethics of Dissensus: Polemos, Embodiment, Obligation," in *Minima*

Moralia: In the Wake of Jean-François Lyotard, ed. Claire Nouvet, Zrinka Stahuljak, and Kent Still (Stanford, CA: Stanford University Press, 2007), 82–83.

91. Lyotard, "Discussions," 377.

92. Rothberg cites Blanchot's vigilance against dramatizations of the Holocaust as a rewriting of Adorno. Blanchot writes,"[T]here can be no fiction-narrative [*récit-fiction*] about Auschwitz." Blanchot, *Vicious Circles*, trans. Paul Auster (Barrytown, NY: Station Hill Press, 1985), 68–69; Rothberg, "After Adorno," 80.

93. Naomi Mandel, *Against the Unspeakable: Complicity, the Holocaust, and Slavery in America* (Charlottesville: University of Virginia Press, 2006), 17.

94. I am referring to Derrida's remarks, transcribed by Lyotard, from a discussion that followed his delivery of this paper in 1980 at Cerisy-la-Salle in the context of the colloquium "Les fins de l'homme: À partir du travail de Jacques Derrida." Derrida's comments as well as a paraphrase of his exchange with Lyotard follow the translation of "Discussions" in *The Lyotard Reader*, 386–89. Derrida obliquely cites these remarks in "Lyotard and Us, " trans. Boris Belay in *Minima Moralia: In the Wake of Jean-François Lyotard*, ed. Claire Nouvet, Zrinka Stahuljak, and Kent Still (Stanford, CA: Stanford University Press, 2007), 1–26 and in *The Work of Mourning*, ed. Pascale-Anne Brault (Chicago: University of Chicago Press, 2001).

95. Lyotard, "Discussions," 386

96. Ibid., 387.

97. Lyotard cites Adorno to this effect: "According to its own concept, metaphysics cannot be a deductive context of judgments about things in being, and neither can it be conceived after the model of an absolute otherness terribly defying thought. It would be possible only as a legible constellation of things in being" (Adorno, *Negative Dialectics*, 407, cited by Lyotard, "Discussions," 362).

98. On the figurative importance of the image prohibition (the Second Commandment) in Adorno's aesthetic, see Gertrud Koch, *Die Einstellung ist die Einstellung: Visuelle Konstruktionen des Judentums* (Frankfurt am Main: Suhrkamp, 1992).

99. Immanuel Kant, "Analytic of the Sublime," *Critique of Judgment*, trans. Werner S. Pluhar (Indianapolis: Hackett, 1987), 97–140.

100. It is significant that Lyotard denounces the indignation that he anticipates arising in response to his designation of "Auschwitz" as an anonym that refers to "an experience of language." His defense is that such indignation, "with its claim to realism," insults the name of "Auschwitz" by not doubting "that there is a result (namely itself)" ("Discussions," 364). This is a particularly problematic criticism for Lyotard because, in *The Differend*, he himself affirms the need to bear witness to the "feeling" that the silences attending names such as *Auschwitz* evoke. What is indignation if it is not a "feeling" that the moral stature of the event has not been properly respected?

101. Lyotard, *Differend*, 22 (section 3).

102. Apart from the analytic lineage, Louis Hjelmslev, Roman Jakobson, and Charles Sanders Peirce also inflect Lyotard's critique of reference and designation. Saul Kripke's *Naming and Necessity* (Cambridge, MA: Harvard University Press, 1972) is the transcription of a series of three lectures delivered at Princeton in January 1970. Kripke's principal argument is that "we have a direct intuition of the rigidity of names, exhibited in our understanding of the truth conditions of particular sentences" (14).

In his preface, he lists three theses that ground the premise that names function as rigid designators: "identical objects are necessarily identical"; "true identity statements between rigid designators are necessary"; and "identity statements between what we call 'names' in actual language are necessary" (4). Notably, this is a premise in which Kripke is not himself invested insofar as he claims not to be logically committed to any thesis about names. I cite these theses because they offer a useful shorthand for the philosophical assumptions underpinning the "necessity" of stable designation as a condition of truth; they are helpful to keep in mind while considering Lyotard's disarticulation of the concept of an invariable referent.

103. Kripke, *Naming and Necessity*, 41.

104. Ibid., 49.

105. Lyotard, *Differend*, 12 (section 20).

106. Ibid., 37 (*Antisthenes*).

107. Ibid., 32 (section 47).

108. Pierre Vidal-Naquet, *Assassins of Memory*. Lyotard draws on Vidal-Naquet's arguments throughout *The Differend*.

109. Lyotard, *Differend*, 32 (section 48).

110. Ibid., 32 (section 48).

111. Ibid., 33 (section 50).

112. Ibid., 39 (section 58).

113. Ibid., 41 (section 62) and 43 (section 66).

114. Ibid., 49 (section 80).

115. Ibid., 35 (section 54).

116. Ibid., 44 (section 68).

117. Ibid., 45 (section 69).

118. Ibid., 50 (section 81).

119. Ibid., 51 (sections 84–85).

120. Ibid., 50 (section 81).

121. Ibid., 51 (section 83) and 54–55 (section 90).

122. Ibid., 51 (section 83).

123. Ibid., 55 (section 91).

124. Ibid., 46 (section 71).

125. Ibid., 45–46 (section 71).

126. See Derrida, "Ends of Man," (previously cited).

127. Lyotard, *Differend*, 45–46 (section 71).

128. Ibid., 45 (section 71)

129. Ibid., 46 (section 72). In Hegel's terms, the apparent continuity of the "I" assimilates its various instances into what he calls a "mediated simplicity or universality." See Hegel's *The Phenomenology of Spirit*, trans. A. V. Miller (New York: Oxford University Press, 1977), 58–66. See also Paul Eisenstein's rereading of Hegel's understanding of universality in order to foreground the negativity at the heart of witnessing in *Traumatic Encounters: Holocaust Representation and the Hegelian Subject* (Albany: State University of New York Press, 2003). Against poststructuralist dismissals of Hegel's logic, Eisenstein reminds us that the chapter "Sense-Certainty: or the 'This' and 'Meaning' (*Meinen*)" in the *Phenomenology* acknowledges flux and its mediation through deictic markers ("this," "that," "here," "there," "now," "then"). The empty universality of deictic markers implicates the "I" as such in the process

of marking time as a measure of the effect of shifting contents at particular moments upon perception, knowing, and self. In foregrounding the role of language in this chapter of the *Phenomenology*, Eisenstein indirectly illuminates the dialectic's pivotal significance for Derrida's theorization of *différance* via Saussure to emphasize the spatiotemporal flexibility of signs whose value is differentiated and deferred by changing contexts of reference. It becomes clear that any absolute opposition between a Hegelian dialectic and deconstruction is itself a reductive mediation that forgets the interdependency among identity and difference, and determinacy and indeterminacy as concepts that rely on the notion of their opposites for definition. Eisenstein's reading of Hegel thus arrives at many of the conclusions that propel Lyotard's politicized aesthetics of witnessing.

130. Lyotard, *Differend*, 46 (section 72).

131. Ibid., 46 (section 73).

132. Ibid., 46 (section 73). My emphasis.

133. Ibid.

134. Ibid., 54 (section 90) and 55 (section 91).

135. Ibid., 9 (section 12).

136. Ibid., 10 (section 13).

137. Mandel, *Against the Unspeakable*, 11.

138. Lyotard, *Differend*, 14 (section 26).

139. Carolyn J. Dean, *The Fragility of Empathy after the Holocaust* (Ithaca, NY: Cornell University Press, 2004).

140. Lyotard, *Differend*, 13 (section 22).

141. Ibid., 57 (section 93).

142. Ibid., 13 (section 22).

143. Ibid., 13 (section 22) and 57 (section 93).

144. Ron Katwan, "The Affect in the Work of Jean-François Lyotard," *Surfaces* 3, no. 13 (1993): 4, cited by Claire Nouvet, "The Inarticulate Affect: Lyotard and Psychoanalytic Testimony," in *Minima Moralia: In the Wake of Jean-François Lyotard*, ed. Claire Nouvet, Zrinka Stahuljak, and Kent Still (Stanford, CA: Stanford University Press, 2007), 109.

145. Ziarek, "Toward a Feminist Ethics," 76 and Lyotard, *Differend*, 13 (sections 22 and 23). See also Lyotard, *Le differend*, 30 (section 23).

146. Lyotard, *Differend*, 57 (section 93).

147. Ibid.

148. Ibid.

149. Lyotard gestures toward this problem while ultimately deflecting it at ibid., 18 (section 32).

150. Ibid., 57 (section 93).

151. Ibid.

152. Ibid.

153. Ibid.

154. Ibid., 11 (section 16).

155. Ziarek, "Toward a Feminist Ethics," 80.

156. Lyotard, *Differend*, 22 (*Plato Notice*), citing Plato, *Letters* 7.342a–d.

157. Lyotard, *Differend* 22 (*Plato Notice*), citing *Phaedrus* 261 ff and Plato's *Republic* II, 377e–379a.

158. Lyotard, *Differend*, 14 (section 26).

159. Jacques Derrida, "Poetics and Politics of Witnessing," in *Sovereignties in Question*, ed. Thomas Dutoit and Outi Pasanen (New York: Fordham University Press, 2005), 74.

160. Richard Beardsworth, "Lyotard's Agitated Judgment," in *Judging Lyotard*, ed. Andrew Benjamin (London: Routledge, 1992), 43–80.

161. Lyotard, *Differend*, 109 (section 168).

162. Ibid., 56 (section 93).

163. Lyotard's states that the "addressor must be understood as a situated instance in a phrase universe, on a par with the referent, the addressee, and the sense. 'We' do not employ language" (ibid., 55, section 91).

164. In Lyotard's words, "it seems neither possible, nor even prudent, to follow Habermas in orienting our treatment of the problem of legitimation in the direction of a search for universal consensus" (*Postmodern Condition*, 65).

165. Ibid.

166. Ziarek, "Toward a Feminist Ethics," 74.

167. Jean-François Lyotard, "Answering the Question: What Is Postmodernism?" trans. Régis Durand in *Postmodern Condition*, 82.

168. Mandel, *Against the Unspeakable*, 25.

169. Ibid., 30–31.

170. Ibid., 52.

171. Dean, *Fragility of Empathy*, 5.

172. Ibid., 44.

173. Ibid., 5.

174. See Derrida's "History of the Lie," in *Without Alibi*, trans. and ed. Peggy Kamuf (Stanford, CA: Stanford University Press, 2002). For a more thorough reading of Derrida that counters my claim above, see James Berger's chapter, "The Absent Referent: Derrida and the Holocaust," in *After the End: Representations of Post-Apocalypse* (Minneapolis: University of Minnesota Press, 1999), 106–30. Berger staunchly criticizes Derrida's "poeticization" of the Holocaust in light of his "compromising" debts to Martin Heidegger and Paul de Man.

175. Derrida, "Poetics and Politics of Witnessing," 77.

176. Ibid., 88.

177. Ibid., 83.

178. Derrida, "The Truth that Wounds (From an Interview)," in *Sovereignties in Question*, ed. Thomas Dutoit and Outi Pasanan (New York: Fordham University Press, 2005), 165.

179. Ziarek, "Toward a Feminist Ethics," 77.

180. Ibid., 78.

181. Eaglestone, *Holocaust and the Postmodern*, 66.

182. In Cordelia Edvardson's *Burned Child Seeks the Fire: A Memoir*, trans. Joel Agee (Boston: Beacon Press, 1997), the narrator describes her recalcitrance in the face of a foster family whose happiness on Christmas Eve cannot diminish the recent traumatic experience of surviving Auschwitz.

183. Lawrence W. Langer, *Holocaust Testimonies: The Ruins of Memory* (New Haven, CT: Yale Univesity Press, 1991).

184. Rothberg, *Traumatic Realism*, 124.

185. Ibid., 121, 122.

186. Ibid., 124. Rothberg includes Tzvetan Todorov in this judgment. See Todorov, *Facing the Extreme: Moral Life in the Concentration Camps* (New York: Henry Holt, 1996).

187. Lawrence Langer, *Versions of Survival: The Holocaust and the Human Spirit* (Albany: State University of New York Press, 1982).

188. Gary Weissman, *Fantasies of Witnessing: Postwar Efforts to Experience the Holocaust* (Ithaca, NY: Cornell University Press, 2004), 118, citing Ruth K[lüger] Angress, "Discussing Holocaust Literature," *Simon Wiesenthal Annual* 2 (1985): 187.

189. Jean-François Lyotard, "The Survivor," trans. Robert Harvey and Mark S. Roberts, in *Toward the Postmodern* (Atlantic Highlands, NJ: Humanities Press, 1993), 144–63.

190. Ibid., 144.

191. Ibid., 145.

192. Ibid., 147.

193. Derrida, "Truth that Wounds," 169.

194. Paul Ricoeur has suggested that Aristotle's criteria of unity and wholeness might figure for a transcendental "need" for narrative. Hence, narratives both reflect and foment a desire for unity and wholeness in staging their possibility. See Ricoeur's *Time and Narrative*, trans. Kathleen Mclaughlin and David Pellauer, vols. 1 and 2 (Chicago: University of Chicago Press, 1984; and idem, *Time and Narrative*, trans. Kathleen Blamey and David Pellauer, vol. 3 (Chicago: University of Chicago Press, 1988).

Chapter Four

1. Ruth Klüger, *Landscapes of Memory: A Holocaust Girlhood Remembered* (London: Bloomsbury, 2003), 68–69. See also idem, *weiter leben: eine Jugend* (Munich: Deutsche Taschenbuch Verlag, 1995), 70.

2. In Klüger's German: "Wir erwarten, daß Ungelöstes gelöst wird, wenn man nur beharrlich festhält an dem, was übrig blieb, dem Ort, den Steinen, der Asche . . ." (*Weiterleben*, 70). The elaboration, "Nicht die *Toten* ehren wir mit diesen unschönen, unscheinbaren Resten vergangener Verbrechen, wir sammeln und bewahren sie, weil *wir* sie irgendwie brauchen" (70) is translated as "We don't honor the dead with these unattractive remnants of past crimes; we collect and keep them for the satisfaction of our own necrophilic desires" (*Landscapes of Memory*, 68).

3. Dominick LaCapra, *Writing History, Writing Trauma* (Baltimore: Johns Hopkins University Press, 2001), 22.

4. See Michael Rothberg, "The Barbed Wire of the Postwar World: Ruth Klüger's Traumatic Realism," in *Traumatic Realism: The Demands of Holocaust Representation* (Minneapolis: University of Minnesota Press, 2000), 107–40. As Rothberg has insightfully suggested, Klüger's account provides a concrete instance of how survivors of trauma "grapple continuously with the interplay of the extreme and the everyday" (131). Rothberg employs Klüger's memoir as an example of "a new mode of representation and historical cognition" that he calls the genre of "traumatic realism" (109). This

genre is a means of moving beyond an opposition in Holocaust studies between the realist emphasis on factuality and the antirealist preoccupation with the unrepresentable extremity of the Holocaust. Rothberg proposes that reading realism "under the sign of trauma" (108) will redress the site of violence as a complex borderland between extremity and everydayness. This framework constitutes the traumatic event as "an object of knowledge," which will "program and transform its readers so that they are forced to acknowledge their relationship to posttraumatic culture" (109).

5. See Mark Seltzer, *Serial Killers: Death and Life in America's Wound Culture* (New York: Routledge, 1998).

6. Freud, "Lecture XXV: Anxiety," and "Lecture XXVI: The Libido Theory and Narcissism," in Volume 16 of *The Standard Edition of the Complete Psychological Works of Sigmund Freud*, trans. and ed. James Strachey in collaboration with Anna Freud (London: Vintage, 2001): 392–411 and 412–30, respectively, and here 16: 411, 430. See also "Vorlesung XXV: Angst" and "Vorlesung XXVI: Die Libidotheorie und der Narzissmus," respectively in *Gesammelte Werke* (Frankfurt: Fischer Taschenbuch Verlag, 1999): *Band XI*: 407–26 and 427–46 (Hereafter citations of Freud's works will refer to volumes in the English edition as "SE" and in the German edition as "GW"). There are some inconsistencies that Freud is still attempting to work out between these two lectures. My paraphrasing overrides the confusion that arises as Freud continues to distinguish between "*Ichtrieben*" (ego-drives) and "*Ichlibido*" (ego-libido). Ultimately, Freud cannot sustain a distinction between the *Triebe* [drives] and libido. As I will argue below with recourse to Jean Laplanche, *libido* is the source and motility of the drives as metapsychologically deformed instincts.

7. Freud, "Die Libidotheorie und der Narzissmus," GW XI: 446.

8. On this point, see Max Horkheimer and Theodor W. Adorno in *Dialectic of Enlightenment: Philosophical Fragments*, ed. Gunzelin Schmid Noer, trans. Edmund Jephcott (Stanford, CA: Stanford University Press, 2002), where they trace a dialectic between the production of a reified subjectivity and the subject's mimetic relation to norms that enjoin him or her to repress his or her instincts. For my analysis of this dialectic, see Karyn Ball, "Paranoia in the Age of the World Picture: The Global 'Limits of Enlightenment,'" *Cultural Critique* 61 (2006): 115–47.

9. See Dominick LaCapra, *Representing the Holocaust: History, Theory, Trauma* (Ithaca, NY: Cornell University Press, 1994). See also LaCapra's *History and Memory after Auschwitz* (Ithaca, NY: Cornell University Press, 1998); idem, *Writing History, Writing Trauma*; and idem, *History in Transit: Experience, Identity, Critical Theory* (Ithaca, NY: Cornell University Press, 2004), which revisit many themes broached in the 1994 book.

10. Freud, "Lecture XXVII: Transference," SE 16: 442.

11. Ibid., 444. Even though transference may "constitute the greatest threat to the treatment," in its absence, Freud insists, "the patient would never even give a hearing to the doctor and his arguments" (444, 445).

12. In Jean Laplanche's and J. B. Pontalis' reading of Freud, overwhelming, ambivalent, or frustrating experiences from early childhood are generally considered to be the animating content of this susceptibility that may lead to libidinal fixation. See the entries on "Fixation" (162–65) and "Neurosis" (266–69) in Jean Laplanche and J. B. Pontalis, *The Language of Psycho-Analysis*, trans. Donald Nicholson-Smith (New York: W. W. Norton & Company, 1973).

13. Paul Eisenstein draws similar conclusions about structural trauma in *Traumatic Encounters: Holocaust Representation and the Hegelian Subject* (Albany: State University of New York Press, 2003). In his view, our aim should be to bear witness to what LaCapra has called "structural trauma" to characterize ontological lack and unconscious aggression in contrast to historical traumas. Eisenstein writes: "if our memorial efforts are informed by the fundamental poststructuralist insight regarding the inability to know or master history objectively, then we become *responsible* for the very substance of history in a radically new way, since history is constantly being fashioned and refashioned, made and remade" (4). Eisenstein identifies the unsymbolizeable negativity of the real as the "substance of history"—its essential condition and not merely its effect. Reciprocally, to bear witness to the Holocaust entails a metahistorical encounter with history in its traumatic particularity.

14. LaCapra, *Writing History, Writing Trauma*, 48.

15. A reading of the 1986 Historians' Debate in the former West Germany confirms LaCapra's argument that a historian's positive, negative, or ambivalent transferential relation with the object of study informs his or her interpretation of it as well as his or her reading of work by other scholars in the field. Hence a war-generation German scholar such as Ernst Nolte might act out his desire to disavow the affective legacy of the Holocaust by calling for a revision that diminishes its historical and national significance. Conversely, a historian's desire to protect the Holocaust may lead to its sacralization.

16. This argument articulates my main disagreement with LaCapra's work on the Holocaust. His distinction between empirical and structural trauma bypasses its irrational and imaginary dimensions that do not adhere to the strictures of moral reason nor to the rigor of critical logic. My revision of LaCapra's otherwise compelling analysis is to affirm more insistently the imbrication between structural and empirical trauma and to specify the implications of their mutual determination.

17. For a critical account of the history of this thesis in Freud's theory, see Jeffrey Moussaieff Masson, *The Assault on Truth: Freud's Suppression of the Seduction Theory* (New York: Pocket Books, 1984). See also *The Complete Letters of Sigmund Freud to Wilhelm Fliess, 1887–1904*, trans. and ed. Jeffrey Moussaieff Masson (Cambridge, MA: Harvard University Press, 1985), 264–66.

18. As Freud reiterates in "Lecture XXVI: The Libido Theory and Narcissism": "It is obvious, too, that we shall profit very little if, following Jung's example, we insist on the original unity of all the [drives] [*Triebe*] and give them the name of 'libido' as the energy invested in all of them" (SE 16: 413). See also "Die Libidotheorie und der Narzissmus," GW XI: 428. In "The Libido Theory" essay of 1923, he once again finds fault with Jung's theory of "a single primal libido" (SE 18: 255–56), but then goes on rather reluctantly to acknowledge the pertinence of "Jung's speculation about a primal libido, especially because the transformation of object-libido into narcissism necessarily carried along with it a certain degree of desexualization, or abandonment of the specifically sexual aims. Nevertheless," he cautions, "it has to be borne in mind that the fact that the self-preservative [drives] of the ego [*die Selbsterhaltungstriebe des Ichs*] are recognized as libidinal does not necessarily prove that there are no other [drives] operating in the ego" (SE 18: 256–57). See also " 'Psychoanalyse' und 'Libidotheorie,' " GW XIII: 232.

19. Jean Laplanche, *Life and Death in Psychoanalysis*, trans. Jeffrey Mehlman (Baltimore: Johns Hopkins University Press, 1970), 13.

20. Freud provides a brief historical clarification of his revised understanding of the drives in a footnote appearing at the end of the sixth chapter of *Beyond the Pleasure Principle*. There he restates his finding that the narcissistic ego drives, which he had earlier opposed to reproductive or object drives (*Triebe*), are also sexual at their source. This insight led him to posit a "fresh" opposition between the ego- and object drives and the "destructive" drives, an opposition that he translates into an antagonism between life drives (*Eros*) and death drives (*Thanatos*). Freud, *Beyond the Pleasure Principle*, SE 18: 7–64, here 60–61; idem, *Jenseits des Lustprinzips*, GW XIII: 1–69, here 66. Alongside Freud's writings, my analysis is indebted to Jean Laplanche's *Life and Death in Psychoanalysis* (cited above) and idem, *New Foundations for Psychoanalysis*, trans. David Macey (Oxford: Basil Blackwell, 1989).

21. Laplanche, *Life and Death in Psychoanalysis*, 21.

22. Ibid., 22.

23. Laplanche writes that insofar as instincts are biological, the source lies " 'outside the scope of psychology.' " Laplanche, *Life and Death in Psychoanalysis*, 13, citing Freud, "[Drives] and Their Vicissitudes," SE 14: 110–40, here 123.

24. Freud, *Beyond the Pleasure Principle*, SE 18: 36. In the German, Freud writes: "*Ein Trieb wäre also ein dem belebten Organischen innewohnender Drang zur Wiederherstellung eines früheren Zustandes*, welchen dies Belebte unter dem Einflusse äußerer Störungskräfte aufgeben mußte, eine Art von organischer Elastizität, oder wenn man will, die Äußerung der Trägheit im organischen Leben" (*Jenseits des Lustprinzips*, GW XIII: 38. Freud's emphasis).

25. Laplanche, *Life and Death in Psychoanalysis*, 22.

26. Ibid., 18–20. Laplanche is attempting to redeem Freud's thought from the "errors" committed by theorists (such as Michael Balint) who assert that sexuality has an object from the beginning. By emphasizing the abstract character of sexuality in Freud's writings, Laplanche effectively repudiates the idea that a fixation on certain objects is a "refinding" of a lost object (e.g., the lost breast of the mother); instead, he underscores the object's partiality as a metonym or metaphorical condensation of diffuse sexual tensions in search of an object.

27. Ibid., 21.

28. Sigmund Freud, "The Libido Theory," SE 18: 255.

29. Ibid.

30. John Fletcher, "Recent Developments in the General Theory of Primal Seduction," *new formations* 48 (2002–3): 12. Fletcher also points out that this shift "is not just a case of one less adequate theory being replaced by a later more ad-equate one, but that 'it corresponds to something in the reality of the human being: the movement from one to the other corresponds to the birth of something, the transition between two states or positions perhaps equivalent to what is sometimes called the passage from nature to culture.' " As Fletcher paraphrases Laplanche, the "colonisation of the self-preservative functions and the ego by Eros takes place not just at the level of theory but in the ontogenetic development of the human being." Fletcher, "Recent Developments," 13, citing Jean Laplanche, "Sublimation and/or Inspiration," trans. Luke Thurston and John Fletcher, in "Jean Laplanche and the Theory of Seduction," special issue of *new formations* 48 (Winter 2002–3): 34.

31. Laplanche, "Sublimation and/or Inspiration," 33. This essay was originally published as "Sublimation et/ou inspiration," in Jean Laplanche, *Entre séduction et inspiration: L'homme* (Paris: Quadrige / Presses Universitaries de France, 1999).

32. Laplanche, "Sublimation and/or Inspiration," 36.

33. Ibid.

34. Ibid. This point resonates with Derrida's deconstruction of Freudian desire as Cynthia Willett has articulated it: "Desire is not originally whole and only subsequently is divided by all that has come to be called death. Desire is originally partial, catachrestic, and constituted in the play that marks desire by alien cravings and accidental effects. If desire is partial, however, it cannot be neutralized by the forces of death." Cynthia Willett, "Tropics of Desire: Freud and Derrida," *Research in Phenomenology* vol. 22.1 (Fall 1992): 148.

35. Laplanche, "Sublimation and/or Inspiration," 36.

36. Ibid., 37. This is not to argue that researchers who continuously test their ideas about their objects against the results of other studies produce "merely" subjective interpretations, but it is to repudiate the idea of an impermeable boundary between "empirical" objects and "libidinal" objects. Given his own acknowledgment of this principle, it is surprising that Laplanche invokes a distinction between objects of science and objects of the drive in order to emphasize the latter's status as products of fantasy: "An additional dimension of the object in psychoanalysis is that it is not necessarily an object in the sense of the theory of knowledge: an 'objective' object. We might here distinguish clearly two meanings which unfortunately, in recent psychoanalytic theory, are too often in a state of coalescence: the notion of objectivity in the sense of knowledge and the notion of objectality in which the object, this time, is an object of the drive and not a scientific or perceptual object. I point this out in order to emphasize that the object of the drive can be, without prejudice, a *fantasmatic* object and that it is perhaps essentially such" (*Life and Death in Psychoanalysis*, 12). Laplanche's distinction between "objectivity" and "objectality" elides the power of unconscious desires to motivate scientific inquiry. Freud's theory of sublimation suggests that empirical or scientific objects might obtain an imaginary valence within the memories of researchers, memories that, as I have already emphasized, are shaped by repression as well as unconscious desires and narcissistic identifications. The apparent firmness of Laplanche's distinction between scientific and libidinal objects is baffling in the work of a psychoanalytic theorist who elsewhere readily acknowledges the intimacy between fantasy and memory.

37. LaCapra, *Writing History, Writing Trauma*, 48.

38. Ibid., 50.

39. Eric Santner, *Stranded Objects: Mourning, Memory, and Film in Postwar Germany* (Ithaca, NY: Cornell University Press, 1990).

40. Alexander Mitscherlich and Margarete Mitscherlich, *The Inability to Mourn: Principles of Collective Behavior*, trans. Beverley R. Placzek (New York: Grove Press, 1975).

41. See Theodor W. Adorno, "The Meaning of Working Through the Past," in *Critical Models*, trans. Henry W. Pickford (New York: Columbia University Press, 1998), 89–103. See also Pickford's notes, 337–43.

42. Eric L. Santner, "History beyond the Pleasure Principle: Some Thoughts on the Representation of Trauma," in *Probing the Limits of Representation: Nazism*

and the "Final Solution," ed. Saul Friedlander (Cambridge, MA: Harvard University Press, 1992), 144.

43. Ibid. Santner's use of the term *emplotment* is an adaption from Hayden White's critical work on the poetics and rhetoric of historiography. See in particular White's "Historical Emplotment and the Problem of Truth," a paper that White delivered at the 1990 conference where Santner presented "History Beyond the Pleasure Principle." White's essay appears in Saul Friedlander, ed. *Probing the Limits of Representation: Nazism and the "Final Solution"* (Cambridge, MA: Harvard University Press, 1992), 37–53.

44. Freud, "Mourning and Melancholia (1917[1915])," SE 14: 243–58, here 245.

45. Laplanche, *Life and Death in Psychoanalysis*, 32. The "seduction thesis" refers to Freud's initial belief in his patients' frequent admissions that they had been victims of incest. He later relinquished this belief in favor of the thesis that these confessions reflected oedipal fantasies about fathers seducing and molesting their children. For a critical account of the history of this thesis in Freud's theory, see Masson, *Assault on Truth*.

46. See *Complete Letters of Sigmund Freud to Wilhelm Fliess*, 264–66.

47. Laplanche, *Life and Death in Psychoanalysis*, 32, citing Freud ibid.

48. Janet Walker, *Trauma Cinema: Documenting Incest and the Holocaust* (Berkeley and Los Angeles: University of California Press, 2005), 9. For the term *propping* and her understanding of fantasy, Walker cites Laplanche's *Life and Death in Psychoanalysis* as well as the entry for *phantasy* in Laplanche and Pontalis, *Language of Psycho-Analysis*, 314. It is important to acknowledge with Anne Tomiche that "in spite of the fact that he abandoned the idea that the sole cause of psychoneurosis was the *actual* reality of seduction, Freud never ceased to assert that sometimes it is the repression of real trauma that underlies the formation of symptoms, and sometimes it is the repression of fantasy." See Anne Tomiche, "Rephrasing the Freudian Unconscious: Lyotard's Affect-Phrase," *Diacritics* 24, no. 1 (Spring 1994): 51.

49. Freud, "Libido Theory," SE 18: 256.

50. This misconception holds sway in Gus Van Sant's film, *Good Will Hunting* (Miramax, 1997). With the help of his therapist, Robin Williams, Matt Damon's character is driven to cathartic weeping about his violently abusive upbringing. Following this purgation, Damon's character is suddenly free of his strangulating past. He stops suppressing his feelings for his girlfriend and drives off into the sunset in the direction of California to join her.

51. See Laplanche, *Life and Death in Psychoanalysis*, 130.

52. Freud, *Beyond the Pleasure Principle*, SE 18: 15.

53. Ibid.; idem, *Jenseits des Lustprinzips*, GW XIII: 13.

54. Santner, "History beyond the Pleasure Principle," 146.

55. Ibid. My emphasis.

56. Freud, *Beyond the Pleasure Principle*, SE 18: 8, 9.

57. Ibid., 55–56.

58. This delimitation implies that the difference between pleasure and unpleasure is both qualitative and quantitative; in other words, so-called "organ pleasure" might produce "unpleasure" if it rises to an "untenable" level. It is worth noting that Freud revises his theses from *Beyond the Pleasure Principle* respecting the relation between pleasure and unpleasure in "The Economic Problem of Masochism" (1924), (Freud, SE 19: 159–70). In that context, Freud remarks: "Pleasure and unpleasure,

therefore, cannot be referred to an increase or decrease of a quantity (which we describe as 'tension due to stimulus'), although they obviously have a great deal to do with that factor. It appears that they depend, not on this quantitative factor, but on some characteristic of it which we can only describe as a qualitative one. If we were able to say what this qualitative characteristic is, we should be much further advanced in psychology. Perhaps it is the rhythm, the temporal sequence of changes, rises and falls in the quantity of stimulus. We do not know" (160).

59. Freud, *Beyond the Pleasure Principle*, SE 18: 27. Elsewhere, I have examined Freud's recourse to *vital substance* (*lebende Substanz*) as the figure that pivots his articulation of organic and psychic evolution. One dimension of this recourse is phylogenetic, but implicitly metaphysical in narrating the development of a split psyche. Another dimension is metaphysical and topological insofar as it delineates a transcendental split between conscious and unconscious contents and functions. See Karyn Ball, "The Substance of Psychic Life," *Dreams of Interpretation: A Century down the Royal Road*, ed. Catherine Liu, John Mowitt, Thomas Pepper, and Jakki Spicer (Minneapolis: University of Minnesota Press, 2007), 321–35.

60. Accordingly, when internal excitations produce too much stress there is "a tendency to treat them as though they were acting, not from the inside, but from the outside, so that it may be possible to bring the shield against stimuli into operation as a means of defence against them." Projection as such plays "a large part in the causation of pathological processes," including those associated with trauma as a crack in the protective shield (Freud, *Beyond the Pleasure Principle*, SE 18: 29).

61. Freud, "Lecture XXV: Anxiety," SE 16: 395 and idem, "Vorlesung XXV: Angst," GW 11: 410.

62. Freud, "Lecture XXV: Anxiety," SE 16: 396 and idem, "Vorlesung XXV: Angst," GW 11: 410. In one of his more evocative yet not very persuasive speculations, Freud goes on to pinpoint anxiety as a residual form of birth pangs—the anxiety of the new-born on leaving the womb.

63. Freud, "Lecture XXV: Anxiety," SE 16: 411.

64. Ibid., 403.

65. Ibid., 403–404.

66. Freud, "Lecture XVIII. Fixation to Traumas—the Unconscious," SE 16: 273–85, here 274–75.

67. Freud, "On Narcissism: An Introduction," in SE 14: 73–102.

68. Ibid., 73–74.

69. Freud, "Lecture XXVI: The Libido Theory and Narcissism," SE 16: 414–15. I am paraphrasing the editors' explanatory note 2 on 414–15.

70. Freud, *Beyond the Pleasure Principle*, SE 18: 52, cited by Strachey (ed.) in ibid., SE 16: 415, note 2.

71. Ibid., "On Narcissism," SE 14: 77.

72. Ibid., 95. Freud writes that the formation of the ego-ideal "heightens the demands on the ego and is the most powerful factor favouring repression" (Ibid., 95).

73. Ibid., 95.

74. Extrapolating from Freud's figuration of the *ideal ego* as the focal point of self-love, I have previously proposed the term *ideal memory* to describe a charged image of the traumatic past that establishes a primary narcissistic orientation for individual or group identity. The companion term *memory ideal* represents a secondary narcissistic memory-composite whose contents reflect the subject's investment in social acceptance as a condition of continuing self-love. The memory ideal would

thus derive from the subject's anticipation of critical expectations about what he or she should or should not remember in light of his or her status in a particular context. A quintessential example of this dynamic is the Memorial to the Murdered Jews of Europe, which consolidated an official state vision of how the Holocaust should be remembered, what I have previously designated the "Holocaust proper," as a regulative memory ideal for Germans. See also Karyn Ball, "For and Against the *Bilderverbot*: The Rhetoric of 'Unrepresentability' and Remediated "Authenticity' in the German Reception of Steven Spielberg's *Schindler's List*" in David Bathrick, Brad Prager, and Michael D. Richardson, eds., *Visualizing the Holocaust: Aesthetics, Documents, Memory* (Rochester: Camden House, 2008).

75. Judith Butler, *The Psychic Life of Power* (Stanford, CA: Stanford University Press, 1997), 85, citing Michel Foucault, *Discipline and Punish: The Birth of the Prison*, trans. Alan Sheridan (New York: Random House, 1979), 30.

76. Foucault, *Discipline and Punish*, 30.

77. Butler, *Psychic Life of Power*, 91.

78. Ibid., 92, 90.

79. Arnold Davidson, "Structures and Strategies of Discourse: Remarks towards a History of Foucault's Philosophy of Language," in *Foucault and His Interlocutors*, ed. Arnold Davidson (Chicago: University of Chicago Press, 1997), 15, 7.

80. Butler, *Psychic Life of Power*, 96–97.

81. Butler, *Psychic Life of Power*, 104. For a critique of Butler's model of subjection, see Kelly Oliver, *Witnessing beyond Recognition* (Minneapolis: University of Minnesota Press, 2001), 61–81.

82. Oliver, *Witnessing beyond Recognition*, 219.

83. Ibid., 17.

84. Ibid., 219.

85. Michael Bernard-Donals, "Beyond the Question of Authenticity: Witness and Testimony in the *Fragments* Controversy," in *Witnessing the Disaster: Essays on Representation and the Holocaust* (Madison: University of Wisconsin Press, 2003), 196–217, 206.

86. Jacques Derrida, *Dissemination*, trans. Barbara Johnson (Chicago: University of Chicago Press, 1981), 61–71. First version published in *Tel Quel*, nos. 32 and 33, 1968.

87. I am thinking in particular here of Derrida's *Speech and Phenomena, and Other Essays on Husserl's Theory of Signs*, trans. David B. Allison (Evanston: Northwestern University Press, 1973) and *Of Grammatology*, trans. Gayatri Spivak (Baltimore: Johns Hopkins University Press, 1974).

88. Derrida writes: "If the *pharmakon* is 'ambivalent,' it is because it constitutes the medium in which opposites are opposed, the movement and the play that links them among themselves, reverses them or makes one side cross over into the other (soul/body, good/evil, inside/outside, memory/forgetfulness, speech/writing, etc.)" (*Dissemination*, 127).

89. On the theme of memory as writing, see Freud's "Note on the 'Mystic Writing-Pad' (1925)," SE 14: 227–32 in light of Derrida's "Freud and the Scene of Writing" in *Writing and Difference*, trans. Alan Bass (Chicago: University of Chicago Press, 1978), 196–231. It is not coincidental to my analysis here that Derrida himself has acknowledged the debt that deconstruction owes to Freud's analysis of the repetition compulsion in *Beyond the Pleasure Principle*. In *Resistances: Of Psychoanalysis*, Derrida writes: "there is nothing fortuitous about the fact that the most decisive and

difficult stakes between, let's say, 'psychoanalysis' and 'deconstruction' should have taken a relatively organized form around the question of the repetition compulsion. The great reference texts here are *Beyond the Pleasure Principle* and Lacan's 'Seminar on "The Purloined Letter."' " Derrida, *Resistances: Of Psychoanalysis* (Stanford, CA: Stanford University Press, 1998), 32. This acknowledgment suggests a profound resonance between deconstruction and Freud's death drive, which serves a primal urge to return the psychic apparatus to a state of inorganic calm. The inanimate state figures for an ossification of the psyche freed of vital tensions; from a deconstructive standpoint, the compulsion to reach this state via repetition is parallel to the desire to achieve a closure of interpretation, to secure signs against the flux of interpretation.

90. Willett, "Tropics of Desire" (cited in note 34 above).

91. Ibid., 138.

92. Ibid., 139.

93. Ibid.

94. Ibid., 142.

95. Ibid., 140.

96. Ibid., 141.

97. Ibid., 143.

98. Paul de Man, " 'Conclusions': Walter Benjamin's 'The Task of the Translator,' " in *The Resistance to Theory* (Minneapolis: University of Minnesota Press), 73–105.

99. De Man writes: "All these activities—critical philosophy, literary theory, history—resemble each other in the fact that they do not resemble that from which they derive. But they are all intralinguistic: they relate to what in the original belongs to language, and not to meaning as an extralinguistic correlate susceptible of paraphrase and imitation. They disarticulate, they undo the original, they reveal that the original was always already disarticulated. They reveal that their failure, which seems to be due to the fact that they are secondary in relation to the original, reveals an essential failure, an essential disarticulation which was already there in the original. They kill the original, by discovering that the original was already dead" (De Man, 84, Santner, *Stranded Objects*, 27. My citation adds a sentence that was paraphrased by Santner).

100. De Man, " 'Conclusions,' " 92.

101. Santner, *Stranded Objects*, 26.

102. Ibid., 29.

103. Ibid.

104. Ibid.

105. Ibid.

106. Ibid., citing de Man, " 'Conclusions,' " 92.

107. Santner, *Stranded Objects*, 29. As Santner suggests, de Man's historical tasks of mourning "were substantial and complex" alluding, of course, to his war time journalistic writings supporting Nazi rhetoric against the Jews. To the extent that de Man's concept of "inhuman" history effaces the social dimensions of mourning, he extenuates his own responsibility for acknowledging and mitigating historical suffering. For a redemptive elaboration of the connection between de Man's activities during the war and his post-war deconstructive writings see Shoshana Felman's "After the Apocalypse: Paul de Man and the Fall to Silence" in *Testimony: Crises of Witnessing in Literature, Psychoanalysis, and History* (New York: Routledge, 1992), 120–64.

Santner and LaCapra share an investment in using the Holocaust as a litmus test for the intellectual legacy of literary and cultural criticism after the linguistic turn and the "rampant" liberties of posthumanist theory in particular. By delimiting trauma and working through proper, LaCapra and Santner would redress the conceptual injustices committed against the memory of historical victims through a deconstructive blurring of distinctions and identities.

LaCapra is not reacting to Derrida's and de Man's work per se, but rather to what he views as exaggerated strains in recent theories of trauma that have been heavily influenced by Lacanian psychoanalysis and/or the linguistic turn. For example, Slavoj Žižek's "return" to Lacan constructs the traumatic real as a dialectical sublation and a transcendental condition of psychosocial existence. LaCapra also argues that Cathy Caruth's work emphasizes the figurative dimensions of trauma in a manner that elides the difference between absent objects and lost objects. To my mind, her work is important for following through on Derrida's and de Man's attention to the errancy of the signifier as well as the hermeneutical insight that the interpretation of the past is determined by present concerns.

LaCapra's moral grounds for separating empirical and structural trauma, on the one hand, and lost and absent objects, on the other, presumably authorize him to set the critical parameters for an evaluation of traumatic discourse; yet it should be recognized that this intervention also allows him to discount the psychoanalytic complexity of deconstructive readings such as Caruth's that highlight the reciprocal influences between historical and structural trauma. In *Representing the Holocaust: History, Theory, Trauma* and *History and Memory after Auschwitz*, LaCapra relegates his discussion of Caruth's work to footnotes. In this respect, his polemic does not simply serve to protect the moral and historical specificity of the Holocaust as a traumatic object of inquiry; it also defers the issue of LaCapra's own considerable investment in instituting a "proper" interpretation of traumatic history. See LaCapra, *Representing the Holocaust*, 14, n. 10 and *History and Memory after Auschwitz*, 208, n. 22. Naomi Mandel views such criticisms along with Ruth Leys's and Amy Hungerford's attacks on Caruth and Shoshana Felman, respectively, as a demonstration of how the "alignment of trauma with ethics renders criticism subject to a certain policing activity; the limits of the argument are made manifest when moral distinctions have been breached." Naomi Mandel, *Against the Unspeakable: Complicity, the Holocaust, and Slavery in America* (Charlottesville: University of Virginia Press, 2006), 57. As I have hopefully made clear, I share Mandel's concern about the disciplinary orientation of trauma studies when it is deployed as a means of accruing moral capital.

108. Santner, *Stranded Objects*, 28. It is worth remarking the symptomatic redundancy of Santner's recourse to the phrase "human subjectivity," which betrays his anxiety about the paradoxical possibility of an "inhuman" subjectivity. The idea of an "inhuman" subjectivity moves in the perilous direction of a "reason in history" that precedes and conditions human agency. Santner's impulse to safeguard the human against this possibility is, thus, a symptom of a long-standing philosophical opposition between freedom and historical necessity.

To his credit, Santner does acknowledge the historical dimensions of the linguistic turn through his attention to the twin "posts" that unite the post-Holocaust era with "postmodern" thought. In the French context, the historically motivated antitotalitarian impetus to move away from ideas that favored deterministic views of identity fostered a repudiation of the allegedly result-driven tendency of Hegel's dialectic as well as Marx's revolutionary class narrative and Freud's biological determinism. At the same time, French thinkers were also responding critically to the legacy of structuralism à la Ferdinand de Saussure, Claude Lévi-Strauss, and the early Roland Barthes. Ludwig Wittgenstein and Bertrand Russell provided models for what would become a formal analytic attention to questions of language, meaning, truth, and knowledge. The question remains as to whether the postwar philosophical turn toward language contradicted the political and moral desire to avoid a deterministic or normative logic. Certainly, the desire to disarticulate determinisms resonated historically with the parallel desire to resist theories that assumed closed and totalizing systems of judgment. Such systems of thought were assumed to reiterate the instrumental logics of Hitler and Stalin's dictatorships or the Fordist disposition of American capitalism. To resist this conceptual threat in their own work, theorists such as Derrida emphasized the errancy or play in acts of interpretation and signification that undermined any final or normative determination of identity. Paradoxically, then, the idea of arbitrary and amoral signifying structures paved the way for a political affirmation of freedom against determinism. Ultimately, however, if deconstruction errs on the side of granting the conditions for "too much" freedom over and against the evidence of historical necessity, as its critics claim, then this freedom is impersonal and itself quasi-deterministic, since it is a structural effect of the circulation of the signifier.

109. Oliver, *Witnessing beyond Recognition*, 110.

110. "Testimony is false," Oliver claims, "if it is merely acting-out rather than working-through the ways in which the indebtedness to others is repressed" (ibid. 109).

111. Ibid., 110.

112. De Man, " 'Conclusions,' " 96.

113. It is worth pointing out that Julia Kristeva's formulation of the *semiotic* to speak about the ways in which the drives are not simply excluded by language but may permeate and fracture it, effectively counters de Man's distinction here. In conversation, Ewa Ziarek proposed an understanding of Kristeva's semiotic as the "hinge" between the pulsations of the drives and the demands of the symbolic. See Kristeva's "The Subject in Process," in *The Tel Quel Reader*, ed. Patrick Ffrench and Roland-François Lack (New York: Routledge, 1998), 133–78. See also Kristeva, *Revolution in Poetic Language*, trans. Margaret Roudiez (New York: Columbia University Press, 1984).

114. Freud, "Lecture XVIII: Fixation to Traumas—the Unconscious," SE 16: 275.

115. See Cathy Caruth, *Unclaimed Experience: Trauma, Narrative, and History* (Baltimore: Johns Hopkins University Press, 1996).

116. See Ruth Leys, *Trauma: A Genealogy* (Chicago: University of Chicago Press, 2000), 266, 229. In Leys's view, this elision makes Caruth's model "an inadvertent parody" of the mimetic model (17). While I am committed to moving beyond the rhetoric of unrepresentability in trauma studies and while I follow Leys in repudiating the notion of "literal" registration, I am reluctant to throw out all aspects of the mimetic model—at the very least, because it is useful for characterizing a subject's experience of his or her own investment in certain traumatic images.

117. See in particular Leys, *Trauma*, 1–17, 153–89. See also Mikkel Borch-Jacobsen, *The Freudian Subject*, trans. Catherine Porter (Stanford, CA: Stanford University Press, 1988).

118. Leys, *Trauma*, 9.

119. Ibid., 10.

120. Mikkel Borch-Jacobsen, *The Emotional Tie: Psychoanalysis, Mimesis, Affect*, trans. Douglas Brick and others (Stanford, CA: Stanford University Press, 1993), 24.

121. Butler, *Psychic Life of Power*, 99.

122. Ibid., 93.

123. Judith Butler, *Precarious Life: The Powers of Mourning and Violence* (New York: Verso, 2004).

124. Ibid., 137, paraphrasing Emmanuel Lévinas, "Peace and Proximity," in *Basic Philosophical Writings*, ed. Adriaan T. Peperzak, Simon Critchley, and Robert Bernasconi (Bloomington: Indiana University Press, 1996).

125. Butler, *Precarious Life*, 136–37.

126. Giorgio Agamben, *Homo Sacer: Sovereign Power and Bare Life*, trans. Daniel Heller-Roazen (Stanford, CA: Stanford University Press, 1998).

127. Jacqueline Rose, *Sexuality in the Field of Vision* (London: Verso, 1987), 91, cited by Butler, *Psychic Life of Power*, 97.

128. LaCapra, *History and Memory after Auschwitz*, 45.

129. Klüger, *Landscapes of Memory*, 27–28. See also Klüger, *weiter leben*, 28.

130. Klüger, *Landscapes of Memory*, 28.

131. Freud, *Beyond the Pleasure Principle*, SE 18: 13–14.

132. Ibid., 20 and idem, *Jenseits des Lustprinzips*, GW XIII: 18.

133. Laplanche, *Life and Death in Psychoanalysis*, 13.

134. Freud, *Beyond the Pleasure Principle*, SE 18: 62.

135. Freud, "Economic Problem of Masochism," SE 19: 163.

136. Ibid., 163–64.

137. Freud's identification of the "feminine" form of masochism was ostensibly based on his experiences in a more intensely patriarchal society where women were largely restricted to domestic roles in the family and to service positions outside of it. Without dismissing continuing inequalities, I suggest that both men and women might differentially fantasize about assuming a passive subject position in ways determined by their relation to changing gender and sexual norms as well as personal differences. While it would be interesting to explore the question of how passivity continues to be "feminized" in a "postfeminist" society, on principle, I would prefer to abandon the designation *feminine* in favor of the more gender-neutral term *passive* masochism, which women and men experience differently. The question that remains is whether men and women continue to see passivity as "feminine." Is a genuinely "liberated" form of passive masochism possible for either men or women?

138. Jean Laplanche, "Narrativity and Hermeneutics: Some Propositions," trans. John Fletcher, in "Jean Laplanche and the Theory of Seduction," special issue of *new formations* (Winter 2002–3): 26. This essay originally appeared as "Narrativité et herméneutique: Quelques propositions," *Revue française de psychanalyse* 3 (1998).

139. Laplanche, "Narrativity and Hermeneutics," 27.

140. Ibid., 29.

141. Ibid.

142. Ibid.

143. Fletcher, "Recent Developments," 10.

144. Laplanche, "Sublimation and/or Inspiration," 38. Laplanche opposes "the stupidity of narcissistic-gestaltist binding" to the "complexity of symbolising forms of binding and of symbolic systems" that correlate objects and concepts with "scenarios, propositions, and judgments" (38).

145. Ibid., 40. The implication for the therapeutic practice is that analysis will primarily entail a restrained work of *unbinding* the sexual death drive (50).

146. Freud, *Beyond the Pleasure Principle*, SE 18: 52; idem, *Jenseits des Lustprinzips*, GW XIII: 56.

147. Charles Shepherdson, *Vital Signs: Nature, Culture, Psychoanalysis* (New York: Routledge, 2000), 177.

148. Herbert Marcuse, *Eros and Civilization: A Philosophical Inquiry into Freud* (Boston: Beacon Press, 1955), 35. Marcuse contrasts this "irrational" repression with its "rational" form as "the 'modifications' of the instincts necessary for the perpetuation of the human race in civilization" (35). While I regret not devoting more space to explaining Marcuse's revision of Freud, I hope I will be forgiven for retaining his term *surplus-repression* even as I prefer to distance myself from some of his more ecstatically utopian proclamations about the sociopolitical potentials of Eros. It is worth noting that, already in the 1950s, Marcuse, who is sometimes celebrated as the father of the New Left, anticipated and contributed to an inclination in the 1960s and 1970s to naively link fascism and sexual repression. Though he emigrated to the United States in 1934, his ideas found a receptive audience among the generation of 1968 in Europe.

As Dagmar Herzog has recently suggested in *Sex after Fascism: Memory and Morality in Twentieth-Century Germany* (Princeton, NJ: Princeton University Press, 2005), the generation that came of age in West Germany in the 1960s had grown up in a milieu inundated by stern Christian voices in the 1950s that contributed to a repressive code where sexual matters were concerned. This code targeted premarital and homosexual relations while encouraging masochism among women, who were enjoined to sacrifice their own needs and desires for their men. Herzog interprets this repressive milieu as a symptomatic counterformation against the exhortations of some Nazi ideologues for the racial elite to celebrate their own "natural" beauty and to encourage sexual relations in and out of marriage to augment the health of the German *Volk* while furthering the policy of aryanization. This 1950s milieu is symptomatic because it allowed postwar Germans to identify with a hypocritical sexual morality as a means of managing and deflecting the profound immorality of mass murder. Jewish re-émigrés such as Max Horkheimer and Theodor W. Adorno made this hypocrisy still more intelligible by citing the recurrence of "Nazi" references to the health of the *Volk* as well as residual eugenic logics in arguments for certain policies restricting birth control and forbidding homosexuality, which were retained from the Nazi period. Yet in the face of the emerging sexual radicalism of the 1960s, Adorno in 1963 already warned that "[t]he liberation of sex in the present society is only superficial. . . . In an unfree society, sexual freedom is as unthinkable as any other." Adorno, "Sexualtabus und Recht heute," in *Sexualität und Verbrechen*, ed. Fritz Bauer et al. (Frankfurt am Main: Fischer, 1963), 300–301, cited by Herzog, *Sex after Fascism*, 155–56.

Though Adorno was a teacher to many of the leading New Leftists, Herzog notes that overall the '68ers tended to appropriate writings by the Frankfurt School rather selectively, so that Horkheimer, Adorno, and Erich Fromm were invoked in a way that "ended up sounding a great deal like Wilhelm Reich," whose "influence on the New Left was unparalleled" (158–59). One of Herzog's key claims is that the sexual radicals of the post-postfascist generation did not realize their moralistic parents were distancing themselves from a partial liberalization of sexual practices and conceptions of pleasure under the Nazis, albeit as the privilege and duty of the racially fit. West German '68ers therefore tended to associate sexual repression with fascism and even to "argue that sexual repression was at the root of all evil" (134). Hence the slogan "Make Love, Not War" "was not just a recommendation for a more decent and pleasurable activity than slaughtering other human beings while risking one's own life; it was also a theory of human nature, a deeply held conviction that those who made a lot of love simply would not be interested in hurting or killing others" (159). Of course, as Herzog also demonstrates, "The near-obsessive reference to the power of parents in writings that were supposedly theorizing Nazism suggests what else was being worked through as 68ers tackled the topic of sexual politics" (160).

149. Marcuse, *Eros and Civilization*, 87.

150. Shepherdson, *Vital Signs*, 177.

151. Freud, "Mourning and Melancholia," SE 14: 244.

152. Shepherdson, *Vital Signs*, 175–76. And, as Shepherdson implies, it is as if the symbolic order, including the rule of law, "somehow depended upon a level of malfunction and perverse enjoyment" that Freud formulates as the 'death drive' and Lacan as *jouissance* (177).

153. The ideational character of masochistic identifications has important implications for a theory of cinematic voyeurism as a forum of sadomasochistic pleasure. Films that depict or dramatize the Holocaust provide spectators from various groups with an occasion to occupy the position of a voyeur who might safely contemplate the historical suffering of others, and identify sadistically with the perpetrators and masochistically with the victims. This observation partially explains how both Jewish and non-Jewish spectators born after the Holocaust might be entertained by a film like Steven Spielberg's *Schindler's List* even while they consciously abhor the persecution and murder it depicts. In this connection, Freud's 1924 theses on the sadomasochistic deformations of the death drive to some extent clarify the charged character of Holocaust memory as well as the desire among various critics to institute its "unrepresentability."

154. LaCapra, *Writing History, Writing Trauma*, 59.

155. Mandel, "Against the Unspeakable," 58.

156. My configuration of the disciplinary imaginary is indebted to Butler's theorization of *performativity*, but here also to her discussions of Nietzsche, Freud, Lacan, Foucault, and Althusser in *The Psychic Life of Power*. On the relationship between Foucault and psychoanalysis, see John Rajchman, *Michel Foucault: The Freedom of Philosophy* (New York: Columbia University Press, 1985); Jacques Derrida, " 'To do justice to Freud': The History of Madness in the Age of Psychoanalysis," trans. Pascale-Anne Brault and Michael Naas, in *Foucault and His Interlocutors*, ed. Arnold Davidson (Chicago: University of Chicago Press, 1997), 57–96; Christopher Lane, "The Experience of the Outside," in *Lacan in America*, ed. Jean-Michel Rabaté (New York: Other Press, 2000), 309–48; Shepherdson, *Vital Signs*, 153–85; and my attempts to think through Foucault's "psychoanalytic unconscious" in Karyn Ball, "Introduction: Traumatizing Psychoanalysis," in *Traumatizing Theory: The Cultural Politics of Affect in*

and beyond Psychoanalysis (New York: Other Press, 2007); and idem, "A Democracy Is Being Beaten," *English Studies in Canada* 32, no. 1 (2006): 45–76.

157. Shepherdson, *Vital Signs*, 162. See also Slavoj Žižek, *For They Know Not What They Do: Enjoyment as a Political Factor* (New York: Routledge, 1992).

158. Shepherdson, *Vital Signs*, 170.

159. Hannah Arendt, *The Origins of Totalitarianism* (San Diego: Harcourt, 1976), 468.

160. Laplanche, "Sublimation and/or Inspiration," 37.

161. See Gillian Rose, "Beginnings of the Day: Fascism and Representation," *Modernity, Culture and "the Jew,"* ed. Bryan Cheyette and Laura Marcus (Oxford: Polity, 1998), 242–56. Giorgio Agamben has also cited Primo Levi in situating this zone of irresponsibility "not *beyond* good and evil but rather, so to speak, *before* them." See Agamben, *Remnants of Auschwitz: The Witness and the Archive*, trans. Daniel Heller-Roazen (Cambridge, MA: Zone Books, 1999), 21.

Chapter Five

I am grateful to Lisa Disch, Marjorie Gelus, Ruth-Ellen Joeres, Leslie Morris, and Heather Zwicker for their detailed comments on prior drafts of a shorter version of this chapter, which originally appeared in *Women in German Yearbook* 19 (2003): 20–49.

1. In her discussion of Thomas Eakins's realism, Marcia Pointon remarks that *The Agnew Clinic*—which centers on a "performance or demonstration (a public enactment)—parallels the conditions of viewing in Hollywood cinema in which the foreclosed real and the concealed site of production (studio and operating theater) produce the conditions of lack." Marcia Pointon, *Naked Authority: The Body in Western Painting, 1830–1908* (Cambridge: Cambridge University Press, 1990), 51.

2. See Shoshana Felman and Dori Laub, *Testimony: Crises of Witnessing in Literature, Psychoanalysis, and History* (New York: Routledge, 1992); Lawrence Langer, *Holocaust Testimonies: The Ruins of Memory* (New Haven, CT: Yale University Press, 1991); Michael Bernard-Donals and Richard Glejzer, *Between Witness and Testimony: The Holocaust and the Limits of Representation* (Albany: State University of New York Press, 2001); and Kelly Oliver, *Witnessing beyond Recognition* (Minneapolis: University of Minnesota Press, 2001). See also Bernard-Donals and Glejzer, eds., *Witnessing the Disaster: Essays on Representation and the Holocaust* (Madison: University of Wisconsin Press, 2003); and Felman, "Education, or Crisis: The Vicissitudes of Teaching," and Laub, "Truth and Testimony: The Process and the Struggle," in *Trauma: Explorations in Memory*, ed. Cathy Caruth (Baltimore: Johns Hopkins University Press, 1995), 13–60 and 61–75, respectively. Caruth's own work on trauma is also important in this connection. In "Social Bonds and Psychical Order: Testimony," *Cultural Values* 5, no. 1 (January 2001): 59–78, Susannah Radstone attributes the extraordinary impact of Felman's and Laub's 1992 *Testimony* book along with Caruth's studies of trauma to "the recent ascendancy of Holocaust Studies, as well as to a theoretical consonance between their theoretical concerns with the transmission of the untransmittable, and the themes of postmodernist theory more generally" (61). Her observations are consonant with the trajectory I map in "Trauma and Its Institutional Destinies," *Cultural Critique* 46 (Fall 2000): 3–44, where I argue that a desire to

reclaim the power of experience while heeding the poststructuralist repudiation of its metaphysical and humanist attachments entailed a terminological shift. Hereafter experience would need to be represented as multifaceted and contradictory, if not also partial, mediated, and/or belated. Memory consequently entered into this juncture as a more "poststructurally correct" substitute for experience, while traumatic memory in particular became the hinge of identity politics in a postidentitarian milieu that nonetheless continued to look to individual and collective suffering as its moral fulcrum. Holocaust studies helped to bring about this turning point by rendering explicit the historiographical, hermeneutical, and moral issues that vex victim and perpetrator memories and the ways in which denial, disavowal, and guilt affect the contours of traumatic history.

3. Michael Bernard-Donals, "Beyond the Question of Authenticity: Witness and Testimony in the *Fragments* Controversy," in Bernard-Donals and Glejzer, *Witnessing the Disaster*, 210. See, in this connection, Binjamin Wilkomirski, *Fragments: Memories of a Wartime Childhood*, trans. Carol Brown Janeway (New York: Schocken Books, 1996).

4. Janet Walker, *Trauma Cinema: Documenting Incest and the Holocaust* (Berkeley and Los Angeles: University of California Press, 2005), xviii.

5. Michel Bernard-Donals and Richard Glejzer, "The Epistemology of Witness: Survivor Narratives and the Holocaust," in *Between Witness and Testimony: The Holocaust and the Limits of Representation* (Albany: State University of New York Press, 2001), 52.

6. In *Witnessing Beyond Recognition*, Kelly Oliver suggests that what testimony performs are "the silences and the blindnesses inherent in the event that, at bottom, also make eyewitness testimony impossible" (Oliver, *Witnessing beyond Recognition*, 86).

7. Agamben, *Remnants of Auschwitz*, 157. Agamben writes: "The modal categories—possibility, impossibility, contingency, necessity—are not innocuous logical or epistemological categories that concern the structure of propositions or the relation of something to our faculty of knowledge. They are ontological operators, that is, the devastating weapons used in the biopolitical struggle for Being in which a decision is made each time on the human and the inhuman, on 'making live' or 'letting die.'" Giorgio Agamben, *Remnants of Auschwitz: The Witness and the Archive*, trans. Daniel Heller-Roazen (Cambridge, MA: Zone Books, 1999), 146–47.

8. To this end, Laub suggests that the analyst's ability to grant such lessons their affective weight and intelligibility might be more strategically served by a dearth rather than by a wealth of factual knowledge about the circumstances surrounding the witness's testimony: "[I]n the process of the testimony to a trauma, as in psychoanalytic practice, in effect, you often do not want to know anything except what the patient tells you, because what is important is the situation of *discovery* of knowledge—its evolution, and its very *happening*. Knowledge in the testimony is, in other words, not simply a factual given that is reproduced and replicated by the testifier, but a genuine advent, an event in its own right" (Laub, in Felman and Laub, *Testimony*, 62).

9. Gary Weissman, *Fantasies of Witnessing: Postwar Efforts to Experience the Holocaust* (Ithaca, NY: Cornell University Press, 2004), 136, citing Laub, "Truth and Testimony," 65.

10. Weissman, *Fantasies of Witnessing*, 136, citing Laub, *Truth and Testimony*, 69.

11. This is a false opposition that Roland Barthes dispatched in his attention to historians' recourse to realist conventions to promote an illusion of referential intimacy and neutrality. See "The Discourse of History" and "The Reality Effect" in *The Rustle of Language*, trans. Richard Howard (Berkeley and Los Angeles: University of California Press, 1989), 127–40 and 141–48, respectively. In extending Barthes's insights, Hayden White foregrounds how historians' respective "emplotments" of historical phenomena as narratives encode particular moral standpoints. Of particular relevance to my discussion here is White's *The Content of the Form: Narrative Discourse and Historical Representation* (Baltimore: Johns Hopkins University Press, 1999).

12. See Ellie Ragland, "The Psychical Nature of Trauma: Freud's Dora, the Young Homosexual Woman, and the *Fort! Da!* Paradigm," in *Topologies of Trauma: Essays on the Limit of Knowledge and Memory*, ed. Linda Belau and Petar Ramadanovic (New York: Other Press, 2002), 75–100. Ragland argues that by hearing the "traumatic truth" of the survivor's testimony, a sympathetic listener acts on behalf of the Other (the social order) to confirm a traumatized subject's damaged sense of continuity in relation to it. Ragland notes that when the Other exposes the visceral underside of fantasy (and the real as such), it traumatizes the split subject by annihilating the power of his or her object *a* to serve its function of suturing appearance and reality. Compassionate listening must then enter into the unbearable void left by a concrete brush with the palpability of this separation—a breach in the possibility of making meaning. Paraphrasing Caruth in Lacanian terms, Ragland writes: "[T]he Other—the social order—must *hear* what is actually being said: a transference relation must be engaged such that a representative listener from the social order believes the *truth* that seeps through the imaginary dimensions of a narrative" (79). See also Cathy Caruth, "Trauma and Experience: Introduction," in Caruth, ed., *Trauma: Explorations in Memory* (Baltimore: Johns Hopkins University Press, 1995), 3–12.

13. Dominick LaCapra, *Representing the Holocaust: History, Theory, Trauma* (Ithaca, NY: Cornell University Press, 1994), 72.

14. LaCapra also asks us not to presume that we are therapists "working in intimate contact with survivors or other traumatized people." LaCapra, *Writing History, Writing Trauma* (Baltimore: Johns Hopkins University Press, 2001), 98.

15. I develop this conception of "disciplinary mimesis" in the first and fourth chapters of this book. See also LaCapra's *Representing the Holocaust* and *History and Memory after Auschwitz* (Ithaca, NY: Cornell University Press, 1998); and John Mowitt, *Text: The Genealogy of an Antidisciplinary Object* (Durham, NC: Duke University Press, 1992). Also useful in theorizing scholarly investments is Saul Friedlander, "Trauma, Memory, Transference," and Michael Geyer and Miriam Hansen, "German-Jewish Memory and Historical Consciousness," in *Holocaust Remembrance: The Shapes of Memory*, ed. Geoffrey Hartman (Cambridge, MA: Blackwell, 1994), 252–63 and 175–90, respectively.

16. Marianne Hirsch, "Surviving Images: Holocaust Photographs and the Work of Postmemory," *Yale Journal of Criticism* 14, no. 1 (2001): 5–37. For Hirsch, postmemory "need not be *strictly* an identity position." It is, instead, "an intersubjective transgenerational space of remembrance, linked specifically to cultural or collective trauma. It is defined through an identification with the victim or witness of trauma, modulated by an unbridgeable distance that separates the participant from one born after" (10).

17. Ibid., 10.

18. See Cathy Caruth, "Unclaimed Experience: Trauma and the Possibility of History (Freud, *Moses and Monotheism*)," in *Trauma: Explorations in Memory* (Baltimore: Johns Hopkins University Press, 1996), 10–24.

19. Hirsch, "Surviving Images," 12.

20. Ibid., 23–24.

21. Michel Foucault, *Discipline and Punish: The Birth of the Prison*, trans. Alan Sheridan (New York: Vintage Books, 1979).

22. Jean-François Lyotard, *The Differend: Phrases in Dispute*, trans. Georges Van Den Abbeele (Minneapolis: University of Minnesota Press, 1988). Originally published by Les Éditions de Minuit, 1983. See also Felman and Laub, *Testimony*.

23. Gertrud Koch, "The Aesthetic Transformation of the Image of the Unimaginable: Notes on Claude Lanzmann's *Shoah*," trans. Jamie Owen Daniel and Miriam Hansen, *October* 48 (Spring 1989): 16.

24. Ibid., 17.

25. Ibid., 21.

26. Yosefa Loshitzky, "Holocaust Others: Spielberg's *Schindler's List* versus Lanzmannn's *Shoah*," in *Spielberg's Holocaust: Critical Perspectives on "Schindler's List,"* ed. Yosefa Loshitzky (Bloomington: Indiana University Press, 1997), 107–8.

27. Ibid., 108. Loshitzky appreciates Lanzmann's respect for "the boundary between what is aesthetically and humanly imaginable and the unimaginable dimension of the annihilation" (Loshitzky, "Holocaust Others," 111). Ultimately, however, Loshitzky is seemingly persuaded by Lanzmann's notion of authenticity that utilizes oral testimony and "the evocation of expressive faces and landscapes" in contrast to the posthistorical cinematic memory repertoire "recycled by the movie industry" that Spielberg enlists. Rothberg, in contrast, emphasizes the inconsistencies in Lanzmann's theory of representation as evinced in the latter's criticism of Spielberg. "On the one hand," Rothberg writes, "he demands historical authenticity. . . . On the other hand, historical authenticity is not what Lanzmann really demands," since there is "something radically *antihistorical* about his position that the Holocaust is unique," that its absoluteness cannot be transmitted, fictionalized, or breached. Michael Rothberg, "'Touch an Event to Begin': Americanizing the Holocaust," in *Traumatic Realism: The Demands of Holocaust Representation* (Minneapolis: University of Minnesota Press, 2000), 232. Rothberg's analysis suggests that both Lanzmann and Spielberg lend credence to Adorno's declaration in "Commitment" that "[t]hose works that through their very existence become the advocates of the victims of a nature-dominating rationality are in their protest by their very nature also always interwoven with the process of rationalization." Theodor W. Adorno, "Commitment," in *Notes to Literature Volume Two*, trans. Shierry Weber Nicholsen (New York: Columbia University Press, 1992), 91. Even if it favors the "evocation" of the imagined versus Spielberg's "real-like" images, Lanzmann's activation of the "relived" (especially when it is orchestrated and edited) actually stylizes unrepresentability (Loshitzky, "Holocaust Others," 123).

28. Michel Foucault, *The History of Sexuality: An Introduction (Volume 1)*, trans. Robert Hurley (New York: Vintage Books, 1990).

29. Radstone, "Social Bonds and Psychical Order," 59. Radstone's thesis is that "the ungraspability and *unidentifiability* of contemporary authority exacerbates aggressivity while attenuating possibilities for identification. Under these circumstances, the transformation of aggression against an external authority into intra-psychic

conflict becomes yet more deeply unmanageable and threatening than in the age of confession. This, I think, is a danger of our times. In these dangerous moments, memories flash up, but they are memories *shaped* by our present dangers, dangers that our testimonies and witnessings can either re-inforce or mitigate" (71).

30. Ibid., 60.

31. Dagmar Herzog offers a revealing historicization of the rise of a radical "antiauthoritarian" confessional culture connected with the battle cry that "the personal is political" in the 1960s among West German feminists and the New Left, which she reads as a counterformation against the 1950s. This "now-familiar slogan," she writes, "remains most usually associated with the women's liberation movements that grew out of and reacted against the various male-dominated New Lefts that had formed in Western nations in the late 1960s. But as New Left pronouncements on sex from the late 1960s and early 1970s make palpably clear," Herzog observes, "the urgent desire to transform both one's self and interpersonal relations was, at least in West Germany, very much a male New Left agenda as well." One would therefore be "hard pressed, for instance, to find as many examples in other Western countries as there were in West Germany of New Left activists demanding that private quarrels between lovers be worked through in group settings. . . . One would also be hard pressed to find as many examples of activists airing in print their most intimate personal shames and hurts. . . ." Among the practices Herzog documents are the Frankfurt Collective's commitment to analyze publicly their sexual difficulties along with their societal implications and Berlin Kommune 1's decision to remove their bathroom door from its hinges. She emphasizes that "[n]one of this makes any sense except against the background of a postwar culture that idealized family values, overemphasized the importance of guarding family secrets, and treated the bodies of its young punitively." Hence the utterly claustrophobic "sexual and familial conservatism advanced in that decade was interpreted as so wholly dishonest and reprehensible, that it seemed that only the strongest and most outrageous counterarguments and counteractions would do." If such "extremity appeared not only justified but mandated," it was in light of the postwar tendency to "present the concerns of morality as being above all about sex, not about murder—or in some cases even to present sex as being as bad as murder." Such hypocrisy "could not fail to make a tremendous impression especially on socially critical young people." See Dagmar Herzog, *Sex after Fascism: Memory and Morality in Twentieth-Century Germany* (Princeton, NJ: Princeton University Press, 2005), 161.

32. Oliver, *Witnessing beyond Recognition*, 98.

33. Wilhelm Dilthey, *Pattern and Meaning in History: Thoughts on History and Society*, ed. H. P. Rickman (London: George Allen & Unwin, 1961), 67–68.

34. Susannah Radstone, "The War of the Fathers: Trauma, Fantasy, and September 11," *Signs: Journal of Women in Culture and Society* 28, no. 1 (2002): 457–59.

35. Ibid., 458. Radstone is writing in the wake of September 11 against certain commonplaces of trauma theory that imply a passive or short-circuited response to the impact of an "unimaginable" or "unprecedented" event.

36. Radstone's definition of the gray zone borrows from Primo Levi's *The Drowned and the Saved* (London: Abacus, 1989).

37. Agamben, *Remnants of Auschwitz*, 21.

38. Radstone, "Social Bonds and Psychical Order," 70, quoting Ian Craib, *The Importance of Disappointment* (London: Routledge, 1994), 109.

39. "The Economic Problem of Masochism (1924)," in Volume 19 of *The Complete Psychological Works of Sigmund Freud*, trans. and ed. James Strachey in collaboration with Anna Freud (London: Vintage, 2001): 159–70. As I mentioned in the previous chapter, Freud distinguishes between *erotogenic*, *feminine*, and *moral* masochism. The erotogenic form involves sexual arousal in the course of suffering pain or identifying with the position of suffering. This form is "original" because it underlies the other two masochisms he delineates. So-called *feminine* masochism designates the pleasure of occupying a passive position. *Moral* masochism is characterized by an investment in self-punishing guilt, which is linked to the masochist's sense that he has failed or has committed some ambiguous crime.

40. Radstone, "Social Bonds and Psychical Order" 66. Radstone borrows the term *Holocaust piety* from Gillian Rose, "Beginnings of the Day: Fascism and Representation," in *Modernity, Culture and "the Jew,"* ed. Bryan Cheyette and Laura Marcus (Oxford: Polity, 1998), 242–56.

41. Laura Frost, *Sex Drives: Fantasies of Fascism in Literary Modernism* (Ithaca, NY: Cornell University Press, 2002).

42. Michel Foucault, "Film and Popular Memory," in *Foucault Live: Collected Interviews, 1961–1984,* ed. Sylvère Lotringer (Brooklyn: Semiotext(e), 1996). Foucault observes that power has an erotic charge that needs to be accounted for in the case of Nazism, which was "represented by shabby, pathetic, puritanical characters, laughably Victorian old maids, or, at best, smutty individuals." He questions how Nazism in "all pornographic literature throughout the world" could become the "ultimate symbol of eroticism." His contention is that in the porn shops' obsession with Nazi insignia, we are witnessing a "re-eroticization of power, taken to a pathetic, ridiculous extreme" to fill the void effected by insufficiently erotic leaders such as Brezhnev, Pompidou, or Nixon (127).

43. Susan Sontag, "Fascinating Fascism," in *Under the Sign of Saturn* (New York: Anchor, 1974), 103. "Sadomasochism," Sontag claims, "has always been the furthest reach of the sexual experience: when sex becomes most purely sexual, that is, severed from personhood, from relationships, from love" (105). Hence, "Sadomasochism is to sex what war is to civil life: the magnificent experience" (103).

44. Ibid., 105.

45. Frost employs *disavowal* rather than *foreclosure*, which would be my preference, to emphasize the systemic quality of the feminist interdiction of erotic fantasies about Nazis. She also acknowledges that this repression is not restricted to feminism as "only one variant of liberal and democratic politics, with the same disavowal of those libidinal impulses that run counter to its ideology" (*Sex Drives*, 150).

46. Ibid., 150.

47. What Althusser called *interpellation* refers to the constitution of individuals as ideological subjects, which transpires at the intersection between the symbolic and the imaginary where a subject recognizes and visualizes himself or herself as the addressee of socioeconomic codes. As Althusser's employment of psychoanalytic terminology implies, interpellation activates a secondary narcissistic identification with an aesthetics of personality that produces "properly" socialized subjects from the cracks of their impossible containment. Foucault distances himself from the notion of individual consciousness that precedes ideological interpellation in Althusser's model. In a reversal of Althusser, Foucault views individuation as an apparent compensation for subjection that actually reinforces disciplinary technologies that isolate and hierarchically categorize subjects in relation to norms. My observations

here echo Judith Butler's readings of Michel Foucault and Louis Althusser in "Subjection, Resistance, Resignification: *Between Freud and Foucault*" and " 'Conscience Doth Make Subjects of Us All': *Althusser's Subjection*," in *The Psychic Life of Power: Theories in Subjection* (Stanford, CA: Stanford University Press, 1997), 83–105 and 106–31, respectively.

48. Theodor W. Adorno, *Negative Dialectics*, trans. E. B. Ashton (New York: Seabury, 1973), 362–63, cited by Naomi Mandel, *Against the Unspeakable: Complicity, the Holocaust, and Slavery in America* (Charlottesville: University of Virginia Press, 2006), 67. The quotation in full reads: "Perennial suffering has as much right to expression as a tortured man has to scream; hence it may have been wrong to say that after Auschwitz you could no longer write poems. But it is not wrong to raise the less cultural question whether after Auschwitz you can go on living—especially whether one who escaped by accident, one who by rights should have been killed, may go on living. His mere survival calls for the coldness, the basic principle of bourgeois subjectivity, without which there could have been no Auschwitz; this is the drastic guilt of him who was spared." In the German, Adorno employs something like a middle voice here rather than the second-person pronoun *you* as suggested by the English translation. See Adorno, *Negative Dialektik* (Frankfurt am Main: Suhrkamp, 1966), 355–56.

49. Adorno, *Negative Dialectics*, 363.

50. Mandel, *Against the Unspeakable*, 70.

51. Ibid., 39.

52. Ibid., 25–26.

53. Ibid., 19.

54. Ibid., 26.

55. Adorno, *Negative Dialectics*, 362.

56. In her *New York Times* editorial "Swastikas for Sweeps" (July 17, 2002), Maureen Dowd comments on the controversy surrounding CBS's plans to air a miniseries based on Ian Kershaw's biography *Hitler, 1899–1936: Hubris*, which, as Dowd wryly noted, would cover the crucial years between eighteen and thirty-four, the same age span as the network's target demographic. While CBS's president, Leslie Moonves, defended the untapped dramatic potential of a miniseries exploring the early years of this "fascinating character" (because it will give us insight into the evolution of contemporary evildoers), critics saw the prospective miniseries as trivializing the figure of Hitler and his crimes for commercial purposes. As Dowd put it: "It's a stretch to argue that understanding an old evildoer would shed light on the new evildoers. There's a big difference between genocide and terrorism. But there's no denying Hollywood's eternal reliance on two subjects: evil and sex."

57. Emmanuel Lévinas, *Alterity and Transcendence*, trans. Michel B. Smith (London: Athlone Press, 1999), 84, cited by Robert Eaglestone, *The Holocaust and the Postmodern* (Oxford: Oxford University Press, 2004), 252.

58. Mandel, *Against the Unspeakable*, 31.

59. Thomas Trezise, "Unspeakable," *Yale Journal of Criticism* 14, no. 1 (2001): 39–66.

60. Ibid., 41, citing Thomas Nagel, *The View from Nowhere* (New York: Oxford University Press, 1986).

61. Anton Kaes notes, "The insistence on the impossibility of adequately comprehending and describing the Final Solution has by now become a *topos* of Holocaust research" that has steered North American discussions in Holocaust and

trauma studies in recent decades. See Anton Kaes, "Holocaust and the End of History: Postmodern Historiography in Cinema," in *Probing the Limits of Representation*, ed. Saul Friedlander (Cambridge, MA: Harvard University Press, 1992), 207.

62. Claude Lanzmann, "Ihr sollt nicht weinen: Einspruch gegen *Schindlers Liste*," *Frankfurter Allgemeine Zeitung*, March 5, 1994, in *"Der Gute Deutsche." Dokumente zur Diskussion um Steven Spielbergs "Schindlers Liste" in Deutschland*, ed. Christoph Weiss (St. Ingbert, Germany: Werner J. Röhrig Universitätsverlag, 1995), 175. Translated from the French by Grete Osterwald from the March 3, 1994, edition of *Le Monde*.

63. Mandel, *Against the Unspeakable*, 57, 39.

64. Ibid., 7.

65. Hirsch, "Surviving Images," 7.

66. Ibid., citing Barbie Zelizer, *Remembering to Forget: Holocaust Memory Through the Camera's Eye* (Chicago: University of Chicago Press, 1998).

67. Hirsch, "Surviving Images," 16. Writing about the displacement of the historical referent by posthistorical memory, Thomas Elsaesser demonstrates that the appropriation of iconic images may serve the affective interests of one past at the expense of another, as when a famous photograph of a Sinti girl caught in the small opening of a cattle car on her way to Auschwitz is circulated as the quintessential image of a Jewish victim. See Thomas Elsaesser, "One Train May Be Hiding Another: History, Memory, Identity, and the Visual Image," in *Topologies of Trauma: Essays on the Limit of Knowledge and Memory*, ed. Linda Belau and Petar Ramadanovic (New York: Other Press, 2002), 70.

68. The impact of the critique of essentialism was observable during the feminist historians' debate of 1989. Claudia Koonz notes that this debate exposed fault lines between the essentalist tendencies of German feminist historians of the Nazi period and their North American counterparts, whose praxis was informed by poststructuralist views of identity and agency. See Gisela Bock, "Die Frauen und der Nationalsozialismus: Bemerkungen zu einem Buch von Claudia Koonz," *Geschichte und Gesellschaft: Zeitschrift für Historische Sozialwissenschaft* 15 (1989): 563–79; Claudia Koonz, "Erwiderung auf Gisela Bocks Rezension von *Mothers in the Fatherland*," trans. Susanne Nitzscke, *Geschichte und Gesellschaft* 18 (1992): 394–99; idem, *Mothers in the Fatherland: Women, the Family and Nazi Politics* (New York: St. Martin's Press, 1987); and Atina Grossmann, "Feminist Debates about Women and National Socialism," *Gender & History* 3 (Autumn 1991): 350–58.

69. Ellie Ragland, *Essays on the Pleasures of Death: From Freud to Lacan* (New York: Routledge, 1995), 21.

70. See Wendy Brown, "The Desire to Be Punished: Freud's 'A Child Is Being Beaten,'" in *Politics Out of History* (Princeton, NJ: Princeton University Press, 2001), 56. See also Brown's chapter "Subjects of Tolerance: Why We Are Civilized and They Are Barbarians," in *Regulating Aversion: Tolerance in the Age of Identity and Empire* (Princeton, NJ: Princeton University Press, 2006), 149–75. See in addition my reading of Brown in "A Democracy Is Being Beaten," *English Studies in Canada*, 32, no. 1 (2006): 45–76.

71. Butler, "Subjection, Resistance, Resignification," 104.

72. Ibid., 102.

73. Weissman, *Fantasies of Witnessing*, 4.

74. As Charles Shepherdson points out, Foucault did not wish to erase the difference between the repression or liberation of sex, as certain commentators have claimed. Rather, he wanted to consider how "the promise of liberation takes part in the same conceptual arrangement that produced the idea of repression, to such a degree that the very aim of liberation often 'ends up repressing' (as in the case of psychoanalysis, perhaps)." Ultimately, then, "the question is whether psychoanalysis indeed remains trapped within the modern discourses of liberation that were born alongside what Foucault regards as the 'monarchical' theories of power (what he also speaks of as the 'repressive hypothesis'), or whether, as Foucault sometimes suggests, psychoanalysis in fact amounts to a disruption of that paradigm, just as genealogy does." Charles Shepherdson, *Vital Signs: Nature, Culture, Psychoanalysis* (New York: Routledge, 2000), 235 n. 17.

Index

Abbeele, Georges van den, 253 n. 18
acting out. *See* working through
Adorno, Theodor W., xv, 12, 14,
18, 41, 80–85, 88, 96, 116, 126,
142–43, 151–52, 158, 160, 186,
197, 210–11, 226 n. 17, 235 n.
121, 236 n. 12, 238 n. 28, n. 30,
n. 35, 239 n. 44, 240 n. 56, 253 n.
12, 264 n. 8, 275–76 n. 148; "after
Auschwitz" and Auschwitz, 9–10,
51–52, 55, 61, 80–81, 93, 97–116
passim, 118, 122–24, 137–39, 142,
152, 160–61, 202, 210, 222 n. 28, n.
29, n. 30, 253 n. 10, n. 22. 283 n.
48; and Derrida, 14, 82–83, 93, 99,
105–8, 111, 113–16, 122–24, 126,
142; on working through as critical
reflection/remembrance (*verarbeiten*),
47, 49, 52, 57, 60–61, 67–68, 139;
151–52, 253–54 n. 22; and lyric prohibition (*Lyrikverbot*), 9–10, 51, 222
n. 28, n. 30, 253 n. 10; on micrology, 107; and the negative sublime,
83–84, 88, 92–93, 97–98, 123; vs.
logics of redemption and *Sinnstiftung*,
48, 51, 55, 60, 84, 98, 100–1, 103–8,
113–14, 116, 118, 123, 142, 151,
158, 160; and the image prohibition
or Second Commandment (*Bilderverbot*), 9, 48, 222 n. 30, 259 n. 98. *See
also* aesthetics: negative; Habermas:
Adorno's influence on; Lyotard: on
Adorno

Adorno, Theodor W., works by: *Aesthetic Theory*, 9, 123; "Commitment,"
222 n. 28, 280 n. 27; "Education
after Auschwitz," 52, 253 n. 22;
"On Lyric Poetry and Society," 9;
"The Meaning of Working Through
the Past," 52, 238 n. 30, 253 n. 22;
Negative Dialectics, 9, 10, 51, 84, 93,
97–101, 103–4, 106, 109, 118, 123,
160, 222 n. 29, 238 n. 35, 253 n.
22, 259 n. 97, 283 n. 48; "What
Does Coming to Terms with the Past
Mean?" 47, 238 n. 28; with Horkheimer, *Dialectic of Enlightenment*, 54,
115–16, 235 n. 121, 239 n. 44, 264
n. 8
aesthetics, 8, 11–15, 37, 42, 48–49, 65,
72, 74, 80–85, 88–90, 92, 96–98,
101, 122–26, 141, 208, 212, 219
n. 3, 236 n. 12, 254 n. 40, 260–61
n. 129, 282–83 n. 47; negative:
Adorno's conception, 9–10, 12, 48,
51, 81, 83–85, 88, 92, 98, 122–23,
136, 138; Lyotard's conception, 10,
14–15, 98; 109, 123–24, 134–39, 224
n. 56. *See also* antimemorial genre;
image prohibition; sublime; unrepresentability and unspeakability
affect: 15; and anxiety, 151, 157–59,
165–67; and collective memory, 12,
42, 72, 86, 279 n. 16, 284 n. 67;
and disciplinarity, 3–4, 14–17, 23,
33–34, 40–43, 187; and/as